T0180540

Lecture Notes in Computer Science   14307

Founding Editors

Gerhard Goos
Juris Hartmanis

Editorial Board Members

Elisa Bertino, *Purdue University, West Lafayette, IN, USA*
Wen Gao, *Peking University, Beijing, China*
Bernhard Steffen ⓘ, *TU Dortmund University, Dortmund, Germany*
Moti Yung ⓘ, *Columbia University, New York, NY, USA*

The series Lecture Notes in Computer Science (LNCS), including its subseries Lecture Notes in Artificial Intelligence (LNAI) and Lecture Notes in Bioinformatics (LNBI), has established itself as a medium for the publication of new developments in computer science and information technology research, teaching, and education.

LNCS enjoys close cooperation with the computer science R & D community, the series counts many renowned academics among its volume editors and paper authors, and collaborates with prestigious societies. Its mission is to serve this international community by providing an invaluable service, mainly focused on the publication of conference and workshop proceedings and postproceedings. LNCS commenced publication in 1973.

Zhiyun Xue · Sameer Antani · Ghada Zamzmi ·
Feng Yang · Sivaramakrishnan Rajaraman ·
Sharon Xiaolei Huang ·
Marius George Linguraru · Zhaohui Liang
Editors

Medical Image Learning with Limited and Noisy Data

Second International Workshop, MILLanD 2023
Held in Conjunction with MICCAI 2023
Vancouver, BC, Canada, October 8, 2023
Proceedings

Editors
Zhiyun Xue 🆔
National Library of Medicine, National
Institutes of Health
Bethesda, MD, USA

Sameer Antani 🆔
National Library of Medicine, National
Institutes of Health
Bethesda, MD, USA

Ghada Zamzmi 🆔
National Library of Medicine, National
Institutes of Health
Bethesda, MD, USA

Feng Yang 🆔
National Library of Medicine, National
Institutes of Health
Bethesda, MD, USA

Sivaramakrishnan Rajaraman 🆔
National Library of Medicine, National
Institutes of Health
Bethesda, MD, USA

Sharon Xiaolei Huang 🆔
College of Information Sciences
and Technology
Penn State University
University Park, PA, USA

Marius George Linguraru 🆔
Sheikh Zayed Institute for Pediatric Surgical
Innovation, Children's National Hospital
Washington, DC, USA

Zhaohui Liang 🆔
National Library of Medicine, National
Institutes of Health
Bethesda, MD, USA

ISSN 0302-9743   ISSN 1611-3349 (electronic)
Lecture Notes in Computer Science
ISBN 978-3-031-47196-4   ISBN 978-3-031-44917-8 (eBook)
https://doi.org/10.1007/978-3-031-44917-8

© The Editor(s) (if applicable) and The Author(s), under exclusive license
to Springer Nature Switzerland AG 2023

This work is subject to copyright. All rights are reserved by the Publisher, whether the whole or part of the material is concerned, specifically the rights of translation, reprinting, reuse of illustrations, recitation, broadcasting, reproduction on microfilms or in any other physical way, and transmission or information storage and retrieval, electronic adaptation, computer software, or by similar or dissimilar methodology now known or hereafter developed.
The use of general descriptive names, registered names, trademarks, service marks, etc. in this publication does not imply, even in the absence of a specific statement, that such names are exempt from the relevant protective laws and regulations and therefore free for general use.
The publisher, the authors, and the editors are safe to assume that the advice and information in this book are believed to be true and accurate at the date of publication. Neither the publisher nor the authors or the editors give a warranty, expressed or implied, with respect to the material contained herein or for any errors or omissions that may have been made. The publisher remains neutral with regard to jurisdictional claims in published maps and institutional affiliations.

This Springer imprint is published by the registered company Springer Nature Switzerland AG
The registered company address is: Gewerbestrasse 11, 6330 Cham, Switzerland

Paper in this product is recyclable.

Preface

Deep learning (DL) techniques have been widely used for processing and analyzing various medical image modalities such as chest X-rays, computed tomography, ultrasound, and microscopic imagery. DL-based medical image analysis can help doctors and researchers in several aspects, such as segmenting organs of interest or clinically important regions, localizing and measuring disease manifestations, identifying and classifying disease patterns, enhancing image quality for better/easier manual interpretation, and recommending therapies based on the predicted stage of the disease. Although DL approaches have a huge potential to advance medical imaging technologies and improve quality and access to healthcare, their performance relies heavily on the quality, variety, and size of training data sets as well as appropriate high-quality annotations. Obtaining such data sets in the medical domain is challenging due to several factors including privacy constraints, rare or complex diseases, and tedious annotation processes. Distribution/domain shifts which can significantly degrade the generalization performance of models are common and considerable for limited medical data given the variability of populations, disease manifestations, and imaging devices. Further, real-world medical data tends to be noisy and incomplete and there might exist noisy labels due to ambiguity in annotations, human fatigue, and large inter/intra-user variations. Limited data may also lead to model bias, a particularly critical issue for medical applications in which DL decisions are of high consequence. To mitigate or overcome training challenges in imperfect or data-limited scenarios, several training techniques have been proposed. Despite the promise of these techniques in a wide range of applications, there are still significant challenges as well as a lack of theoretical and practical understanding of their learning characteristics and decision-making behavior when applied to medical images. Hence, new frameworks, algorithms, and techniques for coping with and learning from noisy data or data with limited annotations should be proposed to advance real-world modeling in medical image applications and improve the state of the art of such research.

This volume presents some novel approaches for handling noisy and limited medical image data sets. It consists of full papers presented at the 2nd Workshop on Medical Image Learning with Noisy and Limited Data (MILLanD), held in conjunction with the 26th International Conference on Medical Image Computing and Computer Assisted Intervention (MICCAI 2023). The workshop brought together machine learning scientists, biomedical engineers, and medical doctors to discuss the challenges and limitations of current deep learning methods applied to limited and noisy medical data and to present new methods for training models using such imperfect data. The workshop received 38 submissions in various topics including efficient data annotation and training strategies, new approaches for learning with noisy/corrupted data or uncertain labels, and new methods in weakly-supervised learning, semi-supervised learning, self-supervised learning, contrastive learning, multitask learning, active learning, and transfer learning. Each submission was reviewed by 2–3 reviewers and further assessed by the workshop's chairs. The workshop's reviewing process was double-blind, i.e., both the reviewer and author identities were concealed throughout the review process. This process resulted in the selection of 24 high-quality full papers that are included in this volume.

August 2023

Zhiyun Xue
Sameer Antani
Ghada Zamzmi
Feng Yang
Sivaramakrishnan Rajaraman
Sharon Xiaolei Huang
Marius George Linguraru
Zhaohui Liang

Organization

General Chair

Zhiyun Xue   National Institutes of Health, USA

Program Committee Chairs

Sameer Antani	National Institutes of Health, USA
Ghada Zamzmi	National Institutes of Health, USA
Feng Yang	National Institutes of Health, USA
Sivaramakrishnan Rajaraman	National Institutes of Health, USA
Sharon Xiaolei Huang	Pennsylvania State University, USA
Marius George Linguraru	Children's National Hospital, USA
Zhaohui Liang	National Institutes of Health, USA
Zhiyun Xue	National Institutes of Health, USA

Program Committee

Amogh Adishesha	Penn State University, USA
Syed Anwar	Children's National Hospital, USA
Somenath Chakraborty	West Virginia University Institute of Technology, USA
Kexin Ding	University of North Carolina at Charlotte, USA
Prasanth Ganesan	Stanford Medicine, USA
Zhifan Gao	Sun Yat-sen University, China
Alba García Seco Herrera	University of Essex, UK
Peng Guo	Massachusetts General Hospital, USA
Mustafa Hajij	University of San Francisco, USA
Zhifan Jiang	Children's National Hospital, USA
Alexandros Karargyris	Institute of Image-Guided Surgery of Strasbourg, France
Eung-Joo Lee	Massachusetts General Hospital, USA
Xiang Li	Massachusetts General Hospital, USA
Sheng Lian	Fuzhou University, China
Ismini Lourentzou	Virginia Tech University, USA
Haomiao Ni	Penn State University, USA

Nguyen Phuoc Nguyen	University of Missouri at Columbia, USA
Anabik Pal	SRM University, Andhra Pradesh, India
Harshit Parmar	Texas Tech University, USA
Rahul Paul	Harvard Medical School, USA
Sudipta Roy	Jio Institute, India
Md Sirajus Salekin	Amazon, USA
Rory Sayres	Google, USA
Ahmed Sayed	Milwaukee School of Engineering, USA
Mennatullah Siam	York University, Canada
Elena Sizikova	Food and Drug Administration, USA
Bella Specktor	Hebrew University of Jerusalem, Israel
Paolo Soda	University Campus Bio-Medico di Roma, Italy
Lihui Wang	Guizhou University, China
Yuan Xue	Johns Hopkins University, USA
Miaomiao Zhang	Capital Normal University, China
Qilong Zhangli	Rutgers University, USA

Contents

Weakly-Supervised, Semi-supervised, and Multitask Learning

Active Learning

Transfer Learning

Efficient Annotation and Training Strategies

Reducing Manual Annotation Costs for Cell Segmentation by Upgrading Low-Quality Annotations

Şerban Vădineanu[1]([✉])([iD]), Daniël M. Pelt[1], Oleh Dzyubachyk[2],
and K. Joost Batenburg[1]

[1] Leiden Institute of Advanced Computer Science, Leiden, The Netherlands
s.vadineanu@liacs.leidenuniv.nl
[2] Leiden University Medical Center, Leiden, The Netherlands

Abstract. Deep learning algorithms for image segmentation typically require large data sets with high-quality annotations to be trained with. For many domains, the annotation cost for obtaining such sets may prove to be prohibitively expensive. Our work aims to reduce the time necessary to create high-quality annotated images by using a relatively small well-annotated data set for training a convolutional neural network to upgrade lower-quality annotations, produced at lower annotation costs. We apply our method to the task of cell segmentation and investigate the performance of our solution when upgrading annotation quality for labels affected by three types of annotation errors: omission, inclusion, and bias. We observe that our method is able to upgrade annotations affected by high error levels from 0.3 to 0.9 Dice similarity with the ground-truth annotations. Moreover, we show that a relatively small well-annotated set enlarged with samples with upgraded annotations can be used to train better-performing segmentation networks compared to training only on the well-annotated set.

Keywords: annotation enhancement · annotation errors · cell segmentation · deep learning

1 Introduction

Deep learning algorithms have been providing effective solutions for many tasks, contributing to the advancement of domains such as speech recognition [11] and computer vision [24]. One important computer vision task that is being tackled with such algorithms is image segmentation [16], a process that aims to provide a separation between the entities present within a given image. However, deep learning models require large quantities of annotated data for training. In

Supplementary Information The online version contains supplementary material available at https://doi.org/10.1007/978-3-031-44917-8_1.

© The Author(s), under exclusive license to Springer Nature Switzerland AG 2023
Z. Xue et al. (Eds.): MILLanD 2023, LNCS 14307, pp. 3–13, 2023.
https://doi.org/10.1007/978-3-031-44917-8_1

addition, the provided annotations should also be of high quality. Specifically, the annotations should be correct by providing information that reflects the reality within the input, and complete, meaning that the annotations provide all the information required by the given task, e.g., all pixels from an image have an associated label in a segmentation task.

For many biomedical imaging tasks, including cell imaging [10], the annotations have to be created manually by domain experts. Due to the limited availability of experts, the annotation process is often time-consuming [27], limiting the capacity for annotating the large quantities of data required by deep learning algorithms. Thus, the general adoption of deep learning for such specialized domains may be considerably hindered. Fewer quality constraints for the annotations could significantly reduce the burden on expert annotators, enabling them to annotate more quickly. For instance, the boundary of every object in a segmentation mask has to be carefully delineated. By providing coarser delineations or only annotating a subset of all objects, a much faster annotation process can be achieved. However, directly training on low-quality annotations is generally detrimental to the performance of deep learning algorithms [25].

This work proposes a framework for effectively obtaining large amounts of high-quality training data with limited required human annotation time for the task of cell segmentation. Our approach is based on manually annotating a small training set of high quality, which we then augment with a much larger amount of low-quality annotations (possibly produced with considerably less human effort). In order to leverage the low-quality annotations, we train a convolutional neural network to learn the mapping for upgrading a low-quality annotation to a high-quality one by presenting it with both high-quality annotations as well as low-quality versions of these annotations. We create erroneous annotations by perturbing the high-quality annotations with a function that approximates potential errors resulting from a low-quality annotation process. Moreover, we show that this perturbation function does not need to exactly replicate the annotation errors present in the low-quality annotations in order for a good mapping to be trained. The training process requires pairs between the perturbed annotations and their corresponding images as input for the upgrade network with the unperturbed, high-quality, annotations as targets. We apply the learned mapping to the large low-quality set to enhance its annotations. Finally, we combine the initial small set of well-annotated data together with the larger set with upgraded annotations and we use them for training accurate deep-learning models for the task of cell segmentation. We show an overview of our method in Fig. 1.

2   Related Work

Among the solutions developed for biomedical image segmentation that use imperfect labels, we highlight weakly-supervised learning and implicit and explicit inconsistency correction methods.

Weakly supervised learning aims to train deep learning algorithms to produce complete segmentation masks by only providing the models with partially-annotated labels. Such techniques can include bounding boxes [20], rough

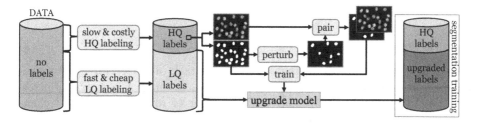

Fig. 1. We consider a high-quality annotator that produces labels in a slow and costly manner and a low-quality annotator, yielding labels faster and cheaper. In a given time frame, the annotators would generate a small data set with high-quality labels and a larger lower-quality set. We perturb the well-annotated labels and we use the perturbed labels together with their corresponding images as input to train an upgrade model. We employ the upgrade model to enhance the labels of the larger data set, which we use in conjunction with the well-annotated samples to train the final segmentation model.

sketches of shape contours [2], geometrical shape descriptors in the form of cen-tre points and lines [14], or partially-annotated segmentation areas [19]. Our solution can also be applied to upgrade partially-annotated labels. However, our framework has broader applicability since it can also compensate for other annotation errors, such as inconsistent border delineation or inclusion of foreign objects in the segmentation mask.

Implicit consistency correction methods compensate for annotation inaccu-racies during the training process by, for instance, reducing the influence of gradients coming from segmentation areas of lower confidence [15], or by using adversarial training to only annotate high-confidence areas of unlabeled data [17]. Explicit consistency correction solutions provide fine adjustments to the output of trained deep learning models [1,4,6]. Our work differs from both cat-egories since we separate the inconsistency correction step, i.e., upgrading the low-quality annotations, from the training process. When it comes to directly improving the provided labels, Yang et al. [26] developed a solution for itera-tively adjusting manual annotations of retinal vessels by employing generative adversarial networks. Our framework differs from their approach, performing the upgrade step only once per label. Moreover, we consider a wider set of errors whose impact on the quality of the annotation is more severe than in Yang et al. [26]. Also, their adjustment framework relies on a relatively large amount of high-quality annotations and may suffer from the challenges associated with generative models, e.g., mode collapse and convergence failure [5].

Another approach related to our method is few-shot segmentation, where the aim is to segment new query images by leveraging information from relatively few support images with a limited amount of annotations. However, these approaches generally require an additional training task with a large set of semantic classes [8,9], whereas our solution only requires data for the current task.

3   Method

3.1   Setup

We apply our framework to the segmentation task of 2D vector-valued (e.g., RGB, grayscale) images. In this paper, we define an image as a matrix of pixels $x \in \mathbb{R}^{N \times M \times C}$, with N, M, and C the number of rows, columns, and channels, respectively. The goal of segmentation is to create a mapping from an input x to the target $y \in \mathbb{Z}^{N \times M}$ to provide a separation between the different entities within that image. Essentially, a label is attributed to each pixel according to the entity that it belongs to. When using deep learning for image segmentation, this mapping is approximated using convolutional neural networks (CNNs) $f_\delta : \mathbb{R}^{N \times M \times C} \to \mathbb{Z}^{N \times M}$, which require a set of image-target pairs $X = \{(x_1, y_1), (x_2, y_2), \ldots, (x_{N_t}, y_{N_t})\}$ to train their parameters δ. The process of training neural networks usually involves successive predictions based on the input x and adjusting the parameters to minimize the loss between the predictions and the labels. In order to achieve the desired results, the network requires well-annotated training samples. We describe the annotation process that produced high-quality labels as the output of the high-quality annotator $A^{HQ} : \mathbb{R}^{N \times M \times C} \to \mathcal{A}^{HQ}$ that receives an input image x and produces a label that is both complete and correct, i.e., belongs to the set of high-quality annotations $\mathcal{A}^{HQ}$. Such an annotation can be the result of a consensus between multiple experts or can require a slow and careful delineation of the shape of each element in x by a single expert. Additionally, we define the set of well-annotated images $X^{HQ} = \{(x, A^{HQ}(x))\}$ needed to train the network parameters $\widehat{\delta} = \underset{\delta}{\mathrm{argmin}} \sum_{(x,y) \in X^{HQ}} L(f_\delta(x), y)$. Due to their large parameter count, CNN-based models are generally prone to overfitting, therefore, requiring large quantities of well-annotated samples.

3.2   Perturbation-Removal Framework

Since producing a sufficient amount of high-quality annotations may prove unfeasible for many specialized domains, the required annotations may be supplied via a less rigorous annotation process. A low-quality annotation process would, for instance, result from an individual expert who quickly produces the annotation, without spending additional time on finer shape details or on removing ambiguities. Also, for setups that require consensus, the label can come from a single expert, a person in training, or a non-expert, thus reducing the annotation costs. We define the low-quality annotator $A^{LQ} : \mathbb{R}^{N \times M \times C} \to \mathcal{A}^{LQ}$ as a function that produces labels that are either incorrect or incomplete or both, thus, being included in the set of low-quality annotations $\mathcal{A}^{LQ}$.

Training solely with low-quality annotations generally leads to inaccurate results [25]. We propose a solution to enhance the quality of a larger set of low-quality annotations, which we utilize to augment an initially small set of high-quality annotations. Our framework requires a low number of well-annotated images X^{HQ} together with a substantially larger set of images that have low-quality annotations $X^{LQ} = \{(x, A^{LQ}(x))\}$, with $|X^{HQ}| < |X^{LQ}|$.

We aim to enhance the low-quality annotation $A^{LQ}(x)$ to $\mathcal{A}^{HQ}$ by finding the upgrade function $U : (\mathbb{R}^{N \times M \times C}, \mathcal{A}^{LQ}) \rightarrow \mathcal{A}^{HQ}$, which translates an annotation of the input image created by the low-quality annotator to an annotation belonging to the space of high-quality annotations. In order to create low-quality versions of annotations, we utilize a perturbation function which aims to approximate the unknown mapping from a high-quality annotation to a low-quality one. We handcraft function $P : \mathcal{A}^{HQ} \rightarrow \mathcal{A}^{LQ}$, that applies perturbations to a high-quality annotation to create an annotated image that approximates a faster, but lower-quality, annotation process. The choice for such a function can vary by task and data set, with implementations that can include heuristics or even learning the perturbations from the data. In our work, we assume we can approximate the perturbation function P by implementing a custom stochastic version of it. Additionally, we also assume that the function U that maps the low-quality label to a high-quality one is a learnable function. We employ the high-quality set to generate many $(x, P(A^{HQ}(x)))$ pairs. Given the stochastic nature of our chosen perturbation function, we can generate multiple perturbed versions of the same high-quality annotation. Thus, we only require a small number of $(x, A^{HQ}(x))$ pairs. We utilize the generated pairs to train an upgrade network u_θ, parameterized by θ, which approximates U by finding $\widehat{\theta} = \underset{\theta}{\operatorname{argmin}} \sum_x L(u_\theta(x, P(A^{HQ}(x))), A^{HQ}(x))$, where L is a loss function. After training u_θ, we apply it to our lower-quality set, which we enhance by adding $(x, u_\theta(x, A^{LQ}(x)))$ pairs. Finally, we use both the enhanced $(x, u_\theta(x, A^{LQ}(x)))$ pairs and the initial high-quality $(x, A^{HQ}(x))$ pairs as training samples for our final segmentation task. Therefore, the CNN-based segmentation f_δ will be obtained as $\widehat{\delta} = \underset{\delta}{\operatorname{argmin}}(\sum_{(x,y) \in X^{HQ}} L(f_\delta(x), y) + \sum_{(x,y) \in X^{LQ}} L(f_\delta(x), u_{\widehat{\theta}}(x, y)))$.

4 Experiments

4.1 Experimental Setup

We designed our experimental setup around a PyTorch [18] implementation of UNet [22], closely resembling the original architecture. We treat both the segmentation and upgrade tasks as binary pixel-wise classification tasks. We train the network until there is no improvement in the validation score for 10 consecutive epochs, at which point we only keep the model with the highest score. Our loss function is the Dice loss and we update the network's parameters according to ADAM optimization algorithm [12]. We partition our data into training and testing with an additional 80/20 split of the training data into training and validation. Finally, we present our results by reporting the Dice coefficient computed over the entire test set and averaged over 5 runs. We validated our comparisons by using the Wilcoxon non-parametric test [21].

4.2   Data

We focus on the cell segmentation task, which fits well within our framework since it requires expertise for annotating and can suffer from insufficiently annotated data. Also, creating the segmentation masks for the right type of cells can be an error-prone process since cell microscopy images contain many different entities with similar characteristics [7]. We use three synthetic data sets, which consist of microscopy images of HL60 nuclei cells, granulocytes, and both cell types, respectively [23], each comprised of 30 volumes (25 for training, 5 for testing) with an average of 84 slices per volume. We also employ manually-annotated data from the EPFL Hippocampus data set [13], containing a training and a testing volume, each having 165 slices. For all data sets, we assume their ground-truth annotations to be of high quality. For each data set, we select a small subset whose annotations remain of high-quality $A^{HQ}(x)$, while perturbing the annotations of the remaining samples to generate $A^{LQ}(x)$. This perturbation step is performed only once per annotation.

4.3   Perturbations for Cell Segmentation

We apply three types of perturbations (omission, inclusion, and bias), described in [25], which can describe potential annotation errors for cell segmentation. Omission refers to the random elimination of a fixed proportion of cell labels from the segmentation mask. Inclusion refers to the random addition to the segmentation mask of a certain proportion of labels belonging to other objects from the input image. Bias refers to the over-coverage or under-coverage of the cells in the segmentation masks. When inclusion is among the perturbations, we employ the synthetic data set containing both HL60 and granulocytes, otherwise, to isolate the effect of the perturbations for each cell type, we use the data sets containing individual cells. In order to perform the perturbations, we require instance labels, some of which we consequently remove (omission), add (inclusion), or modify by performing morphological operations (bias). Given the relatively ill-defined distinction between low-quality and high-quality annotations, we will further consider as low-quality annotations only the ones affected by large degrees of perturbations, i.e., 70% omission, 70% inclusion, a bias of 6, or a combination of perturbations.

4.4   Results

Upgrading Low-Quality Annotations. We evaluated the performance of our upgrade network by upgrading annotations that presented large perturbation values. The results reported in Table 1 are produced after choosing the number of high-quality training slices and their originating volumes as a trade-off between a low slice count and performance (comparison presented in Supplementary Material). The remaining slices from the chosen volumes were used to form the low-quality set. Since different data sets are affected differently by the same level of perturbations, the number of chosen high-quality slices varies with both the data set and the perturbation type.

We notice that, except for inclusion for mitochondria, our framework is able to improve the annotation quality for all data sets and error types. The results for mitochondria with 70% inclusion may be caused by the relatively low impact that inclusion had on the similarity between the perturbed and ground truth annotations (Dice score > 0.9). Also, considering that the data set was shown to contain inconsistencies [3], some included shapes may actually belong to the ground truth. Thus, the efficacy of the upgrade network might suffer when presenting it with high-quality annotations as both perturbation and target.

Table 1. The Dice similarity with the ground truth test set of the annotations affected by perturbations and the upgraded annotations, the Dice similarity of the predictions produced by segmentation networks trained only on the high-quality data, on the high-quality data enhanced with upgraded annotations, and the results of thresholding. The largest value in each row is shown in bold. The training setup indicates the data set on which the upgrade network was trained, the total number of slices used for training, and the number of volumes from which the slices were selected.

| | Training setup for upgrade network | | | Quality of training annotations | | Quality of segmentation network | | |
| | | | | | | Training data | | |
Perturb.	Data set	Volumes	Slices	LQ	Upgraded	HQ only	HQ + upgraded	Thrs.
70% omission	HL60	10	10	0.462	**0.939**	0.876	**0.929**	0.887
	gran.	10	80	0.495	**0.92**	0.892	**0.894**	0.732
	mito.	1	40	0.463	**0.845**	0.803	**0.868**	-
70% inclusion	HL60	10	10	0.925	**0.992**	0.913	**0.962**	0.892
	gran.	10	10	0.381	**0.98**	0.856	**0.898**	0.214
	mito.	1	80	**0.909**	0.87	**0.882**	0.876	-
bias 6	HL60	10	10	0.857	**0.909**	0.876	**0.923**	0.887
	gran.	10	40	0.675	**0.865**	0.868	**0.877**	0.732
	mito.	1	40	0.809	**0.885**	0.803	**0.867**	-
30% om. 30% incl. bias 4	HL60	10	10	0.71	**0.929**	0.913	**0.93**	0.892
	gran.	10	10	0.54	**0.86**	**0.856**	0.847	0.214
	mito.	1	20	0.703	**0.874**	0.782	**0.854**	-

Table 2. The Dice similarity with the ground truth test set of the upgraded network trained on various degrees of perturbations. The perturbations present in the low-quality set are 30% omission, 30% inclusion, and a bias severity of 4, respectively. For each perturbation type, the highest score is shown in bold.

| | Training perturbation for upgrade network | | | | | | | | |
| | omission | | | inclusion | | | bias | | |
	20%	30%	50%	20%	30%	50%	2	4	6
HL60	0.955	**0.972**	0.952	0.973	0.972	**0.986**	0.915	0.918	**0.926**
gran.	0.838	0.86	**0.93**	**0.984**	0.98	0.981	0.821	0.837	**0.884**
mito.	0.878	**0.88**	0.861	0.847	0.848	**0.866**	0.782	0.84	**0.865**

We also observe that, for a combination of perturbations, a relatively small set of well-annotated samples, i.e., 20 slices, is able to train an u_θ whose upgraded annotations show Dice similarity gains of 31% for HL60, 59% for granulocytes, and 24% for mitochondria when compared with the perturbed annotations. Comparisons for different numbers of slices are shown in the Supplementary Material.

Segmentation Improvements. In Table 1 we report the effect of enlarging the training set with the upgraded annotations generated by u_θ when training the segmentation network f_δ. In order to verify that the simulated data cannot be easily segmented based on the pixel intensity levels, we use as baseline a simple thresholding solution in which the input images are segmented by selecting a threshold via grid search with a step of 1% of the maximum pixel intensity. For each data set, we select a single threshold that yields the highest Dice score on the training set. The low baseline results in Table 1 reflect the complexity of the simulated data sets. Our results show that, for most cases where u_θ improved the quality of annotations, the addition of samples with upgraded labels translated into a higher segmentation performance of the final segmentation network on the test data. For the synthetic data sets, the highest gain is seen when augmenting the training data with upgraded annotations from 70% inclusion, with 16% increase in Dice score for HL60 cells and a 5% increase for granulocytes, while mitochondria achieved an increase of 8% when the additional low-quality annotations had 70% omission.

Perturbation Mismatch. So far, the upgrade network was trained on the same level of perturbation as the perturbation present in X^{LQ}. However, in practice, it might be difficult to exactly match the type and severity of the perturbations present in the data. We present in Table 2 the effect of such mismatch on the performance of the upgrade function when the annotations of X^{LQ} contain 30% omission, 30% inclusion, and a bias severity of 4, respectively. We observe that matching the exact amount of omission as in X^{LQ} achieves the best result only for HL60 cells and mitochondria, whereas for granulocytes the highest score is obtained when training u_θ on a higher omission level. Moreover, even when not reaching the highest Dice score, the upgraded annotations of HL60 cells and mitochondria still show, respectively, a 16% and 4% improvement over the baseline annotations for 50% omission in X^{LQ}. This implies that varying the presence of a large proportion of the cell masks can be overall more beneficial for training u_θ than aiming to exactly match the omission present in the annotations. Similarly for inclusion and bias, u_θ trained with a larger error than in X^{LQ} produced either better or comparable results to u_θ trained with the same error as in X^{LQ}. The Supplementary Material contains additional comparisons.

5   Conclusion

We presented our framework for enlarging training data sets with limited human annotation costs by only requiring a small set of data with high-quality annotations and a larger set with low-quality annotations. We use a small high-quality data set to train an upgrade network that enhances the annotation quality of the larger set. We showed that the networks trained on data sets enlarged by our method show considerably higher segmentation scores than only training on high-quality data for both synthetic and real-world data sets. In the future, we intend to compare our framework with other solutions that apply corrections to segmentation masks such as partial labeling [19] and confident learning [28]. Such comparison will provide a more objective assessment of the performance of our approach. Here we limited ourselves to a somewhat simplified validation due to space constraints.

Our results indicate that we only require a relatively low number of well-annotated images for improving low-quality annotations to a level comparable with the ground truth. Also, we noticed that the best results are obtained when the upgrade model is trained with large perturbation levels and is applied to annotations that present high errors. Thus, our solution may be more suitable for embedding into an annotation process where large errors in annotation are expected, rather than for annotations with a relatively limited amount of errors.

Acknowledgment. This research was supported by the SAILS program of Leiden University. DMP is supported by The Netherlands Organisation for Scientific Research (NWO), project number 016.Veni.192.235.

References

1. Araújo, R.J., Cardoso, J.S., Oliveira, H.P.: A deep learning design for improving topology coherence in blood vessel segmentation. In: Shen, D., Liu, T., Peters, T.M., Staib, L.H., Essert, C., Zhou, S., Yap, P.-T., Khan, A. (eds.) Medical Image Computing and Computer Assisted Intervention – MICCAI 2019: 22nd International Conference, Shenzhen, China, October 13–17, 2019, Proceedings, Part I, pp. 93–101. Springer, Cham (2019). https://doi.org/10.1007/978-3-030-32239-7_11
2. Can, Y.B., Chaitanya, K., Mustafa, B., Koch, L.M., Konukoglu, E., Baumgartner, C.F.: Learning to segment medical images with scribble-supervision alone. In: Stoyanov, D., et al. (eds.) DLMIA/ML-CDS -2018. LNCS, vol. 11045, pp. 236–244. Springer, Cham (2018). https://doi.org/10.1007/978-3-030-00889-5_27
3. Casser, V., Kang, K., Pfister, H., Haehn, D.: Fast mitochondria detection for connectomics. In: Arbel, T., Ayed, I.B., de Bruijne, M., Descoteaux, M., Lombaert, H., Pal, C. (eds.) MIDL 2020. Proceedings of Machine Learning Research, vol. 121, pp. 111–120. PMLR (2020)
4. Chen, S., Juarez, A.G., Su, J., van Tulder, G., Wolff, L., van Walsum, T., de Bruijne, M.: Label refinement network from synthetic error augmentation for medical image segmentation. CoRR abs/2209.06353 (2022)
5. Creswell, A., White, T., Dumoulin, V., Arulkumaran, K., Sengupta, B., Bharath, A.A.: Generative adversarial networks: an overview. IEEE Signal Process. Mag. **35**(1), 53–65 (2018)
6. Dai, W., Dong, N., Wang, Z., Liang, X., Zhang, H., Xing, E.P.: SCAN: structure correcting adversarial network for organ segmentation in chest x-rays. In: Stoyanov, D., et al. (eds.) DLMIA/ML-CDS -2018. LNCS, vol. 11045, pp. 263–273. Springer, Cham (2018). https://doi.org/10.1007/978-3-030-00889-5_30

7. Diem, K., Magaret, A.S., Klock, A., Jin, L., Zhu, J., Corey, L.: Image analysis for accurately counting cd4+ and cd8+ t cells in human tissue. J. Virol. Methods **222**, 117–21 (2015)
8. Feng, R., et al.: Interactive few-shot learning: limited supervision, better medical image segmentation. IEEE Trans. Med. Imaging **40**(10), 2575–2588 (2021)
9. Feyjie, A.R., Azad, R., Pedersoli, M., Kauffman, C., Ayed, I.B., Dolz, J.: Semi-supervised few-shot learning for medical image segmentation. arXiv preprint arXiv:2003.08462 (2020)
10. Greenwald, N.F., et al.: Whole-cell segmentation of tissue images with human-level performance using large-scale data annotation and deep learning. Nat. Biotechnol. **40**(4), 555–565 (2022)
11. Kamath, U., Liu, J., Whitaker, J.: Deep Learning for NLP and Speech Recognition. Springer, Cham (2019). https://doi.org/10.1007/978-3-030-14596-5
12. Kingma, D.P., Ba, J.: Adam: A method for stochastic optimization. In: Bengio, Y., LeCun, Y. (eds.) ICLR 2015 (2015)
13. Lucchi, A., Smith, K., Achanta, R., Knott, G., Fua, P.: Supervoxel-based segmentation of mitochondria in EM image stacks with learned shape features. IEEE Trans. Medical Imaging **31**(2), 474–486 (2012)
14. Matuszewski, D.J., Sintorn, I.M.: Minimal annotation training for segmentation of microscopy images. In: ISBI 2018, pp. 387–390. IEEE (2018)
15. Min, S., Chen, X., Zha, Z.J., Wu, F., Zhang, Y.: A two-stream mutual attention network for semi-supervised biomedical segmentation with noisy labels. In: AAAI. vol. 33, pp. 4578–4585 (2019)
16. Minaee, S., Boykov, Y., Porikli, F., Plaza, A., Kehtarnavaz, N., Terzopoulos, D.: Image segmentation using deep learning: a survey. IEEE Trans. Pattern Anal. Mach. Intell. **44**(7), 3523–3542 (2022)
17. Nie, D., Gao, Y., Wang, L., Shen, D.: ASDNet: attention based semi-supervised deep networks for medical image segmentation. In: Frangi, A.F., Schnabel, J.A., Davatzikos, C., Alberola-López, C., Fichtinger, G. (eds.) MICCAI 2018. LNCS, vol. 11073, pp. 370–378. Springer, Cham (2018). https://doi.org/10.1007/978-3-030-00937-3_43
18. Paszke, A., et al.: Pytorch: An imperative style, high-performance deep learning library. In: NeurIPS 2019, pp. 8024–8035 (2019)
19. Peng, L., et al.: Semi-supervised learning for semantic segmentation of emphysema with partial annotations. IEEE J. Biomed. Health Inform. **24**(8), 2327–2336 (2020)
20. Rajchl, M., et al.: Deepcut: object segmentation from bounding box annotations using convolutional neural networks. IEEE Trans. Med. Imaging **36**(2), 674–683 (2017)
21. Rey, D., Neuhäuser, M.: Wilcoxon-signed-rank test. In: Lovric, M. (ed.) International Encyclopedia of Statistical Science, pp. 1658–1659. Springer (2011)
22. Ronneberger, O., Fischer, P., Brox, T.: U-Net: convolutional networks for biomedical image segmentation. In: Navab, N., Hornegger, J., Wells, W.M., Frangi, A.F. (eds.) Medical Image Computing and Computer-Assisted Intervention – MICCAI 2015: 18th International Conference, Munich, Germany, October 5-9, 2015, Proceedings, Part III, pp. 234–241. Springer, Cham (2015). https://doi.org/10.1007/978-3-319-24574-4_28
23. Svoboda, D., Kozubek, M., Stejskal, S.: Generation of digital phantoms of cell nuclei and simulation of image formation in 3D image cytometry. Cytometry Part A 75A (2009)

24. Voulodimos, A., Doulamis, N., Doulamis, A.D., Protopapadakis, E.: Deep learning for computer vision: a brief review. Comput. Intell. Neurosci. 2018, 7068349:1–7068349:13 (2018)
25. Vădineanu, S., Pelt, D.M., Dzyubachyk, O., Batenburg, K.J.: An analysis of the impact of annotation errors on the accuracy of deep learning for cell segmentation. In: Proceedings of The 5th International Conference on Medical Imaging with Deep Learning. Proceedings of Machine Learning Research, vol. 172, pp. 1251–1267. PMLR (06–08 Jul 2022)
26. Yang, Y., Wang, Z., Liu, J., Cheng, K.T., Yang, X.: Label refinement with an iterative generative adversarial network for boosting retinal vessel segmentation. arXiv preprint arXiv:1912.02589 (2019)
27. Zhang, L., et al.: Disentangling human error from ground truth in segmentation of medical images. Adv. Neural. Inf. Process. Syst. **33**, 15750–15762 (2020)
28. Zhang, M., et al.: Characterizing label errors: confident learning for noisy-labeled image segmentation. In: Martel, A.L., et al. (eds.) Medical Image Computing and Computer Assisted Intervention – MICCAI 2020: 23rd International Conference, Lima, Peru, October 4–8, 2020, Proceedings, Part I, pp. 721–730. Springer, Cham (2020). https://doi.org/10.1007/978-3-030-59710-8_70

ScribSD: Scribble-Supervised Fetal MRI Segmentation Based on Simultaneous Feature and Prediction Self-distillation

Yijie Qu[1], Qianfei Zhao[1], Linda Wei[2], Tao Lu[3], Shaoting Zhang[1,4],
and Guotai Wang[1,4(✉)]

[1] University of Electronic Science and Technology of China, Chengdu, China
guotai.wang@uestc.edu.cn
[2] Shanghai Jiao Tong University, Shanghai, China
[3] Sichuan Provincial People's Hospital, Chengdu, China
[4] Shanghai AI Lab, Shanghai, China

Abstract. Automatic segmentation of different organs in fetal Magnetic Resonance Imaging (MRI) plays an important role in measuring the development of the fetus. However, obtaining a large amount of high-quality manually annotated fetal MRI is time-consuming and requires specialized knowledge, which hinders the widespread application that relies on such data to train a model with good segmentation performance. Using weak annotations such as scribbles can substantially reduce the annotation cost, but often leads to poor segmentation performance due to insufficient supervision. In this work, we propose a Scribble-supervised Self-Distillation (ScribSD) method to alleviate this problem. For a student network supervised by scribbles and a teacher based on Exponential Moving Average (EMA), we first introduce prediction-level Knowledge Distillation (KD) that leverages soft predictions of the teacher network to supervise the student, and then propose feature-level KD that encourages the similarity of features between the teacher and student at multiple scales, which efficiently improves the segmentation performance of the student network. Experimental results demonstrate that our KD modules substantially improve the performance of the student, and our method outperforms five state-of-the-art scribble-supervised learning methods.

Keywords: Fetal MRI · Segmentation · Scribble Annotation · Knowledge Distillation

1 Introduction

As a non-invasive medical imaging technique, Magnetic Resonance Imaging (MRI) has been widely used in clinical diagnosis and treatment, and fetal MRI has become an important diagnostic tool for prenatal examination [21,25]. Automatic segmentation of the placenta and brain in fetal MRI helps more accurate assessment of the development of the fetus, detection of fetal diseases, malformations, and developmental abnormalities at an early time [1,25]. Recently,

© The Author(s), under exclusive license to Springer Nature Switzerland AG 2023
Z. Xue et al. (Eds.): MILLanD 2023, LNCS 14307, pp. 14–23, 2023.
https://doi.org/10.1007/978-3-031-44917-8_2

deep learning with Convolutional Neural Networks (CNNs) has been used for accurate fetal brain and placenta segmentation from fetal MRI [3,16,20]. However, most of these methods require large-scale images with accurate pixel-level dense annotations for model training. Unfortunately, medical image annotation is a time-consuming, expensive, and expert-dependent process, making obtaining large-scale annotated datasets difficult.

Weak annotations (e.g., image-level labels [23], bounding boxes [14] and scribbles [8,22]) are more accessible to obtain than pixel-level dense annotations, and can effectively reduce the annotation cost. Compared with image-level labels and bounding boxes, scribbles are more flexible to annotate targets with various shapes and often lead to better performance [8]. Therefore, this work focuses on exploring using scribble annotations to efficiently and robustly train high-performance fetal MRI segmentation models.

To learn from scribble annotations for segmentation, existing methods are mainly based on introducing regularization or pseudo labels for unlabeled pixels. For regularization-based methods, Kim et al. [6] proposed a level set-based Mumford-Shah function to regularize the segmentation results. Scribble2D5 [2] expands the scribbles based on super-pixels and uses active contours to constrain the prediction results. Conditional Random Field (CRF) [18] loss and normalized cut loss [17] has also been proposed for regularization. Additionally, pseudo-label-based methods utilize weak annotations to generate pseudo labels for network training. Scribble2Label [7] generates pseudo labels based on the Exponential Moving Average (EMA) of the predictions and filters out low-quality labels for robust learning. Luo et al. [10] proposed Dynamically Mixed Pseudo Label Supervision (DMPLS) where the predictions of two decoders are mixed randomly to serve as pseudo labels. The Uncertainty-aware Self-ensembling and Transformation-consistent Mean Teacher Model (USTM) [9] leverages an uncertainty-aware mean teacher to generate pseudo labels for supervising the student based on a Mean Square Error (MSE) loss. However, the pseudo labels may not be accurate with a lot of noise, which may limit the performance of the learned model. Luo et al. [10] directly took the hard pseudo labels for supervision without considering the noise, and USTM [9] used uncertainty estimation based on Monte Carlo Dropout to suppress predictions with high uncertainties, which requires multiple forward passes for each iteration, making the training stage time-consuming.

In this work, we propose an efficient scribble-based learning method called Scribble-supervised Self-Distillation (ScribSD) for fetal MRI segmentation. The contributions are three-fold. Firstly, we introduce a KD-based method for robustly learning from scribbles for segmentation. Compared with existing works using hard pseudo labels [10], we introduce prediction-level Knowledge Distillation (KD) that uses soft prediction obtained by a teacher to supervise the student, as soft predictions are more noise-robust, and hard labels tend to contain more noise [24]. Secondly, to better transfer knowledge from the teacher to the student for higher performance, we introduce multi-scale feature distillation that encourages feature consistency between the teacher and student at

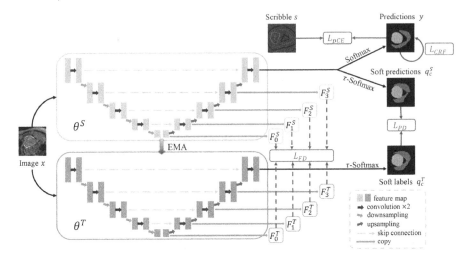

Fig. 1. The proposed Scribble-supervised Self-Distillation (ScribSD) framework. Prediction-level Distillation (L_{PD}) based on soft labels and multi-scale feature distillation (L_{FD}) are combined for supervising the student on unannotated pixels.

different resolution levels. In addition, compared with classic KD methods [5,24] that require pre-training a teacher model, we use self-distillation that efficiently generates the teacher on-the-fly based on the EMA of model parameters. Experimental results on a fetal brain and placenta segmentation dataset demonstrated that our method outperformed several state-of-the-art scribble-supervised segmentation methods.

2   Method

Our proposed Scribble-supervised Self-Distillation (ScribSD) is illustrated in Fig. 1. For a student model supervised by the scribbles and a regularization loss based on CRF, we generate a teacher model based on EMA for self-distillation, where prediction-level distillation and multi-scale feature-level distillation are combined to better transfer the knowledge from the teacher to the student.

2.1   Student Model with Scribble Supervision

In this work, we consider a UNet [15]-like structure for segmentation due to its high performance in a wide range of tasks. For a training set with scribble annotations, a partial cross-entropy (pCE) loss is used to learn from the scribbles:

$$L_{pCE} = -\frac{1}{|\omega_s|} \sum_{i \in \omega_s} \sum_{c=0}^{C} s_i^c log(p_i^c) \tag{1}$$

where p is the probability map predicted by the student model, s is the one-hot scribble annotation map, and w_s is the set of labeled pixels. C denotes the class number for segmentation. s_i^c and p_i^c are probabilities of pixel i being class c in the network prediction and scribble annotation, respectively.

Since just applying L_{pCE} on the sparse annotations usually does not provide enough supervision around boundaries [13], we further use a CRF loss (L_{CRF}) to regularize the network output, which encourages prediction consistency between neighboring pixels with similar features:

$$L_{CRF} = \sum_{c=0}^{C} \sum_{(i,j) \in \Phi} G(i,j) p_i^c (1 - p_j^c) \tag{2}$$

where Φ denotes the set of pixel pairs in the image. $G(i,j)$ refers to the Gaussian kernel bandwidth filter:

$$G(i,j) = \frac{1}{\omega} exp \left(-\frac{\|H_i - H_j\|^2}{2\sigma_H^2} - \frac{\|I_i - I_j\|^2}{2\sigma_I^2} \right) \tag{3}$$

where H_i and I_i denote the spatial position and the spectral value of pixel i, respectively. ω is the weight for normalization, σ_H and σ_I are hyper-parameters to control the scale of Gaussian kernels.

2.2 Scribble-Supervised Self-distillation

Instead of pre-training an extra teacher model offline for KD [5,24], we obtain the teacher model during the training process on the fly, where the teacher has the same structure as the student model, but with different model weights. As shown in Fig. 1, let θ^S and θ^T denote the weights of the student and teacher models, respectively. The teacher is updated as an EMA of the student: $\theta_t^T = \lambda \theta_{t-1}^T + (1 - \lambda)\theta_t^S$, where θ_t^S and θ_{t-1}^T are weights of the teacher and student at iteration t and $t-1$, respectively. $\lambda = min(1 - \frac{1}{t+1}, 0.99)$ is the EMA momentum that gradually increases to 0.99, where t denotes the current number of iteration.

Prediction Distillation (PD). With the teacher network, we use a temperature-calibrated Softmax (τ-Softmax) to obtain soft labels that are more noise-tolerant [12] for supervision.

$$q_{c,n}^T = \frac{exp(z_{c,n}^T / \tau)}{\sum_c exp(z_{c,n}^T / \tau)} \tag{4}$$

where $z_{c,n}^T$ is the logit output on the c-th channel at the n-th pixel obtained by the teacher. $q_{c,n}^T$ is the probability value in the c-th channel of the soft label. $\tau \geq 1$ is a hyper-parameter to control the softness, where a larger τ leads to a softer output, i.e., the probability for each class is less likely to be the extreme values of 0.0 or 1.0. Note that $\tau = 1$ corresponds to the standard softmax operation.

Similarly, we use $q_{c,n}^S$ to represent the student's soft prediction obtained by τ-Softmax. As the KL-Divergence is more sensitive and precise in measuring the difference between two probability distributions, and is better able to capture the knowledge of the teacher model. The prediction-level distillation loss L_{PD} is defined as the KL-Divergence between the soft predictions:

$$L_{PD} = \frac{1}{N} \sum_{n=0}^{N} \sum_{c=0}^{C} q_{c,n}^T log(q_{c,n}^T / q_{c,n}^S) \tag{5}$$

where N denotes the number of pixels in the image.

Feature Distillation (FD). In addition to PD which focuses on prediction-level distillation, we also use feature-level distillation at multiple scales to encourage the student to mimic the teacher's feature extraction ability. Let D denote the number of scales based on up-sampling in the decoder ($D = 4$ in this work). The feature maps at scale d for the teacher and student are denoted as F_d^T and F_d^S, respectively. Note that $d = 0$ represents the bottleneck, and the bigger d is, the further away we get from the bottleneck. The FD loss is defined as:

$$L_{FD} = - \sum_{d=0}^{D-1} \gamma_d \cdot sim(F_d^T, F_d^S) = - \sum_{d=0}^{D-1} \gamma_d \frac{F_d^T \cdot F_d^S}{||F_d^T|| \times ||F_d^S||} \tag{6}$$

where sim is the cosine similarity. γ_d is the weight at scale d. As a larger d value corresponds to a higher resolution for accurate segmentation, we make γ_d gradually increase with d, i.e., 0.1, 0.2, 0.3, and 0.4 respectively for γ_0 to γ_3.

Overall Loss. Based on L_{PD} and L_{FD}, the overall loss for student training is:

$$L = L_{pCE} + \alpha \cdot L_{CRF} + \beta_t \cdot (L_{PD} + \delta L_{FD}) \tag{7}$$

where α is the weight for L_{CRF}, following [13] and based on the result of the validation set, α is set to 0.01 in our method. β_t is a weight for the KD terms, and δ is the weight of L_{FD}. Note that β_t ramps up from 0 to its maximum value β according to sigmoid ramp up function $\beta_t = \beta * e^{-5(1-t/t_{max})^2}$, where t denotes the current iteration number and t_{max} is the maximum iteration number for ramp-up. Since the teacher network uses the EMA weights of successive student networks, the performance of the teacher model is poor at the early stage of training. As the training progresses, the teacher's performance gradually improves, which is leveraged by a larger β_t.

3   Experiment and Results

3.1   Dataset and Implementation Details

MRI scans of 88 fetuses in the second trimester for fetal brain and placenta segmentation were collected by Single Shot Fast Spin Echo (SSFSE) with pixel size

Table 1. Comparison between our method and existing weakly-supervised methods with the same backbone of UNet [15]. ∗ denotes significantly higher performance than the existing methods (p-value < 0.05 based a paired t-test).

Method	Dice(%)↑			ASSD(mm)↓		
	Placenta	Brain	Average	Placenta	Brain	Average
pCE	77.73±9.25	87.06±5.48	82.40 ± 6.14	5.72 ± 4.26	3.63 ± 2.18	4.67 ± 2.45
DMPLS [10]	78.18 ± 7.15	86.94 ± 7.10	82.56 ± 5.53	7.25 ± 5.80	2.84 ± 1.30	5.04 ± 3.03
EM [4]	76.92 ± 19.47	89.34 ± 4.39	83.13 ± 10.34	10.37 ± 22.33	2.58 ± 1.29	6.47 ± 11.16
MLoss [6]	76.87 ± 8.78	86.76 ± 6.09	81.81 ± 6.17	5.89 ± 4.37	3.52 ± 1.91	4.71 ± 2.52
TV [11]	76.61 ± 9.51	87.25 ± 5.96	81.93 ± 6.45	5.98 ± 4.33	3.30 ± 1.93	4.64 ± 2.44
USTM [9]	80.92 ± 6.62	88.78 ± 4.84	84.85 ± 4.55	4.42 ± 3.22	3.07 ± 2.04	3.74 ± 2.00
Ours	**82.91 ± 8.87***	**92.46 ± 3.94***	**87.68 ± 5.49***	3.68 ± 2.96	**1.48 ± 0.88***	**2.58 ± 1.70***

0.60–1.24mm and slice thickness 3.00–7.15mm. The image size was 256×256, and each volume had 25–100 slices. We used scribbles for the training set and pixel-level annotations for the validation and testing sets. The images were randomly split into 40, 10, and 38 scans for training, validation, and testing, respectively.

The experiments were conducted on a Ubuntu desktop with PyTorch and an NVIDIA GeForce RTX 3090Ti GPU. Due to the large slice thickness, we employed 2D CNNs for slice-level segmentation and stacked the results in a volume for 3D evaluation. 2D UNet [15] was used for segmentation, with Adam optimizer for training. Dropout was used in the lower two levels and the dropout ratio was 0.5. Random flipping and random cropping were used for data augmentation. The learning rate was initialized as 0.001 and reduced by half for every 150 epochs. The batch size was 4 and the total epoch number was 800. The maximum iteration number for ramp-up t_{max} was 5000. Post-processing was used for all the compared methods by only keeping the largest connected component in the 3D space for each class. Based on the best performance on the validation set, the hyper-parameter setting was: $\tau = 5$, $\alpha = 0.01$, $\beta = 1$ and $\delta = 1$. Following [13], the parameters for CRF loss were $\omega = 1$, $\sigma_H = 5$ and $\sigma_I = 0.1$. For quantitative evaluation of the 3D segmentation results, we measured the Dice score and Average Symmetric Surface Distance (ASSD).

3.2   Results

Comparison with Existing Scribble-Supervised Methods. Our method was compared with six existing methods: 1) only pCE, 2) Dynamically Mixed Pseudo Labels Supervision (DMPLS) [10], 3) Entropy Minimization (EM) [4], 4) Mumford-Shah Loss (MLoss) [6], 5) Total Variation (TV) [11] for regularization and 6) USTM [9]. Table 1 presents a quantitative comparison between these methods. Using pCE loss only obtained an average Dice of 77.73% and 87.06% for the placenta and fetal brain, respectively. Our method achieved the best performance and improved it to 82.91% and 92.46% for the two classes, respectively. Compared with the best existing method USTM [9], our method significantly improved the average Dice by 2.83% percent points and reduced the ASSD by

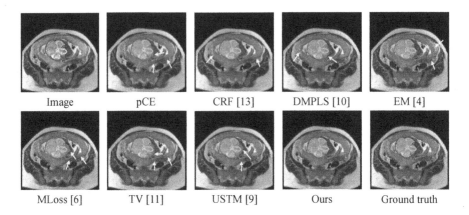

| Image | pCE | CRF [13] | DMPLS [10] | EM [4] |

| MLoss [6] | TV [11] | USTM [9] | Ours | Ground truth |

Fig. 2. Qualitative comparison of our proposed method and several existing methods.

Table 2. Ablation study on different supervision strategies.

Loss functions						Dice(%)↑			ASSD(mm)↓		
pCE	CRF	MSE	PD	FD*	FD	Placenta	Brain	Average	Placenta	Brain	Average
✓						81.24 ± 6.45	83.81 ± 9.46	82.53 ± 6.37	4.83 ± 2.71	7.07 ± 8.92	5.95 ± 4.64
✓	✓					79.34 ± 11.10	88.26 ± 5.28	83.80 ± 6.14	9.07 ± 12.24	2.62 ± 1.33	5.85 ± 6.00
✓	✓	✓				79.87 ± 11.36	87.15 ± 7.29	83.51 ± 6.49	8.04 ± 12.55	2.77 ± 1.95	5.40 ± 6.09
✓	✓		✓			83.66 ± 4.76	87.53 ± 6.03	85.59 ± 4.31	3.75 ± 1.56	2.70 ± 1.42	3.22 ± 0.96
✓	✓		✓	✓		**85.34 ± 4.75**	90.66 ± 5.87	88.00 ± 4.52	3.57 ± 1.49	2.03 ± 1.39	2.80 ± 0.94
✓	✓		✓		✓	85.19 ± 4.94	**91.08 ± 5.29**	**88.14 ± 4.26**	**3.16 ± 1.48**	**1.80 ± 1.29**	**2.48 ± 0.94**

1.16 mm, with p-value < 0.05 according to a paired t-test. Figure 2 presents a visual comparison of segmentation results obtained by these methods, where red and green colors show the placenta and fetal brain, respectively. It shows that the segmentation result obtained by our proposed method was the closest to the ground truth. In contrast, the other methods obtained more under-segmented or over-segmented regions, as highlighted by yellow arrows.

Ablation Study. To investigate the effectiveness of each of the supervision terms used in our method, we set pCE as the baseline, and gradually added the CRF loss, PD loss, and FD loss, respectively. The PD loss based on soft predictions obtained by τ-Softmax was compared with an MSE loss applied to the probability predictions obtained by standard Softmax, which corresponds to the typical mean teacher method [19]. Our FD based on multi-scale feature distillation was also compared with FD* which means only applying feature distillation at the bottleneck.

The results of different settings of the training loss on the validation set are shown in Table 2. pCE only obtained an average Dice of 82.53% and introducing the CRF loss improved it to 83.80%. Applying our PD further improved it to 85.59%, while replacing PD with MSE led to a lower performance (83.51%). Finally, combining CRF loss with our PD and FD led to the best average Dice

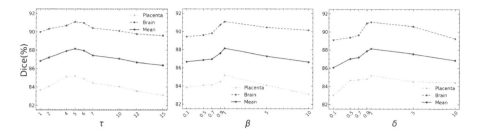

Fig. 3. Sensitivity analysis of hyper-parameter τ, β and δ, respectively.

of 88.14% with ASSD of 2.48 mm. Replacing our FD with FD* obtained average Dice and ASSD values of 88.00% and 2.80 mm, respectively, showing the effectiveness of the proposed multi-scale feature distillation.

Figure 3 shows the analysis of hyper-parameter settings for τ, β and δ. It shows that the performance gradually increases when τ changes from 1.0 to 5.0, demonstrating that distillation with a softer prediction based on τ-Softmax is more effective than a standard Softmax (τ=1) considering the noise in the teacher's output. However, when $\tau > 5.0$, the performance decreased, which is mainly because an extremely soft (i.e., highly uncertain) prediction is less informative about the class membership of pixels. Fig. 3 also shows that the highest Dice was achieved when $\delta = 1$, and $\beta = 1$. Note that poor performance was obtained when setting β and δ to very large values, which enforces the student to over-fit the teacher and limits its performance.

4 Conclusion

In this work, we proposed a Scribble-supervised Self-Distillation (ScribSD) method for weakly supervised fetal MRI segmentation. The proposed KD strategy combines Prediction Distillation based on soft predictions to deal with noisy pseudo labels and multi-scale Feature Distillation that transfers the high-quality knowledge contained in the teacher model to the student. Experimental results on the placenta and fetal brain segmentation demonstrated the superiority of our method over five state-of-the-art scribble-supervised methods. Our method has the potential for achieving accurate segmentation models based on scribbles, which can largely reduce the annotation cost. In the future, it is of interest to implement our method with 3D CNNs and apply it to more multi-class segmentation tasks.

Acknowledgment. This work was supported by the National Natural Science Foundation of China under Grant 62271115.

References

1. Budd, S., et al.: Detecting hypo-plastic left heart syndrome in fetal ultrasound via disease-specific atlas maps. In: de Bruijne, M., et al. (eds.) MICCAI 2021. LNCS,

vol. 12907, pp. 207–217. Springer, Cham (2021). https://doi.org/10.1007/978-3-030-87234-2_20

2. Chen, Q., Hong, Y.: Scribble2d5: weakly-supervised volumetric image segmentation via scribble annotations. In: MICCAI, pp. 234–243. Springer Nature Switzerland, Cham (2022). https://doi.org/10.1007/978-3-031-16452-1_23

3. Fidon, L., et al.: Label-set loss functions for partial supervision: application to fetal brain 3D MRI parcellation. In: de Bruijne, M., et al. (eds.) MICCAI 2021. LNCS, vol. 12902, pp. 647–657. Springer, Cham (2021). https://doi.org/10.1007/978-3-030-87196-3_60

4. Grandvalet, Y., Bengio, Y.: Semi-supervised learning by entropy minimization. In: NeurIPS, pp. 281–296 (2005)

5. Hinton, G., Vinyals, O., Dean, J.: Distilling the knowledge in a neural network. In: NeurIPS, pp. 1–9 (2015)

6. Kim, B., Ye, J.C.: Mumford-Shah loss functional for image segmentation with deep learning. IEEE Trans. Image Process. **29**, 1856–1866 (2019)

7. Lee, H., Jeong, W.-K.: Scribble2Label: scribble-supervised cell segmentation via self-generating pseudo-labels with consistency. In: Martel, A.L., et al. (eds.) MICCAI 2020. LNCS, vol. 12261, pp. 14–23. Springer, Cham (2020). https://doi.org/10.1007/978-3-030-59710-8_2

8. Lin, D., Dai, J., Jia, J., He, K., Sun, J.: Scribblesup: scribble-supervised convolutional networks for semantic segmentation. In: CVPR, pp. 3159–3167 (2016)

9. Liu, X., et al.: Weakly supervised segmentation of COVID19 infection with scribble annotation on CT images. Pattern Recogn. **122**, 108341 (2022)

10. Luo, X., et al.: Scribble-supervised medical image segmentation via dual-branch network and dynamically mixed pseudo labels supervision. In: MICCAI, pp. 528–538. Springer (2022). https://doi.org/10.1007/978-3-031-16431-6_50

11. Luo, X., et al.: WORD: A large scale dataset, benchmark and clinical applicable study for abdominal organ segmentation from CT image. Med. Image Anal. **82**, 102642 (2022)

12. Müller, R., Kornblith, S., Hinton, G.E.: When does label smoothing help? In: NeurIPS, pp. 1–10 (2019)

13. Obukhov, A., Georgoulis, S., Dai, D., Van Gool, L.: Gated CRF loss for weakly supervised semantic image segmentation. In: NeurIPS, pp. 1–9 (2019)

14. Rajchl, M., et al.: Deepcut: object segmentation from bounding box annotations using convolutional neural networks. IEEE Trans. Med. Imaging **36**(2), 674–683 (2016)

15. Ronneberger, O., Fischer, P., Brox, T.: U-Net: convolutional networks for biomedical image segmentation. In: Navab, N., Hornegger, J., Wells, W.M., Frangi, A.F. (eds.) MICCAI 2015. LNCS, vol. 9351, pp. 234–241. Springer, Cham (2015). https://doi.org/10.1007/978-3-319-24574-4_28

16. Salehi, S.S.M., et al.: Real-time automatic fetal brain extraction in fetal MRI by deep learning. In: ISBI, pp. 720–724. IEEE (2018)

17. Tang, M., Djelouah, A., Perazzi, F., Boykov, Y., Schroers, C.: Normalized cut loss for weakly-supervised cnn segmentation. In: CVPR, pp. 1818–1827 (2018)

18. Tang, M., et al.: On regularized losses for weakly-supervised CNN segmentation. In: Ferrari, V., Hebert, M., Sminchisescu, C., Weiss, Y. (eds.) ECCV 2018. LNCS, vol. 11220, pp. 524–540. Springer, Cham (2018). https://doi.org/10.1007/978-3-030-01270-0_31

19. Tarvainen, A., Valpola, H.: Mean teachers are better role models: weight-averaged consistency targets improve semi-supervised deep learning results. In NeurIPS, pp. 1195–1204 (2017)

20. Torrents-Barrena, J., et al.: Fully automatic 3D reconstruction of the placenta and its peripheral vasculature in intrauterine fetal MRI. Med. Image Anal. **54**, 263–279 (2019)

21. Uus, A.U., et al.: Automated 3D reconstruction of the fetal thorax in the standard atlas space from motion-corrupted MRI stacks for 21–36 weeks GA range. Med. Image Anal. **80**, 102484 (2022)

22. Valvano, G., Leo, A., Tsaftaris, S.A.: Learning to segment from scribbles using multi-scale adversarial attention gates. IEEE Trans. Med. Imaging **40**(8), 1990–2001 (2021)

23. Wu, K., Du, B., Luo, M., Wen, H., Shen, Y., Feng, J.: Weakly supervised brain lesion segmentation via attentional representation learning. In: Shen, D., et al. (eds.) MICCAI 2019. LNCS, vol. 11766, pp. 211–219. Springer, Cham (2019). https://doi.org/10.1007/978-3-030-32248-9_24

24. Xu, K., Rui, L., Li, Y., Gu, L.: Feature normalized knowledge distillation for image classification. In: Vedaldi, A., Bischof, H., Brox, T., Frahm, J.-M. (eds.) ECCV 2020. LNCS, vol. 12370, pp. 664–680. Springer, Cham (2020). https://doi.org/10.1007/978-3-030-58595-2_40

25. Zhang, X., et al.: Confidence-aware cascaded network for fetal brain segmentation on MR images. In: de Bruijne, M., et al. (eds.) MICCAI 2021. LNCS, vol. 12903, pp. 584–593. Springer, Cham (2021). https://doi.org/10.1007/978-3-030-87199-4_55

Label-Efficient Contrastive Learning-Based Model for Nuclei Detection and Classification in 3D Cardiovascular Immunofluorescent Images

Nazanin Moradinasab[1]([✉])[ID], Rebecca A. Deaton[2][ID], Laura S. Shankman[2][ID], Gary K. Owens[3][ID], and Donald E. Brown[4][ID]

[1] Department of Engineering Systems and Environment,
University of Virginia, Charlottesville, VA, USA
nm4wu@virginia.edu

[2] Laboratory of Dr. Gary Owens Cardiovascular Research Center,
University of Virginia, Charlottesville, VA, USA
{rad5x,lss4f}@virginia.edu

[3] Department of Molecular Physiology and Biological Physics,
University of Virginia, Charlottesville, VA, USA
gko@virginia.edu

[4] School of Data Science, University of Virginia, Charlottesville, VA, USA
deb@virginia.edu

Abstract. Recently, deep learning-based methods achieved promising performance in nuclei detection and classification applications. However, training deep learning-based methods requires a large amount of pixel-wise annotated data, which is time-consuming and labor-intensive, especially in 3D images. An alternative approach is to adapt weak-annotation methods, such as labeling each nucleus with a point, but this method does not extend from 2D histopathology images (for which it was originally developed) to 3D immunofluorescent images. The reason is that 3D images contain multiple channels (z-axis) for nuclei and different markers separately, which makes training using point annotations difficult. To address this challenge, we propose the Label-efficient Contrastive learning-based (LECL) model to detect and classify various types of nuclei in 3D immunofluorescent images. Previous methods use Maximum Intensity Projection (MIP) to convert immunofluorescent images with multiple slices to 2D images, which can cause signals from different z-stacks to falsely appear associated with each other. To overcome this, we devised an Extended Maximum Intensity Projection (EMIP) approach that addresses issues using MIP. Furthermore, we performed a Supervised Contrastive Learning (SCL) approach for weakly supervised settings. We conducted experiments on cardiovascular datasets and found that our proposed framework is effective and efficient in detecting and classifying various types of nuclei in 3D immunofluorescent images.

Keywords: Nuclei detection · Classification · Point annotations

© The Author(s), under exclusive license to Springer Nature Switzerland AG 2023
Z. Xue et al. (Eds.): MILLanD 2023, LNCS 14307, pp. 24–34, 2023.
https://doi.org/10.1007/978-3-031-44917-8_3

1   Introduction

Analyzing immunofluorescent images is crucial for understanding the underlying causes of myocardial infarctions (MI) and strokes [1,12], which are leading global causes of death [14]. Clinical studies suggest that plaque composition, rather than lesion size, is more indicative of plaque rupture or erosion events [4,9]. However, determining plaque composition from 3D immunofluorescent images manually is time-consuming and prone to human error. To address these challenges, an automated algorithm is needed to detect and classify nuclei in 3D immunofluorescent images. Deep learning algorithms have shown significant success in medical image segmentation and classification tasks, including histopathology and fluorescent microscopy images [5]. However, these methods typically require a large number of pixel-level annotations, which can be time-consuming and labor-intensive, especially for 3D images. To address this issue, weak-annotation methods have emerged, such as labeling each nucleus with a single point [2,6,10,11,13,16]. While all these studies focus on developing weakly supervised models for nuclei detection in 2D images, our study is the first to leverage weakly annotated data while preserving the 3D nature of the images.

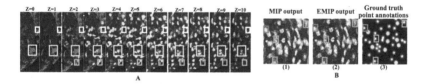

Fig. 1. A) Challenges: **(1) nucleus in the yellow square:** Even though the ground truth labels for the nucleus in the yellow and green squares are positive, they are only coincident in the second slice, **(2) nucleus in the white square:** it shows an example of nonoverlapping marker and nucleus, (B-1) The MIP approach's output, (B-2) The EMIP approach's output, (B-3) Ground truth point annotations: green color represents nuclei labeled as positive, and white color represents nuclei labeled as negative. (Color figure online)

The study conducted by Moradinasab *et al.* [6] is highly relevant to our work. They introduce a weakly supervised approach for nuclei detection via point annotations and employ the HoVer-Net model. To tackle the challenge of training with point annotations, they adopt the cluster labeling approach [11] to derive pixel-level labels. Nevertheless, their proposed method does not classify the type of detected nuclei, which is crucial for determining plaque composition in 3D cardiovascular immunofluorescent images. Additionally, the authors converted the multichannel 3D images into z-stacked images using the Maximum Intensity Projection (MIP) technique and trained the HoVer-Net model on the resulting z-stack images. The MIP approach is a common technique used to reduce the computational burden in image analysis. Several studies, such as Noguchi et al.

(2023) [8] and Nagao et al. (2020) [7], have successfully employed the MIP technique for image preprocessing to convert 3D images into 2D format in tasks like cell segmentation and cell cycle phase classification. Nevertheless, it's important to consider that the MIP approach might not be the optimal option for nuclei detection and classification models, as elaborated in the subsequent section.

To address these challenges, this paper proposes the Label-efficient Contrastive learning-based (LECL) model for nuclei detection/classification in 3D multichannel fluorescent images. The model aims to detect nuclei and assign them a classification label based on specific markers (e.g., Lineage Tracing) with minimum labeling cost. We assign the label "positive" if and only if the given detected nucleus overlaps with the given marker, otherwise, it is labeled as "negative". It is notable that training the model to classify the type of each nucleus using weak annotations in these images is a difficult task because these images contain multiple channels (Z-axis) for nuclei and different markers, as shown in Fig. 4-a in Appendix. The main challenges of nuclei detection/classification in 3D images are described in detail in Sect. 2. To address these challenges, we developed a new approach called Extended Maximum Intensity Projection (EMIP) that partially performs the maximum intensity projection per nucleus where z levels contain the given nucleus to convert multi-channel images to 2D z-stack images. Furthermore, to improve the performance of the model further in a weakly setting, we perform the supervised contrastive learning approach.

2 Challenges

The main challenges associated with detecting and classifying the types of nuclei in fluorescent images can be categorized into three groups as follows:

1. **One specific nucleus might spread over multiple z-slices, as shown in Fig. 1-A, but only have a point annotation in one z-slice.** For example, the blue color nucleus in the orange square spreads over z-slices from two to eight, but the experts are asked to only annotate that nucleus in one of the slices to minimize the labeling cost.
2. **The marker and nucleus might not be coincident in all z-slices.** In fluorescent images, the given nucleus is labeled as positive if that nucleus and the marker overlap at least in one of the z-slices. In other words, even though the ground truth label for the nucleus is positive, the nucleus might not contain the marker in some slices as shown in Fig. 1-A.
3. **Maximum Intensity Projection (MIP) can cause objects to appear coincident that are actually separated in space.** Some studies use MIP to convert multi-channel 3D images into 2D z-stack images [8], as shown in Fig. 4-b in Appendix. This approach utilizes MIP over nuclei/marker channels to convert these 3D images to 2D images (i.e., collapse images along with the z-axis). Then, the 2D nuclei image is combined with the 2D marker image using the linear combination method. However, this approach can be problematic when there are non-overlapping nuclei and markers in the same

x and y, but at different z-axis. Figure 1-A illustrates this, where the blue nucleus and red marker in the white square indicate non-overlapping objects that could be falsely shown as overlapping using the MIP approach.

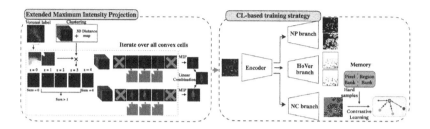

Fig. 2. Schematic representation of the LECL model

3   Method

In this section, we describe the proposed Label-efficient Contrastive learning-based (LECL) model (Fig. 2), which consists of two components: a) Extended Maximum Intensity Projection (EMIP) and b) Supervised Contrastive Learning-based (SCL) training strategy.

3.1   Extended Maximum Intensity Projection (EMIP)

The EMIP method is proposed to address the issue of non-overlapping nuclei and markers in the MIP approach. It uses maximum intensity projection for each nucleus separately, only considering the z-slices containing that nucleus. For example, if a nucleus spans z-slices from seven to ten, EMIP applies MIP only to those slices. This ensures an accurate representation of the nucleus without mistakenly overlapping with the marker. Figure 1-B compares the outputs of the MIP and EMIP approaches for an example image (Fig. 3-A). The EMIP approach prevents the lineage tracing marker (in red) from falsely appearing over nuclei with the ground truth label negative. The nuclei in the pink and orange squares with the ground truth label negative falsely contain signals of the marker in the output of MIP, whereas EMIP avoids this issue.

Algorithm 1 outlines the steps of the EMIP approach. To perform the EMIP approach, two types of information are necessary: (a) which z-slices are associated with each individual nucleus and (b) the boundaries of each nucleus along the x- and y-axes. To determine approximate boundaries using point annotations, we propose using k-means clustering and Voronoi label methods (Steps 1-6 in Algorithm 1). It's essential to note that all nuclei have been annotated with points located at their centers, ensuring we have ground truth point annotations for all nuclei in the dataset. However, due to the nature of 3D images,

---

Algorithm 1: Extended Maximum Intensity Projection

---

linenosize= **input**: multi-channel images, Point-level annotations

for $i = 1 : N$ *(Number of images)* **do**

1. Generate the 3D distance map (D_i) using point annotations
2. Create the feature map by combining the distance map and nuclei z-slices
3. Apply k-mean clustering on the feature map
4. Identify background cluster (i.e., Min overlap with the dilated point labels)
5. Generate 3D binary masks
6. Generate the 2D Voronoi label using point annotations

    for $j = 1 : N_{cell}$ *(Number of convex cells in the 2D Voronoi label)* **do**

      (a) Generate the Voronoi Cell (VC) binary mask for cell j
      (b) Find the intersection between VC mask and 3D binary mask (I_j^{3D})
      (c) Determine the set of slices (S_j) containing the $Nuclous_j$ by taking summation over the z-slices in I_j^{3D}
      (d) Find the intersection between VC and the nuclei/marker z-slice
      (e) Compute the maximum intensity projection for nuclei and marker channels only over the corresponding slices (S_j) for convex cell j

end **end**

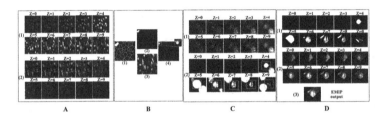

Fig. 3. (A-1) The nuclei z-slices, (A-2) The marker z-slices, (B-1) The Voronoi label, (B-2) The Voronoi Cell (VC) binary mask associated to convex cell j that assigns label 1 to convex cell j and zero to others, (B-3) The z-slice 6 of nuclei channel, (B-4) The multiplication's output of VC mask and z-slice 6 which depicts the nucleus located in convex cell j, (C-1) nuclei z-slices, (C-2) The 3D binary mask, (D-1) The intersection between VC mask (B-2) and 3D binary mask (C-2), (D-2) the intersection between the VC binary mask and the nuclei/marker z-slices, (D-3) EMIP output

nuclei are often spread across multiple slices, and the center of each nucleus is only located in one of the slices. Therefore, while every nucleus has a point annotation, these annotations are limited to the z-slice where the nucleus center is present. Consequently, point annotations for all nuclei per slice are unavailable. Using k-means clustering, we generate 3D binary masks (steps 3–5). First, we create a 3D distance map from the distance transform of point annotations (step 1). This map represents distances to the nearest nuclear point. Combining the distance map with nuclei channels of the multi-channel nuclei/marker image creates a features map (step 2). Next, k-means clustering (k=3) is applied to the feature maps, resulting in 3D binary masks. Label 0 represents the background cluster with minimal overlap with dilated point labels, and label 1 corresponds to nuclei pixels. An example of the nuclei channels and the 3D binary mask is shown in Fig. 3-C. As shown, the binary mask indicates that the given nucleus in the orange square is spreading only over z-slices from four to nine (i.e., it approximates the nucleus' boundaries over the z-axis). To find the nuclei boundaries on the x- and y-axes, Voronoi labels are created (step 6) using point annotations (Fig. 3-B-(1)). Assuming that each Voronoi convex cell contains only one nucleus, the Voronoi edges separate all nuclei from each other well. Next, we iterate through Voronoi convex cells (steps a–e) and create a Voronoi Cell (VC) binary mask for each cell, approximating nuclei boundaries on the x- and y-axes. Figure 3-B-(2) shows the VC binary mask for convex cell j. Since each cell is assumed to contain only one nucleus, the intersection of the VC binary mask with nuclei/marker channels reveals the nucleus in that cell (Fig. 3-B-(4)). Likewise, the intersection of the VC and 3D binary masks will reveal only the nucleus mask (represented by the color white) within the corresponding cell (Fig. 3-D-(1)). As nuclei and background take values of one (i.e., white color) and zero (i.e., black color) respectively, simply, summation over the z-slices can be used as a detector of the presence of the nucleus. If the sum is greater than one, it implies the nucleus is present in that z-slice. Figure 3-D-(1) shows that the nucleus corresponding to the convex cell j is spreading over z-slices four to nine, and its boundaries over the x- and y- axes can be determined using the given convex cell edges. Figure 3-D-(3) illustrates that a MIP is performed over the z-slices spanning from four to nine for the nucleus situated within the convex cell. This technique avoids the lineage tracing marker, which spreads over slices zero to three, from overlapping with the nucleus.

3.2 Supervised Contrastive Learning-Based (SCL) Training Strategy

The Hover-Net model [3] is used for nuclei detection and classification due to its strong generalizability and instance detection performance. The generated pixel-wise masks contain three regions: nuclei, background, and an unlabeled area. For training the NC branch, Eq. 1 is used, employing the cross-entropy (L^{CE}), Dice (L^{Dice}), SCL (L^{SCL}), and entropy-minimization ($L^{entropy}$) loss functions. The Hover and NP branches were trained using the approach from [6]. The entropy-minimization loss is applied to the unlabeled area.

$$
\begin{aligned}
L &= L^{CE} + L^{Dice} + L^{SupCon} + L^{entropy} \\
L^{CE} &= -\frac{1}{n}\Sigma_{i=1}^{N}\Sigma_{k=1}^{K}X_{i,k}(I)logY_{i,k}(I) \\
L^{Dice} &= 1 - \frac{2\Sigma_{i=1}^{N}(X_i(I)\times Y_i(I))+\epsilon}{\Sigma_{i=1}^{N}X_i(I)+\Sigma_{i=1}^{N}Y_i(I)+\epsilon} \\
L^{SCL} &= \frac{-1}{|P(q)|}\sum_{q^+\in P(q)}log\frac{exp(q\cdot q^+/\tau)}{exp(q\cdot q^+/\tau)+\sum_{q^-\in N(i)}exp(q\cdot q^-/\tau)} \\
L^{entropy} &= -\Sigma_{i=1}^{N}\Sigma_{k=1}^{K}Y_{i,k}(I)logY_{i,k}(I)
\end{aligned}
\tag{1}
$$

where Y, X, K, N, and $\epsilon(1.0e-3)$ are the prediction, ground truth, number of classes, number of images, and smoothness constant, respectively. The Cross-Entropy Loss function has two limitations: 1) It penalizes pixel-wise predictions independently without considering their relationships, and 2) It does not directly supervise the learned representations. HoVer-Net improves upon the Cross-Entropy Loss function by incorporating the Dice loss function, which considers pixel dependencies within an image. However, the Dice loss function does not account for global semantic relationships across images. To address the issue, we enhance our model's performance by incorporating Pixel-to-Pixel and Pixel-to-Region Supervised Contrastive Learning (SCL) [15] techniques alongside cross-entropy and Dice losses in the third branch. We introduce a projection head in the NC branch, outputting the embedding q per pixel, which is optimized using the last row of Eq. 1. Where, $p(q)$ and $N(q)$ indicate the set of positive and negative embedding samples, respectively.

4 Experimental Results

Metrics: To evaluate the model's performance, we utilize the popular detection/classification metrics: precision $(P = \frac{TP}{TP+FP})$, recall $(R = \frac{TP}{TP+FN})$, and F1-score $(F1 = \frac{2TP}{2TP+FP+FN})$.

Datasets: We experimented with three datasets: **Cardiovascular dataset 1 (D1)** and **Cardiovascular dataset 2 (D2)**, containing advanced atherosclerotic lesion images from two mouse models. D1 has 13 images, with 11 used for training and 2 for testing. These images vary in size along the z-axis (8 to 13). We extract 256×256-pixel patches with 10% overlap. The train and test sets have 370 and 74 patches respectively. Additionally, we have a separate evaluation set called D2 (29 images) that are used for further evaluation. Our aim was to propose a label-efficient model that achieves comparable results with minimum labeling effort, so we trained our model on the smaller dataset. Please refer to Appendix (Table 3) for more details. Additionally, we used the **CoNSeP dataset** [1] [3], which contains 24,332 nuclei from 41 whole slide images (26 for training and 14 for testing), with 7 different classes: fibroblast, dysplastic/malignant epithelial, inflammatory, healthy epithelial, muscle, other, and endothelial.

Table 1. The performance of proposed methods on D1 and D2

Model	Branch	D1			D2		
		Precision	Recall	F1	Precision	Recall	F1
HoVer-Net [3] (MIP)	NP	**0.8898**	0.8894	0.8883	**0.9233**	0.8455	0.8816
	NC	0.6608	0.8511	0.7424	0.7150	0.6663	0.6703
HoVer-Net [3] (EMIP)	NP	0.8551	**0.9353**	0.8880	0.9064	0.8743	0.8894
	NC	0.7694	0.7800	0.7718	0.8114	0.7718	0.7760
Qu et al. [11] (EMIP)	NP	0.7774	0.8489	0.8084	0.6525	0.877	0.7431
	NC	**0.8548**	0.6048	0.6881	0.8140	0.5749	0.6577
LECL	NP	0.8764	0.9154	**0.8942**	0.9215	0.877	**0.8978**
	NC	0.8277	**0.7668**	**0.7890**	**0.8392**	**0.7840**	**0.7953**

---

[1] https://warwick.ac.uk/fac/cross_fac/tia/data/hovernet/

Test Time: We combine nuclei and marker channels per slice using the linear combination method (Fig. 4-a in Appendix). The model detects and classifies nuclei in each slice individually. The final output is integrated over the slices with this rule: If a nucleus is predicted positive in at least one slice, it is labeled positive, otherwise negative.

Results: Table 1 shows the performance of different approaches on D1 and D2. The first row shows the results of using regular MIP during both the training and test stages, while the second row shows the model's performance trained using EMIP. The NP branch indicates the model's performance in detecting nuclei, and the NC branch denotes the model's performance in classifying the type of detected nuclei. As observed, the EMIP approach improves precision and F1 score metrics by 16.43% and 3.96% on D1, respectively, indicating a decrease in false positives. To ensure a comprehensive evaluation of our proposed method, we have included Dataset D2 in our study. The selection of D2 was based on its larger size and representativeness, making it suitable for robust performance assessment. As observed, the proposed EMIP approach achieves higher precision, recall, and F1 scores than the MIP method. The study found that the EMIP approach reduces false positives in lineage tracing markers overlapping with nuclei. Furthermore, we compare the performance of the HoVer-Net [3] model with Qu *et al.* [11] on both datasets D1 and D2. Hyper-parameters for Qu *et al.* [11] was borrowed from [11]. As observed, the HoVer-Net model [3] outperforms Qu*et al.* [11] in both nuclei detection and classification. We investigate the benefits of combining SCL-based training and EMIP in the LECL model. The SCL loss enhances the model's performance by capturing global semantic relationships between pixel samples, resulting in better intra-class compactness and inter-class separability. On both D1 and D2, the LECL model outperforms other models. For visualization examples, refer to Fig. 5 in the Appendix. Furthermore, the hyperparameters for all experiments have been provided in Table 4 in the Appendix.

Table 2. The effect of SCL based training approach on the CoNSep dataset

Model	F_d	F_c^e	F_c^i	F_c^s	F_c^m
HoVer-Net [3] w/o SCL (Weakly)	0.735	0.578	0.542	0.461	0.147
HoVer-Net [3] w SCL (Weakly)	0.738	0.576	0.551	0.480	0.212

Ablation Study: To investigate further the performance of the SCL-based HoVer-Net, we evaluate the model on the ConSep dataset (Table 2). Here, F_d represents the F1-score for nuclei detection, while F_c^e, F_c^i, F_c^s, and F_c^m indicate the F1-scores for epithelial, inflammatory, spindle-shaped, and miscellaneous, respectively. The SCL-based model achieves better performance.

5   Discussion

Developing an automated approach for 3D nuclei detection and classification in fluorescent images requires expensive pixel-wise annotations. To overcome this, we propose a LECL model, which includes the EMIP and SCL components. The EMIP approach improves upon the limitations of the MIP approach, while the SCL learning approach enhances the model's performance by learning more discriminative features. However, a limitation of this study is that it relies on point annotations performed by domain experts during training and testing, which can be challenging and prone to human error. To address this, future work could explore generating synthetic data with reliable labels and using domain adaptation techniques to improve performance on real-world datasets. Moreover, the study focuses solely on lineage tracing markers, leaving room for exploring the proposed method's performance on other markers, like LGALS3.

Acknowledgments. This work was supported by an American Heart Association Predoctoral Fellowship (23PRE1028980), NIH R01 HL155165, NIH R01 156849, and National Center for Advancing Translational Science of the National Institutes of Health Award UL1 TR003015. Furthermore, we would like to thank Simon Graham, Quoc Dang Vu, Shan E Ahmed Raza, Ayesha Azam, Yee Wah Tsang, Jin Tae Kwak, and Nasir Rajpoot for providing the public CoNSep dataset.

A   Appendix

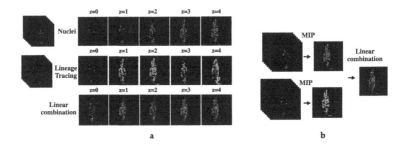

Fig. 4. a) It presents the sequence of channels (i.e. z=0,..,n) for the nuclei (first row) and the Lineage Tracing marker (second row). The nuclei and Lineage Tracing marker channels are associated with each other in order. The third row indicates the linear combination of the nuclei and Lineage Tracing marker per slice.

Table 3. Cardiovascular datasets

Characteristics	Dataset	Value
Model	D1	$Myh11 - CreER_{T2} - RADROSA26 - STOP_{flox} - tdTomApoe - /-$
	D2	$Myh11 - CreER_{T2} - RADROSA26 - STOP_{flox} - tdTomIrs1_{\Delta/\Delta}Irs2_{\Delta/\Delta}$
Diet	D1	Western diet for 18 weeks
	D2	Western diet for 18 weeks

Table 4. Training setup for all experiments

Characteristic	Value	Characteristic		Value
Pytorch	1.10	**Loss function weights**	Entropy	0.5
			Cross-entropy	1
			Dice loss	1
GPU	Tesla p100	**Number of epochs**		100
Projection head	Two convolutional layers, outputting a 256 *l*2-normalized feature vector			

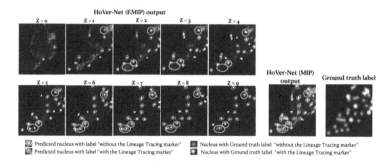

Fig. 5. The model's output trained using the HoVer-Net(MIP) and HoVer-Net(EMIP). The HoVer-Net (EMIP) model correctly predicts label positive for nuclei in the yellow circle, which is consistent with the ground truth labels. In contrast, HoVer-Net (MIP) incorrectly predicts these nuclei as negative. Both models incorrectly predict the nuclei's labels in the blue circle. (Color figure online)

References

1. Biccard, B.M., et al.: Perioperative patient outcomes in the African surgical outcomes study: a 7-day prospective observational cohort study. Lancet **391**(10130), 1589–1598 (2018)
2. Chamanzar, A., Nie, Y.: Weakly supervised multi-task learning for cell detection and segmentation. In: 2020 IEEE 17th International Symposium on Biomedical Imaging (ISBI), pp. 513–516. IEEE (2020)
3. Graham, S., et al.: Hover-net: simultaneous segmentation and classification of nuclei in multi-tissue histology images. Med. Image Anal. **58**, 101563 (2019)
4. Libby, P.: Inflammation in atherosclerosis. Arterioscler. Thromb. Vasc. Biol. **32**(9), 2045–2051 (2012)
5. Liu, X., et al.: Advances in deep learning-based medical image analysis. Health Data Science 2021 (2021)
6. Moradinasab, N., Sharma, Y., Shankman, L.S., Owens, G.K., Brown, D.E.: Weakly supervised deep instance nuclei detection using points annotation in 3D cardiovascular immunofluorescent images (2022)
7. Nagao, Y., Sakamoto, M., Chinen, T., Okada, Y., Takao, D.: Robust classification of cell cycle phase and biological feature extraction by image-based deep learning. Mol. Biol. Cell **31**(13), 1346–1354 (2020)

8. Noguchi, Y., Murakami, M., Murata, M., Kano, F.: Microscopic image-based classification of adipocyte differentiation by machine learning. Histochem. Cell Biol. **159**(4), 313–327 (2023)

9. Pasterkamp, G., Den Ruijter, H.M., Libby, P.: Temporal shifts in clinical presentation and underlying mechanisms of atherosclerotic disease. Nat. Rev. Cardiol. **14**(1), 21–29 (2017)

10. Qu, H., et al.: Joint segmentation and fine-grained classification of nuclei in histopathology images. In: 2019 IEEE 16th International Symposium on Biomedical Imaging (ISBI 2019), pp. 900–904. IEEE (2019)

11. Qu, H., et al.: Weakly supervised deep nuclei segmentation using points annotation in histopathology images. In: International Conference on Medical Imaging with Deep Learning, pp. 390–400. PMLR (2019)

12. Rickard, J.L., Ntakiyiruta, G., Chu, K.M.: Associations with perioperative mortality rate at a major referral hospital in Rwanda. World J. Surg. **40**(4), 784–790 (2016)

13. Tian, K., et al.: Weakly-supervised nucleus segmentation based on point annotations: a coarse-to-fine self-stimulated learning strategy. In: Martel, A.L., et al. (eds.) Medical Image Computing and Computer Assisted Intervention – MICCAI 2020: 23rd International Conference, Lima, Peru, October 4–8, 2020, Proceedings, Part V, pp. 299–308. Springer International Publishing, Cham (2020). https://doi.org/10.1007/978-3-030-59722-1_29

14. Virmani, R., Kolodgie, F.D., Burke, A.P., Farb, A., Schwartz, S.M.: Lessons from sudden coronary death: a comprehensive morphological classification scheme for atherosclerotic lesions. Arterioscler. Thromb. Vasc. Biol. **20**(5), 1262–1275 (2000)

15. Wang, W., Zhou, T., Yu, F., Dai, J., Konukoglu, E., Van Gool, L.: Exploring cross-image pixel contrast for semantic segmentation. In: Proceedings of the IEEE/CVF International Conference on Computer Vision, pp. 7303–7313 (2021)

16. Yoo, I., Yoo, D., Paeng, K.: PseudoEdgeNet: nuclei segmentation only with point annotations. In: Shen, D., et al. (eds.) Medical Image Computing and Computer Assisted Intervention – MICCAI 2019: 22nd International Conference, Shenzhen, China, October 13–17, 2019, Proceedings, Part I, pp. 731–739. Springer, Cham (2019). https://doi.org/10.1007/978-3-030-32239-7_81

Affordable Graph Neural Network Framework Using Topological Graph Contraction

Christopher Adnel and Islem Rekik[✉]ⓘ

BASIRA Lab, Imperial-X and Department of Computing,
Imperial College London, London, UK
i.rekik@imperial.ac.uk
http://basira-lab.com

Abstract. Graph neural networks (GNNs) have many applications, including the medical field (e.g., neuroscience), thanks to their flexibility and expressiveness in handling unstructured graph-based data. However, one major issue in applying GNNs for medical applications is their unscalability in handling large and complex graphs, primarily due to their high memory usage. This high memory usage is controlled mainly by the data points' interconnectivity and the neighbourhood expansion problem, which causes non-trivial mini-batching, unlike standard neural networks. While many recent publications are focusing on mini-batching GNN using sub-graph sampling/partitioning methods, there are many other directions to take in terms of reducing memory usage, such as quantisation and graph reduction methods. In this paper, we propose a novel topological graph contraction method using centrality measure and a memory-efficient GNN training framework (C-QSIGN), which incorporates our proposed contraction method along with several other state-of-the-art (SOTA) methods. Furthermore, we benchmarked our proposed model performance in terms of prediction quality and GPU usage against other SOTA methods. We show that C-QSIGN requires the least GPU memory compared to benchmark SOTA models (54% of SIGN and 18% of GCN on the Organ C dataset), allowing more efficient learning on complex, large-scale graphs. Our codes are publicly available at https://github.com/basiralab/CQSIGN.

Keywords: graph neural network · GNN memory efficient training · graph centralitiy measure · graph contraction · SIGN · quantisation

1 Introduction

GNNs represent a class of artificial neural networks specifically designed to handle graph-based data (e.g., social networks, molecule structure [1], and protein interactions [2]) and to solve graph-related tasks such as node classification, clustering, and link prediction [3]. Although GNNs have already been the popular methods for tasks like recommendation system [4] and fraud detections

© The Author(s), under exclusive license to Springer Nature Switzerland AG 2023
Z. Xue et al. (Eds.): MILLanD 2023, LNCS 14307, pp. 35–46, 2023.
https://doi.org/10.1007/978-3-031-44917-8_4

Fig. 1. Proposed four-stage GNN memory improvement framework

[5], recently, they also started gaining traction in medical fields [6], especially neuroscience, where brains are modelled as graphs consisting of the anatomical region of interests (ROI) as nodes and edges that model either morphological, functional, or structural connections between ROIs [7]. Furthermore, being a generalised version of convolutional neural network (CNN) [3], GNN can also be used to solve computer vision-related tasks such as image segmentation [8] including those for medical applications (e.g., liver tumour classification [9]).

The main benefit of GNN over standard neural networks is that in addition to utilising the feature of each data point (node embedding), it also utilises the connection information (represented by edges) between data points which can lead to improved prediction performance. However, the interconnected nature of the data points also introduces some limitations regarding computational efficiency (i.e., GPU memory complexity), which limits the scalability of GNNs for real-world applications, including medical applications. [6] supports this, highlighting graph complexity and training efficiency as one of the seven major limitations in applying GNNs for medical and healthcare data analysis. Most GNN methods such as Graph Convolutional Network (GCN) [10], Neural Message Passing Scheme (NPMS) [1], and Graph Attention Network (GAT) [11] rely on embedding aggregation from connected neighbouring nodes along with embedding transformation on each layer which creates a strong coupling between the aggregation and transformation phase. This leads to non-trivial mini-batched stochastic gradient descent (SGD) training, as it is challenging to construct a mini-batch while maintaining the inter-batch connections. Conversely, full-batched gradient descent (GD) training does not have this issue, but it does not scale well with large and complex graphs due to GPU memory limitation [12].

In this present work, we introduce a novel topological graph contraction method along with a simple memory-efficient GNN training framework which combines various SOTA methods in memory-efficient GNN training as shown in Fig 1. The framework presents four types of improvements, each corresponding to a different stage in the GNN training process. Since each of these improvements applies to a different stage of the training process, they can theoretically be applied on top of each other. Our work focuses on the first three training stages: graph preprocessing, mini-batch construction, and model compression.

While many of the recently published methods on memory-efficient GNN training focus on mini-batch construction [12–15] or implementing quantisation on the layers [16,17], graph reduction is still relatively under-explored. Graph reduction aims to reduce or contract the number of nodes in the input sample graph while preserving only the most essential nodes to maintain the prediction performance. Some of the most notable works in this direction utilise neighbourhood similarity measures of posterior probability such as KL divergence and cross-entropy [18], and another uses graph coarsening algorithms [19]. However, the use of classical graph centrality measures to drive the reduction has yet to be explored thoroughly, even though it is one of the simplest methods for quantifying node importance. [20] mentioned using centrality to select nodes to label for GNN training in a high labelling cost scenario, but no mention of memory usage is made. Hence, our work explores various centrality measures to drive the graph contraction in the proposed framework.

Related Work. Moving towards the mini-batch construction stage, a well-known computational difficulty in this stage is the neighbourhood expansion problem. Precisely, to compute an embedding of node v_i in layer l, we need to store the embeddings of its neighbours $v_j \in N(v_i)$ in layer $l - 1$, which subsequently requires the embeddings of $v_k \in N(v_j)$ in layer $l - 2$ and so on. This recursive neighbourhood access causes a time complexity exponential to GCN layer depth should we compute the exact embedding for out-of-batch nodes in the mini-batched training [12]. One of the first partitioning methods, Cluster-GCN [12], constructs the batch using sub-graph partitions through graph clustering algorithms (e.g., METIS [21]), and inter-batch connections are neglected. A clustering algorithm is used to drive the partitioning such that it minimises the number of inter-batch edges, and thus, its removal should pose a minimal impact on performance. However, removing inter-batch edges might remove otherwise meaningful topological information from the graph [13]. Improving upon Cluster-GCN [12], GNN Auto Scale [13] combines Cluster-GCN [12] with the concept of historical embedding by [22], which is defined as previous node embedding values computed in the last iteration. In GNN Auto Scale [13], instead of neglecting the inter-batch edges, we are approximating the out-of-batch node embedding values using its historical embedding. Therefore, unlike Cluster-GCN [12], GNN Auto Scale [13] is able to maintain all edges in the graph. However, one downside is that it gives us the same memory complexity as full-batched training, which we want to avoid in the first place. To avoid this, GNN Auto Scale [13] stores the historical embeddings in the main memory (RAM) and communicates the embedding information to GPU to retrieve and update the historical embeddings when needed. However, this will add some communication overheads for CPU to GPU transfer along with some approximation errors due to stale embedding computations. A more recent work, LMC-GNN [14], improves upon GNN Auto Scale [13] by using a convex combination of incomplete up-to-date messages along with the historical messages to approximate the inter-batch messages more accurately. LMC-GNN [14] shows that although it minimally affects GPU memory efficiency, getting more accurate inter-batch messages approximation leads to faster training convergence. Another recent work which will be adopted in the present framework is SIGN [15], which took a different approach by decoupling feature aggregation and transformation phase. SIGN [15] allows the pre-computation of the aggregation phase as it does not contain any trainable parameters, which leaves only MLP training for the feature transformation phase. Hence, this greatly simplifies the mini-batching process equivalent to those of a standard neural network.

Moving towards the quantisation stage, although not as widely researched as other neural network models (e.g., CNNs), quantisation methods in GNNs have recently gained attention. One of the most recent publications in this direction is EXACT [16], which applies an activation compression method by ActNN [23] that is initially intended for CNNs and on top of that, they also apply a random projection by [24] for feature dimensionality reduction. Another related work in GNN quantisation, VQ-GNN [17], combines mini-batch construction with vector quantisation by approximating out-of-batch messages using the vector quantisation while using original messages for in-batch messages. In the present framework, however, we are only interested in a simple linear layer quantisation as adopting SIGN as our backbone model only requires us to train MLP in the GPU. Hence, we can adapt the activation compressed linear layers by ActNN [23] for our framework (C-QSIGN).

2   Proposed Efficient GNN Framework Using Centrality Based Contraction

Problem Statement. In this work, we primarily aim to minimise GPU memory usage for node-level classification problems. Given an input graph $\mathcal{G} = \{\mathcal{V}, \mathcal{E}\}$ with nodes $\mathcal{V}$, unweighted edges $\mathcal{E}$ which can be converted into binary adjacency matrix representation of the node connectance $A \in \mathbb{R}^{|\mathcal{V}| \times |\mathcal{V}|}$, and the computation node budget (maximum number of nodes that can fit in GPU memory), the goal is to predict $Y \in \mathbb{R}^{|\mathcal{V}| \times F_{out}}$ that corresponds to each node's predicted class or label. Here, each node also has an embedding vector with dimension F_{in} which, when grouped across all of the nodes, gives us the embedding matrix $X \in \mathbb{R}^{|\mathcal{V}| \times F_{in}}$. In Fig. 2, we present our proposed framework flowchart for node-level classification, which consists of the graph contraction stage, mini-batch construction stage, and quantisation stage.

Graph Contraction Stage with Centrality Driven Contraction. In this stage, we use various node centrality measures along with edge contraction to reduce the input graph size. The first and simplest centrality measure is the degree centrality (DC) which is simply the node's degree or the count of non-zero entries along the row of the adjacency matrix. DC can be computed using $C_D(v_i) = deg(v_i) = \sum_{i \neq j} A_{ij}^b$, with A^b as a binary adjacency matrix. Another centrality measure we use is the betweenness centrality (BC) which measures the number of shortest paths between any pair of nodes that crosses the node of interest (the more shortest paths crossing the node means that the node has higher importance). However, computing BC can be quite expensive with an $O(|\mathcal{V}||\mathcal{E}|)$ time complexity [25]. Fortunately, an approximation can be made by sampling K number of nodes and limiting computation using the K sampled nodes only [26] (higher K leads to better approximation). The formula for BC is $C_B(v_i) = \sum_{i \neq j \neq k} \frac{\sigma_{jk}(v_i)}{\sigma_{jk}}$, where $\sigma_{jk}(v_i)$ denotes the number of shortest paths between v_j and v_k that crosses v_i, and σ_{jk} denotes the number of shortest paths between v_j and v_k. As a third hubness measure, we use closeness centrality (CC),

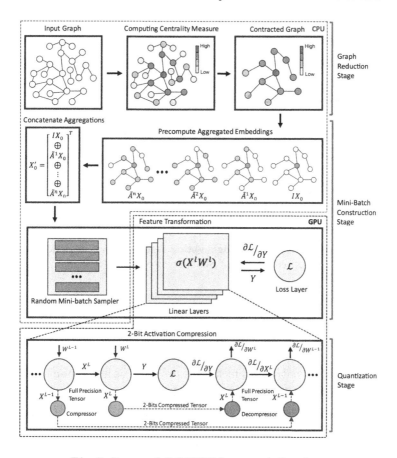

Fig. 2. Proposed C-QSIGN framework flowchart

which measures the closeness of the node of interest to all other nodes in the graph. The computation of CC can be costly as it involves computing the shortest distance between all pairs of nodes using the Floyd-Warshall algorithm with an $O(|\mathcal{V}|^3)$ time complexity. CC can be computed using $C_C(v_i) = \frac{|\mathcal{V}|-1}{\sum_{i \neq j} l_{ij}}$, where l_{ij} denotes the closest distance between v_i and v_j. The fourth centrality measure we use in our framework is the eigenvector centrality (EC) which measures the connectance of a node similar to degree centrality. However, different from degree centrality, the eigenvector centrality can distinguish between connections to strong (e.g., hub nodes) and weak (e.g., leaf nodes) nodes [27], thereby examining the quality of neighbouring nodes in addition to their quantity. Therefore, EC is an improved version of DC with higher computational costs. EC can be computed using $C_E(v_i) = \frac{1}{\lambda_1} \sum_j A_{ij} x_j$, where λ_1 denotes the highest eigenvalue of the adjacency matrix A and x_j denotes the eigenvector corresponding to node v_j. The last centrality measure we are exploring is the PageRank centrality (PR) introduced by Google [28] and is originally used to rank websites. PR itself can be seen as a variant of EC with added random jump probability [29]. The formula for PR is $C_{PR}(v_i) = (I - \alpha A D^{-1})^{-1} \mathbf{1}_i$, where D is a diagonal matrix consisting of node degrees and α denotes the damping factor which is usually set to 0.85.

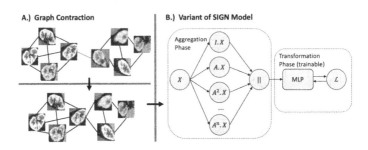

Fig. 3. A.) Graph contraction (red highlighting denotes the nodes and edges to be contracted) and B.) Adopted variant of SIGN architecture (Color figure online)

In our graph contraction stage, instead of directly removing the nodes, we contract the edges by merging the least important node with its strongest neighbour. This merging will also be done while keeping only the most important node's embeddings along with all other edges connected to both nodes as shown in Fig. 3A. This edge contraction method is preferred as it maintains the graph's connectivity and avoids fragmenting the graph.

Mini-Batch Graph Construction with SIGN [15] Model. Here, we adopt a variation of SIGN [15] as our backbone model as shown in Fig. 3B. Notice that the aggregation phase is decoupled from the transformation phase, allowing us to precompute the aggregated embeddings. Therefore, we can trivially construct the aggregated embedding mini-batches for the MLP. In SIGN [15], embedding aggregation to an arbitrary number of hops can be done using various k-hop adjacency matrices, which are essentially the power matrices A^k as shown in the aggregation phase of Fig. 3B. Next, the various k-hop aggregations are concatenated before being passed to the MLP. Note that from the previous contraction up until this aggregation, the pre-computation phase is done in the CPU as shown in Fig. 2, while from the MLP onwards will be done by the GPU.

Quantisation Stage with Activation Compression [23]. The final stage is the quantisation stage in the linear layers of the MLP which we adopt from the 2-bit activation compressed linear layer of ActNN [23]. As shown in the quantisation stage of Fig. 2, forward propagation is done using the original full precision embeddings. At the same time, instead of storing these original full precision embeddings for the gradient computation later (backward pass), we store the compressed version of the embeddings with 2 Bit quantisation. These compressed 2-bit embeddings are then decompressed back to full precision, albeit with information loss, as this is a lossy compression. The main benefit of this activation compression is the reduction of GPU memory usage for storing the activation map by up to a factor of 16 (2-bit compressed vs 32-bit full precision). However, this also comes at an additional computational time overhead as quantisation and dequantisation must be done at each layer during the forward and backward pass. The quantisation will be done on a per-group basis according to [23] with the quantisation equation defined as $quant(\mathbf{h_{ig}}) = \frac{\mathbf{h_{ig}}-Z_{ig}}{R_{ig}}.B$, where h_{ig} denotes the embeddings of node v_i belonging to group g, $Z_{ig} =\min(\mathbf{h_{ig}})$, $R_{ig} =\max(\mathbf{h_{ig}})-\min(\mathbf{h_{ig}})$, $B = 2^b - 1$, with b denoting the number of compression bits which in our case is 2. Dequantisation is the inverse of the function and is written as $dequant(\mathbf{h_{ig}}) = Z_{ig} + quant(\mathbf{h_{ig}}).\frac{R_{ig}}{B}$.

3   Results and Discussion

Dataset Details and Hyperparameters. We evaluated our proposed framework on various public datasets (e.g., PPI [2] and Organ C & S [9]). Protein-Protein Interaction (PPI) was introduced by [30], which represents different human tissues. Here, each node denotes a protein with gene sets and immunological signatures as its embeddings [30], whereas the edge represents the interaction between pair of proteins. Organ S & C [9] datasets are abdominal CT scan images (28 × 28 pixels) of liver tumours. The suffix C and S denote the coronal and sagittal views of the scan, respectively. To represent the images as graph data, we vectorise the pixels and use this as the node feature. The edges are formed based on the cosine similarity of all pair of images which are then sparsified to the top ∼1.2 million edges to reduce the graph complexity. The dataset details and hyperparameters used are given in Table 1.

Table 1. Dataset details and hyperparameters.

	PPI	Organ-S	Organ-C
# of Nodes	56944	25221	23660
# of Edges	1587264	1276046	1241622
# of Features	50	784	784
# of Labels	121	11	11
Task Type	Multi-label	Multi-class	Multi-class
Training Nodes	44906	13940	13000
Validation Nodes	6514	2452	2392
Test Nodes	5524	8829	8268
# of layers	3	3	3
Hidden channels	1024	2048	2048
Dropouts	0.2	0.5	0.5
# of Hops	2	1	1
# of Mini-batch	10	3	3
Learning Rate	0.005	0.0005	0.0005

Node Budget Convergence. First, we experimented with the contraction's node budget to see its impact on the validation accuracy. For this, we trained multiple GCN models with EC contraction on various node budgets as depicted in Fig. 4. Experiment shows that the validation accuracy converges with only 15000 nodes for PPI and 8000 nodes for both Organ C & S dataset, suggesting that these public datasets are highly contractable. Consequently, we can train our GNN model on the contracted graph for a potentially lower GPU memory footprint.

C-QSIGN Benchmarks. Next, we benchmarked C-QSIGN against various memory-efficient GNN models as shown in Table 2. Here, we compare GPU memory footprint and prediction quality (e.g., accuracy, micro F1, micro sensitivity, and micro specificity). Benchmark shows that our proposed C-QSIGN framework have the least GPU memory footprint compared to the other benchmarked method with equivalent hyperparameters. Moreover, C-QSIGN is able to maintain prediction quality similar to the other models. Depending on the centrality measure, the contracted variant of each models is shown to achieve very close performance to the original graph (e.g., EC and CC for PPI). However, the optimum choice of centrality to use is largely dataset dependent as shown by the experiment. Hence, centrality type of the contraction can be treated as a hyperparameter. We initially also intended to benchmark against the other graph reduction methods [18,19]. However, we encountered memory errors when trying to coarsen our datasets using the graph coarsening algorithm by [19], whereas [18] does not publish their source code at the time of writing.

Fig. 4. Valdiation accuracy convergence of C-GCN (EC).

Table 2. Performance and GPU memory efficiency benchmark on various models and datasets (PPI are collapsed to 15000 nodes, while Organ-C & Organ-S to 8000 nodes). All datasets are trained inductively, and all results are based on a 95 confidence interval of 5 runs. GPU memory is in MB (overall lowest is **bolded**).

Methods	PPI					MedMNIST Organ-S			MedMNIST Organ-C		
	GPU Memory	ACC	F1	Sensitivity	Specificity	GPU Memory	ACC	Specificity	GPU Memory	ACC	Specificity
GCN	2347.3	$99.44_{.01}$	$99.06_{.01}$	$98.84_{.03}$	$99.70_{.01}$	1175.4	$60.12_{.08}$	$96.01_{.01}$	1102.4	$77.68_{.35}$	$97.77_{.04}$
C-GCN (DC)	810.2	$77.93_{.18}$	$63.45_{.56}$	$64.00_{1.37}$	$83.88_{.58}$	693.0	$58.81_{.50}$	$95.88_{.05}$	693.7	$76.10_{.37}$	$97.61_{.04}$
C-GCN (BC)	808.0	$87.55_{.07}$	$78.48_{.16}$	$75.83_{.33}$	$92.56_{.10}$	691.1	$58.75_{.45}$	$95.88_{.05}$	693.0	$76.08_{.47}$	$97.61_{.05}$
C-GCN (PR)	808.7	$79.08_{.04}$	$64.93_{.15}$	$64.68_{.33}$	$85.23_{.11}$	691.6	$58.81_{.50}$	$95.88_{.05}$	693.5	$76.10_{.37}$	$97.61_{.04}$
C-GCN (CC)	807.6	$97.19_{.03}$	$95.24_{.03}$	$94.03_{.20}$	$98.53_{.12}$	692.9	$58.81_{.50}$	$95.88_{.05}$	693.3	$76.10_{.37}$	$97.61_{.04}$
C-GCN (EC)	806.3	$98.72_{.01}$	$97.85_{.02}$	$97.10_{.05}$	$99.41_{.01}$	692.9	$58.81_{.50}$	$95.88_{.05}$	693.7	$76.10_{.37}$	$97.61_{.04}$
GAS	427.3	$99.53_{.01}$	$99.22_{.02}$	$99.05_{.03}$	$99.74_{.02}$	545.5	$58.19_{.29}$	$95.82_{.03}$	519.6	$76.03_{1.16}$	$97.60_{.12}$
C-GAS (DC)	180.9	$73.83_{.49}$	$53.01_{2.84}$	$49.67_{5.84}$	$84.16_{2.84}$	363.3	$56.88_{.32}$	$95.69_{.03}$	381.9	$73.80_{1.18}$	$97.38_{.12}$
C-GAS (BC)	176.9	$86.82_{.09}$	$76.99_{.25}$	$73.66_{.68}$	$92.45_{.24}$	355.6	$57.15_{.51}$	$95.72_{.05}$	377.6	$74.85_{.61}$	$97.49_{.06}$
C-GAS (PR)	184.4	$76.44_{.16}$	$57.30_{.63}$	$52.81_{1.26}$	$86.54_{.58}$	354.2	$56.88_{.32}$	$95.69_{.03}$	375.6	$73.80_{1.18}$	$97.38_{.12}$
C-GAS (CC)	252.3	$96.28_{.12}$	$93.70_{.23}$	$92.44_{.55}$	$97.92_{.11}$	357.5	$56.88_{.32}$	$95.69_{.03}$	381.9	$73.80_{1.18}$	$97.38_{.12}$
C-GAS (EC)	239.3	$98.41_{.06}$	$97.33_{.11}$	$96.58_{.15}$	$99.20_{.06}$	360.5	$56.88_{.32}$	$95.69_{.03}$	382.4	$73.80_{1.18}$	$97.38_{.12}$
ClusterGCN	366.4	$99.40_{.01}$	$98.99_{.01}$	$98.79_{.02}$	$99.66_{.01}$	699.4	$60.11_{.41}$	$96.01_{.04}$	627.2	$78.09_{1.37}$	$97.81_{.14}$
C-ClusterGCN (DC)	149.9	$83.31_{.09}$	$72.63_{.22}$	$73.99_{.55}$	$87.29_{.21}$	437.4	$58.95_{.52}$	$95.90_{.05}$	438.8	$75.84_{.72}$	$97.58_{.07}$
C-ClusterGCN (BC)	154.0	$89.82_{.16}$	$83.00_{.24}$	$83.02_{.27}$	$92.73_{.21}$	432.7	$59.45_{.43}$	$95.95_{.04}$	433.9	$76.42_{.40}$	$97.64_{.04}$
C-ClusterGCN (PR)	152.5	$82.67_{.09}$	$71.78_{.19}$	$73.63_{.55}$	$86.53_{.26}$	446.1	$59.06_{.67}$	$95.91_{.07}$	436.3	$76.10_{.38}$	$97.61_{.04}$
C-ClusterGCN (CC)	149.0	$96.69_{.02}$	$94.44_{.03}$	$93.88_{.10}$	$97.89_{.05}$	432.3	$58.71_{.26}$	$95.87_{.03}$	434.4	$75.25_{1.24}$	$97.52_{.12}$
C-ClusterGCN (EC)	148.3	$98.10_{.03}$	$96.81_{.04}$	$96.38_{.11}$	$98.84_{.05}$	444.6	$58.81_{.42}$	$95.88_{.04}$	441.1	$75.36_{.94}$	$97.54_{.09}$
SIGN	177.3	$99.45_{.01}$	$99.08_{.02}$	$98.83_{.02}$	$99.72_{.01}$	402.3	$61.37_{.47}$	$96.14_{.05}$	382.9	$79.21_{.23}$	$97.92_{.02}$
C-SIGN (DC)	81.4	$80.55_{.08}$	$66.37_{.06}$	$64.11_{.26}$	$87.58_{.22}$	275.6	$60.44_{.19}$	$96.04_{.02}$	275.7	$77.61_{.15}$	$97.76_{.01}$
C-SIGN (BC)	81.4	$87.47_{.05}$	$77.73_{.05}$	$73.03_{.32}$	$93.64_{.19}$	275.6	$60.01_{.23}$	$96.00_{.04}$	275.6	$77.86_{.38}$	$97.79_{.04}$
C-SIGN (PR)	81.4	$80.19_{.07}$	$64.44_{.17}$	$59.97_{.24}$	$88.83_{.03}$	275.6	$60.44_{.19}$	$96.04_{.02}$	275.7	$77.61_{.15}$	$97.76_{.01}$
C-SIGN (CC)	81.4	$97.17_{.03}$	$95.20_{.05}$	$93.65_{.02}$	$98.67_{.04}$	275.6	$60.44_{.19}$	$96.04_{.02}$	275.7	$77.61_{.15}$	$97.76_{.01}$
C-SIGN (EC)	81.4	$98.66_{.01}$	$97.75_{.02}$	$96.94_{.07}$	$99.40_{.02}$	275.6	$60.44_{.19}$	$96.04_{.02}$	275.7	$77.61_{.15}$	$97.76_{.01}$
QSIGN	116.9	$99.42_{.01}$	$99.03_{.02}$	$98.76_{.02}$	$99.71_{.02}$	278.4	$61.80_{.57}$	$96.18_{.06}$	269.4	$79.25_{.32}$	$97.93_{.03}$
C-QSIGN (DC)	**69.1**	$80.26_{.09}$	$66.52_{.22}$	$65.51_{.39}$	$86.56_{.10}$	**216.7**	$59.93_{.49}$	$95.99_{.05}$	**216.7**	$77.37_{.26}$	$97.74_{.03}$
C-QSIGN (BC)	**69.1**	$87.29_{.05}$	$77.59_{.09}$	$73.49_{.35}$	$93.19_{.18}$	**216.7**	$60.01_{.45}$	$96.00_{.04}$	**216.7**	$77.80_{.56}$	$97.78_{.06}$
C-QSIGN (PR)	**69.1**	$79.78_{.11}$	$64.41_{.19}$	$61.13_{.72}$	$87.75_{.44}$	**216.7**	$59.93_{.49}$	$95.99_{.05}$	**216.7**	$77.37_{.26}$	$97.74_{.03}$
C-QSIGN (CC)	**69.1**	$97.13_{.02}$	$95.13_{.03}$	$93.70_{.06}$	$98.59_{.04}$	**216.7**	$59.93_{.49}$	$95.99_{.05}$	**216.7**	$77.37_{.26}$	$97.74_{.03}$
C-QSIGN (EC)	**69.1**	$98.63_{.03}$	$97.68_{.05}$	$96.83_{.06}$	$99.39_{.03}$	**216.7**	$59.93_{.49}$	$95.99_{.05}$	**216.7**	$77.37_{.26}$	$97.74_{.03}$

4 Conclusion

In this work, we introduced a novel centrality-based graph contraction method along with a memory-efficient GNN training framework which generalises to multiple SOTA methods (SIGN [15] and quantisation [23]) to form C-QSIGN. We benchmarked C-QSIGN and showed that our proposed framework could compete with other SOTA methods in prediction performance while using significantly lower memory. The current limitation of the proposed C-QSIGN method is the addition of hyperparameters to be tuned, especially the type of centrality and the node budgets for the topological contraction. However, for node budget, as a higher node budget generally means better training quality, we can maximise the budget based on available GPU memory.

5 Appendix

Computational Time Comparison of Benchmarked Models. In this section, we show the epoch time comparison of our benchmarked models (Table 3). Experiments show that C-SIGN methods has the least epoch time compared to other mini-batched methods. The delay in C-QSIGN methods are attributable the quantization and dequantization processes, which adds more processing time as depicted in the experiment.

Table 3. Complete computational resources benchmarks. Epoch time is defined as the time for one complete pass of the dataset. Therefore, full-batched methods (i.e., GCN) will have a much shorter epoch time than mini-batched methods as no CPU to GPU data transfer is necessary on each epoch, and the gradient descent step is only done once per epoch. The GPU memory is in MB (overall lowest is **bolded**), and the epoch time is in milliseconds.

Methods	PPI		MedMNIST Organ-S		MedMNIST Organ-C	
	GPU Memory	Epoch Time	GPU Memory	Epoch Time	GPU Memory	Epoch Time
GCN	2347.3	3.01.9	1175.4	1.70.0	1102.4	1.90.1
C-GCN (DC)	810.2	2.20.7	693.0	1.70.1	693.7	1.90.2
C-GCN (BC)	808.0	2.20.7	691.1	1.70.1	693.0	1.90.1
C-GCN (PR)	808.7	2.20.7	691.6	1.70.0	693.5	1.90.2
C-GCN (CC)	807.6	2.10.7	692.9	1.80.2	693.3	1.80.2
C-GCN (EC)	806.3	2.10.7	692.9	1.80.2	693.7	1.80.2
GAS	427.3	737.34.2	545.5	329.31.9	519.6	308.21.0
C-GAS (DC)	180.9	294.2 4.1	363.3	196.9 1.1	381.9	211.2 0.7
C-GAS (BC)	176.9	274.6 4.5	355.6	192.9 2.4	377.6	207.7 1.6
C-GAS (PR)	184.4	284.95.8	354.2	193.92.4	375.6	210.00.7
C-GAS (CC)	252.3	373.76.7	357.5	197.00.7	381.9	211.71.5
C-GAS (EC)	239.3	389.62.8	360.5	196.91.4	382.4	211.22.4
ClusterGCN	366.4	660.33.0	699.4	377.90.9	627.2	368.83.2
C-ClusterGCN (DC)	149.9	274.30.8	437.4	229.52.6	438.8	262.72.9
C-ClusterGCN (BC)	154.0	258.51.2	432.7	233.910.1	433.9	255.32.8
C-ClusterGCN (PR)	152.5	277.81.9	446.1	240.46.6	436.3	260.92.8
C-ClusterGCN (CC)	149.0	227.03.0	432.3	229.62.3	434.4	261.73.1
C-ClusterGCN (EC)	148.3	218.24.2	444.6	232.31.8	441.1	262.42.7
SIGN	177.3	176.10.9	402.3	173.71.7	382.9	164.61.6
C-SIGN (DC)	81.4	64.90.1	275.6	99.60.9	275.7	99.20.6
C-SIGN (BC)	81.4	65.10.6	275.6	99.20.6	275.6	99.0.5
C-SIGN (PR)	81.4	65.20.6	275.6	99.30.6	275.7	99.40.6
C-SIGN (CC)	81.4	64.80.6	275.6	98.40.3	275.7	98.50.5
C-SIGN (EC)	81.4	64.9 0.8	275.6	98.9 0.3	275.7	99.0 0.6
QSIGN	116.9	273.80.5	278.4	229.11.0	269.4	218.41.0
C-QSIGN (DC)	**69.1**	101.00.5	**216.7**	136.50.7	**216.7**	136.20.4
C-QSIGN (BC)	**69.1**	101.40.5	**216.7**	136.50.7	**216.7**	136.30.2
C-QSIGN (PR)	**69.1**	101.50.5	**216.7**	136.80.7	**216.7**	136.50.4
C-QSIGN (CC)	**69.1**	101.40.4	**216.7**	135.60.3	**216.7**	135.50.3
C-QSIGN (EC)	**69.1**	101.40.6	**216.7**	136.00.5	**216.7**	136.10.2

References

1. Gilmer, J., Schoenholz, S.S., Riley, P.F., Vinyals, O.: Dahl, p. 199. Message passing neural networks. Machine Learning Meets Quantum Physics, G.E. (2020)
2. Zitnik, M., Leskovec, J.: Predicting multicellular function through multi-layer tissue networks. Bioinformatics **33**, i190–i198 (2017)
3. Wu, Z., Pan, S., Chen, F., Long, G., Zhang, C., Yu, P.S.: A comprehensive survey on graph neural networks. IEEE Trans. Neural Netw. Learn. Syst. **32**, 4–24 (2021)
4. Gao, C., et al.: A survey of graph neural networks for recommender systems: challenges, methods, and directions. ACM Trans. Recommender Syst. **1**, 1–51 (2023)

5. Wu, Q., Chen, Y., Yang, C., Yan, J.: Energy-based out-of-distribution detection for graph neural networks. In: International Conference on Learning Representations (ICLR) (2023)
6. Ahmedt-Aristizabal, D., Armin, M.A., Denman, S., Fookes, C., Petersson, L.: Graph-based deep learning for medical diagnosis and analysis: past, present and future. Sensors **21**, 4758 (2021)
7. Bessadok, A., Mahjoub, M.A., Rekik, I.: Graph neural networks in network neuroscience. IEEE Trans. Pattern Anal. Mach. Intell. (2022)
8. Krzywda, M., Lukasik, S., Gandomi, A.H.: Graph neural networks in computer vision - architectures, datasets and common approaches. In: 2022 International Joint Conference on Neural Networks (IJCNN). IEEE (2022)
9. Yang, J., et al.: Medmnist v2-a large-scale lightweight benchmark for 2d and 3d biomedical image classification. Scientific Data **10**, 41 (2023)
10. Kipf, T.N., Welling, M.: Semi-supervised classification with graph convolutional networks. In: International Conference on Learning Representations (ICLR) (2017)
11. Veličković, P., Cucurull, G., Casanova, A., Romero, A., Liò, P., Bengio, Y.: Graph attention networks. In: International Conference on Learning Representations (ICLR) (2018)
12. Chiang, W.L., Liu, X., Si, S., Li, Y., Bengio, S., Hsieh, C.J.: Cluster-gcn: an efficient algorithm for training deep and large graph convolutional networks. In: ACM SIGKDD Conference on Knowledge Discovery and Data Mining (KDD) (2019)
13. Fey, M., Lenssen, J.E., Weichert, F., Leskovec, J.: GNNAutoScale: scalable and expressive graph neural networks via historical embeddings. In: International Conference on Machine Learning (ICML) (2021)
14. Shi, Z., Liang, X., Wang, J.: LMC: fast training of GNNs via subgraph sampling with provable convergence. In: International Conference on Learning Representations (ICLR) (2023)
15. Frasca, F., Rossi, E., Eynard, D., Chamberlain, B., Bronstein, M., Monti, F.: Sign: scalable inception graph neural networks. In: ICML 2020 Workshop on Graph Representation Learning and Beyond (2020)
16. Liu, Z., Zhou, K., Yang, F., Li, L., Chen, R., Hu, X.: EXACT: scalable graph neural networks training via extreme activation compression. In: International Conference on Learning Representations (ICLR), (2022)
17. Ding, M., Kong, K., Li, J., Zhu, C., Dickerson, J.P., Huang, F., Goldstein, T.: Vq-gnn: a universal framework to scale up graph neural networks using vector quantization (2021)
18. Prochazka, P., Mares, M., Dedic, M.: Scalable graph size reduction for efficient gnn application. In: Information Technologies - Applications and Theory (2022)
19. Huang, Z., Zhang, S., C.X.T.L., Zhou, M.: Scaling up graph neural networks via graph coarsening. In: In Proceedings of the 27th ACM SIGKDD Conference on Knowledge Discovery and Data Mining (KDD 2021) (2021)
20. Sandeep, C., Salim, A., Sethunadh, R., Sumitra, S.: An efficient scheme based on graph centrality to select nodes for training for effective learning (2021)
21. Karypis, G., Kumar, V.: Kumar, V.: A fast and high quality multilevel scheme for partitioning irregular graphs. SIAM J. Sci. Comput. **20**(1), 359–392 (1999)
22. Chen, J., Zhu, J., Song, L.: Stochastic training of graph convolutional networks with variance reduction (2018)
23. Chen, J., et al.: Actnn: reducing training memory footprint via 2-bit activation compressed training. In: International Conference on Machine Learning (ICML) (2021)

24. Achlioptas, D.: Database-friendly random projections. In: Proceedings of the Twentieth ACM SIGMOD-SIGACT-SIGART Symposium on Principles of Database Systems, PODS 2001, pp. 274–281. Association for Computing Machinery, New York (2001)
25. Brandes, U.: A faster algorithm for betweenness centrality. J. Math. Soc. 25 (2004)
26. Brandes, U., Pich, C.: Centrality estimation in large networks. Inter. J. Bifurcation Chaos **17**, 2303–2318 (2007)
27. Newman, M.: In: Mathematics of Networks, pp. 1–8 (2008)
28. Page, L., Brin, S., Motwani, R., Winograd, T.: The pagerank citation ranking: bringing order to the web. In: The Web Conference (1999)
29. Zaki, M.J., Jr., W.M.: Data Mining and Analysis: Fundamental Concepts and Algorithms. Cambridge University Press, USA (2014)
30. Hamilton, W.L., Ying, R., Leskovec, J.: Inductive representation learning on large graphs. In: NIPS (2017)

Approaches for Noisy, Missing, and Low Quality Data

Dual-Domain Iterative Network with Adaptive Data Consistency for Joint Denoising and Few-Angle Reconstruction of Low-Dose Cardiac SPECT

Xiongchao Chen[1]($\boxtimes$), Bo Zhou[1], Huidong Xie[1], Xueqi Guo[1], Qiong Liu[1],
Albert J. Sinusas[1,2,3], and Chi Liu[1,2]

[1] Department of Biomedical Engineering, Yale University, New Haven, USA
{xiongchao.chen,chi.liu}@yale.edu
[2] Department of Radiology and Biomedical Imaging,
Yale University, New Haven, USA
[3] Department of Internal Medicine, Yale University, New Haven, USA

Abstract. Myocardial perfusion imaging (MPI) by single-photon emission computed tomography (SPECT) is widely applied for the diagnosis of cardiovascular diseases. Reducing the dose of the injected tracer is essential for lowering the patient's radiation exposure, but it will lead to increased image noise. Additionally, the latest dedicated cardiac SPECT scanners typically acquire projections in fewer angles using fewer detectors to reduce hardware expenses, potentially resulting in lower reconstruction accuracy. To overcome these challenges, we propose a dual-domain iterative network for end-to-end joint denoising and reconstruction from low-dose and few-angle projections of cardiac SPECT. The image-domain network provides a prior estimate for the projection-domain networks. The projection-domain primary and auxiliary modules are interconnected for progressive denoising and few-angle reconstruction. Adaptive Data Consistency (ADC) modules improve prediction accuracy by adaptively fusing the outputs of the primary and auxiliary modules. Experiments using clinical MPI data show that our proposed method outperforms existing image-, projection-, and dual-domain techniques, producing more accurate projections and reconstructions. Ablation studies confirm the significance of the image-domain prior estimate and ADC modules in enhancing network performance. Our source code is available at https://github.com/XiongchaoChen/DuDoNet-JointLD.

Keywords: Cardiac SPECT · Dual-domain · Denoising · Few-angle reconstruction · Adaptive data consistency

Supplementary Information The online version contains supplementary material available at https://doi.org/10.1007/978-3-031-44917-8_5.

ⓒ The Author(s), under exclusive license to Springer Nature Switzerland AG 2023
Z. Xue et al. (Eds.): MILLanD 2023, LNCS 14307, pp. 49–59, 2023.
https://doi.org/10.1007/978-3-031-44917-8_5

1   Introduction

Myocardial perfusion imaging (MPI) through Single-Photon Emission Computed Tomography (SPECT) is the most commonly employed exam for diagnosing cardiovascular diseases [13]. However, exposure to ionizing radiation from SPECT radioactive tracers presents potential risks to both patient and healthcare provider [14]. While reducing the injected dose can lower the radiation exposure, it will lead to increased image noise [16]. Additionally, acquiring projections in fewer angles using fewer detectors is a viable strategy for shortening scanning time, reducing hardware expenses, and lowering the possibility of SPECT-CT misalignment [8,9]. However, fewer-angle projections can lead to lower reconstruction accuracy and higher image noise [18].

Many deep learning methods by Convolutional Neural Networks (CNNs) have been developed for denoising or few-angle reconstruction in nuclear medicine. Existing techniques for denoising in nuclear medicine were implemented either in the projection or image domain. Low-dose (LD) projection or image was input to CNN to predict the corresponding full-dose (FD) projection [1,25] or image [21,24,26]. Previous approaches for few-angle reconstruction were developed based on projection-, image-, or dual-domain frameworks [6]. In the projection- or image-domain methods, the few-angle projection or image was input to CNN to generate the full-angle projection [23,27] or image [2], respectively. The dual-domain method, Dual-domain Sinogram Synthesis (DuDoSS), utilized the image-domain output as an initial estimation for the prediction of the full-angle projection in the projection domain [10].

The latest dedicated cardiac SPECT scanners tend to employ fewer detectors to minimize hardware costs [28]. Although deep learning-enabled denoising or few-angle reconstruction in nuclear medicine has been extensively studied in previous works, end-to-end joint denoising and few-angle reconstruction for the latest dedicated scanners still remains highly under-explored. Here, we present a dual-domain iterative network with learnable Adaptive Data Consistency (ADC) modules for joint denoising and few-angle reconstruction of cardiac SPECT. The image-domain network provides a prior estimate for the prediction in the projection domain. Paired primary and auxiliary modules are interconnected for progressive denoising and few-angle restoration. ADC modules are incorporated to enhance prediction accuracy by fusing the predicted projections from primary and auxiliary modules. We evaluated the proposed method using clinical data and compared it to existing projection-, image-, and dual-domain methods. In addition, we also conducted ablation studies to assess the impact of the image-domain prior estimate and ADC modules on the network performance.

2   Methods

2.1   Dataset and Pre-processing

A dataset consisting of 474 anonymized clinical hybrid SPECT-CT MPI studies was collected. Each study was conducted following the injection of ^{99m}Tc-tetrofosmin on a GE NM/CT 570c [28]. The clinical characteristics of enrolled patients are listed in supplementary Table S1.

The GE 530c/570c scanners comprise of 19 pinhole detectors arranged in three columns on a cylindrical surface [3]. The few-angle projections were generated by selecting the 9 angles (9A) in the central column, simulating the configurations of the latest cost-effective MyoSPECT ES few-angle scanner [15] as shown in supplementary Fig. S1. The 10%-dose LD projections were produced by randomly decimating the list-mode data at a 10% downsampling rate. The simulated LD&9A projection is the input, and the original FD&19A projection is the label. We used 200, 74, and 200 cases for training, validation, and testing.

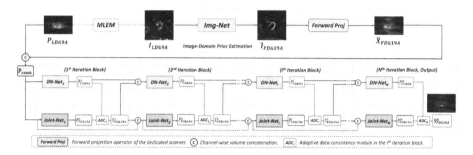

Fig. 1. Dual-domain iterative network Joint-DuDo. The forward projection of the image-domain output (top row) serves as a prior estimate for the projection domain (bottom row). The primary (*Joint-Net*) and the auxiliary modules (*DN-Net*) are interconnected in every iteration for progressive denoising and few-angle restoration.

2.2 Dual-Domain Iterative Network

The dual-domain iterative network for joint estimation, designated as Joint-DuDo, is shown in Fig. 1. The LD&9A projection $P_{LD\&9A}$ is first input into a Maximum-Likelihood Expectation Maximization (MLEM, 30 iterations) module, producing the reconstructed LD&9A image $I_{LD\&9A}$.

Image-Domain Prior Estimation. $I_{LD\&9A}$ is then input to the image-domain network *Img-Net*, i.e. a CNN module, to produce the predicted image $\hat{I}_{FD\&19A}$, supervised by the ground-truth FD&19A image $I_{FD\&19A}$. The image-domain loss $\mathcal{L}_I$ can be formulated as:

$$\mathcal{L}_I = \left\| \hat{I}_{FD\&19A} - I_{FD\&19A} \right\|_1. \tag{1}$$

Then, $\hat{I}_{FD\&19A}$ is fed into a forward projection (FP) operator derived from the system matrix of GE 530c/570c, producing $\widetilde{X}_{FD\&19A}$ as the prior estimate of the ground-truth FD&19A projection $P_{FD\&19A}$. The image-domain output can be formulated as:

$$\widetilde{X}_{FD\&19A} = \mathcal{F}(\mathcal{I}(I_{LD\&9A})), \tag{2}$$

where $\mathcal{I}(\cdot)$ is the *Img-Net* operator and $\mathcal{F}(\cdot)$ is the system FP operator.

Projection-Domain Iterative Prediction. The prior estimate $\widetilde{X}_{FD\&19A}$ is then channel-wise concatenated with $P_{LD\&9A}$ to generate $\widetilde{P}_{comb}$, which serves as the dual-channel input to the projection-domain networks, formulated as:

$$\widetilde{P}_{comb} = \left\{ \widetilde{X}_{FD\&19A}, P_{LD\&9A} \right\}, \tag{3}$$

where $\{\cdot\}$ refers to channel-wise concatenation of 3D projections.

Given the difficulty in performing joint denoising and few-angle restoration directly, we split and assign the two tasks to two parallel Attention U-Net modules [22]: the auxiliary module (*DN-Net*) employed for denoising and the primary module (*Joint-Net*) employed for joint prediction. Specifically, *DN-Net* solely focuses on denoising and produces an auxiliary projection. *Joint-Net* performs both denoising and few-angle restoration, producing the primary projection. The auxiliary and primary projections are then fused in an ADC module (described in Subsect. 2.3), producing a fused projection of higher accuracy.

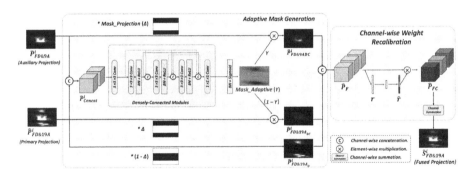

Fig. 2. Adaptive data consistency (ADC) is composed of an Adaptive Mask Generation module (left) to fuse the auxiliary and the primary projections and a Channel-wise Weight Recalibration module (right) to adjust weights of the combined projections.

In the 1st iteration block, $\widetilde{P}_{comb}$ is first input to *DN-Net*$_1$ to produce the auxiliary projection $\hat{P}^1_{FD\&9A}$. It is also input to *Joint-Net*$_1$ to produce the primary projection $\hat{P}^1_{FD\&19A}$. Then, $\hat{P}^1_{FD\&9A}$ and $\hat{P}^1_{FD\&19A}$ are fused in the ADC_1 module, producing the fused projection $\hat{S}^1_{FD\&19A}$, formulated as:

$$\hat{S}^1_{FD\&19A} = \mathcal{A}_1(\mathcal{D}_1(\widetilde{P}_{comb}), \mathcal{J}_1(\widetilde{P}_{comb})), \tag{4}$$

where $\mathcal{A}_1(\cdot)$ is the ADC_1 operator to be described in Subsect. 2.3. $\mathcal{D}_1(\cdot)$ is the *DN-Net*$_1$ operator, and $\mathcal{J}_1(\cdot)$ is the *Joint-Net*$_1$ operator.

In the $i^{th}(i \geq 2)$ iteration block, the output of the $(i-1)^{th}$ iteration, $\hat{S}^{(i-1)}_{FD\&19A}$, was added to the input of *DN-Net*$_i$ to assist the denoising of the auxiliary module. $\hat{S}^{(i-1)}_{FD\&19A}$ is concatenated with the output of *DN-Net*$_{(i-1)}$ and then fed into $DN\text{-}Net_i$ to produce the auxiliary projection $\hat{P}^i_{FD\&9A}$ in the i_{th} iteration:

$$\hat{P}^i_{FD\&9A} = \mathcal{D}_i(\{\hat{S}^{(i-1)}_{FD\&19A}, \hat{P}^{(i-1)}_{FD\&9A}\}),\tag{5}$$

where $\mathcal{D}_i(\cdot)$ is the $DN\text{-}Net_i$ operator. Then, the outputs of all the $(i-1)$ previous iterations, $\hat{S}^m_{FD\&19A}(m < i)$, are densely connected with $\widetilde{P}_{comb}$ as the input to $Joint\text{-}Net_i$ to produce the primary projection in the i_{th} iteration:

$$\hat{P}^i_{FD\&19A} = \mathcal{J}_i(\{\widetilde{P}_{comb}, \hat{S}^1_{FD\&19A}, \hat{S}^2_{FD\&19A}, \cdots, \hat{S}^{(i-1)}_{FD\&19A}\}),\tag{6}$$

where $\mathcal{J}_i(\cdot)$ is the $Joint\text{-}Net_i$ operator. Then, the auxiliary and primary projections are fused in ADC_i for recalibration, generating the fused $\hat{S}^i_{FD\&19A}$ as:

$$\hat{S}^i_{FD\&19A} = \mathcal{A}_i(\hat{P}^i_{FD\&9A}, \hat{P}^i_{FD\&19A}),\tag{7}$$

where $\mathcal{A}_i(\cdot)$ is the ADC_i operator. The overall network output $\hat{S}^N_{FD\&19A}$ is the output of the Nth iteration, where N is the total number of iterations with a default value of 4. The projection-domain loss is formulated as:

$$\mathcal{L}_P = \sum_{i=1}^N (\left\| \hat{P}^i_{FD\&9A} - P_{FD\&9A}\right\|_1 + \left\|\hat{S}^i_{FD\&19A} - P_{FD\&19A}\right\|_1),\tag{8}$$

where $P_{FD\&9A}$ is the FD&9A projection. The total loss function $\mathcal{L}$ is the weighted summation of the image-domain loss $\mathcal{L}_I$ and the projection-domain loss $\mathcal{L}_P$:

$$\mathcal{L} = w_I\mathcal{L}_I + w_P\mathcal{L}_P,\tag{9}$$

where the weights w_I and w_P were set as 0.5 to achieve the optimal performance.

2.3   Adaptive Data Consistency

The initial data consistency (DC) was used to fuse the predicted and ground-truth k-spaces, thereby ensuring the consistency of the MRI image in k-space [12,29]. It is also utilized in the DuDoSS for the few-angle reconstruction of nuclear medicine imaging [10]. However, in our study, the ground-truth FD&9A projection $P_{FD\&9A}$, which is a pre-requisite for applying DC to $\hat{P}_{FD\&19A}$, is not available as input. Thus, we generate $\hat{P}^i_{FD\&9A}$ using $DN\text{-}Net_i$ as the intermediate auxiliary information to improve $\hat{P}_{FD\&19A}$. The proposed ADC generates a voxel-wise adaptive projection mask for the fusion of $\hat{P}^i_{FD\&9A}$ and $\hat{P}^i_{FD\&19A}$.

As presented in Fig. 2, in the ith iteration, $\hat{P}^i_{FD\&9A}$ and $\hat{P}^i_{FD\&19A}$ are first concatenated and input to a densely-connected CNN module for spatial feature extraction. Then, a voxel-wise adaptive projection mask γ is generated from the extracted features using a Sigmoid operator, which determines the voxel-wise weights (ranges from 0 to 1) for the adaptive summation of $\hat{P}^i_{FD\&9A}$ and $\hat{P}^i_{FD\&19A}$. The weighted projections of the central columns are:

$$\hat{P}^i_{FD\&9A_{DC}} = \hat{P}^i_{FD\&9A} * \Delta * \gamma,\tag{10}$$

$$\hat{P}^i_{FD\&19A_{DC}} = \hat{P}^i_{FD\&19A} * \Delta * (1 - \gamma), \tag{11}$$

where $*$ is the voxel-wise multiplication, and Δ refers to the binary mask of the few-angle projection (shown in Fig. 2). In addition, the outer columns of $\hat{P}_{FD\&19A}$ is computed as: $\hat{P}^i_{FD\&19A_O} = \hat{P}^i_{FD\&19A} * (1 - \Delta)$.

Then, the above three weighted projections are concatenated and input to a Channel-wise Weight Recalibration module, a squeeze-excitation [17] self-attention mechanism, to generate a channel recalibration vector $\hat{r} = [r_1, r_2, r_3]$. The output of ADC is the weighted summation of recalibrated projections as:

$$\hat{S}^i_{FD\&19A} = r_1\hat{P}^i_{FD\&9A_{DC}} + r_2\hat{P}^i_{FD\&19A_{DC}} + r_3\hat{P}^i_{FD\&19A_O}. \tag{12}$$

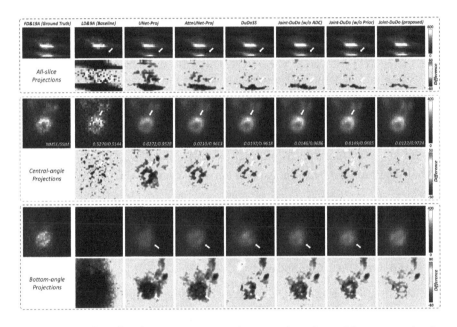

Fig. 3. Predicted FD&19A projections in side, central-angle, and bottom-angle views with NMSE/SSIM annotated. White arrows denote prediction inconsistency.

2.4 Implementation Details

We evaluated Joint-DuDo against various deep learning methods in this study. Projection-domain methods using U-Net (designated as UNet-Proj) [22] or Attention U-Net (designated as AttnUNet-Proj) [19], the image-domain method using Attention U-Net (designated as AttnUNet-Img) [27], and the dual-domain method DuDoSS [10] were tested. We also included ablation study groups without ADC (but with normal DC, designated as Joint-DuDo (w/o ADC)) or without the image-domain prior estimate (designated as Joint-DuDo (w/o Prior)).

Networks were developed using PyTorch [20] and trained with Adam optimizers. The initial learning rate was 10^{-3} for image and projection modules and

10^{-4} for ADC modules, with a decay rate of 0.99 per epoch to avoid overfitting. Joint-DuDo and ablation groups were trained for 50 epochs and the other groups were trained for 200 epochs. The default number of iterations of Joint-DuDo was 4. Evaluations of Joint-DuDo using multiple iterations (1 to 6) are shown in Sect. 3 (Fig. 5 left). Evaluations of more datasets with different LD levels (1 to 80%, default 10%) are shown in Sect. 3 (Fig. 5 mid, right).

Table 1. Evaluation of the predicted FD&19A projections using normalized mean square error (NMSE), normalized mean absolute error (NMAE), structural similarity (SSIM), and peak signal-to-noise ratio (PSNR). The best results are in red.

Methods	NMSE(%)	NMAE(%)	SSIM	PSNR	P-values[†]
Baseline LD-9A	54.46 ± 2.46	62.44 ± 2.53	0.4912 ± 0.0260	19.23 ± 1.68	< 0.001
UNet-Proj [22]	4.26 ± 1.58	16.65 ± 2.42	0.9247 ± 0.0248	30.54 ± 1.79	< 0.001
AttnUNet-Proj [19]	3.43 ± 1.17	15.34 ± 2.40	0.9372 ± 0.0193	31.47 ± 1.65	< 0.001
DuDoSS [10]	3.10 ± 0.78	14.54 ± 1.59	0.9429 ± 0.0153	31.82 ± 1.50	< 0.001
Joint-DuDo (w/o ADC)	2.42 ± 0.81	13.04 ± 1.89	0.9509 ± 0.0156	32.97 ± 1.60	< 0.001
Joint-DuDo (w/o Prior)	2.43 ± 0.82	13.36 ± 1.90	0.9507 ± 0.0150	32.95 ± 1.68	< 0.001
Joint-DuDo (proposed)	2.16 ± 0.71	12.51 ± 1.73	0.9548 ± 0.0137	33.47 ± 1.67	–

[†]P-values of the paired t-tests of NMSE between the current method and Joint-DuDo (proposed).

3 Results

Figure 3 presents the qualitative comparison of the predicted FD&19A projections in different projection views. It can be observed that Joint-DuDo generates more accurate predicted projections at all views compared to the projection- and dual-domain approaches. Joint-DuDo also demonstrates higher accuracy compared to the ablation study groups without the image-domain prior estimate or ADC modules, proving the roles of the prior estimate and ADC in enhancing network performance. Table 1 outlines the quantitative evaluations of the predicted projections. Joint-DuDo outperforms existing projection- and dual-domain approaches and the ablation study groups ($p < 0.001$).

Table 2. Evaluation of the reconstructed or predicted FD&19A SPECT images w/ or w/o attenuation correction (AC). The best results are marked in red.

Methods	Reconstructed Images w/o AC			Reconstructed Images w/ AC		
	NMSE(%)	NMAE(%)	PSNR	NMSE(%)	NMAE(%)	PSNR
Baseline LD-9A	30.66 ± 11.27	47.76 ± 6.74	25.41 ± 2.12	22.57 ± 9.42	42.23 ± 7.02	26.17 ± 2.05
UNet-Proj [22]	7.00 ± 2.56	23.59 ± 3.75	31.77 ± 1.94	5.39 ± 2.02	20.85 ± 3.34	32.26 ± 1.75
AttnUNet-Proj [19]	6.14 ± 2.08	22.32 ± 3.29	32.33 ± 1.96	4.70 ± 1.65	19.61 ± 2.94	32.85 ± 1.76
AttnUNet-Img [27]	6.07 ± 1.44	21.80 ± 2.26	32.29 ± 1.87	4.66 ± 1.05	19.50 ± 1.95	32.78 ± 1.59
DuDoSS [10]	5.57 ± 1.77	21.70 ± 3.11	32.61 ± 1.93	4.44 ± 1.40	18.89 ± 2.84	33.09 ± 1.75
Joint-DuDo (w/o ADC)	5.32 ± 1.78	20.57 ± 3.12	32.95 ± 1.91	4.22 ± 1.44	18.42 ± 2.83	33.32 ± 1.73
Joint-DuDo (w/o Prior)	5.45 ± 1.83	20.75 ± 3.20	32.84 ± 1.93	4.34 ± 1.51	18.60 ± 2.85	33.20 ± 1.76
Joint-DuDo (proposed)	4.68 ± 1.46	19.27 ± 2.70	33.49 ± 1.87	3.72 ± 1.19	17.32 ± 2.48	33.85 ± 1.71

Figure 4 shows the qualitative comparison of the reconstructed or predicted FD&19A images with or without the CT-based attenuation correction (AC) [4,5,7,11]. Joint-DuDo results in more accurate SPECT images compared to other image-domain, projection-domain, and dual-domain approaches as well as the ablation groups. Segment-wise visualizations of the images in Fig. 4 are shown in supplementary Fig. S2 and S3. With or without AC, Joint-DuDo outperforms the other methods ($p < 0.001$) as indicated by the quantitative comparison in Table 2.

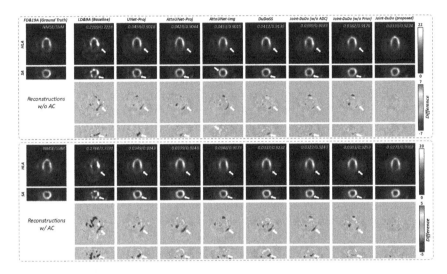

Fig. 4. Reconstructed or predicted FD&19A SPECT images w/ or w/o the CT-based attenuation correction (AC). White arrows denote the prediction inconsistency. (Colour figure online)

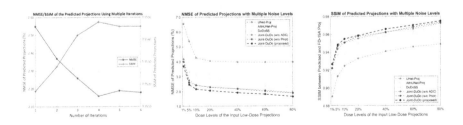

Fig. 5. Evaluation of Joint-DuDo using multiple iterations (left). Evaluation of various approaches based on datasets with different LD levels (mid, right).

As shown in Fig. 5 (left), the performance of Joint-DuDo improves as the number of iterations (N) increases and reaches convergence at $N = 4$. In addition, we generated more datasets with different LD levels (1% to 80%) to test the network performance as shown in Fig. 5 (mid and right). It can be observed that our proposed Joint-DuDo demonstrates consistently higher prediction accuracy across various LD levels compared to other testing methods.

4 Discussion and Conclusion

In this work, we propose Joint-DuDo, a novel dual-domain iterative network with learnable ADC modules, for the joint denoising and few-angle reconstruction of low-dose cardiac SPECT. Joint-DuDo employs the output of the image domain as an initial estimate for the projection prediction in the projection domain. This initial estimate enables the input closer to the target, thus enhancing the overall prediction accuracy. The ADC modules produce adaptive projection masks to fuse the predicted auxiliary and primary projections for higher output accuracy. Experiments using clinical data showed that the proposed Joint-DuDo led to higher accuracy in the projections and reconstructions than existing projection-, image-, and dual-domain approaches.

The potential clinical significance of our work is that it shows the feasibility of simultaneously performing denoising and few-angle reconstruction in low-dose cardiac SPECT. Using the proposed method, we could potentially promote the clinical adoption and market coverage of the latest cost-effective fewer-angle SPECT scanners with reduced radiation dose.

References

1. Aghakhan Olia, N., et al.: Deep learning–based denoising of low-dose SPECT myocardial perfusion images: quantitative assessment and clinical performance. Eur. J. Nucl. Med. Mol. Imaging **49**(5), 1508–1522 (2021). https://doi.org/10.1007/s00259-021-05614-7
2. Amirrashedi, M., Sarkar, S., Ghadiri, H., Ghafarian, P., Zaidi, H., Ay, M.R.: A deep neural network to recover missing data in small animal pet imaging: comparison between sinogram-and image-domain implementations. In: 2021 IEEE 18th International Symposium on Biomedical Imaging (ISBI), pp. 1365–1368. IEEE (2021)
3. Chan, C., et al.: The impact of system matrix dimension on small FOV SPECT reconstruction with truncated projections. Med. Phys. **43**(1), 213–224 (2016)
4. Chen, X., et al.: Cross-vender, cross-tracer, and cross-protocol deep transfer learning for attenuation map generation of cardiac SPECT. J. Nucl. Cardiol. **29**(6), 3379–3391 (2022)
5. Chen, X., Liu, C.: Deep-learning-based methods of attenuation correction for SPECT and PET. J. Nucl. Cardiol. 1–20 (2022). https://doi.org/10.1007/s12350-022-03007-3
6. Chen, X., Peng, Z., Valadez, G.H.: DD-CISENet: dual-domain cross-iteration squeeze and excitation network for accelerated MRI reconstruction. arXiv preprint arXiv:2305.00088 (2023)
7. Chen, X., et al.: Ct-free attenuation correction for dedicated cardiac SPECT using a 3d dual squeeze-and-excitation residual dense network. J. Nucl. Cardiol. **29**(5), 2235–2250 (2022)

8. Chen, X., et al.: Dusfe: dual-channel squeeze-fusion-excitation co-attention for cross-modality registration of cardiac SPECT and CT. Med. Image Anal. **88**, 102840 (2023)

9. Chen, X., et al.: Dual-branch squeeze-fusion-excitation module for cross-modality registration of cardiac SPECT and ct. In: International Conference on Medical Image Computing and Computer-Assisted Intervention. pp. 46–55. Springer (2022). https://doi.org/10.1007/978-3-031-16446-0_5

10. Chen, X., et al.: Dudoss: Deep-learning-based dual-domain sinogram synthesis from sparsely sampled projections of cardiac SPECT. Med. Phys. **50**, 89–103 (2022)

11. Chen, X., et al.: Direct and indirect strategies of deep-learning-based attenuation correction for general purpose and dedicated cardiac spect. Eur. J. Nucl. Med. Mol. Imaging **49**(9), 3046–3060 (2022)

12. Chlemper, J., Caballero, J., Hajnal, J., Price, A., Rueckert, D.: A deep cascade of convolutional neural networks for dynamic MR image reconstructio. IEEE Trans. Med. Imaging **37**, 491–503 (2017)

13. Danad, I., et al.: Comparison of coronary CT angiography, SPECT, pet, and hybrid imaging for diagnosis of ischemic heart disease determined by fractional flow reserve. JAMA Cardiol. **2**(10), 1100–1107 (2017)

14. Einstein, A.J.: Effects of radiation exposure from cardiac imaging: how good are the data? J. Am. College Cardiol. **59**(6), 553–565 (2012)

15. GE-HealthCare: Ge myospect es: A perfect fit for today's practice of cardiology. Available at https://www.gehealthcare.com/products/molecular-imaging/myospect (2023)

16. Henzlova, M.J., Duvall, W.L., Einstein, A.J., Travin, M.I., Verberne, H.J.: ASNC imaging guidelines for SPECT nuclear cardiology procedures: Stress, protocols, and tracers. J. Nucl. Cardiol. **23**, 606–639 (2016)

17. Hu, J., Shen, L., Sun, G.: Squeeze-and-excitation networks. In: Proceedings of the IEEE Conference on Computer Vision and Pattern Recognition, pp. 7132–7141 (2018)

18. Niu, S., et al.: Sparse-view x-ray CT reconstruction via total generalized variation regularization. Phys. Med. Bio. **59**(12), 2997 (2014)

19. Oktay, O., et al.: Attention u-net: learning where to look for the pancreas. arXiv preprint arXiv:1804.03999 (2018)

20. Paszke, A., et al.: Pytorch: an imperative style, high-performance deep learning library. Adv. Neural Inf. Process. Syst. **32** (2019)

21. Ramon, A.J., Yang, Y., Pretorius, P.H., Johnson, K.L., King, M.A., Wernick, M.N.: Improving diagnostic accuracy in low-dose SPECT myocardial perfusion imaging with convolutional denoising networks. IEEE Trans. Med. Imaging **39**(9), 2893–2903 (2020)

22. Ronneberger, O., Fischer, P., Brox, T.: U-Net: convolutional networks for biomedical image segmentation. In: Navab, N., Hornegger, J., Wells, W.M., Frangi, A.F. (eds.) MICCAI 2015. LNCS, vol. 9351, pp. 234–241. Springer, Cham (2015). https://doi.org/10.1007/978-3-319-24574-4_28

23. Shiri, I., et al.: Standard SPECT myocardial perfusion estimation from half-time acquisitions using deep convolutional residual neural networks. J. Nucl. Cardiol. **28**(6), 2761–2779 (2020). https://doi.org/10.1007/s12350-020-02119-y

24. Sun, J., Du, Y., Li, C., Wu, T.H., Yang, B., Mok, G.S.: Pix2pix generative adversarial network for low dose myocardial perfusion SPECT denoising. Quant. Imaging Med. Sur. **12**(7), 3539 (2022)

25. Sun, J., et al.: Deep learning-based denoising in projection-domain and reconstruction-domain for low-dose myocardial perfusion SPECT. J. Nucl. Cardiol. 1–16 (2022)
26. Wang, Y., et al.: 3D conditional generative adversarial networks for high-quality pet image estimation at low dose. Neuroimage **174**, 550–562 (2018)
27. Whiteley, W., Gregor, J.: CNN-based pet sinogram repair to mitigate defective block detectors. Phys. Med. Bio. **64**(23), 235017 (2019)
28. Wu, J., Liu, C.: Recent advances in cardiac SPECT instrumentation and imaging methods. Phys. Med. Bio. **64**(6), 06TR01 (2019)
29. Zhou, B., Zhou, S.K.: Dudornet: learning a dual-domain recurrent network for fast mri reconstruction with deep t1 prior. In: Proceedings of the IEEE/CVF Conference on Computer Vision and Pattern Recognition, pp. 4273–4282 (2020)

A Multitask Framework for Label Refinement and Lesion Segmentation in Clinical Brain Imaging

Yang Yu[1], Jiahao Wang[2], Ashish Jith Sreejith Kumar[1], Bryan Tan[1],
Navya Vanjavaka[3], Nurul Hafidzah Rahim[3], Alistair Koh[1], Shaheen Low[1],
Yih Yian Sitoh[3], Hanry Yu[2], Pavitra Krishnaswamy[1], and Ivan Ho Mien[1,3(✉)]

[1] Institute for Infocomm Research (I²R), A*STAR, Singapore, Singapore
{yu_yang,Ivan_Ho}@i2r.a-star.edu.sg
[2] National University of Singapore (NUS), Singapore, Singapore
[3] National Neuroscience Institute (NNI), Singapore, Singapore

Abstract. Supervised deep learning methods offer the potential for automating lesion segmentation in routine clinical brain imaging, but performance is dependent on label quality. In practice, obtaining high-quality labels from experienced annotators for large-scale datasets is not always feasible, while noisy labels from less experienced annotators are often available. Prior studies focus on either label refinement methods or on learning to segment with noisy labels, but there has been little work on integrating these approaches within a unified framework. To address this gap, we propose a novel multitask framework for end-to-end noisy-label refinement and lesion segmentation. Our approach minimizes the discrepancy between the refined label and the predicted segmentation mask, and is highly customizable for scenarios with multiple sets of noisy labels, incomplete ground truth coverage and/or 2D/3D scans. In extensive experiments on both proprietary and public clinical brain imaging datasets, we demonstrate that our end-to-end framework offers strong performance improvements over prevailing baselines on both label refinement and lesion segmentation. Our proposed framework maintains performance gains over baselines even when ground truth labels are available for only 25–50% of the dataset. Our approach has implications for effective medical image segmentation in settings that are replete with noisy labels but sparse on ground truth annotation.

Keywords: Multitask learning · Noisy labels · Label refinement · Lesion segmentation

Y. Yu and J. Wang—Contributed equally to this work.

Supplementary Information The online version contains supplementary material available at https://doi.org/10.1007/978-3-031-44917-8_6.

© The Author(s), under exclusive license to Springer Nature Switzerland AG 2023
Z. Xue et al. (Eds.): MILLanD 2023, LNCS 14307, pp. 60–70, 2023.
https://doi.org/10.1007/978-3-031-44917-8_6

1   Introduction

The importance of accurate lesion segmentation in clinical brain imaging goes beyond disease diagnosis to treatment decisions and surgical/radiotherapeutic planning [1,13]. Automation saves immense time and manpower resources and to that end, supervised deep learning approaches have achieved state-of-the-art performance in segmenting lesions on brain MRI and CT scans [16–18]. However, these approaches still require large image datasets that must be accurately and laboriously labelled at the pixel level. Compounding this difficulty is the challenge of obtaining high-quality ground truth labels arising from intrinsic (e.g., morphological complexity) to human (e.g., clinical experience) factors.

A practical compromise in the balance between label quality and cost is to achieve full dataset annotation from less experienced annotators while strategically using a limited number of more experienced annotators to review and correct a subset of the acquired lower-quality or noisy labels. To mitigate adverse effects on segmentation accuracy from training models with noisy labels [15], there is a need for an end-to-end capability that automatically refines noisy labels and/or segment lesions, guided by higher-quality ground truth labels.

Some studies develop label refinement methods to map noisy label inputs to ground truth label distributions [11,26] while others design methods to perform segmentation with noisy labels by learning the noise distributions [22,23]. However, the literature on combining label refinement and learning with noisy labels within a unified framework is still in its nascency [4]. Furthermore, there is little work demonstrating these novel methods for complex clinical image segmentation tasks in scenarios with noisy labels from less experienced annotators.

Here, we propose a novel multitask framework that simultaneously refines noisy labels and segments lesions in an end-to-end fashion. We treat the noisy label as an additional input and define a multitask problem to jointly predict the ground truth label distribution and segment lesions of interest. We develop a multitask learning strategy that inherently minimizes the discrepancy between the refined labels and the predicted segmentation mask. Our approach is scalable to multiple sets of noisy labels and/or different levels of specialized ground truth guidance. Our main contributions are:

1. We introduce a novel multitask framework to leverage cross-label discrepancy minimization for end-to-end noisy-label refinement and lesion segmentation.
2. We perform a series of experiments on both proprietary and public brain MRI datasets to demonstrate substantial performance improvements over prevailing baselines. Further, we show that our multitask strategy provides a substantial boost in performance over each of the component networks.
3. We demonstrate that our framework is readily adapted for practical scenarios where specialized ground truth labels can only be obtained for a portion of the dataset, and maintains the improved performance over the baselines even with a 50% drop in ground truth coverage.
4. We also validate the scalability of our modular framework on a 3D lesion segmentation task to show its capability for supporting customized 3D deep learning models.

2   Related Work

Label Refinement on Noisy Labels. To refine noisy labels from multiple annotators, the medical image segmentation community employs techniques such as Simultaneous Truth and Performance Level Estimation (STAPLE) [19]. However, these label fusion approaches require multiple noisy label sets and do not readily incorporate information from associated ground truth labels [8]. Others have developed label refinement methods to map noisy label inputs to ground truth label distributions [11,26] but these have yet to be demonstrated for complex clinical image segmentation tasks. A recent study explored generative adversarial networks (GANs) based on a conditional generative model for ophthalmological conditions [21] but this method is not designed to deal with scenarios with incomplete coverage of associated ground truth labels.

Lesion Segmentation with Noisy Labels. In recent years, various approaches have been proposed to handle noisy or incorrect pixel labels in medical image segmentation tasks [9,24]. Some studies have also proposed and further extended methods that leverage noisy labels for pixel-wise loss correction through meta-guided networks, mask-guided attention, and superpixel-guided learning mechanisms [3,5,12]. However, these methods assume a simple mapping between noisy and ground truth labels, and it is unclear whether such functions can adequately handle the significant real-world variations in distributions of labels (across location, size, and shape for example) from different annotators.

There has also been little work on approaches integrating the refinement of noisy labels with lesion segmentation. To our knowledge, only one study has explored this important combination [4]. This work proposed a GAN-based segmentation framework to integrate label correction and sample reweighting strategies but does not address the inherent discrepancy between the refined labels and the predicted segmentation masks, it would have been helpful as a baseline comparison but their official implementation was not released. Differently, we leverage a cross-label discrepancy minimization strategy [25] and adapt this strategy within a novel multi-task framework for noisy label refinement and lesion segmentation.

3   Methods

Problem Formulation. We denote the n samples as $\mathcal{X} = \{x_1, \ldots, x_n\}$ and $\widetilde{\mathcal{Y}} = \{\widetilde{y}_1, \ldots, \widetilde{y}_n\}$, where x_j and $\widetilde{y}_j$ represent the j-th data input for images and noisy labels respectively. Each data input is also associated with a ground truth label denoted as $\mathcal{Y} = \{y_1, \ldots, y_n\}$. Given a paired testing input, the task is to both refine the noisy label $\widetilde{y}^T$ and segment lesions in the image x^T.

Multitask Learning Framework. Figure 1 illustrates the proposed framework. Our aim is to learn the network-specific transformation in various tasks.

We accomplish this with two encoder-decoder networks trained in a joint manner for label refinement and lesion segmentation. For both networks, we use the similarity loss to eliminate the cross-label discrepancy, and the supervision loss to leverage the ground truth labels.

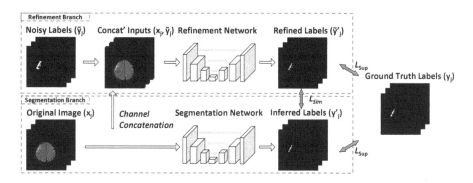

Fig. 1. Proposed end-to-end multitask learning framework for simultaneous label refinement and lesion segmentation.

Specifically, for the j-th input data x_j and $\widetilde{y}_j$, we denote the outputs of the refinement network and segmentation network as $\widetilde{y}'_j$ and y'_j respectively. The similarity loss $\mathcal{L}_{\text{Sim}}$ for both networks is constructed as follows:

$$\mathcal{L}_{\text{Sim}}(x_j, \widetilde{y}_j) = \frac{1}{n} \sum_{j=1}^{n} [(\widetilde{y}'_j - y'_j)^2] \tag{1}$$

The supervision loss $\mathcal{L}_{\text{Sup}}$ for both networks is calculated by:

$$\mathcal{L}_{\text{Sup}}(x_j, \widetilde{y}_j) = \frac{1}{n} \sum_{j=1}^{n} [(1 - \frac{2y_j \widetilde{y}'_j}{\text{Max}((y_j + \widetilde{y}'_j), \epsilon)}) + (1 - \frac{2y_j y'_j}{\text{Max}((y_j + y'_j), \epsilon)})] \tag{2}$$

where hyper-parameter ϵ is set to prevent zero-valued denominators. The final objective function across the two networks is then formulated as:

$$\mathcal{L}_{\text{Tot}} = \lambda \mathcal{L}_{\text{Sim}} + \mathcal{L}_{\text{Sup}} \tag{3}$$

where hyper-parameter λ controls the relative importance of the similarity loss. As our proposed framework trains both networks simultaneously in an end-to-end manner, it enables joint refinement of the noisy labels with the prediction of the lesion masks. During testing, the end-to-end refinement and segmentation networks can be used together or separately. The refinement network takes test images with its corresponding noisy labels $\{x^T, \widetilde{y}^T\}$ as inputs and outputs refined labels $\{\widetilde{y}'^T\}$; the segmentation network takes test images $\{x^T\}$ as inputs and outputs inferred labels $\{y'^T\}$.

4   Experiment Setup

Datasets. We evaluated our multitask framework on both proprietary (dwMRI) and public (BraTS 2019, BraTS 2021) MRI datasets (Details in Supplementary Table S1, Figure S1). The dwMRI dataset comprises 298 anonymized diffusion-weighted imaging (DWI) brain studies acquired at a tertiary healthcare institution (National Neuroscience Institute, Singapore) between 2009 to 2019 as part of routine clinical care. Data collection and use were approved by the relevant institutional review boards (SingHealth CIRB Ref 2019/2804). Abnormalities were segmented using ITK-SNAP by two groups of annotators with different experience levels (two radiography students and two neuroradiology fellows) whose annotations yielded one set of noisy labels and ground truth labels respectively. After excluding 7690 images without any DWI abnormalities, 470 images were randomly selected for training/validation (internal splitting ratio 4:1), leaving the remaining 141 images for testing on the 2D task. The BraTS 2019/2021 datasets comprise 335/1251 pre-operative multimodal MRI brain studies of high- and low-grade gliomas with pixel-level annotations categorized into necrotic and non-enhancing tumor (label-1), peritumoral edema (label-2), and enhancing tumor (label-4) [13]. For our experiments, we investigated segmentation of the tumor core (TC) on various sequences by removing label-2 and combining label-4 and label-1 into a single ground truth label. For BraTS 2019, we randomly sampled 500 images for training/validation and 200 images for testing to match with the dwMRI dataset on the 2D task. For BraTS 2021 with more studies provided, we randomly sampled 1000 studies for training/validation and 251 studies for testing on the 3D tasks. To simulate label noise, we applied similar methods used in previous literature [12,23,24,26], namely random shift, random rotation, dilation, and random noise, to the ground truth labels of selected images/studies. Examples of differences between paired ground truth labels and real/simulated noisy labels for both datasets are provided in Supplementary Figure S1.

Implementation Details. The proposed method includes a conventional UNet [18] (2D tasks) and a volumetric UNet [14] (3D tasks) for both refinement and segmentation networks. We demonstrated the results using ResNeXt-50 [20] (2D tasks) and ResNet-110 [6] (3D tasks) as encoder backbones. We implemented all experiments in PyTorch with two Nvidia A5000 GPUs. Hyperparameters are shown in Supplementary Table S2.

Baselines. To compare the performance of our proposed method against other state-of-the-art (SOTA) approaches, we implemented the Conditional GAN algorithm [21], Confident Learning algorithm [24], Attention Module algorithm [9], and volumetric UNet algorithm [14]. We investigate the performance of Conditional GAN for label refinement and the performance of Confident Learning and Attention Module for lesion segmentation on the 2D task. We also examine the performance of Volumetric UNet [14] for lesion segmentation on the 3D task. Hyperparameters are shown in Supplementary Table S3.

Experiments. We performed four experiments to assess the efficacy of our proposed approach for label refinement and image segmentation. In the first experiment, we compared our technique with the aforementioned 2D baselines. In the second experiment, we performed ablation studies to systematically evaluate the effect of each network and similarity loss in our framework. In the third experiment, we simulated scenarios where only a portion (25%, 50%, or 75%) of images have corresponding ground truth labels and assessed performance compared to the fully-paired experiment. In this experiment, we first trained the networks using images with paired noisy and ground truth labels and used the generated pseudo-labels from refined labels as ground truth labels for images with noisy labels only. We further trained the model on both paired and unpaired images using a pseudo-labeling strategy coupled with a deterministic annealing process [10]. In the fourth experiment, we investigated the scalability of our proposed technique to a 3D task with performance compared to the 3D baseline [14].

Table 1. Comparison of refinement and segmentation accuracy for different methods. The means and standard deviations of the DSC (%)/HSD are reported. Best in **bold**.

Task (Methods)	dwMRI		BraTS 2019	
	DSC↑	HSD↓	DSC↑	HSD↓
Refinement (Conditional GAN [21])	49.44 ± 0.45	2.16 ± 0.10	79.84 ± 0.82	3.07 ± 0.03
Refinement (Ours)	$\mathbf{51.46 \pm 0.29}$	$\mathbf{2.13 \pm 0.05}$	$\mathbf{80.22 \pm 0.07}$	$\mathbf{3.02 \pm 0.05}$
Segmentation (Confident Learning [24])	34.29 ± 1.62	2.62 ± 0.38	44.13 ± 1.38	3.69 ± 0.11
Segmentation (Attention Module [9])	39.83 ± 1.48	2.47 ± 0.07	56.61 ± 1.38	$\mathbf{3.01 \pm 0.06}$
Segmentation (Ours)	$\mathbf{41.96 \pm 2.07}$	$\mathbf{2.07 \pm 0.11}$	$\mathbf{58.43 \pm 1.29}$	3.07 ± 0.03

Evaluation Metrics. We evaluated the Dice Similarity Coefficient (DSC) [2] and Hausdorff Surface Distance (HSD) [7] to quantify the performance of label refinement and lesion segmentation. (Higher DSC and/or lower HSD values indicate better performance.) We employed multiple seeds to compute averaged values and standard deviations for both DSC and HSD metrics.

5   Results

Comparison with SOTA Baselines on Label Refinement. We first benchmarked our results against the recent SOTA baselines for label refinement in Table 1. Our proposed multitask learning approach provides a 2.02%/0.03 boost for the dwMRI dataset and a 0.38%/0.05 improvement for the BraTS 2019 dataset in DSC/HSD over the Conditional GAN refinement baseline. Although simulated noise in the BraTS 2019 dataset is more easily corrected compared with real noise in the dwMRI dataset, the results still display consistently substantial improvements in both actual and simulated noisy labels.

Comparison with SOTA Baselines on Lesion Segmentation. We also benchmarked our results against the recent SOTA baselines for lesion segmentation in Table 1. The Confident Learning approach achieves DSC/HSD of 34.29±1.62 (%)/2.62±0.38 and 44.13±1.38 (%)/3.69±0.11 on dwMRI and BraTS 2019, respectively. When combined with ground truth labels that could better guide the model training process, the Attention Module approach achieves higher DSC of 39.83±1.48 (%)/2.47±0.07 and 56.61±1.38 (%)/3.01±0.06 on dwMRI and BraTS 2019, respectively. Our proposed framework improved over both of these methods with DSC/HSD of 41.96±2.07 (%)/2.07±0.11 and 58.43±1.29 (%)/3.07±0.03 on dwMRI and BraTS 2019, respectively. Our results suggest that the inclusion of noisy labels in our multitask learning approach is able to further enhance semantic consistency among labels with various quality levels.

Table 2. Comparison of refinement and segmentation accuracy for ablation studies. The means and standard deviations of the DSC (%)/HSD are reported. Best in **bold**.

Task (Networks)	dwMRI		BraTS 2019	
	DSC↑	HSD↓	DSC↑	HSD↓
Refinement (Refinement Network)	48.05 ± 0.89	2.23 ± 0.12	78.83 ± 0.25	3.17 ± 0.07
Refinement (Multitask Network w/o $\mathcal{L}_{\mathrm{Sim}}$)	50.37 ± 0.29	2.23 ± 0.02	80.06 ± 0.80	3.08 ± 0.03
Refinement (Multitask Network w/ $\mathcal{L}_{\mathrm{Sim}}$)	$\mathbf{51.46 \pm 0.10}$	$\mathbf{2.13 \pm 0.05}$	$\mathbf{80.22 \pm 0.07}$	$\mathbf{3.02 \pm 0.05}$
Segmentation (Segmentation Network)	38.53 ± 2.05	2.05 ± 0.07	55.25 ± 3.16	$\mathbf{3.03 \pm 0.12}$
Segmentation (Multitask Network w/o $\mathcal{L}_{\mathrm{Sim}}$)	40.16 ± 2.16	$\mathbf{2.01 \pm 0.26}$	55.87 ± 2.58	3.49 ± 0.33
Segmentation (Multitask Network w/ $\mathcal{L}_{\mathrm{Sim}}$)	$\mathbf{41.96 \pm 2.07}$	2.07 ± 0.11	$\mathbf{58.43 \pm 1.29}$	3.07 ± 0.03

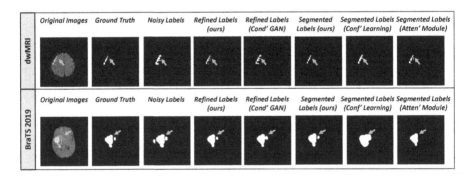

Fig. 2. Visualisation of label refinement and image segmentation on two datasets (dwMRI and BraTS 2019). Subtle differences are indicated by red arrows. (Color figure online)

Visualization of Refined and Segmented Images. For further characterization, we present exemplary results on two images (one from dwMRI and one from BraTS 2019) from the testing sets in Fig. 2. These results demonstrate the potential of our proposed method to correct subtle noises, particularly in connected areas, and also accurately identify semantic lesions, especially when accuracy relies on fine details.

Ablation Studies. Next, we performed ablation studies to systematically assess the contribution of each component in our proposed framework. The results, in Table 2, indicate that injection of the segmentation and refinement paths through a multitask learning framework yields a 3.41% and 3.43% increase in DSC, as well as comparable performance in HSD for the dwMRI dataset; and 1.39% and 3.18% improvement in DSC as well as comparable performance in HSD for the BraTS 2019 dataset on label refinement and lesion segmentation, respectively, compared to using only the refinement or segmentation network alone. The results also show that integration of the similarity loss further improves model performance on lesion detection.

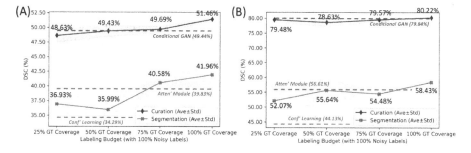

Fig. 3. Performance results in DSC (%) for label refinement and lesion segmentation accuracy on (A) dwMRI (left) and (B) BraTS 2019 (right) datasets in scenarios with incomplete ground truth label coverage, as indicated by the percentage of images paired with ground truth labels. The base DSC (%) for refined labels (green dashed line) and segmented lesions (blue dashed lines) using previous SOTAs with 100% ground truth coverage (%) are also shown for comparison. (Color figure online)

Performance with Incomplete Coverage of Ground Truth Labels. Figure 3 presents the results of the proposed multitask learning framework trained with incomplete labels. In real-world scenarios, it is common to only have a limited percentage of ground truth labels, although ideally, having more ground truth labels would result in better performance. The results show improved performance for the dwMRI and BraTS 2019 datasets with more ground truth labels, due to benefits from pixel information of images providing additional lesion-level information. There are certain fluctuations in DSC values at lower ground truth coverage, but the general trend still remains the same as DSC values increase with greater coverage of paired ground truth labels. Even in the scenario with ground truth labels being available for only 25% of the images, the DSCs for refined labels and segmented lesions still show comparable performance to the baseline DSCs from previous SOTA(s) with 100% ground truth coverage, for the two respective datasets. For lesion segmentation, when only 50–75% of the images have paired ground truth labels, the proposed framework also outperforms the baseline DSCs from previous SOTA(s) with 100% ground truth coverage, by up to 1.70–6.29%/10.35–11.51% for the two respective datasets.

Scalability on 3D Task. We further investigated the scalability of our proposed technique on a 3D task against the recent volumetric UNet baseline for 3D lesion segmentation of the tumor core (TC) in Table 3. When combined with the multitask learning strategy that simultaneously refines noisy labels and segments lesions, the DSC improves from 73.44±0.76 (%) to 76.96±0.80 (%) for lesion segmentation on BraTS 2021. The results also demonstrate that our multitask framework is a general modular framework which can be further adapted to customized 3D deep learning models for enhancement of segmentation accuracy.

Table 3. Comparison of refinement and segmentation accuracy for a 3D task. The means and standard deviations of the DSC (%) are reported. Best in **bold**.

Dataset (Networks)	Refinement (Ours) DSC↑	Segmentation (Ours) DSC↑	Segmentation (Volumetric UNet [14]) DSC↑
BraTS 2021	**88.37** ± 2.14	**76.96** ± 0.80	73.44 ± 0.76

6   Conclusion

In summary, we proposed a novel multitask framework that simultaneously refines noisy labels and segments lesions in an end-to-end manner by leveraging cross-label discrepancy minimization, and conducted extensive experiments on both proprietary and public datasets in 2D and 3D settings to demonstrate its effectiveness. Our work has implications for addressing challenges in brain lesion segmentation that arise from difficulties in acquiring high-quality labels.

Acknowledgements. Research efforts were supported by funding and infrastructure for deep learning and medical imaging research from the Institute for Infocomm Research, Science and Engineering Research Council, A*STAR, Singapore and the National Neuroscience Institute, Singapore.

References

1. Akkus, Z., Galimzianova, A., Hoogi, A., Rubin, D.L., Erickson, B.J.: Deep learning for brain MRI segmentation: state of the art and future directions. J. Digital Imaging **30**, 449–459 (2017)

2. Bertels, J., et al.: Optimizing the dice score and jaccard index for medical image segmentation: theory and practice. In: Shen, D., et al. (eds.) MICCAI 2019. LNCS, vol. 11765, pp. 92–100. Springer, Cham (2019). https://doi.org/10.1007/978-3-030-32245-8_11

3. Cai, Z., Xin, J., Shi, P., Zhou, S., Wu, J., Zheng, N.: Meta pixel loss correction for medical image segmentation with noisy labels. In: Medical Image Learning with Limited and Noisy Data: First International Workshop, MILLanD 2022, Held in Conjunction with MICCAI 2022, Singapore, September 22, 2022, Proceedings. pp. 32–41. Springer (2022). https://doi.org/10.1007/978-3-031-16760-7_4

4. Cheng, G., Ji, H., Tian, Y.: Walking on two legs: learning image segmentation with noisy labels. In: Conference on Uncertainty in Artificial Intelligence, pp. 330–339. PMLR (2020)

5. Guo, R., Pagnucco, M., Song, Y.: Learning with noise: mask-guided attention model for weakly supervised nuclei segmentation. In: de Bruijne, M., et al. (eds.) MICCAI 2021. LNCS, vol. 12902, pp. 461–470. Springer, Cham (2021). https://doi.org/10.1007/978-3-030-87196-3_43

6. He, K., Zhang, X., Ren, S., Sun, J.: Identity Mappings in Deep Residual Networks. In: Leibe, B., Matas, J., Sebe, N., Welling, M. (eds.) ECCV 2016. LNCS, vol. 9908, pp. 630–645. Springer, Cham (2016). https://doi.org/10.1007/978-3-319-46493-0_38

7. Huttenlocher, D.P., Klanderman, G.A., Rucklidge, W.J.: Comparing images using the hausdorff distance. IEEE Trans. Pattern Anal. Mach. Intell. 15(9), 850–863 (1993)

8. Karimi, D., Dou, H., Warfield, S.K., Gholipour, A.: Deep learning with noisy labels: exploring techniques and remedies in medical image analysis. Med. Image Anal. 65, 101759 (2020)

9. Kim, J., Kim, M., Kang, H., Lee, K.: U-gat-it: Unsupervised generative attentional networks with adaptive layer-instance normalization for image-to-image translation. arXiv preprint arXiv:1907.10830 (2019)

10. Lee, D.H., et al.: Pseudo-label: The simple and efficient semi-supervised learning method for deep neural networks. In: Workshop on challenges in representation learning, ICML. p. 896 (2013)

11. Lee, J., et al.: A pixel-level coarse-to-fine image segmentation labelling algorithm. Sci. Reports 12(1), 8672 (2022)

12. Li, S., Gao, Z., He, X.: Superpixel-Guided Iterative Learning from Noisy Labels for Medical Image Segmentation. In: de Bruijne, M., et al. (eds.) MICCAI 2021. LNCS, vol. 12901, pp. 525–535. Springer, Cham (2021). https://doi.org/10.1007/978-3-030-87193-2_50

13. Menze, B.H., et al.: The multimodal brain tumor image segmentation benchmark (brats). IEEE Trans. Med. Imaging 34(10), 1993–2024 (2014)

14. Myronenko, A.: 3D MRI Brain Tumor Segmentation Using Autoencoder Regularization. In: Crimi, A., Bakas, S., Kuijf, H., Keyvan, F., Reyes, M., van Walsum, T. (eds.) BrainLes 2018. LNCS, vol. 11384, pp. 311–320. Springer, Cham (2019). https://doi.org/10.1007/978-3-030-11726-9_28

15. Obuchowicz, R., Oszust, M., Piorkowski, A.: Interobserver variability in quality assessment of magnetic resonance images. BMC Med. Imaging 20, 1–10 (2020)

16. Rajpurkar, P., et al.: Deep learning for chest radiograph diagnosis: a retrospective comparison of the chexnext algorithm to practicing radiologists. PLoS Med. 15(11), e1002686 (2018)

17. Ranjbarzadeh, R., Bagherian Kasgari, A., Jafarzadeh Ghoushchi, S., Anari, S., Naseri, M., Bendechache, M.: Brain tumor segmentation based on deep learning and an attention mechanism using MRI multi-modalities brain images. Sci. Reports **11**(1), 1–17 (2021)
18. Ronneberger, O., Fischer, P., Brox, T.: U-Net: Convolutional Networks for Biomedical Image Segmentation. In: Navab, N., Hornegger, J., Wells, W.M., Frangi, A.F. (eds.) MICCAI 2015. LNCS, vol. 9351, pp. 234–241. Springer, Cham (2015). https://doi.org/10.1007/978-3-319-24574-4_28
19. Warfield, S.K., Zou, K.H., Wells, W.M.: Simultaneous truth and performance level estimation (staple): an algorithm for the validation of image segmentation. IEEE Trans. Med. Imaging **23**(7), 903–921 (2004)
20. Xie, S., Girshick, R., Dollár, P., Tu, Z., He, K.: Aggregated residual transformations for deep neural networks. In: Proceedings of the IEEE Conference on Computer Vision and Pattern Recognition, pp. 1492–1500 (2017)
21. Yang, Y., Wang, Z., Liu, J., Cheng, K.T., Yang, X.: Label refinement with an iterative generative adversarial network for boosting retinal vessel segmentation. arXiv preprint arXiv:1912.02589 (2019)
22. Zhang, L., et al.: Learning to Segment When Experts Disagree. In: Martel, A.L., et al. (eds.) MICCAI 2020. LNCS, vol. 12261, pp. 179–190. Springer, Cham (2020). https://doi.org/10.1007/978-3-030-59710-8_18
23. Zhang, L., et al.: Disentangling human error from the ground truth in segmentation of medical images. In: Proceedings of the 34th International Conference on Neural Information Processing Systems, pp. 15750–15762. ACL (2020)
24. Zhang, M., et al.: Characterizing label errors: confident learning for noisy-labeled image segmentation. In: Martel, A.L., et al. (eds.) MICCAI 2020. LNCS, vol. 12261, pp. 721–730. Springer, Cham (2020). https://doi.org/10.1007/978-3-030-59710-8_70
25. Zhen, L., Hu, P., Wang, X., Peng, D.: Deep supervised cross-modal retrieval. In: Proceedings of the IEEE/CVF Conference on Computer Vision and Pattern Recognition, pp. 10394–10403 (2019)
26. Zheng, G., Awadallah, A.H., Dumais, S.: Meta label correction for noisy label learning. In: Proceedings of the AAAI Conference on Artificial Intelligence, pp. 11053–11061 (2021)

COVID-19 Lesion Segmentation Framework for the Contrast-Enhanced CT in the Absence of Contrast-Enhanced CT Annotations

Maryna Kvasnytsia[✉][iD], Abel Díaz Berenguer[iD], Hichem Sahli[iD],
and Jef Vandemeulebroucke[iD]

Vrije Universiteit Brussel (VUB), Brussels, Belgium
mkvasnyt@etrovub.be

Abstract. Medical imaging is a dynamic domain where new acquisition protocols are regularly developed and employed to meet changing clinical needs. Deep learning models for medical image segmentation have proven to be a valuable tool for medical image processing. Creating such a model from scratch requires a lot of effort in terms of annotating new types of data and model training. Therefore, the amount of annotated training data for the new imaging protocol might still be limited. In this work we propose a framework for segmentation of images acquired with a new imaging protocol(contrast-enhanced lung CT) that does not require annotating training data in the new target domain. Instead, the framework leverages the previously developed models, data and annotations in a related source domain. Using contrast-enhanced lung CT data as a target data we demonstrate that unpaired image translation from the non-contrast enhanced source data, combined with self-supervised pretraining achieves 0.726 Dice Score for the COVID-19 lesion segmentation task on the target data, without the necessity to annotate any target data for the model training.

1 Introduction

Deep learning methods for medical image segmentation achieve state-of-the-art performance [17]. Despite an increased research interest in semi-supervised and unsupervised approaches, segmentation networks still require many manual delineations for training. Annotation of medical images remains a challenge due to the sensitive nature of the medical data and the specialized domain knowledge necessary to accurately delineate objects of interest. Medical imaging is a dynamically developing domain where new imaging protocols are being regularly developed. Developing a segmentation model for the new image type (target data) from scratch requires a lot of effort in terms of annotating and model training. At the same time, deep learning models are sensitive to the distribution difference

Supplementary Information The online version contains supplementary material available at https://doi.org/10.1007/978-3-031-44917-8_7.

© The Author(s), under exclusive license to Springer Nature Switzerland AG 2023
Z. Xue et al. (Eds.): MILLanD 2023, LNCS 14307, pp. 71–81, 2023.
https://doi.org/10.1007/978-3-031-44917-8_7

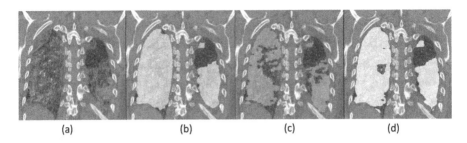

(a)   (b)   (c)   (d)

Fig. 1. Example of segmentation improvement due to combination of self-supervised pretraining and image to image translation compared to utilizing the model developed for NC-CT images. (a) - CE-CT coronal CT slice, (b) - corresponding ground truth mask (green), (c) - segmentation mask(red) obtained with method developed for NC-CT, (d) - segmentation mask obtained with suggested framework. (Color figure online)

between training and test datasets (domain shift) [14], therefore the straight-forward application of a segmentation model previously developed on original source data is often unsuccessful. Non-contrast CT imaging (NC-CT) has proven to be a valuable tool for the assessment of the severity of COVID-19 induced pathological processes in the lungs. It has been shown that COVID-19 also manifests itself with co-occurring vascular pathologies [1]. This invokes the necessity to perform a CT scan with contrast to better visualize vascular structures in the lungs. The appearance of contrast-enhanced CT image(CE-CT) changes the texture visualization of lungs due to enhanced vascular structures, also causing increased local CT values of specific organs, such as the heart and aorta. Many successful models for COVID-19 lesion segmentation based on NC-CT were developed and deployed in the hospitals. There is an abundance of publicly available annotated NC-CT data for this task. However, due to the differences between CE-CT and NC-CT images straightforward application of the models developed for the NC-CT produces suboptimal results. An illustrative example of this problem is shown in Fig 1. One can observe mostly undersegmentation of lesions estimated with NC-CT model applied without adaptations to CE-CT image. In this work, we focus on the problem of facilitated transitioning to the new imaging protocol by effectively leveraging previously acquired data and previously developed models for COVID-19 lesion segmentation. Our contributions are summarized as follows:

1. We propose a framework combining self-supervised pretraining on the unlabelled data followed by fine-tuning on the data generated by means of unsupervised image translation methods.
2. We compare two methods of unsupervised image translation, CUT and cycle-GAN, in respect to final segmentation accuracy.
3. We demonstrate on the example of CE-CT images that proposed framework allows to approach segmentation accuracy of the well-annotated source domain without annotating the data from a new target domain.

2   Related Work

Using Synthetic Data to Alleviate Segmentation with Limited or Absent Annotations. Creating a model from scratch requires a lot of effort in terms of annotating new data and model training. When developing the model for a new imaging modality or protocol the amount of training data might still be limited. There is an incentive to use synthetic data in order to alleviate the problem of limited data. A number of publications demonstrate that GANs are able to generate realistically-looking medical images [4,6,7,19]. However, the usefulness of such images for segmentation task remains uncertain. Skandarani et al. [27] evaluated several GAN architectures in order to test if GANs are able to generate workable medical images. Despite achieving good results in terms of realistically looking medical images, their conclusion is that segmentation results based on generated images are still inferior to those produced with full medical dataset. Similarly, in [26], segmentation networks trained with exclusively generated images do not reach the performance of networks trained with real images. Existing GAN models utilized for the generation of medical images have some limitations. The Pix2Pix model [18] relies on aligned paired datasets. To overcome this limitation unpaired image-to-image translation is implemented via cycle-consistency method [32], which learns an inverse mapping from the output domain back to the input and estimates reconstruction loss for the input image. Cycle-consistency may produce multiple solutions, therefore can be challenging to apply for medical image-to-image translation tasks where high accuracy is important. The CUT model introduced in [24] is based on multilayer patchwise contrastive learning and adversarial learning. This method does not rely on cycle-consistency and performs one-sided image translation by maximizing the mutual information between an input patch and a generated patch. Choi et al [10] demonstrated the successful application of an out-of-the-box CUT model for domain adaptation from contrast-enhanced T1 MR to high-resolution T2 MR.

Self-supervised Learning. Training deep neural networks on a limited dataset may cause the risk of overfitting. To address the overfitting problem, it is possible to pretrain the network on large-sized data based on images acquired with established imaging protocol (source task data), and then fine-tune the model on the target data (images acquired with new imaging protocol). Pretraining can be implemented via self-supervised learning(SSL) [30] that derives supervision from the source data itself, and therefore does not require a laborious annotation step and gives the opportunity to exploit more data since unannotated data is more abundant. Self-supervised learning attempts to derive a good feature representation while solving pretext tasks such as predicting relative positions [12], solving jigsaw puzzle [23], reconstructing part of the image, anatomical location prediction [3]. Model Genesis [31] achieved state-of-the-art segmentation performance by solving image reconstruction tasks starting from images transformed by random combinations of several transformations. Another branch of self-supervised learning, contrastive learning, aims to learn a feature embedding where associated or similar samples are close to each other while far from the dissimilar samples. The associated samples include images or image patches and their transformed versions. The choice of positive and negative samples is an important design decision, especially in the medical imaging domain. Chaitanya et al [9] investigate different strategies for selecting negative and positive samples by taking into account domain-specific cues. Contrastive learning has been successfully applied to a number of segmentation problems with limited annotations [21,29].

3   Proposed Framework

The workflow consists of three steps, starting with unsupervised pretraining using unannotated CT images. The second step is generation of synthetic contrast-enhanced images using unpaired image translation. In the next step, the generated CE-CT images together with corresponding labels are used for training the segmentation model based on nnUnet architecture [17]. Detailed information about the steps is presented in the following subsections. The entire workflow is illustrated in Fig 2.

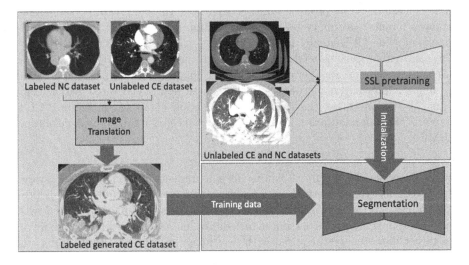

Fig. 2. Illustration of the workflow. In step 1, we train the image translation model to generate CE-CT images from NC-CT. In step 2, we pretrain nnUnet by solving the reconstruction task using unlabeled NC-CT and CE-CT. Finally, we train the segmentation model using generated CE-CT images and labels inherited from NC-CT as training data and weights initialization from the SSL pretraining.

4   Methods

4.1   Image Translation

We compare performance of 2 image translation models, CUT and cycle-GAN, with their default configurations, using the same datasets in order to choose the most optimal method of generation of the synthetic CE-CT images. Both models were trained with data described in Table 1 to perform image translation from NC-CT to CE-CT using default configurations. Consequently, the trained translation models were used to generate corresponding CE-CT images using labelled non-contrast datasets. CE-CT images can highlight different structures depending on the acquisition moment in respect to the contrast agent administration as illustrated in Supplementary material. This can pose a challenge for cycle-GAN since the method assumes one-to-one correspondence between source and target image.

4.2   SSL Pretraining and Segmentation

Self-supervised pretraining included in the proposed workflow was inspired by the model Genesis [31] and implemented by solving image restoration tasks. 3D patches of size $128 \times 128 \times 32$ of input images were transformed using local pixel value shuffling, image in-painting, image out-painting, and nonlinear intensity transformation as illustrated in the Supplementary material. We created several models to explore the influence of the amount and type of the pretraining data on segmentation performance.Two baseline nnUnet segmentation models were trained with random weights initialization, using CE-CT images generated by CUT(SL_{CUT}) and by cycle-GAN(SL_{cGAN}). The $SL_{CUT}^{SSL(NC)}$ model is nnUnet initialized with weights obtained from self-supervised pretraining of 2106 on NC-CT images.The $SL_{CUT}^{SSL(CE)}$ model is a nnUnet initialized with weights obtained from self-supervised pretraining of 222 on CE-CT images. The $SL_{CUT}^{SSL(NC-CE)}$ is a nnUnet initialized with weights obtained from self-supervised pretraining of on 2106 NC CT images, the pretraining was subsequently continued on real unannotated 222 CE-CT images. For all pretrained models fine-tuning for the segmentation task has been performed using CE-CT images generated by CUT.

5   Experiments and Results

Data. Five datasets were included in this work: 4 datasets of no-contrast enhanced data and one dataset of contrast-enhanced data. The contrast-enhanced images(total amount, 251) used in this work were acquired at the University hospital of Brussels(UZB) with dual-energy CT protocol using iodine contrast agent. The dual-energy CT protocol allows to reconstruct high-energy CT images resembling non-contrast CT data. It is possible therefore to apply a segmentation nnUnet model [17] developed with full supervision for non-contrast CT images to such high-energy reconstructions to obtain masks which after review are used as "silver" ground truth segmentations. Since our goal is to investigate a strategy to develop models for CE-CT images that provide segmentation results consistent with NC-based models already in use, we consider such "silver" ground truth masks as acceptable for testing. 29 CE-CT datasets were set aside for testing of the entire framework. For unsupervised training of the image translation model and unsupervised pretraining of the segmentation model we use 2106 unlabeled NC-CT datasets acquired in various hospitals(hospitals pool2). For fine-tuning stage we applied trained image translation model to generate CE-CT images using 2 labeled public datasets [25,28] and labeled data from 4 hospitals(hospitals pool1) for fine-tuning of the segmentation model. We used 50 healthy lung CT images from public MosMedData [22] dataset for the training of the related fully unsupervised reference model(referred to as CH-GAN) following the [11]. The summary of the training data is presented in the Table 1.

Table 1. Data used for training and validation in this work. NC-CT stands for non-contrast enhanced CT, CE-CT stands for contrast-enhanced CT. "GAN/SSL" means that data was used for training image translation model and for self-supervised pretraining, "Generation" means that the data was used for generation of the training datataset for the final segmentation model. For "Hospitals pool2" data was collected from 10 institutions throughout Europe and Latin America, it includes scans of COVID-19 related pathologies and lung pathologies acquired prior to November 2019. For "Hospitals pool1" data was collected from 4 hospitals in Europe, all datasets were acquired from COVID-19-positive patients.

Data origin	Type	Pathology	Amount	Labeled	Usage
Public datasets [25,28]	NC-CT	COVID-19	260	Yes	Generation
Hospitals pool1	NC-CT	COVID-19	79	Yes	Generation
Hospitals pool2	NC-CT	Various	2106	No	GAN/SSL
UZB	CE-CT	Covid-19	222	No	GAN/SSL
MosMedData [22]	NC-CT	Healthy	50	No	CH-GAN

Preprocessing and Implementation Details. All CT datasets are resampled to an isotropic resolution of 1mm. Image intensities were clipped to [-1000, 1000] HU and scaled to the range of [0,1]. Lung masks are calculated using publicly available algorithm [16]. In our workflow, we use the 3D nnUnet architecture for image restoration and segmentation, implemented within the MONAI framework [8]. All training patches are derived by random cropping of input images to $128 \times 128 \times 32$. We use the Adam optimizer with a learning rate of 0.0001 and weight decay of 0.00001. MSE loss was used during training of the image reconstruction task, Dice loss was used for the image segmentation task. The preprocessing for image translation included clipping image intensities to [-1000, 1000] HU, scaling to [0,1] and resampling images to 256×256 in axial orientation. In the post-processing step for segmentation, we additionally overlap predicted lesion masks with lung masks to reduce false positives.

Quantitative and Qualitative Analysis. We have calculated the Frechet Inception Distance(FID) that uses a pre-trained Inception network to assess the quality of images generated by GAN [15]. The lower value of FID usually indicates a good visual correspondence of generated images. In our experiment, the value of FID is quite high for CUT, 178, with even higher value of 217 for cycle-GAN. Though FID is an accepted measure for distinguishing the best and less effective generation methods in computer vision, there is some critique of using it for medical images since the InceptionNet used for the calculation of FID was trained on non-medical images [27]. In the evaluation of the entire workflow, we put emphasis on the segmentation metrics such as Dice Score. Visual comparison of generated images suggests that CUT achieves more realistic appearance of generated CE-CT compared to cycle-GAN in the same amount of epochs as illustrated in the supplementary material. We observe enhanced appearance of vascular and cardiac structures on the CUT-generated images while the shape and locations of the organs are preserved. The models adapted for the domain differences were evaluated on the test dataset which consisted of 29 real CE-CT images with annotations generated according to the method described in the Data section. To illustrate the domain gap we applied the nnUnet initialised with weights from SSL pretrainning on NC-CT data and fine-tuned on NC-CT data without adaptation for CE-CT domain, $SL_{NC}^{SSL(NC)}$, on the CE-CT test set. The state-of-the-art models evaluated on NC-CT data report segmentation accuracy of 0.77 Dice Score [28], which we consider a target accuracy for segmentation model developed for a new imaging protocol.

We compared proposed framework to the related fully unsupervised COVID-19 lesion segmentation approach proposed in [11] based on subtracting synthetic healthy CT generated by cycle-GAN from original CT images and consequent thresholding of the derived difference maps (CH-GAN). Following [11], we trained CUT model to perform unsupervised translation of CE-CT images to healthy lung CT using dataset [22]. Unlike [11] where only lower threshold is used to produce lesion segmentations, we define both lower and upper thresholds to binarize the difference maps to eliminate differences not related to pathology but originating from translating contrast enhanced image to non-contrasted image. Average Dice Scores and Hausdorff distances calculated for the test dataset are summarized in Table 2 and in Fig 3. Both baseline models, SL_{CUT} and SL_{cGAN}, are nnUnets trained with random weights initialization on generated CE-CT images by CUT or cycle-GAN correspondingly, already provide good results in terms of Dice Score, 0.677 and 0.675, significantly outperforming the reference CH-GAN model. Initializing the model with weights derived from pretraining on a limited amount of CE-CT data improves performance by 0.012 Dice. Using a rich unlabeled NC dataset for pretraining gives a 0.05 Dice boost in segmentation performance. The best Dice Score is accomplished with $SL_{CUT}^{SSL(NC-CE)}$ model which was initialized with weights obtained via consequent pretraining on the rich NC dataset and continued with additional pretraining on a smaller CE dataset. Examples of segmentation masks produced by implemented models are presented in Supplementary material.

Table 2. Mean Dice Score and Hausdorff distance (95%, HD95) calculated on the test set. In the "Generation step" column image translation method is indicated if applicable, in the "Pretraining step" type of data for pretraining.

Model name	Generation step	Pretraining step	Dice/std	HD95(mm)/std
$SL_{NC}^{SSL(NC)}$	no	NC	0.606/0.1634	44.77/36.34
SL_{CUT}	CUT	no	0.677/0.1390	32.04/28.21
SL_{cGAN}	cycle-GAN	no	0.675/0.1424	20.68/18.74
$SL_{CUT}^{SSL(NC)}$	CUT	NC	0.721/0.1408	33.40/30.00
$SL_{CUT}^{SSL(CE)}$	CUT	CE	0.689/0.1331	**26.85/27.11**
$SL_{CUT}^{SSL(NC-CE)}$	CUT	NC and CE	**0.726/0.1402**	34.47/36.59
CH-GAN	CUT	no	0.444/0.2094	32.48/17.04

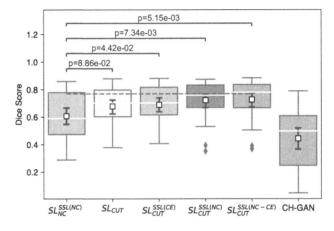

Fig. 3. Boxplot visualization of Dice Scores achieved by different models, together with mean(white square) and a 95% confidence intervals(black errorbar) and corresponding p-values calculated comparing to the the model trained on NC-CT without domain adaptation, $SL_{NC}^{SSL(NC)}$. The models combining self-supervised pretraining with fine-tuning on generated data provide improvement in terms of the segmentation performance. The dashed line represents a goal accuracy, average Dice Score achieved by state-of-the-art fully-supervised models on NC-CT data.

6   Discussion

We proposed a framework for COVID-19 lesion segmentation on CE-CT images without annotation by utilizing image translation methods in combination with self-supervised pretraining. Using image translation methods we leverage available annotated datasets to generate a training dataset for the new imaging protocol. We believe that the proposed framework can find its application in clinics for less effortful transitioning to new imaging protocols while preserving the ability to segment lesions with comparable accuracy as with a supervised model based on non-contrast CT. The limitations of the current work include a relatively small test dataset with imperfect ground truth masks, restricting us from generalizing our findings. We assume there is room for improvement with respect to the quality of generated CE-CT, since, in this work, the image translation models were used without any optimization and modifications taking the medical domain into consideration. For example, out-of-the-box configuration of CUT required resampling of the images to 256×256 which could lead to small image details being lost in generated images. The original CUT model works with 2D images, while 3D image information is essential in the medical domain. Generating each slice separately may lead to discrepancies in intensity along the z-direction as illustrated in Supplementary material. Therefore, modifying the image translation model to process 3D volumes can be beneficial for optimal image translation. Assessment of the quality of generated data in this work was done by visual inspection. Automated methods of synthetic medical imaging data quality control would be beneficial for future work. Our experiments did not reveal any significant benefit of CUT over cycle-GAN or vice versa using their default configurations. Comparing the performance of different image-to-image translation schemes [2,5,13,20] would be an interesting analysis in future works. Evaluating such a workflow for more challenging multi-modality (MRI-CT) scenarios would be of interest.

References

1. Ackermann, M., et al.: Pulmonary vascular endothelialitis, thrombosis, and angiogenesis in COVID-19. N. Engl. J. Med. **383**(2), 120–128 (2020)
2. Amodio, M., Krishnaswamy, S.: Travelgan: image-to-image translation by transformation vector learning. In: 2019 IEEE/CVF Conference on Computer Vision and Pattern Recognition (CVPR), pp. 8975–8984 (2019)
3. Bai, W., et al.: Self-supervised learning for cardiac MR image segmentation by anatomical position prediction. In: Shen, D., et al. (eds.) MICCAI 2019. LNCS, vol. 11765, pp. 541–549. Springer, Cham (2019). https://doi.org/10.1007/978-3-030-32245-8_60
4. Baur, C., Albarqouni, S., Navab, N.: Generating highly realistic images of skin lesions with GANs. In: Stoyanov, D., et al. (eds.) CARE/CLIP/OR 2.0/ISIC - 2018. LNCS, vol. 11041, pp. 260–267. Springer, Cham (2018). https://doi.org/10.1007/978-3-030-01201-4_28
5. Benaim, S., Wolf, L.: One-sided unsupervised domain mapping. Adv. Neural Inf. Proc. Syst. **30** (2017)
6. Bermúdez, C., Plassard, A.J., Davis, L.T., Newton, A.T., Resnick, S.M., Landman, B.A.: Learning implicit brain MRI manifolds with deep learning. In: Medical Imaging (2018)
7. Calimeri, F., Marzullo, A., Stamile, C., Terracina, G.: Biomedical data augmentation using generative adversarial neural networks. In: Lintas, A., Rovetta, S., Verschure, P.F.M.J., Villa, A.E.P. (eds.) ICANN 2017. LNCS, vol. 10614, pp. 626–634. Springer, Cham (2017). https://doi.org/10.1007/978-3-319-68612-7_71
8. Cardoso, M.J., et al.: MONAI: an open-source framework for deep learning in healthcare. ArXiv:2211.02701 (2022)

9. Chaitanya, K., Erdil, E., Karani, N., Konukoglu, E.: Contrastive learning of global and local features for medical image segmentation with limited annotations. ArXiv:2006.10511 (2020)

10. Choi, J.W.: Using out-of-the-box frameworks for contrastive unpaired image translation for vestibular schwannoma and cochlea segmentation: an approach for the CrossMoDA challenge. In: Crimi, A., Bakas, S. (eds.) Brainlesion: Glioma, Multiple Sclerosis, Stroke and Traumatic Brain Injuries: 7th International Workshop, BrainLes 2021, Held in Conjunction with MICCAI 2021, Virtual Event, September 27, 2021, Revised Selected Papers, Part II, pp. 509–517. Springer, Cham (2022). https://doi.org/10.1007/978-3-031-09002-8_44

11. Connell, M., et al.: Unsupervised segmentation and quantification of COVID-19 lesions on computed tomography scans using cyclegan. Methods **205**, 200–209 (2022). https://doi.org/10.1016/j.ymeth.2022.07.007

12. Doersch, C., Gupta, A.K., Efros, A.A.: Unsupervised visual representation learning by context prediction. In: 2015 IEEE International Conference on Computer Vision (ICCV), pp. 1422–1430 (2015)

13. Fu, H., Gong, M., Wang, C., Batmanghelich, K., Zhang, K., Tao, D.: Geometry-consistent generative adversarial networks for one-sided unsupervised domain mapping. In: 2019 IEEE/CVF Conference on Computer Vision and Pattern Recognition (CVPR), pp. 2422–2431 (2018)

14. Guan, H., Liu, M.: Domain adaptation for medical image analysis: a survey. IEEE Trans. Biomed. Eng. **69**, 1173–1185 (2021)

15. Heusel, M., Ramsauer, H., Unterthiner, T., Nessler, B., Hochreiter, S.: GANs trained by a two time-scale update rule converge to a local nash equilibrium. Adv. Neural Inf. Proc. Syst. **30** (2017)

16. Hofmanninger, J., Prayer, F., Pan, J., Röhrich, S., Prosch, H., Langs, G.: Automatic lung segmentation in routine imaging is primarily a data diversity problem, not a methodology problem. Eur. Radiol. Exp. **4**(1), 1–13 (2020). https://doi.org/10.1186/s41747-020-00173-2

17. Isensee, F., Jaeger, P.F., Kohl, S.A.A., Petersen, J., Maier-Hein, K.H.: nnU-Net: a self-configuring method for deep learning-based biomedical image segmentation. Nat. Methods **18**(2), 203–211 (2021). https://doi.org/10.1038/s41592-020-01008-z

18. Isola, P., Zhu, J.Y., Zhou, T., Efros, A.A.: Image-to-image translation with conditional adversarial networks. In: 2017 IEEE Conference on Computer Vision and Pattern Recognition (CVPR), pp. 5967–5976 (2016)

19. Kazeminia, S., et al.: GANs for medical image analysis. Artif. Intell. Med. **109**, 101938 (2018)

20. Kong, L., Lian, C., Huang, D., Li, Z., Hu, Y., Zhou, Q.: Breaking the dilemma of medical image-to-image translation. Adv. Neural Inf. Proc. Syst. **34**, 1964–1978 (2021)

21. Li, Z., et al.: Contrastive and selective hidden embeddings for medical image segmentation. IEEE Trans. Med. Imaging **41**(11), 3398–3410 (2022)

22. Morozov, S., et al.: MosMedData: chest CT scans with COVID-19 related findings dataset. medRxiv (2020). https://doi.org/10.1101/2020.05.20.20100362

23. Noroozi, M., Favaro, P.: Unsupervised learning of visual representations by solving jigsaw puzzles. In: Leibe, B., Matas, J., Sebe, N., Welling, M. (eds.) ECCV 2016. LNCS, vol. 9910, pp. 69–84. Springer, Cham (2016). https://doi.org/10.1007/978-3-319-46466-4_5

24. Park, T., Efros, A.A., Zhang, R., Zhu, J.-Y.: Contrastive learning for unpaired image-to-image translation. In: Vedaldi, A., Bischof, H., Brox, T., Frahm, J.-M. (eds.) ECCV 2020. LNCS, vol. 12354, pp. 319–345. Springer, Cham (2020). https://doi.org/10.1007/978-3-030-58545-7_19

25. Peng An, Sheng Xu, E.B.T.: CT images in COVID-19 [data set]. Cancer Imaging Arch. **10** (2020), https://doi.org/10.7937/TCIA.2020.GQRY-NC81

26. Shin, H.-C., et al.: Medical image synthesis for data augmentation and anonymization using generative adversarial networks. In: Gooya, A., Goksel, O., Oguz, I., Burgos, N. (eds.) SASHIMI 2018. LNCS, vol. 11037, pp. 1–11. Springer, Cham (2018). https://doi.org/10.1007/978-3-030-00536-8_1

27. Skandarani, Y., Jodoin, P.M., Lalande, A.: GANs for medical image synthesis: an empirical study. ArXiv:2105.05318 (2021)

28. Wang, G., et al.: A noise-robust framework for automatic segmentation of COVID-19 pneumonia lesions from CT images. IEEE Trans. Med. Imaging **39**(8), 2653–2663 (2020)

29. Yan, K., et al.: SAM: Self-supervised learning of pixel-wise anatomical embeddings in radiological images. IEEE Trans. Med. Imaging **41**(10), 2658–2669 (2020)

30. Yang, X., He, X., Liang, Y., Yang, Y., Zhang, S., Xie, P.: Transfer learning or self-supervised learning? a tale of two pretraining paradigms. ArXiv:2007.04234 (2020)

31. Zhou, Z., et al.: Models Genesis: generic autodidactic models for 3d medical image analysis. In: Shen, D., et al. (eds.) MICCAI 2019. LNCS, vol. 11767, pp. 384–393. Springer, Cham (2019). https://doi.org/10.1007/978-3-030-32251-9_42

32. Zhu, J.Y., Park, T., Isola, P., Efros, A.A.: Unpaired image-to-image translation using cycle-consistent adversarial networks. In: 2017 IEEE International Conference on Computer Vision (ICCV), pp. 2242–2251 (2017)

Feasibility of Universal Anomaly Detection Without Knowing the Abnormality in Medical Images

Can Cui[1], Yaohong Wang[2], Shunxing Bao[1], Yucheng Tang[3], Ruining Deng[1],
Lucas W. Remedios[1], Zuhayr Asad[1], Joseph T. Roland[2], Ken S. Lau[2], Qi Liu[2],
Lori A. Coburn[2], Keith T. Wilson[2], Bennett A. Landman[1],
and Yuankai Huo[1(✉)]

[1] Vanderbilt University, Nashville, TN 37235, USA
yuankai.huo@vanderbilt.edu
[2] Vanderbilt University Medical Center, Nashville, TN 37215, USA
[3] NVIDIA Corporation, Santa Clara, Bethesda, USA

Abstract. Many anomaly detection approaches, especially deep learning methods, have been recently developed to identify abnormal image morphology by only employing normal images during training. Unfortunately, many prior anomaly detection methods were optimized for a specific "known" abnormality (e.g., brain tumor, bone fraction, cell types). Moreover, even though only the normal images were used in the training process, the abnormal images were often employed during the validation process (e.g., epoch selection, hyper-parameter tuning), which might leak the supposed "unknown" abnormality unintentionally. In this study, we investigated these two essential aspects regarding universal anomaly detection in medical images by (1) comparing various anomaly detection methods across four medical datasets, (2) investigating the inevitable but often neglected issues on how to unbiasedly select the optimal anomaly detection model during the validation phase using only normal images, and (3) proposing a simple decision-level ensemble method to leverage the advantage of different kinds of anomaly detection without knowing the abnormality. The results of our experiments indicate that none of the evaluated methods consistently achieved the best performance across all datasets. Our proposed method enhanced the robustness of performance in general (average AUC 0.956).

Keywords: Anomaly detection · medical images · ensemble learning

1 Introduction

In the context of human perception, it is observed that individuals possess the ability to summarize and store normal patterns, thereby enabling them to recognize the abnormal patterns upon first encounter by comparing them to the normal patterns stored in memory. Especially when existing certain abnormal

© The Author(s), under exclusive license to Springer Nature Switzerland AG 2023
Z. Xue et al. (Eds.): MILLanD 2023, LNCS 14307, pp. 82–92, 2023.
https://doi.org/10.1007/978-3-031-44917-8_8

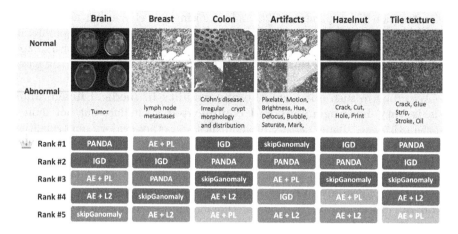

Fig. 1. The upper panels show the 4 medical image datasets and 2 natural image datasets that are used for anomaly detection in this study. The lower panels show the ranking of their performance across different image cohorts (corresponding to the results in Table 2). None of these methods consistently achieved the best performance across all datasets.

cases are infrequent or unknown, the ability to discriminate between normal and abnormal patterns must be acquired through learning from normal data. This has driven the research in the area of anomaly detection in machine learning, which has been further enhanced by the advances in deep learning techniques, improving the generalization ability of more complex patterns and leading to more effective detection of abnormality. Different from the regular classification problems, anomaly detection is a kind of one-class classification, where normal and abnormal patterns are binary classifications, but trained solely on normal data and are tested on their ability to detect abnormal patterns [16, 18].

In the medical domain, vast amounts of data are routinely processed, with the identification of abnormal cases being of great value. For instance, images with poor quality or artifacts should be discarded or require repetition, and patterns in images that deviate from normal patterns may indicate a rare disease. Due to the scarcity of labeled data and the infrequency of abnormal cases, conventional classification methods may not be appropriate. Therefore, there is a need for the development of anomaly detection techniques for medical image data.

Numerous anomaly detection methods have already been proposed, with distribution-based and pretext-task-based strategies being two of the primary approaches [18]. Distribution-based methods estimate the distribution of normal data or compact the feature space of normal data, allowing abnormal data that lies outside the distribution or boundary of normal data to be recognized as abnormal. Examples of distribution-based methods include One-Class Support Vector Machines (OCSVM) [9], Deep Support Vector Data Description (DeepSVDD) [14], and Variational Autoencoder (VAE) [3]. On the other hand, pretext-task-based methods involve training models for specific tasks, such as reconstruction [7], inpainting [12], and denoising [8], etc., using normal data only. It is expected that the model can achieve good performance in completing these tasks using normal data but perform poorly when presented with abnormal data. Previous works have explored the effectiveness of pretext-task-based methods for anomaly detection.

According to such prior arts, **the abnormality in medical image analysis is very heterogeneous and complicated**, including, but not limited to, the existence, shape, density of anomalies and other sensory abnormalities. The abnormalities in sensory attributes can also lead to content abnormalities, such as local abnormalities (use pixel-wise reconstruction loss) or more global abnormalities (use perceptual loss at the content level). Unfortunately, **most of the prior anomaly detection methods were optimized for a specific "known" abnormality** (e.g., brain tumor, bone fraction, cell types) [5,17]. Moreover, even though only the normal images were used in the training set, the abnormal images were often employed during the validation process (e.g., epoch selection, hyper-parameter tuning) [17], which might leak the supposed "unknown" abnormality unintentionally. Whether an anomaly detection strategy can perform consistently well for various kinds of anomalies is a problem (Fig. 1).

In this study, we compare the performance of multiple representative anomaly detection methods and introduce a decision-level ensemble to take advantage of different methods to capture multiple kinds of anomalies. Meanwhile, an overlooked but crucial problem in training an anomaly detection model is the hyper-parameter selection of the training epoch [13]. The selection of a suitable training epoch can influence the results significantly but many works only empirically set a fixed number of epochs [1,6,15]. Different from the regular classification problems, there may be no anomaly data available in the training phase, so the classification accuracy of the validation set may not be applicable here. Also, the validation set may introduce the bias to known abnormality. In this work, we investigated different epoch selection strategies including a fixed number of epochs, loss of normal data in the validation set, and a dynamic epoch selection method proposed by Reiss et al. [13]. And their performance was compared with the model selected by a validation set with both normal and abnormal data available.

The contribution of this paper is threefold:

- Firstly, we compare multiple representative anomaly detection methods on various medical datasets.
- Secondly, we investigate the inevitable but often neglected issues on how to unbiasedly select the optimal anomaly detection model during the validation phase using only normal images.
- Thirdly, we propose a simple decision-level ensemble method to leverage anomaly detection without knowing the abnormality. Extensive experiments were done on 6 datasets and 5 different anomaly detection methods.

2 Methods

2.1 Anomaly Detection Benchmarks

In this work, we selected and compared five representative anomaly detection methods for image data. The structures of these methods are displayed in Fig. 2.

1) Autoencoder (AE) with pixel-wise loss. The autoencoder is a basic reconstruction-based method that aims to train a model to be able to reconstruct normal images but performs worse in reconstructing abnormal images. Images are reconstructed from a bottle-neck feature vector downsampled by convolutional and pooling layers. The pixel-wise loss is used to supervise the reconstruction training and used as the anomaly score.

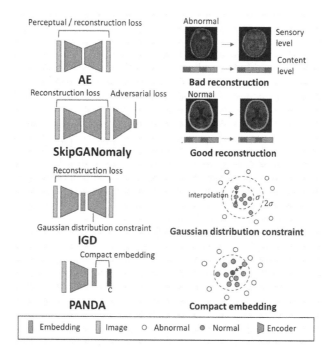

Fig. 2. This figure presents the representative anomaly detection methods.

2) Autoencoder with a perceptual loss. Instead of using the pixel-wised reconstruction loss. The perceptual loss cares about the content similarity of real and reconstructed images. Especially for pathology images, the dense regions with edges are hard to reconstruct, which may confuse the reconstruction errors results from the anomaly input. The similarity in higher-level embedding spaces from a pre-trained network can also benefit anomaly detection [17].

3) SkipGanomaly. [2] SkipGanomaly is an enhanced variant of GANomaly [1], which has been developed to generate normal images through the use of both skip connections and adversarial loss. Compared to the auto-encoder-based method, the generated images were found to be less blurry. Zehnder et al [19] applied it successfully in anomaly detection in pathology images of breast cancer.

4) IGD. [6] The IGD method is based on the density estimation of VAE for anomaly detection. It constrains a smooth Gaussian-shape latent space for normal data with adversarially interpolated training samples. Specifically, it not only constrains the latent space with regular VAE design but also forces the model to predict the interpolation coefficient of normal embeddings.

5) PANDA. [13] The PANDA method draws inspiration from the DeepSVDD method [15]. In PANDA, the encoder used for image embedding is replaced with an ImageNet pre-trained encoder, instead of a learned encoder from reconstruction tasks. The ImageNet pre-trained encoder is preferred over a learned encoder because it already has a strong expression ability. The embedding generated by PANDA is then fine-tuned by a distance loss to a fixed embedding center to compact the embedding space. This approach helps to improve the overall efficiency and effectiveness of the anomaly detection model. Also, an elastic regularization inspired by continual learning was added to combat the collapse of compacted space. The distance of an embedding to the fixed center can be used as the anomaly score.

The above five representative anomaly detection method covers both the pretext-task-based and the distribution-based anomaly detection methods. By covering multiple perspectives, these methods are expected to be effective in detecting various anomalies. As a result, combining them into an ensemble model can increase the overall robustness of the anomaly detection system.

2.2   Model Selection Strategies During the Validation Stage

An important yet overlooked issue in anomaly detection is the selection of a suitable training epoch for the model. Stopping the training process at different epochs can lead to significantly varied outcomes, but previous research did not adequately address how the epochs were chosen. Unlike typical classification tasks that use both normal and abnormal data in a validation set for epoch selection, the ideal setting of an anomaly detection model should only see normal images, even during the validation stage. Not only because the abnormal cases can be rare to get, but also because the model is expected to be a real "unbiased" anomaly detection method that deals with unknown abnormalities. Unfortunately, many prior arts employed abnormal images during the validation phase, which leak the known abnormality to the AI model, while some others set a fixed number of epochs for model training which may not fully exploit the model performance at risk. In this paper, we evaluate (1) the performance gap if we only use normal data in both the training and validation phases and (2) how to select the optimal anomaly detection model by only using the normal images.

The first strategy was to employ two sets of normal and abnormal images during the validation stage. Then, select the best model or tuning hyper-parameters based on the best binary classification performance. This was widely used in the prior arts, yet leaked the abnormality to the AI model. Therefore, the models are selected for the best performance on "known" abnormality. Here, we investigate the alternative strategies that only use the normal images during the validation phase:

Strategy 1) Assessing the loss of normal samples in the validation set, which provides an indication of how well the model has been trained for the pretext task, such as image reconstruction.

Strategy 2) Sample-wise early stopping proposed by Reiss et al. [13]. Firstly, multiple model checkpoints of different epochs are required to save in the training phase. Then, for each sample in the testing phase, its anomaly score at different checkpoints will be normalized by the corresponding average anomaly score of normal samples in the validation sets and denoted as the maximal ratio. The model checkpoint with a maximal ratio indicates the checkpoint has the best separation to this testing sample and the maximal ratio is used as the anomaly score of this sample.

2.3   Model Ensemble

To create an ensemble of different anomaly detection methods, the anomaly scores range of model i on normal data in the validation set $max(N_i) - min(N_i)$ is used to normalize the anomaly score of each testing image α_i as the equation Eq. (1) shown. This is done to eliminate the unnormalized score with a smaller value from being drowned out by the one with much larger values. Once the normalized anomaly scores $\hat{\alpha}_i$ are calculated, the average ensemble strategy is used to combine the scores of k different models (Eq. (2)).

$$\hat{\alpha}_i = \frac{\alpha_i - min(N_i)}{max(N_i) - min(N_i)}, \tag{1}$$

$$\alpha_{ensemble} = \frac{1}{k} \sum_i^k \hat{\alpha}_i, \tag{2}$$

where N_i is the anomaly score set of normal data in the validation set for method i.

Table 1. Datasets and the corresponding data splits used in this work

Dataset	Training	Validation		Testing	
	Normal	Normal	Abnormal	Normal	Abnormal
Brain [11]	1000	400	600	600	600
Colon	213	71	79	80	80
Breast [10]	5462	2150	2169	4000	817
Artifact [10]	5462	2150	2150	4000	4000
Hazelnut [4]	391	9	12	31	58
Tile [4]	201	29	19	33	65

3   Experiments

3.1   Dataset

Four medical datasets and two natural image datasets are used to investigate and evaluate the anomaly detection algorithm in this work. 1) **Camelyon breast dataset** [10]. A public dataset for breast cancer metastase detection in digital pathology. Following the previous work [17], patches in the size of 768×768 were tiled from either the healthy tissue or tumor tissue under 40× magnification and used as normal and abnormal data separately. 2) **Inhouse colon dataset.** A private pathology dataset of healthy colon tissues and Crohn's disease. The patches tile in the size of 1812×1812 were labeled by pathologists to be normal and abnormal (with disease). 3) **Camelyon dataset with artifacts.** Nine kinds of common artifacts/corruptions for pathology images were generated on the normal images on the Camelyon dataset [10] using the toolbox released by Zhang et al. [20]. 4) **Brain tumor dataset.** A public dataset contains 2D MRI slices with tumors or without tumors, in the size of 512×512. [11] 5) **Hazelnut dataset.** A prevalent computer vision anomaly detection benchmark from MVet [4]. 6) **Tile dataset.** A prevalent computer vision anomaly detection benchmark from MVet [4].

Image patches in training, validation and testing sets were split by patients. The number of data is shown in Table 1.

3.2   Experimental Setting

The experiments were divided into three parts.

1) Comparison of different anomaly detection models. In Sect. 2.1, we introduced five anomaly detection methods, which were separately applied to 6 datasets. Each method was trained for 250 epochs, with checkpoints saved every 25 epochs, except for the PANDA method, which was trained for 20 epochs with a checkpoint saved every 2 epochs. For the AE-based methods, the architecture used by Cai et al. [5] was employed in this work. The autoencoder with a bottleneck structure consists of 4 down/up convolutional blocks. When the input images were resized to 64×64 or 256×256, the length of the bottleneck was 16 and 128 separately. The output of the first convolutional layer in the fourth block of the ImageNet pre-trained vgg-16 was used for the perceptual loss to train the reconstruction networks. For the SkipGANanomaly, IGD, and PANDA methods, the official GitHub repositories of these papers were used in this study. The default parameters and experimental configurations outlined in the original papers were adopted unless otherwise specified.

2) Comparison of four training epoch selection strategies. The most common methods are setting a fixed number of training epochs and selecting the epoch in which the complete validation set (with both normal and abnormal data) achieved the highest performance. They were compared with the sample-wise model selection and strategy using the loss of normal validation mentioned in Sect. 2.2.

3) **Comparison of ensemble model and individual models.** The five individual anomaly detection models were ensembled as Sect. 2.3 introduced.

Moreover, all images were processed as a three-channel input, with the channels copied for MRI grayscale images, and then normalized to intensity [0,1]. The batch size for 64×64 resolution and 256×256 resolution were 64 and 8 separately. To evaluate the capability of the model in discerning normal and abnormal data, the Receiver Operating Characteristic Area Under the Curve (ROC-AUC) score was utilized.

4   Results and Discussion

The results of the ensemble anomaly detection are compared with the individual methods and presented in Table 2. It can be seen that none of the individual

Table 2. Comparison of individual and ensembled anomaly detection methods. The AUC scores are computed from the withheld testing data. **Blue** values indicate the best individual model for each cohort. Red value indicates the best overall performance across all cohorts.(The individual models are selected by the sample-wise early stopping.)

Method	Brain	Colon	Breast	Artifact	Hazelnut	Tile	Average AUC
AE + PL (64) [17]	0.945	0.904	0.658	0.636	0.947	0.889	**0.830**
AE + L2 (64)	0.776	0.472	0.302	0.507	0.860	0.719	**0.606**
AE + PL (256) [17]	0.888	0.020	0.962	0.696	0.930	0.670	**0.694**
AE + L2 (256)	0.711	0.224	0.108	0.506	0.876	0.673	**0.516**
SkipGanomaly [2]	0.660	0.634	0.815	0.999	0.942	0.776	**0.804**
IGD [6]	0.934	0.981	0.918	0.557	0.965	0.963	**0.886**
PANDA [13]	0.981	0.931	0.882	0.879	0.959	0.980	**0.935**
Avg. Ensemble (256) (Ours)	0.944	0.744	0.932	0.993	0.995	0.976	**0.931**
Avg. Ensemble (64) (Ours)	0.959	0.931	0.867	0.995	0.998	0.986	0.956

*AE: auto-encoder, *PL: perceptual loss, *L2: L2 loss
*(64): 64×64 resolution, *(256): 256×256 resolution

Table 3. Comparison of different model selection methods. The values **in bold** indicate the best performance among the four methods. The underscore values indicate the second highest performance.

Method		Validation using Only Normal Images		Normal & Abnormal
	Last epoch	Normal Validation	Sample-wise Model	Complete Validation
AE + PL (64)	0.828	0.841	0.830	**0.848**
AE + L2 (64)	0.547	0.562	0.606	**0.644**
AE + PL (256)	0.655	**0.719**	0.694	0.718
AE + L2 (256)	0.446	0.471	0.516	**0.583**
SkipGanomaly	0.648	0.669	0.804	**0.875**
IGD	0.837	0.855	**0.886**	0.886
PANDA	0.942	0.942	0.935	**0.944**

anomaly detection methods outperforms other methods across all datasets. Even though some methods achieved the best performance in some datasets, they may fail in some other datasets. The average ensemble results take advantage of anomaly detection from different aspects and tend to achieve more robust results. Notably, the ensemble method surpasses the best models in Hazelnut and Tile datasets and demonstrates competitive performance in other datasets. Moreover, the average AUC of the ensembled method across all datasets can outperform the best individual anomaly detection method in our experiments. Table 3 is the comparison of different model selection methods for the best training epochs. It is observed that with the help of labeled abnormal data in the validation set, the results always outperformed other methods across most of the datasets. The sample-wise selection method was performed close to the complete validation set, but it requires larger saving memory and multiple times of inferences for better performance. The epoch selected by the validation set with normal data only performed better than the baseline method using the fixed number of epochs, which is an efficient and practical method for model selection in anomaly detection.

5   Conclusion

In this paper, we assess the prevalent anomaly detection approaches on six image cohorts. Based on the experiment results, we draw the following conclusions: (1) None of the evaluated methods consistently attain the best performance across all datasets. (2) Current model selection methods commonly involve abnormal images during the validation stage, inadvertently disclosing the abnormality and consequently yielding better performance compared to a more stringent model selection approach that uses only normal images during validation. (3) Our proposed simple ensemble method improves anomaly detection performance without requiring knowledge of the abnormality.

Acknowledgements. This work is supported by the Leona M. and Harry B. Helmsley Charitable Trust grant G-1903-03793, NSF CAREER 1452485.

References

1. Akcay, S., Atapour-Abarghouei, A., Breckon, T.P.: GANomaly: semi-supervised anomaly detection via adversarial training. In: Jawahar, C.V., Li, H., Mori, G., Schindler, K. (eds.) ACCV 2018. LNCS, vol. 11363, pp. 622–637. Springer, Cham (2019). https://doi.org/10.1007/978-3-030-20893-6_39

2. Akçay, S., Atapour-Abarghouei, A., Breckon, T.P.: Skip-GANomaly: skip connected and adversarially trained encoder-decoder anomaly detection. In: 2019 International Joint Conference on Neural Networks (IJCNN), pp. 1–8. IEEE (2019)

3. An, J., Cho, S.: Variational autoencoder based anomaly detection using reconstruction probability. Special Lect. IE **2**(1), 1–18 (2015)

4. Bergmann, P., Fauser, M., Sattlegger, D., Steger, C.: MVTec AD-a comprehensive real-world dataset for unsupervised anomaly detection. In: Proceedings of the IEEE/CVF Conference on Computer Vision and Pattern Recognition, pp. 9592–9600 (2019)

5. Cai, Y., Chen, H., Yang, X., Zhou, Y., Cheng, K.T.: Dual-distribution discrepancy for anomaly detection in chest X-rays. In: Wang, L., Dou, Q., Fletcher, P.T., Speidel, S., Li, S. (eds.) Medical Image Computing and Computer Assisted Intervention – MICCAI 2022. MICCAI 2022. Lecture Notes in Computer Science, vol. 13433, pp. 584–593. Springer, Cham (2022). https://doi.org/10.1007/978-3-031-16437-8_56

6. Chen, Y., Tian, Y., Pang, G., Carneiro, G.: Deep one-class classification via interpolated gaussian descriptor. In: Proceedings of the AAAI Conference on Artificial Intelligence, vol. 36, pp. 383–392 (2022)

7. Gong, D., et al.: Memorizing normality to detect anomaly: memory-augmented deep autoencoder for unsupervised anomaly detection. In: Proceedings of the IEEE/CVF International Conference on Computer Vision, pp. 1705–1714 (2019)

8. Kascenas, A., Pugeault, N., O'Neil, A.Q.: Denoising autoencoders for unsupervised anomaly detection in brain MRI. In: International Conference on Medical Imaging with Deep Learning, pp. 653–664. PMLR (2022)

9. Li, K.L., Huang, H.K., Tian, S.F., Xu, W.: Improving one-class SVM for anomaly detection. In: Proceedings of the 2003 International Conference on Machine Learning and Cybernetics (IEEE Cat. No. 03EX693), vol. 5, pp. 3077–3081. IEEE (2003)

10. Litjens, G., et al.: 1399 H&E-stained sentinel lymph node sections of breast cancer patients: the CAMELYON dataset. GigaScience **7**(6), giy065 (2018)

11. Nickparvar, M.: Brain tumor MRI dataset (2021). https://doi.org/10.34740/KAGGLE/DSV/2645886 , https://www.kaggle.com/dsv/2645886

12. Pirnay, J., Chai, K.: Inpainting transformer for anomaly detection. In: Sclaroff, S., Distante, C., Leo, M., Farinella, G.M., Tombari, F. (eds.) Image Analysis and Processing – ICIAP 2022. ICIAP 2022. Lecture Notes in Computer Science, vol. 13232, pp. 394–406. Springer, Cham (2022). https://doi.org/10.1007/978-3-031-06430-2_33

13. Reiss, T., Cohen, N., Bergman, L., Hoshen, Y.: Panda: adapting pretrained features for anomaly detection and segmentation. In: Proceedings of the IEEE/CVF Conference on Computer Vision and Pattern Recognition, pp. 2806–2814 (2021)

14. Ruff, L., et al.: Deep one-class classification. In: International Conference on Machine Learning, pp. 4393–4402. PMLR (2018)

15. Ruff, L., et al.: Deep one-class classification. In: Proceedings of the 35th International Conference on Machine Learning, vol. 80, pp. 4393–4402 (2018)

16. Salehi, M., Mirzaei, H., Hendrycks, D., Li, Y., Rohban, M.H., Sabokrou, M.: A unified survey on anomaly, novelty, open-set, and out-of-distribution detection: solutions and future challenges. arXiv preprint arXiv:2110.14051 (2021)

17. Shvetsova, N., Bakker, B., Fedulova, I., Schulz, H., Dylov, D.V.: Anomaly detection in medical imaging with deep perceptual autoencoders. IEEE Access **9**, 118571–118583 (2021)

18. Yang, J., Xu, R., Qi, Z., Shi, Y.: Visual anomaly detection for images: a survey. arXiv preprint arXiv:2109.13157 (2021)

19. Zehnder, P., Feng, J., Fuji, R.N., Sullivan, R., Hu, F.: Multiscale generative model using regularized skip-connections and perceptual loss for anomaly detection in toxicologic histopathology. J. Pathol. Inf. **13**, 100102 (2022)
20. Zhang, Y., Sun, Y., Li, H., Zheng, S., Zhu, C., Yang, L.: Benchmarking the robustness of deep neural networks to common corruptions in digital pathology. In: Wang, L., Dou, Q., Fletcher, P.T., Speidel, S., Li, S. (eds.) Medical Image Computing and Computer Assisted Intervention – MICCAI 2022. MICCAI 2022. Lecture Notes in Computer Science, vol. 13432, pp. 242–252. Springer, Cham (2022). https://doi.org/10.1007/978-3-031-16434-7_24

Unsupervised, Self-supervised, and Contrastive Learning

Decoupled Conditional Contrastive Learning with Variable Metadata for Prostate Lesion Detection

Camille Ruppli[1,3(✉)], Pietro Gori[1], Roberto Ardon[3], and Isabelle Bloch[1,2]

[1] LTCI, Télécom Paris, Institut Polytechnique de Paris, Paris, France
[2] Sorbonne Université, CNRS, LIP6, Paris, France
[3] Incepto Medical, Paris, France
`camille.ruppli@incepto-medical.com`

Abstract. Early diagnosis of prostate cancer is crucial for efficient treatment. Multi-parametric Magnetic Resonance Images (mp-MRI) are widely used for lesion detection. The Prostate Imaging Reporting and Data System (PI-RADS) has standardized interpretation of prostate MRI by defining a score for lesion malignancy. PI-RADS data is readily available from radiology reports but is subject to high inter-reports variability. We propose a new contrastive loss function that leverages weak metadata with multiple annotators per sample and takes advantage of inter-reports variability by defining metadata confidence. By combining metadata of varying confidence with unannotated data into a single conditional contrastive loss function, we report a 3% AUC increase on lesion detection on the public PI-CAI challenge dataset.

Code is available at: https://github.com/camilleruppli/decoupled_ccl.

Keywords: Contrastive Learning · Semi-supervised Learning · Prostate cancer segmentation

1 Introduction

Clinical Context. Prostate cancer is the second most common cancer in men worldwide. Its early detection is crucial for efficient treatment. Multi-parametric MRI has proved successful to increase diagnosis accuracy [21]. Recently, deep learning methods have been developed to automate prostate cancer detection [3,22,33]. Most of these methods rely on datasets of thousands of images, where lesions are usually manually annotated and classified by experts. This classification is based on the Prostate Imaging Reporting and Data System (PI-RADS) score, which ranges between 1 and 5, and associates a malignancy level to each lesion or to the whole exam (by considering the highest lesion score) [27].

Supplementary Information The online version contains supplementary material available at https://doi.org/10.1007/978-3-031-44917-8_9.

© The Author(s), under exclusive license to Springer Nature Switzerland AG 2023
Z. Xue et al. (Eds.): MILLanD 2023, LNCS 14307, pp. 95–105, 2023.
https://doi.org/10.1007/978-3-031-44917-8_9

This score is widely used by clinicians and is readily available from radiology reports. However, it is rather qualitative and subject to low inter-reader reproducibility [25]. Images can also be classified using biopsy results, as in the PI-CAI dataset [23]. This kind of classification is usually considered more precise (hence often taken as ground truth), but is also more costly to obtain and presents a bias since only patients with high PI-RADS scores undergo a biopsy. Building a generic and automatic lesion detection method must therefore deal with the diversity of classification sources, radiology or biopsy, and the variability of classifications for a given exam.

Methodological Context. In the past years, the amount of available medical imaging data has drastically increased. However, images are often either unannotated or weakly-annotated (*e.g.*, a single PI-RADS score for the entire exam), as annotating each lesion is costly and time consuming. This means that usual supervised models cannot be used, since their performance highly depends on the amount of annotated data, as shown in Table 1.

Table 1. AUC at exam level (metrics defined in Sect. 3) on a hold out test set of the PI-CAI dataset of models trained from random initialization with 5-fold cross validation on a private dataset.

	100% ($N_{train} = 1397$)	10% ($N_{train} = 139$)	1% ($N_{train} = 13$)
3D UNet	0.80 (0.03)	0.76 (0.02)	0.71 (0.04)
3D ResUnet	0.79 (0.01)	0.73 (0.02)	0.64 (0.03)

To take advantage of unannotated or weakly-annotated data during a pretraining step, self-supervised contrastive learning methods [7,15,16] have been developed. Recent works have proposed to condition contrastive learning with class labels [18] or weak metadata [8,10,26] to improve latent representations. Lately, some works have also studied the robustness of supervised contrastive learning against noisy labels [30] proposing a new regularization [32].

While contrastive pretraining has been widely applied to classification problems [7,13,15,16], there have been few works about segmentation [2,6]. Recent works [1,6,35] propose to include pseudo labels at the pixel (decoder) level and not after the encoder, but, due to high computational burden, they can only consider 2D images and not whole 3D volumes.

Furthermore, many datasets contain several weak metadata at the exam level (e.g., PI-RADS score) obtained by different annotators. These weak metadata may have high inter- and intra-annotator variability, as for the PI-RADS score [25]. This variability is rarely taken into account into self-supervised pretraining. Researchers usually either use all annotations, thus using the same sample several times, or they only use confident samples, based on the number of annotators and their experience or on the learned representations, as in [19].

Contributions. Here, we aim to train a model that takes as input multi-parametric MRI exam and outputs a map where higher values account for higher lesion probability. *Annotations* are provided by multiple annotators in the form of binary maps: segmentations of observed lesions. Only a small portion of the dataset has annotations. A greater proportion has *metadata* information available from written reports. These metadata, referring to the whole exam, are either a (binary) biopsy grading (presence or absence of malignant lesion) or a PI-RADS score. For each exam, reports with a PI-RADS score are available from several radiologists, but the number of radiologists may differ among exams.

In the spirit of [5,11], we propose to include confidence, measured as a degree of inter-reports variability on metadata, in a contrastive learning framework. Our contributions are the following:

- We propose a new contrastive loss function that leverages weak metadata with multiple annotators per sample and takes advantage of inter-annotators variability by defining metadata confidence.
- We show that our method performs better than training from random initialization and previous pre-training methods on both the PI-CAI [24] public dataset and on a private multi-parametric prostate MRI dataset for prostate cancer lesion detection.

2 Method

We propose to apply contrastive pretraining to prostate lesion detection. A lesion is considered detected if the overlap between the predicted lesion segmentation and the reference segmentation is above 0.1, as defined in [22]. The predicted lesion masks are generated by a U-Net model [20] (since in our experiments this was the best model, see Table 1) fine-tuned after contrastive pretraining. In this section, we describe our contrastive learning framework defining confidence on metadata.

2.1 Contrastive Learning Framework

Contrastive learning (CL) methods train an encoder to bring close together latent representations of images of a positive pair while pushing further apart those of negative pairs. In unsupervised CL [7], where no annotations or metadata are available, a positive pair is usually defined as two transformations of the same image and negative pairs as transformed versions of different images. Transformations are usually randomly chosen among a predefined family of transformations. The final estimated latent space is structured to learn invariances with respect to the applied transformations.

In most CL methods, latent representations of different images are pushed apart *uniformly*. The alignment/uniformity contrastive loss function proposed in [28] is:

$$\mathcal{L}_{NCE} = \underbrace{\frac{1}{N} \sum_{i=1}^{N} d_{ii}}_{\text{Global Alignment}} + \underbrace{\log \Big(\frac{1}{N^2} \sum_{i,j=1}^{N} e^{-d_{ij}}\Big)}_{\text{Global Uniformity}} \quad (1)$$

where $d_{ij} = ||x_1^i - x_2^j||_2$, x_1^i and x_2^j are the encoder outputs of the transformed versions of images i and j, respectively. However, as in many medical applications, our dataset contains discrete clinical features as metadata: PI-RADS scores and biopsy results per exam, that should be used to better define negative and positive samples. To take metadata into account in contrastive pretraining, we follow the work of [9,10]. The authors introduce a kernel function on metadata y to *condition* positive and negative pairs selection, defining the following loss function:

$$\mathcal{L}_w = \underbrace{\frac{1}{N} \sum_{i,j=1}^{N} w(y_i, y_j) d_{ij}}_{\text{Conditional Alignment}} + \underbrace{\log \Big(\frac{1}{N^2} \sum_{i,j=1}^{N} (||w||_\infty - w(y_i, y_j)) e^{-d_{ij}}\Big)}_{\text{Conditional Uniformity}} \quad (2)$$

where w is a kernel function measuring the degree of similarity between metadata y_i and y_j, $0 \leq w \leq 1$ and $||w||_\infty = w(y_i, y_i) = 1$. The conditional alignment term brings close together, in the representation space, only samples that have a metadata similarity greater than 0, while the conditional uniformity term does not repel all samples uniformly but weights the repulsion based on metadata dissimilarity. A schematic view of these two objective functions is shown in Fig. 1 of the supplementary material.

We apply this framework to metadata (PI-RADS scores and biopsy results) that can have high inter-report variability.

To simplify the problem and homogenize PI-RADS and biopsy scores, we decide to binarize both scores, following clinical practice and medical knowledge [12,27]. We set $y = 0$ for PI-RADS 1 and 2, and $y = 1$ for PI-RADS 4 and 5. We do not consider PI-RADS 3, since it has the highest inter-reader variability [14] and low positive predictive value [29]. This means that all exams with a PI-RADS 3 are considered deprived of metadata. For each exam i, a set of y values is available, noted $\mathbf{y}_i$. The number of annotations may differ among subjects (see Eq. (5) for a definition of w in such cases). For a biopsy result (defining an ISUP classification [12]), we set $y = 0$ if ISUP ≤ 1 and $y = 1$ if ISUP ≥ 2.

To take advantage of the entire dataset, we also consider unannotated data for which metadata are not provided. When computing the loss function on an exam without metadata (no $\mathbf{y}$ associated), we use the standard (unsupervised) contrastive loss function, as defined in [7]. This leads to the following contrastive loss function:

$$
\mathcal{L}_w = \left.\begin{array}{l}
\dfrac{1}{|A|}\sum_{i\in A}\left(\sum_{j\in A}w(\mathbf{y}_j,\mathbf{y}_i)\|x_1^i - x_2^j\|\right) \\[2ex]
+ \log\left(\dfrac{1}{|A|^2}\sum_{i,j\in A}(1 - w(\mathbf{y}_i,\mathbf{y}_j))e^{-\|x_1^i - x_2^j\|}\right) \\[2ex]
+ \dfrac{1}{|U|}\sum_{i\in U}\left(\|x_1^i - x_2^i\|\right) + \log\left(\dfrac{1}{|U|^2}\sum_{\substack{i,j\in U \\ i\neq j}}e^{-\|x_1^i - x_2^j\|}\right)
\end{array}\right\}
\begin{array}{l}
\text{with metadata} \\[4ex]
(3) \\[4ex]
\text{without metadata}
\end{array}
$$

where A (resp. U) is the subset with (resp. without) associated $\mathbf{y}$ metadata.

Since the number of annotations may be different between two subjects i and j, we cannot use a standard kernel, as the RBF in [10]. We would like to take into account metadata confidence, namely agreement among annotators. In the following, we propose a new kernel w that takes metadata confidence into account.

Confidence. Our measure of confidence is based on the discrepancy between the elements of vector $\mathbf{y}$ and their most common value (or majority voting). For exam i, if y_i is the most common value in its metadata vector $\mathbf{y}_i = [y_{i0}, y_{i1}, \ldots y_{in-1}]$ with n the number of available scores, confidence c is defined as:

$$
c(\mathbf{y}_i) = \begin{cases}
\epsilon & \text{if } n = 1 \\[3ex]
2 \times \left(\dfrac{\sum_{k=0}^{n-1}\delta(y_{ik}, y_i)}{n} - \dfrac{1}{2}\right) & \text{if } n > 1
\end{cases}
\tag{4}
$$

where δ is the Dirac function and $\epsilon = 0.1$[1]. $c(\mathbf{y}_i) \in [0,1]$, 0 is found when an even number of opposite scores is obtained and the majority voting cannot provide a decision. In that case the associated exam will be considered as deprived of metadata. The proposed kernel then reads :

$$
w(\mathbf{y}_i, \mathbf{y}_j) = \begin{cases}
1 & \text{if } i = j & \text{(exam against its} \\
& & \text{own transformed version)} \\
c_{ij} & \text{if } y_i = y_j \text{ and } i \neq j & \text{(different exams,} \\
& & \text{same majority voting)} \\
0 & \text{if } y_i \neq y_j \text{ and } i \neq j & \text{(different exams,} \\
& & \text{different majority voting)}
\end{cases}
\tag{5}
$$

where $c_{ij} = \min(c(\mathbf{y}_i), c(\mathbf{y}_j))$. For two given exams i and j, the proposed model is interpreted as follows:

---

[1] The maximum number of metadata available for an exam is $n = 7$, the minimal achievable confidence value is thus $c = 2(4/7 - 1/2) > 0.14$. We fix ϵ so that the confidence for $n = 1$ is higher than 0 but less that the minimal confidence when n is odd.

- If both metadata confidences are maximal ($c_{ij} = 1$), $w(\mathbf{y}_i, \mathbf{y}_j)$ will be equal to 1 and full alignment will be computed.
- If either metadata confidence is less than 1, $w(\mathbf{y}_i, \mathbf{y}_j)$ value will be smaller and exams will not be fully aligned in the latent space. The less confidence, the less aligned exams i and j representations will be.
- If confidence drops to zero for either exam, the exam will only be aligned with its own transformed version.

Similarly to decoupled CL [31], we design w such that the second term of Equation (3) does not repel samples with identical metadata most common value and maximal confidence ($c_{ij} = 1$). See Fig. 1 for a schematic view.

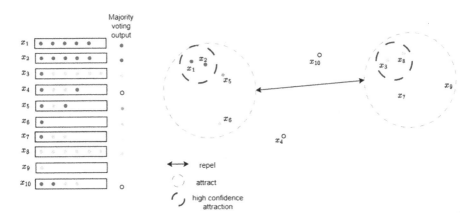

Fig. 1. Given a set of exams $x_{i \in [1,10]}$, $\mathbf{y}_i$ is represented as a list of colored points. Confidence (c) is represented with color saturation: darker means more confident. Exams such that $c(\mathbf{y}_i) = 0$ (no decision from majority voting) are considered as unlabeled and uncolored. Exams such that $c(\mathbf{y}_{i,j}) = 1$ and $y_i = y_j$, e.g. (x_1, x_2) (resp. (x_3, x_8)), will be strongly attracted while less attracted to patients with $c(\mathbf{y}_i) < 1$, e.g. $x_{5,6}$ (resp. $x_{7,9}$). Groups of exams with different y scores are repelled.

2.2   Experimental Settings

Datasets. Experiments were performed on a private dataset of 2415 multi parametric MRI prostate exams among which 1397 have annotations (metadata and manual lesion segmentation) provided by multiple radiologists (up to 7). We also use the public PI-CAI dataset [23] composed of 1500 exams and 1295 annotations. In all learning steps, we used T2 weighted (T2w), apparent diffusion coefficient (ADC) and diffusion weighted (with the highest available b-value in the exam) sequences. As in [22,34], we use the prostate ternary segmentation (background, peripheral zone and central zone), generated from an independent process on T2w sequences. We thus learn from a total of four volumes considered as registered. Pretraining is performed on data from both datasets on 3915 exams. Fine-tuning is performed with 1% and 10% of these exams using cross validation (see **Implementation details**).

Implementation Details. We pretrain the chosen U-Net encoder followed by a projection head. Similarly to nn U-Net [17], the encoder is a fully convolutional network where spatial anisotropy is used (e.g. axial axis is downsampled with a lower frequency since MRI volumes often have lower resolution in this direction). It is composed of four convolution blocks with one convolution layer in each block and takes the four sequences as input in channel dimension. The projection head is a two-layer perceptron as in [7]. We train with a batch size of 16 for 100 epochs and use a learning rate of 10^{-4}. Following the work of [13] on contrastive learning for prostate cancer triage, we use a random sampling of rotation, translation and horizontal flip to generate the transformed versions of the images.

To evaluate the impact of contrastive pretraining at low data regime, we perform fine-tuning with 10% and 1% of annotated exams. The contrastive pretrained encoder is used to initialize the U-Net encoder, the whole encoder-decoder architecture is then fine-tuned on the supervised task. Fine-tuning is performed with **5-fold cross validation** with both datasets using the pretrained encoder. Using 1% (resp. 10%) of annotated data, each fold has 39 (resp. 269) training data and 12 (resp. 83) validation data. We build a hold out test set of 500 volumes[2], not used during any training step with data from both datasets to report our results. We also compared fine-tuning from our pretrained encoder to a model trained from random initialization. Fine-tuning results with 10% of annotated data are reported the in supplementary material.

Computing Infrastructure. Optimizations were run on GPU NVIDIA T4 cards.

3   Results and Discussion

The 3D U-Net network outputs lesions segmentation masks which are thresholded, following the dynamic thresholding proposed in [4], and of which connected components are computed. For each connected component, a detection probability is assigned as the maximum value of the network output in this component. The output of this post-processing is a binary mask associated with a detection probability per lesion. We compute the overlap between each lesion mask and the reference mask. A lesion is considered as a true positive (detection) if the overlap with the reference is above 0.1 as defined in [22]. This threshold is chosen to keep a maximum number of lesions to be analyzed for AUC computation. Different thresholds values are then applied for AUC computation.

As in [22,33], lesion detection probability is used to compute AUC values at exam and lesion levels, and average precision (mAP). To compute AUC at exam level we take, as ground truth, the absence or presence of a lesion mask, and, as a detection probability, the maximum probability of the set of detected lesions. At lesion level, all detection probabilities are considered and thresholded

---

[2]   The 100 validation cases on the PI-CAI challenge website being hidden we could not compare our methods to the leaderboard performances.

with different values, which amounts to limiting the number of predicted lesions. The higher this threshold, the lower are sensitivity and the number of predicted lesions, and the higher is specificity.

Results are presented in Table 2. For both datasets, we see that including metadata confidence to condition alignment and uniformity in contrastive pretraining yields better performances than previous state of the art approaches and random initialization. The discrepancy between PI-CAI and private mAP is due to the nature of the dataset: the PI-CAI challenge was designed to detect lesions confirmed by biopsy, while our private dataset contains lesions not necessarily confirmed by biopsy. Our private dataset contains manually segmented lesions that might be discarded if biopsy was performed. The model being finetuned on both datasets, PI-CAI exams are overly segmented which leads to lower mAP values (since our model tends to over-segment on biopsy ground truths). For our clinical application, which aims to reproduce radiologist responses, this is acceptable. We report significant performance improvement at very low data regime (1% annotated data) compared to existing methods which is a framework often encountered in clinical practice.

To assess the impact of our approach we perform different ablation studies (shown in the second part of Table 2).

High Confidence (HC Row in Table 2). For pretraining, only exams with confidence equal to 1 are considered but are not perfectly aligned ($c_{ij} = 0.8\delta(c_{ij}, 1)$ in Eq. (5)). We can see that considering only confident samples to condition contrastive learning decreased performances.

Majority Voting (Majority Voting Row in Table 2). We removed confidence and used majority voting output for kernel computation. If two different exams have the same majority vote we set : $w(y_i, y_j) = 0.8$ in Eq. (5), other w values are kept unchanged. We can see that using majority voting output without taking confidence into account leads to decreased performances.

Biopsy (Biopsy Row in Table 2). We set the confidence of PI-CAI exams to 1 (increasing biopsy confidence) which amounts to setting $\epsilon = 1$ for PI-CAI exams in Eq. (4). No particular improvement is observed with this approach.

Global Uniformity. We remove the conditioning on uniformity. Exams are uniformly repelled rather than conditioning on metadata similarity for repulsion (which amounts to setting $w(\mathbf{y}_i, \mathbf{y}_j) = 0$ for the second term of Equation (3)). Removing uniformity conditioning yields lower performances than the proposed approach (GlU row in Table 2).

Figure 2 shows the impact of our pretraining method on the finetuned U-Net outputs. Without conditioning, some lesions are missed (cases FN 1, FN 2) and others are falsely detected (cases FP 1, 2 and 3). Adding the conditioned pretraining removed these errors. More examples are provided in the supplementary material.

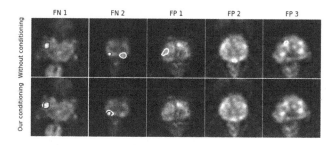

Fig. 2. Examples of false negative (FN) and false positive (FP) cases (first row) corrected by the proposed method (second row). Reference segmentation: green overlay, predicted lesions: red overlay (Color figure online)

Table 2. 5-fold cross validation mean AUC and mAP after fine-tuning on PI-CAI and private datasets with 1% of annotated data (standard deviation in parentheses)

Method	AUC exam		AUC lesion		mAP	
	PI-CAI	Private	PI-CAI	Private	PI-CAI	Private
Random init	0.68 (0.06)	0.74 (0.03)	0.73 (0.11)	0.70 (0.05)	0.27 (0.05)	0.62 (0.03)
Unif Align [28]	0.66 (0.07)	0.72 (0.01)	0.64 (0.13)	0.68 (0.03)	0.28 (0.07)	0.63 (0.03)
simCLR [7]	0.64 (0.07)	0.73 (0.05)	0.65 (0.08)	0.68 (0.05)	0.22 (0.07)	0.60 (0.06)
MoCo [16]	0.63 (0.08)	0.71 (0.04)	0.59 (0.12)	0.64 (0.07)	0.24 (0.10)	0.58 (0.06)
BYOL [15]	0.67 (0.06)	0.72 (0.04)	0.66 (0.16)	0.68 (0.04)	0.26 (0.05)	0.59 (0.04)
nnCLR [11]	0.57 (0.08)	0.73 (0.05)	0.49 (0.09)	0.62 (0.06)	0.21 (0.05)	0.59 (0.05)
Ours	**0.70** (0.05)	**0.75** (0.03)	**0.75** (0.10)	0.71 (0.03)	**0.30** (0.09)	**0.63** (0.04)
GIU	0.60 (0.05)	0.74 (0.03)	0.60 (0.12)	**0.73** (0.02)	0.23 (0.05)	0.63 (0.04)
Biopsy	0.64 (0.06)	0.73 (0.03)	0.69 (0.06)	0.70 (0.03)	0.24 (0.05)	0.62 (0.04)
HC	0.66 (0.08)	0.75 (0.04)	0.60 (0.06)	0.67 (0.03)	0.28 (0.09)	0.62 (0.03)
Majority voting	0.63 (0.06)	0.74 (0.02)	0.62 (0.06)	0.69 (0.04)	0.28 (0.07)	0.61 (0.04)

4   Conclusion

We presented a new method to take the confidence of metadata, namely the agreement among annotators, into account in a contrastive pretraining. We proposed a definition of metadata confidence and a new kernel to condition positive and negative sampling. The proposed method yielded better results for prostate lesion detection than existing contrastive learning approaches on two datasets.

References

1. Alonso, I., Sabater, A., Ferstl, D., Montesano, L., Murillo, A.C.: Semi-supervised semantic segmentation with pixel-level contrastive learning from a class-wise memory bank. In: ICCV, pp. 8199–8208 (2021)

2. Basak, H., Yin, Z.: Pseudo-label guided contrastive learning for semi-supervised medical image segmentation. In: CVPR (2023)
3. Bhattacharya, I., Seetharaman, A., et al.: Selective identification and localization of indolent and aggressive prostate cancers via CorrSigNIA: an MRI-pathology correlation and deep learning framework. Med. Image Anal. **75**, 102288 (2021)
4. Bosma, J.S., Saha, A., et al.: Annotation-efficient cancer detection with report-guided lesion annotation for deep learning-based prostate cancer detection in bpMRI. arxiv:2112.05151 (2021)
5. Bovsnjak, M., Richemond, P.H., et al.: SemPPL: predicting pseudo-labels for better contrastive representations. In: ICLR (2023)
6. Chaitanya, K., Erdil, E., Karani, N., Konukoglu, E.: Local contrastive loss with pseudo-label based self-training for semi-supervised medical image segmentation. Med. Image Anal. **87**, 102792 (2021)
7. Chen, T., Kornblith, S., Norouzi, M., Hinton, G.: A simple framework for contrastive learning of visual representations. In: ICML, vol. 119, pp. 1597–1607 (2020)
8. Dufumier, B., Barbano, C.A., Louiset, R., Duchesnay, E., Gori, P.: Integrating prior knowledge in contrastive learning with kernel. In: International Conference on Machine Learning (ICML) (2023)
9. Dufumier, B., Gori, P., et al.: Conditional alignment and uniformity for contrastive learning with continuous proxy labels. In: MedNeurIPS (2021)
10. Dufumier, B., et al.: Contrastive learning with continuous proxy meta-data for 3D MRI classification. In: de Bruijne, M., et al. (eds.) MICCAI 2021. LNCS, vol. 12902, pp. 58–68. Springer, Cham (2021). https://doi.org/10.1007/978-3-030-87196-3_6
11. Dwibedi, D., Aytar, Y., et al.: With a little help from my friends: nearest-neighbor contrastive learning of visual representations. In: ICCV, pp. 9568–9577 (2021)
12. Epstein, J.I., Egevad, L., Amin, M.B., Delahunt, B., Srigley, J.R., Humphrey, P.A.: The 2014 international society of urological pathology (ISUP) consensus conference on gleason grading of prostatic carcinoma: definition of grading patterns and proposal for a new grading system. Am. J. Surg. Pathol. **40**, 244–252 (2015)
13. Fernandez-Quilez, A., Eftestøl, T., Kjosavik, S.R., Olsen, M.G., Oppedal, K.: Contrasting axial T2W MRI for prostate cancer triage: a self-supervised learning approach. In: ISBI, pp. 1–5 (2022)
14. Greer, M.D., et al.: Interreader variability of prostate imaging reporting and data system version 2 in detecting and assessing prostate cancer lesions at prostate MRI. In: AJR, pp. 1–8 (2019)
15. Grill, J.B., Strub, F., et al.: Bootstrap your own latent: a new approach to self-supervised learning. In: NeurIPS (2020)
16. He, K., Fan, H., Wu, Y., Xie, S., Girshick, R.B.: Momentum contrast for unsupervised visual representation learning. In: CVPR, pp. 9726–9735 (2019)
17. Isensee, F., Jaeger, P.F., Kohl, S.A.A., Petersen, J., Maier-Hein, K.: nnU-Net: a self-configuring method for deep learning-based biomedical image segmentation. Nat. Methods **18**, 203–211 (2020)
18. Khosla, P., Teterwak, P., et al.: Supervised contrastive learning. In: NeurIPS (2020)
19. Li, S., Xia, X., Ge, S., Liu, T.: Selective-supervised contrastive learning with noisy labels. In: CVPR, pp. 316–325 (2022)
20. Ronneberger, O., Fischer, P., Brox, T.: U-net: convolutional networks for biomedical image segmentation. In: Navab, N., Hornegger, J., Wells, W.M., Frangi, A.F. (eds.) MICCAI 2015. LNCS, vol. 9351, pp. 234–241. Springer, Cham (2015). https://doi.org/10.1007/978-3-319-24574-4_28

21. Rouvière, O., et al.: Use of prostate systematic and targeted biopsy on the basis of multiparametric MRI in biopsy-naive patients (MRI-FIRST): a prospective, multicentre, paired diagnostic study. Lancet Oncol. **20**(1), 100–109 (2019)
22. Saha, A., Hosseinzadeh, M., Huisman, H.J.: End-to-end prostate cancer detection in bpMRI via 3D CNNs: effect of attention mechanisms, clinical priori and decoupled false positive reduction. Med. Image Anal. **73**, 102155 (2021)
23. Saha, A., Twilt, J.J., et al.: Artificial intelligence and radiologists at prostate cancer detection in MRI: the PI-CAI challenge (2022)
24. Saha, A., Twilt, J.J., et al.: The PI-CAI challenge: public training and development dataset (2022)
25. Smith, C.P., et al.: Intra- and interreader reproducibility of PI-RADSv2: a multi-reader study. J. Magn. Reson. Imaging **49**, 1694–1703 (2019)
26. Tsai, Y.H.H., Li, T., et al.: Conditional contrastive learning with kernel. In: ICLR (2022)
27. Turkbey, B.I., et al.: Prostate imaging reporting and data system version 2.1: 2019 update of prostate imaging reporting and data system version 2. Eur. Urol. **76**, 340–351 (2019)
28. Wang, T., Isola, P.: Understanding contrastive representation learning through alignment and uniformity on the hypersphere. In: ICML, vol. 119, pp. 9929–9939 (2020)
29. Westphalen, A.C., et al.: Variability of the positive predictive value of PI-RADS for prostate MRI across 26 centers: experience of the society of abdominal radiology prostate cancer disease-focused panel. Radiology, 190646 (2020)
30. Xue, Y., Whitecross, K., Mirzasoleiman, B.: Investigating why contrastive learning benefits robustness against label noise. In: ICML, pp. 24851–24871 (2022)
31. Yeh, C., Hong, C., et al.: Decoupled contrastive learning. In: Avidan, S., Brostow, G., Cisse, M., Farinella, G.M., Hassner, T. (eds.) ECCV 2022. LNCS, vol. 13686, pp. 668–684. Springer, Heidelberg (2022). https://doi.org/10.1007/978-3-031-19809-0_38
32. Yi, L., Liu, S., She, Q., McLeod, A., Wang, B.: On learning contrastive representations for learning with noisy labels. In: CVPR, pp. 16661–16670 (2022)
33. Yu, X., et al.: Deep attentive panoptic model for prostate cancer detection using biparametric MRI scans. In: Martel, A.L., et al. (eds.) MICCAI 2020. LNCS, vol. 12264, pp. 594–604. Springer, Cham (2020). https://doi.org/10.1007/978-3-030-59719-1_58
34. Yu, X., Lou, B., et al.: False positive reduction using multiscale contextual features for prostate cancer detection in multi-parametric MRI scans. In: IEEE 17th International Symposium on Biomedical Imaging (ISBI), pp. 1355–1359 (2020)
35. Zhao, X., et al.: Contrastive learning for label efficient semantic segmentation. In: ICCV, pp. 10603–10613 (2020)

FBA-Net: Foreground and Background Aware Contrastive Learning for Semi-Supervised Atrium Segmentation

Yunsung Chung[1]([✉]), Chanho Lim[2], Chao Huang[2], Nassir Marrouche[2], and Jihun Hamm[1]

[1] Department of Computer Science, Tulane University, New Orleans, USA
{ychung3,jhamm3}@tulane.edu
[2] School of Medicine, Tulane University, New Orleans, USA
{clim,chuang16,nmarrouche}@tulane.edu

Abstract. Medical image segmentation of gadolinium enhancement magnetic resonance imaging (GE MRI) is an important task in clinical applications. However, manual annotation is time-consuming and requires specialized expertise. Semi-supervised segmentation methods that leverage both labeled and unlabeled data have shown promise, with contrastive learning emerging as a particularly effective approach. In this paper, we propose a contrastive learning strategy of foreground and background representations for semi-supervised 3D medical image segmentation (FBA-Net). Specifically, we leverage the contrastive loss to learn representations of both the foreground and background regions in the images. By training the network to distinguish between foreground-background pairs, we aim to learn a representation that can effectively capture the anatomical structures of interest. Experiments on three medical segmentation datasets demonstrate state-of-the-art performance. Notably, our method achieves a Dice score of 91.31% with only 20% labeled data, which is remarkably close to the 91.62% score of the fully supervised method that uses 100% labeled data on the left atrium dataset. Our framework has the potential to advance the field of semi-supervised 3D medical image segmentation and enable more efficient and accurate analysis of medical images with a limited amount of annotated labels. Our code is available at https://github.com/cys1102/FBA-Net.

Keywords: Semi-supervised learning · Contrastive learning · Cardiac Image segmentation

1 Introduction

Medical image segmentation of the left atrium (LA) plays a crucial role in many clinical applications, including diagnosis, treatment planning, and disease monitoring. In recent years, deep learning approaches [6,13,15,23] have shown promising results in medical image segmentation tasks but require a large amount of

© The Author(s), under exclusive license to Springer Nature Switzerland AG 2023
Z. Xue et al. (Eds.): MILLanD 2023, LNCS 14307, pp. 106–116, 2023.
https://doi.org/10.1007/978-3-031-44917-8_10

manually annotated data for training. In addition, manual annotation of medical images is a challenging task that requires expert knowledge and specialized tools, leading to time-consuming and laborious procedures. The need for utilizing unannotated data has motivated researchers to develop semi-supervised learning techniques that can leverage both labeled and unlabeled data to improve accuracy.

As a solution, contrastive learning [3,7,8,11,21] has emerged as a promising approach for downstream tasks with unlabeled data to obtain a better initialization in various computer vision tasks, including medical image processing [1,2,4,9,12,18,27]. This technique leverages unlabeled data to learn meaningful representations that capture the underlying structure of the data. These representations can be used to improve the performance of supervised learning algorithms on labeled data. The contrastive learning strategy has also been employed for semi-supervised learning in medical image segmentation [24,26].

Semi-supervised learning with contrastive learning has gained popularity in recent years for its ability to reduce the burden of annotation. However, we believe that two significant issues have been neglected in existing investigations. Firstly, many of the existing methods focus on relationships between voxels, which require considerable computational resources and depend heavily on augmentation to generate positive pairs. Secondly, most contrastive learning studies disregard the specific characteristics of segmentation tasks when extracting representations. We suggest that tailored representations to meet the requirements of segmentation tasks could enhance performance with minimum additional computational costs.

To address these issues, we propose a semi-supervised learning approach that focuses on discriminating the foreground and background representations (FBA-Net) by contrastive learning. Our approach trains the model to distinguish between the foreground-background regions of target objects by optimizing contrastive loss. This enables the model to identify important foreground features while ignoring the less relevant background features, leading to better performance in segmenting target objects and extracting precise boundaries between them. By utilizing semi-supervised techniques, this approach offers a potential solution for reducing the dependence on labeled data while improving the accuracy of medical image analysis.

In this paper, we make the following contributions: (1) We propose a novel contrasting strategy of foreground and background representations specialized for medical image segmentation and leverage unannotated labels to alleviate the burden of annotation. (2) We introduce a contrastive module that allows the network to distinguish between foreground and background regions of target objects, reducing the reliance on consistency loss. The module is designed to be easily integrated into any network. (3) We evaluate the proposed method on three public datasets and observe that it outperforms existing state-of-the-art methods. Notably, our proposed method, when trained on just 20% of labeled data, shows a minimal dice score difference of only 0.31% compared to fully supervised learning which is trained on 100% of labeled data on the LA dataset.

Related Work. In the field of contrastive learning, Bachman et al. [3] introduced an autoregressive model to generate a context for multi-views of the same data to train a network by predicting the context of one view given the context of another view. Chen et al. [7] used data augmentation to produce different views from the same image to learn representations that are invariant to transformations. He et al. [11] introduced a momentum-based update rule to generate a dynamic dictionary of visual representations.

Semi-supervised learning approaches have been applied to medical image segmentation. Li et al. [14] incorporated a shape prior into the network using the signed distance map to encode the shape information. Luo et al. [16] introduced a dual-task consistency method to enforce consistency between segmentation masks and an auxiliary task. Wu et al. [19] proposed mutual consistency learning approach from multiple different decoders. You et al. [24] introduced a semi-supervised learning framework for volumetric medical image segmentation using momentum contrastive voxel-wise representation learning. Zhao et al. [26] proposed a voxel-level contrastive learning framework with intensity augmentations.

While contrastive learning and semi-supervised learning have shown promising results in medical image segmentation, FBA-Net differs from existing methods in two ways. Firstly, unlike recent works that generate positive pairs via augmentations of identical input and compute the contrastive loss between voxels. Instead, we employ a contrastive module to extract representations of target entities. This not only simplifies the training process by reducing computational resource demands but also lessens the dependence on augmentations techniques. Secondly, while previous contrastive learning methods have used a variation of InfoNCE loss [17], our method adopts loss functions specially designed to differentiate between foreground and background representations in medical image segmentation.

2   Method

2.1   Architecture

FBA-Net is comprised of two major components: a pseudo-label generation module and a contrastive learning module. Given a dataset represented as (X, Y), we have images $x \in X$ and their corresponding labels $y \in Y$. X comprises N labeled and M unlabeled slices ($N \ll M$). From input images $x_i \in X$, the network extracts the foreground regions of target objects, denoted as $M_i \in \mathbb{R}^{H \times W \times C}$. By creating $(1 - M_i) \in \mathbb{R}^{H \times W \times C}$, we can generate corresponding background regions. An encoder $h(\cdot)$ with a projection head is used to map z_i^f and z_i^b to process the foreground and background representations further, respectively. The projection head is responsible for projecting foreground and background maps onto a latent space where contrastive loss can be implemented.

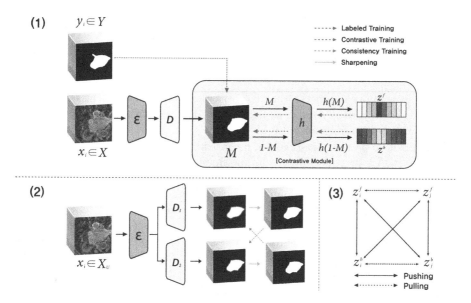

Fig. 1. A overview of FBA-Net includes the following aspects. (A) Our proposed contrastive training strategy: given an image $x \in X$, we can obtain the background from $1 - M$, assuming M is the foreground region. The encoder $h(\cdot)$ creates foreground and background representations, denoted by z^f and z^b, respectively. (B) Mutual consistency training: two different decoders D_1, D_2 generate pseudo labels for each other for unlabeled images, $x_i \in X_U$. These pseudo labels are produced after a sharpening function. (3) Foreground and background representations, z_i^f and z_i^b, respectively, are created as positive and negative contrastive pairs. The positive pairs are pulled closer, while the negative pairs are pushed apart.

2.2   Contrastive Learning

FBA-Net employs contrastive learning, which learns representations of data by contrasting foreground and background representations. This approach can aid in identifying the precise boundaries of targets by maximizing the gap between foreground-background relationships. Additionally, contrastive learning can help alleviate the need for a large number of pixel-wise labels, which is a significant challenge in image segmentation.

Inspired by Xie et al. [21], we introduce two distinct losses for positive and negative pairs. However, instead of channel-wise representations, we extract spatial-wise representations of foreground-background. As noted by [7,8], the network learns faster using contrastive loss with large batch size, which needs high computational costs. To achieve maximum effectiveness with smaller batches, we use ranking weights. We first compute the similarities between representations using the following equation:

$$s_{ij} = sim(z_i, z_j) \tag{1}$$

where sim indicates the cosine similarity function. Given the set of similarities $S_{ij} = \{s_{11}, s_{12}, ..., s_{ij}\}$, the ranking weights are calculated as

$$w_{ij} = \exp(-\alpha \cdot rank(sim(z_i, z_j))) \tag{2}$$

where α is a hyperparameter that controls the smoothness of the exponential function. We empirically set α as 0.25. $rank$ denotes the rank function within $S_{i,j}$ and the weight ranges from 0 to 1.

The positive pairs are responsible for maximizing the similarity between representations. A foreground object in one image should be located closer to the foreground representation of another image in the semantic space. This principle similarly applies to background-background associations as shown in Fig. 1. Given n input images, the contrastive module computes n foreground and background representations, denoted as z_n^f and z_n^b, respectively. Positive pairs are formed between the same foreground or background representations, excluding oneself. We define positive losses for foreground-foreground and background-background pairs as follows

$$\mathcal{L}_{pos}^f = -\frac{1}{n(n-1)} \sum_{i=1}^{n} \sum_{j=1}^{n} \mathbb{1}_{[i \neq j]} \log(w_{ij}^f \cdot sim(z_i^f, z_j^f)) \tag{3}$$

$$\mathcal{L}_{pos}^b = -\frac{1}{n(n-1)} \sum_{i=1}^{n} \sum_{j=1}^{n} \mathbb{1}_{[i \neq j]} \log(w_{ij}^b \cdot sim(z_i^b, z_j^b)) \tag{4}$$

where $\mathbb{1}_{[i \neq j]} \in \{0, 1\}$ represents an indicator function that outputs 1 if $i \neq j$. The positive loss combines each loss of two positive foreground and background pairs.

$$\mathcal{L}_{pos} = \mathcal{L}_{pos}^f + \mathcal{L}_{pos}^b \tag{5}$$

The foreground and background representations have different meanings and play distinct roles in segmentation. To enlarge the difference, we use negative pair loss as part of our training process. The negative pair loss encourages the model to distinguish between foreground and background objects, allowing for more precise and accurate segmentation. The negative pair loss is defined as

$$\mathcal{L}_{neg} = -\frac{1}{n^2} \sum_{i=1}^{n} \sum_{j=1}^{n} \log(w_{ij}^{f,b} \cdot (1 - sim(z_i^f, z_j^b))) \tag{6}$$

The contrastive loss and the overall training loss are provided below:

$$\mathcal{L}_{contra} = \mathcal{L}_{pos} + \mathcal{L}_{neg}, \tag{7}$$

$$\mathcal{L} = \mathcal{L}_{dice} + \mathcal{L}_{contra} + \mathcal{L}_{consist}, \tag{8}$$

where $\mathcal{L}_{dice}$ and $\mathcal{L}_{consist}$ represent Dice loss for labeled training and MSE loss for mutual training.

Table 1. Comparisons of semi-supervised segmentation models on LA, Pancreas-CT, and ACDC datasets. * indicates our re-implementation methods.

Method	Labeled data	LA		Pancreas-CT		ACDC	
		Dice ↑	ASD↓	Dice ↑	ASD↓	Dice ↑	ASD↓
Supervised	100%	91.62	1.64	82.60	1.33	91.65	0.56
SSASSNet [14]	10%	85.81	4.04	68.97	**1.96**	84.14	1.40
DTC [16]		87.91	2.92	66.58	4.16	82.71	2.99
CVRL* [24]		88.06	3.11	69.03	3.95	86.66	3.27
MC-NET [20]		87.92	2.64	69.06	2.28	86.34	2.08
MC-NET+ [19]		88.39	1.99	70.00	3.87	87.10	2.00
RCPS* [26]		**89.24**	2.12	71.24	3.71	88.09	1.96
FBA-Net		88.69	**1.92**	**71.35**	3.00	**88.45**	**0.71**
SSASSNet	20%	89.23	3.15	76.39	1.42	87.04	2.15
DTC		89.39	2.16	76.27	2.20	86.28	2.11
CVRL*		90.15	2.01	77.33	2.18	88.12	2.41
MC-NET		90.11	2.02	78.17	**1.55**	87.83	1.52
MC-NET+		91.09	1.71	79.37	1.72	88.51	1.54
RCPS*		91.15	1.95	80.52	2.19	88.92	1.68
FBA-Net		**91.31**	**1.52**	**80.97**	1.59	**89.81**	**1.11**

3 Experiments and Results

3.1 Dataset

(1) **LA Dataset**[1] is the benchmark dataset from the 2018 MICCAI Atria Segmentation Challenge [22]. This dataset consists of 100 3D GE CMR images, including segmentation labels for the left atrium. The scans were acquired at an isotropic resolution of $0.625 \times 0.625 \times 0.625 \, mm^3$. The dataset was split into two sets: 80 scans for training and 20 scans for evaluation. (2) **Pancreas-CT**[2] [10] contains 82 patients of 3D abdominal contrast-enhanced CT scans. We partitioned this dataset into two sets: 62 samples for training and 20 samples for evaluation. (3) **ACDC dataset**[3] [5] is a collection of cardiac MRIs, containing 100 short-axis cine-MRIs and three classes: left and right ventricle, and myocardium. We applied a fixed data split, where 70, 10, and 20 patients' data for training, validation, and testing sets, respectively. All data splits followed the approach mentioned in [19].

---

[1] https://www.cardiacatlas.org/atriaseg2018-challenge/
[2] https://wiki.cancerimagingarchive.net/display/Public/Pancreas-CT
[3] https://www.creatis.insa-lyon.fr/Challenge/acdc/databases.html

3.2   Implementation

All methods are implemented in PyTorch 1.12 with an NVIDIA 3090Ti GPU. To maintain consistency with the experiment setting outlined in [24], we employed V-Net/U-Net as the backbone network and trained the models for 15,000 iterations. During the training process, we utilized SGD optimizer with a momentum value of 0.9 and weight decay of 0.005. The initial learning rate was set to 0.01. We set the batch size to 4, which contained 2 labeled scans and 2 unlabeled scans. Following previous works [25], we used the Dice similarity coefficient (DSC) and Average Surface Distance (ASD) to evaluate the segmentation performance.

Table 2. The effectiveness of contrastive module as a plug-and-play. CM denotes the contrastive module.

Methods	Dice ↑	ASD ↓
SSASSNet	89.23	3.15
+CM	90.11(+0.88)	2.52(−0.63)
DTC	89.39	2.16
+CM	90.40(+1.01)	2.12(−0.04)
MC-NET	90.11	2.02
+CM	90.47(+0.36)	2.06(+0.04)

Table 3. Comparison between InfoNCE Loss and FBA Loss.

Methods	Dice ↑	ASD ↓
InfoNCE Loss	91.07	1.67
FBA Loss	**91.31**	**1.52**

3.3   Results

Quantitative Result. This section presents the quantitative results of our proposed approach for medical image segmentation on three datasets: LA, Pancreas-CT, and ACDC. As shown in Table 1, our approach is capable of extracting distinguishing features using a minimal number of labels. This results in performance metrics that closely approximate those attained by the fully-supervised method, i.e., 91.31 vs 91.62 on the LA dataset. FBA-Net surpasses other contrastive learning methods, specifically CVRL and RCPS, across most metrics over all datasets. The results on the ACDC dataset outperform all state-of-the-art methods such as SSASSNet, DTC, CVRL, MC-NET, MC-NET+, and RCPS. This indicates the versatile applicability of our approach, which can be effectively employed in binary-class segmentation and extends to multi-class segmentation as well. Significantly, the ASD score yielded by our method is considerably lower than the previously lowest scores (0.71 vs 1.40 and 1.11 vs 1.52), demonstrating the method's efficacy. These findings highlight the usefulness of our approach in improving the segmentation accuracy of medical images through the integration of tailored contrastive learning.

Qualitative Result. The visualizations in Fig. 2 illustrate the segmentation results for FBA-Net and other methods. In particular, FBA-Net has produced highly accurate segmentation results, closely mirroring the ground truths and surpassing other approaches. The results indicate that FBA-Net can efficiently segment even the most challenging parts of the images, as pointed out by the yellow arrow. Notably, other methods either over-segmented or completely missed the regions indicated by the arrow in the first sample, while FBA-Net successfully segmented these areas. These results highlight the precision of the FBA-Net in medical image segmentation, especially in challenging scenarios.

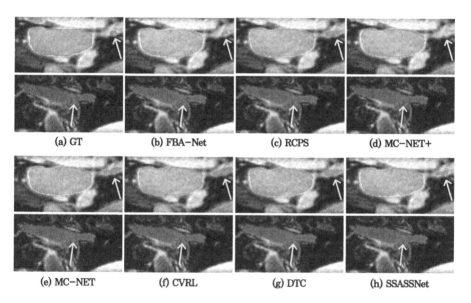

Fig. 2. Visual comparison between FBA-Net and the state-of-the-art methods trained with 20% labeled data. The areas highlighted in red and green represent the ground truth and predicted regions, respectively. (Color figure online)

Ablation Study. In order to assess the utility of our proposed contrastive module as a plug-and-play component, we apply it to other semi-supervised methods including SSASSNet, DTC, and MC-Net. Table 2 reveals that the addition of our contrastive module leads to an improvement in segmentation performance. In particular, the Dice scores for the three models show respective increases of 0.88%, 1.01%, and 0.36%. We further demonstrate the effectiveness of our tailored FBA loss in distinguishing representations for segmentation by comparing it to the InfoNCE loss on the LA dataset, as shown in Table 3. The FBA loss shows superior performance across all metrics when compared to InfoNCE loss, a common choice in other contrastive learning methods such as CVRL and RCPS. Unlike the InfoNCE loss, the FBA loss performs effectively even in low batch-size settings, making it ideal for real-world applications where computational resources are limited. This highlights not only the significance of differentiating feature representation but also the enhanced effectiveness of our loss function in medical image segmentation tasks.

4 Conclusion

In this paper, we proposed a contrastive learning approach that focuses on learning the foreground and background features separately for accurate segmentation. By utilizing the contrastive module, our method has the potential to greatly reduce the costs and time associated with manual annotation, which could have a significant impact by enabling the rapid development of diagnostic tools and treatments. Additionally, our approach demonstrated state-of-the-art performance. The proposed approach can be extended to other medical image segmentation tasks where foreground-background separation is crucial for accurate segmentation.

References

1. Azizi, S., et al.: Robust and efficient medical imaging with self-supervision. arXiv preprint arXiv:2205.09723 (2022)
2. Azizi, S., et al.: Big self-supervised models advance medical image classification. In: Proceedings of the IEEE/CVF International Conference on Computer Vision, pp. 3478–3488 (2021)
3. Bachman, P., Hjelm, R.D., Buchwalter, W.: Learning representations by maximizing mutual information across views. Adv. Neural Inf. Process. Syst. **32**, 1–11 (2019)
4. Bai, W., et al.: Self-supervised learning for cardiac MR image segmentation by anatomical position prediction. In: Shen, D., et al. (eds.) MICCAI 2019. LNCS, vol. 11765, pp. 541–549. Springer, Cham (2019). https://doi.org/10.1007/978-3-030-32245-8_60
5. Bernard, O., et al.: Deep learning techniques for automatic mri cardiac multi-structures segmentation and diagnosis: is the problem solved? IEEE Trans. Med. Imaging **37**(11), 2514–2525 (2018)
6. Chen, J.: Jas-gan: generative adversarial network based joint atrium and scar segmentations on unbalanced atrial targets. IEEE J. Biomed. Health Inf. **26**(1), 103–114 (2021)
7. Chen, T., Kornblith, S., Norouzi, M., Hinton, G.: A simple framework for contrastive learning of visual representations. In: International Conference on Machine Learning, pp. 1597–1607. PMLR (2020)
8. Chen, X., Fan, H., Girshick, R., He, K.: Improved baselines with momentum contrastive learning. arXiv preprint arXiv:2003.04297 (2020)
9. Cho, K., et al.: Chess: chest x-ray pre-trained model via self-supervised contrastive learning. J. Dig. Imaging, 1–9 (2023)
10. Clark, K., et al.: The cancer imaging archive (tcia): maintaining and operating a public information repository. J. Dig. Imaging **26**, 1045–1057 (2013)

11. He, K., Fan, H., Wu, Y., Xie, S., Girshick, R.: Momentum contrast for unsupervised visual representation learning. In: Proceedings of the IEEE/CVF Conference on Computer Vision and Pattern Recognition, pp. 9729–9738 (2020)

12. Kiyasseh, D., Swiston, A., Chen, R., Chen, A.: Segmentation of left atrial MR images via self-supervised semi-supervised meta-learning. In: de Bruijne, M., et al. (eds.) MICCAI 2021. LNCS, vol. 12902, pp. 13–24. Springer, Cham (2021). https://doi.org/10.1007/978-3-030-87196-3_2

13. Li, L., Zimmer, V.A., Schnabel, J.A., Zhuang, X.: Atrialjsqnet: a new framework for joint segmentation and quantification of left atrium and scars incorporating spatial and shape information. Med. Image Anal. **76**, 102303 (2022)

14. Li, S., Zhang, C., He, X.: Shape-aware semi-supervised 3D semantic segmentation for medical images. In: Martel, A.L., et al. (eds.) MICCAI 2020. LNCS, vol. 12261, pp. 552–561. Springer, Cham (2020). https://doi.org/10.1007/978-3-030-59710-8_54

15. Liu, T., Hou, S., Zhu, J., Zhao, Z., Jiang, H.: Ugformer for robust left atrium and scar segmentation across scanners. arXiv preprint arXiv:2210.05151 (2022)

16. Luo, X., Chen, J., Song, T., Wang, G.: Semi-supervised medical image segmentation through dual-task consistency. In: Proceedings of the AAAI Conference on Artificial Intelligence, vol. 35, pp. 8801–8809 (2021)

17. Oord, A.V.D., Li, Y., Vinyals, O.: Representation learning with contrastive predictive coding. arXiv preprint arXiv:1807.03748 (2018)

18. Tang, Y., et al.: Self-supervised pre-training of swin transformers for 3d medical image analysis. In: Proceedings of the IEEE/CVF Conference on Computer Vision and Pattern Recognition, pp. 20730–20740 (2022)

19. Wu, Y., et al.: Mutual consistency learning for semi-supervised medical image segmentation. Med. Image Anal. **81**, 102530 (2022)

20. Wu, Y., Xu, M., Ge, Z., Cai, J., Zhang, L.: Semi-supervised left atrium segmentation with mutual consistency training. In: de Bruijne, M., et al. (eds.) MICCAI 2021. LNCS, vol. 12902, pp. 297–306. Springer, Cham (2021). https://doi.org/10.1007/978-3-030-87196-3_28

21. Xie, J., Xiang, J., Chen, J., Hou, X., Zhao, X., Shen, L.: Contrastive learning of class-agnostic activation map for weakly supervised object localization and semantic segmentation. arXiv preprint arXiv:2203.13505 (2022)

22. Xiong, Z., et al.: A global benchmark of algorithms for segmenting the left atrium from late gadolinium-enhanced cardiac magnetic resonance imaging. Med. Image Anal. **67**, 101832 (2021)

23. Yang, G., et al.: Simultaneous left atrium anatomy and scar segmentations via deep learning in multiview information with attention. Future Gener. Comput. Syst. **107**, 215–228 (2020)

24. You, C., Zhao, R., Staib, L.H., Duncan, J.S.: Momentum contrastive voxel-wise representation learning for semi-supervised volumetric medical image segmentation. In: Wang, L., Dou, Q., Fletcher, P.T., Speidel, S., Li, S. (eds.) Medical Image Computing and Computer Assisted Intervention-MICCAI 2022: 25th International Conference, Singapore, 18–22 September 2022, Proceedings, Part IV, pp. 639–652. Springer, Heidelberg (2022). https://doi.org/10.1007/978-3-031-16440-8_61

25. Yu, L., Wang, S., Li, X., Fu, C.-W., Heng, P.-A.: Uncertainty-aware self-ensembling model for semi-supervised 3D left atrium segmentation. In: Shen, D., et al. (eds.) MICCAI 2019. LNCS, vol. 11765, pp. 605–613. Springer, Cham (2019). https://doi.org/10.1007/978-3-030-32245-8_67

26. Zhao, X., et al.: RCPS: rectified contrastive pseudo supervision for semi-supervised medical image segmentation. arXiv preprint arXiv:2301.05500 (2023)

27. Zhou, H.Y., Lu, C., Yang, S., Han, X., Yu, Y.: Preservational learning improves self-supervised medical image models by reconstructing diverse contexts. In: Proceedings of the IEEE/CVF International Conference on Computer Vision, pp. 3499–3509 (2021)

Masked Image Modeling
for Label-Efficient Segmentation
in Two-Photon Excitation Microscopy

Tony Xu$^{(\boxtimes)}$![ORCID], Matthew Rozak ![ORCID], Edward Ntiri, Adrienne Dorr ![ORCID],
James Mester, Bojana Stefanovic, Anne Martel ![ORCID], and Maged Goubran ![ORCID]

Sunnybrook Research Institute, University of Toronto, Toronto, ON, Canada
`tonylt.xu@mail.utoronto.ca`

Abstract. Generating accurate structural segmentation for 3D two-photon excitation microscopy (TPEM) images affords insights into how cellular-scale networks in living animal models respond to disease. Manual creation of dense segmentation masks is, however, very time-consuming image modeling (MIM) has recently emerged as a highly effective self-supervised learning (SSL) formulation for feature extraction in natural images, reducing reliance on human-created labels. Here, we extend MIM to 3D TPEM datasets and show that a model pre-trained using MIM obtains improved downstream segmentation performance relative to random initialization. We assessed our novel pipeline using multi-channel TPEM data on two common segmentation tasks, neuronal and vascular segmentation. We also introduce intensity-based and channel-separated masking strategies that respectively aim to exploit the intra-channel correlation of intensity and foreground structures, and inter-channel correlations that are specific to microscopy images. We show that these methods are effective for generating representations of TPEM images, and identify novel insights on how MIM can be modified to yield more salient image representations for microscopy. Our method reaches statistically similar performances to a fully-supervised model (using the entire dataset) when only requiring just 25% of the labeled data for both neuronal and vascular segmentation tasks. To the best of our knowledge, this is the first investigation applying MIM methods to microscopy, and we hope our presented SSL pipeline may both reduce the necessary labeling effort and improve downstream analysis of TPEM images for neuroscience investigations. To this end, we plan to make the SSL pipeline, pretrained models and training code available under the following GitHub organization: https://github.com/AICONSlab.

Keywords: Self-supervised learning · Two photon excitation microscopy · 3D image segmentation

1 Introduction

Two-photon excitation microscopy (TPEM) permits high-resolution in-vivo 3D imaging of the brain, allowing for the investigation of cellular changes in neuronal

---

Supplementary Information The online version contains supplementary material available at https://doi.org/10.1007/978-3-031-44917-8_11.

© The Author(s), under exclusive license to Springer Nature Switzerland AG 2023
Z. Xue et al. (Eds.): MILLanD 2023, LNCS 14307, pp. 117–127, 2023.
https://doi.org/10.1007/978-3-031-44917-8_11

or vascular networks. This enables probing of how neural networks in living animal models respond and adapt to disease or injury. Typical analysis pipelines of similar images require the segmentation of structures of interest in multiple fluorescence channels using conventional computer vision algorithms, or more recently convolutional neural networks (CNNs) [14,15,20]. However, these methods rely heavily on detailed and accurate labels, which are exceedingly time-consuming to create in these large 3D volumes. To mitigate this issue, self-supervised learning (SSL) has emerged as a promising subdivision of unsupervised learning, which attempts to learn image representations from large amounts of unlabeled data that can be later transferred to a downstream supervised task [1]. These methods have been shown to generalize well in settings with limited amounts of image labels on computer vision tasks [18]. While SSL techniques have achieved state-of-the-art performance on computer vision tasks, there have been limited studies applying SSL methods to microscopy [13], leaving a critical need to improve model generalizability and efficiency in terms of labeled data via contemporary SSL algorithms; especially with the increasing sizes of microscopy datasets.

Masked image modelling (MIM) has emerged as a powerful SSL pretext task for learning representations of natural images [3,11,21]. MIM techniques involve learning to reconstruct an original signal from a partially masked input. This concept can be intuitively adapted to 3D microscopy images, where a model would learn to reconstruct probable structures by exploiting correlations in different locations in a volume. In order for MIM to formulate a useful pretraining task, the ratio of masked patches to total patches [11] and strategy for mask generation are key parameters to optimize [3,12]. To extend the methodology to microscopy images, here we develop a 3D MIM-based SSL pipeline employing the Vision Transformer (ViT) architecture [9]. We then introduce and investigate two types of simple modality-specific masking strategies. Firstly, since the presence of foreground structures in microscopy are highly correlated to image intensity, we introduce intensity masking and inverse intensity masking. These masking strategies relate masking probability to patch intensities, allowing for preferential masking of foreground or background regions. The second type are channel-together versus channel-separated masking. The former masks both input channels of a microscopy image identically, while channel-separated masking independently masks each input channel. This could encourage a model to learn correlations between channels on top of spatial correlations between masked input patches.

Our main contributions are:

- Developing the first MIM-based SSL pipeline for 3D microscopy images.
- Optimizing masking parameters for multi-channel microscopy data via extensive studies on masking strategies and ratios.
- Validating and testing our methodology on a large multi-channel TPEM dataset for both neuronal and vascular segmentation.

Our models will enhance the generalizability of 3D microscopy segmentation models and reduce their reliance on densely labelled masks. The presented

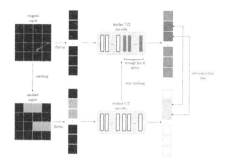

Fig. 1. Overview of the proposed methodology.

SSL pipeline can be extended to other TPEM datasets and segmentation tasks, optimizing the analysis and investigation of TPEM in a wide range of studies (Fig. 1).

2   Related Work

Self-Supervised Learning. SSL is a subset of unsupervised learning that has been exceptionally popular in recent computer vision studies [6,7,11]. It typically breaks the traditional training procedure of a deep learning model into two separate stages: self-supervised pretraining, and finetuning. The pretraining stage applies a pretext task, which can be automatically performed prior to or during experiment runtime, to large amounts of unlabeled data. In the finetuning stage, the model is commonly initialized using weights learned during pretraining and trained again using labeled data for a downstream task. The SSL training regime has been shown to be particularly effective when limited amounts of labels are available for finetuning - a common occurrence with medical imaging datasets, and specifically 3D microscopy data.

There have been several investigations focused on extending SSL to 3D medical images, though they were generally applied to modalities such as computed tomography (CT) and magnetic resonance imaging (MRI) [8,16,17]. To our knowledge, there has been a limited number of studies applying SSL to 3D microscopy images, with Klinghoffer et al. [13] investigating the shuffling pretext task for axon segmentation. This work specifically demonstrated that SSL applied to a single channel microscopy dataset can improve segmentation performance. However, this work only tested their pipeline on a small test set and on a single task, and did not investigate multi-channel interactions in microscopy. Additionally, the presented improvements were not substantial, while significant performance improvements over the shuffle pretext task have been achieved in other 3D imaging domains [16].

Masked Image Modelling. MIM falls under generative pretext tasks, where an input is corrupted by masking out a portion of it, and a model learns to restore the masked regions [11]. This has been done in natural images by directly predicting pixel values [11,21] or by predicting representations of inputs [2]. MIM has been shown to benefit representations for a variety of classic vision tasks and medical images [22]. However, to our knowledge, there has been no investigation on the application of MIM to microscopy datasets. To address this gap, we apply the MIM self-supervised pretext task to TPEM microscopy datasets. We specifically adopt a scheme of predicting masked representations of input data via the data2vec [2] formulation and extend it to microscopy inputs, while investigating modality-specific masking strategies.

3   Methodology

3.1   Target Formulation

Three-dimensional ViT inputs can be extended from the standard ViT used for natural images by splitting a larger input volume into non-overlapping patch volumes. Following standard practice from previous studies, we employed a 3D volume input size of $96 \times 96 \times 96$, and a patch input size of $16 \times 16 \times 16$, resulting in a sequence input of $6 \times 6 \times 6 = 216$ patches to the encoder network.

For this work, we employed the data2vec self-supervised pretraining scheme [2], which functions by passing through the *unmasked* input into an exponential moving average (EMA) teacher model that tracks the weights of a student model. The input to the student model is a *masked* version of the original image, and the pretraining task is to regress the teacher representation of the masked patches. Specifically, the prediction target is the layer-normalized average of the outputs of the top $K = 6$ transformer layers of the teacher model. Following the original paper, we also use Smoothed L1 loss as the loss function for this investigation.

3.2   Masking

Masking was performed by replacing masked patches with a learnable mask token. He et al. found that, for natural images, a high ratio of masked to unmasked patches is important for reducing redundancy and creating a complex pretraining task [11]. In this work, we developed several masking strategies specifically for microscopy datasets, and investigated their interactions with the masking ratio. Specifically, we investigated three strategies for selecting masked patches. The first is the standard random masking, which randomly selects patches to mask in an image from a uniform distribution. As a domain-specific extension to this approach for microscopy imaging, we also investigate intensity masking, and inverse intensity masking strategies. For intensity masking, the selection probability was computed by taking the average intensity of the raw input of each patch and smoothing out probability of selection by linearly mapping the minimum mean (I_{min}) and maximum mean patch intensity (I_{max}), between $[0.5, 1.5]$ in arbitrary units. We performed this linear mapping to increase the likelihood of selecting key patches while still permitting random selection of all patches. We normalized these values to a probability mass function by dividing by the sum over all mean patch intensities comprising an image. For inverse intensity masking, the element-wise reciprocal was calculated prior to normalization.

Typical MIM formulations involve predicting spatially masked regions based on nearby unmasked regions. For microscopy images, different fluorescence channels correspond to separately labelled structures, which may also be mutually correlated and formulate a useful prediction task. To incorporate this into the masking methodology, we introduce channel separated masking, which simply involves independently generating a set of masked regions (using intensity, inverse-intensity, or random masking strategies) for each input channel. To facilitate this, we adjust the vanilla ViT patch embedding layer to compute patch embeddings of different microscopy channels separately before being concatenated and input into the Transformer [19] blocks in a ViT. We hypothesize that this could aid the pretext task in learning correlations between channels and create richer pretraining representations that will benefit downstream task performance.

3.3   Segmentation Finetuning

After SSL pretraining experiments, we transferred the learned weights of the ViT-base into the encoder of a UNet Transformer (UNETR) model [10]. This model was then further trained on structural segmentation tasks, which will be referred to as finetuning. As a comparison, baseline supervised performance was obtained with a randomly initialized ViT encoder, henceforth referred to as fully supervised learning (FSL).

3.4   Implementation Details

We implemented our SSL pretraining and segmentation finetuning in PyTorch, and use MONAI [5] for data loading and preprocessing. Our encoder employs a ViT-base model [9] with number of layers, $L = 12$, a hidden size $D = 768$, and a feed-forward inner dimension of $4 \times D = 3072$. Additional hyperparameters used to train the model are included as supplementary material. We used the Dice overlap coefficient as an evaluation metric to compare experiments as commonly performed, and the best performing epoch on the validation set was selected for test evaluation. Notably, we finetuned the neuron and vessel channels separately to explore the isolated effects of pretraining on each channel.

3.5   Dataset Description

We used an internally acquired TPEM dataset consisting of 42 volumes drawn from 25 Thy1-YFP mice, with lectin stain to label the vasculature, and a resolution of $0.99\,\mu\mathrm{m}/\mathrm{px}$, $0.99\,\mu\mathrm{m}/\mathrm{px}$, and $2.64\,\mu\mathrm{m}/\mathrm{px}$. Ninety six slices were acquired in the axial (z) dimension, which were later upsampled to 254 pixels to achieve an approximately isotropic image. Both neuronal and vascular structures are semi-automatically labeled using the Ilastik software [4] that relies on manual initialization followed by random forest-based segmentation, which took approximately 88 h for a domain specialist.

Table 1. TPEM SSL Masking strategy and ratio ablation results.

Masking strategy	Random			Intensity			Inverse intensity		
Masking Ratio	0.25	0.50	0.75	0.25	0.50	0.75	0.25	0.50	0.75
Dice	0.7395	0.7439	0.7470	0.7319	0.7364	0.7492	0.7467	**0.7524**	0.7469
Precision	0.7115	0.7189	0.7274	0.7780	0.7672	0.6885	0.6908	0.7021	0.7254
Recall	0.8004	0.8027	0.7910	0.7201	0.7350	0.8439	0.8400	0.8412	0.7934

The volumes were randomly split on the subject-level into train (N = 24), validation (N = 10) and test (N = 8) sets. To conduct SSL pretraining, the 24 train volumes were further split into 13 volumes (~55%) reserved for SSL experiments and 11 volumes (~45%) for experiments probing robustness of pretrained weights to smaller labeled dataset sizes. Though all of the train dataset is labeled, only the raw microscopy volume is used during SSL pretraining (i.e., labels are discarded).

4   Experiments and Results

4.1   Masking Ratio and Strategy

To investigate the effects of masking extent (ratio) and strategy during MIM on downstream model performance, we performed optimization experiments using 25% of the labeled dataset size, and finetuned on the neuron channel (segmentation task). We specifically investigated low, medium, and high masking ratios (25%, 50% and 75% respectively) for each masking strategy (random, intensity and inverse intensity). For these experiments, the channel separated masking policy was used (Table 1).

We found that the best intensity and inverse intensity masking experiments improved model performance slightly over the random masking strategy. For random and intensity masking strategies, results improved with increasing masking ratio, consistent with results found in previous MIM studies. We found good performance with all masking ratios using inverse intensity masking, with the best results across all experiments achieved when using a 0.5 masking ratio.

4.2   Channel-Wise Masking Policy

We conducted optimization experiments using 45% of the labeled dataset size, and finetuned on both the neuron and vessel channels to elucidate the optimal channel-wise masking policy for microscopy data (i.e., perform channel separated or channel together masking). Inverse-intensity masking with a ratio of 50% was used. For the channel-separated experiments, inverse-intensity masking probability was computed for each channel separately, while for channel-together, the finetuning channel was used to compute probabilities.

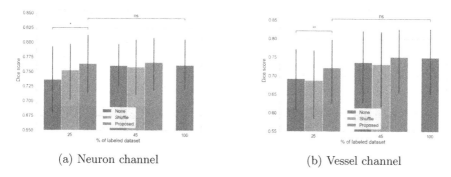

(a) Neuron channel   (b) Vessel channel

Fig. 2. Model performance for neuronal and vascular segmentation without SSL, using the shuffle pretext task [13] and using the proposed MIM method. Statistical significance assessed using the Wilcoxon signed rank test on Dice scores, "ns" is a non-significant result, * indicates a p-value < 0.05, and ** indicates a p-value < 0.01.

We found that the best strategy for masking varies depending on the fine-tuning channel. The optimal strategy for the neuron channel was to mask both channels together by a reasonably small margin, which obtained a Dice overlap of 0.766 vs. 0.759 for channels apart. Conversely, channel separated masking performed considerably better for vessel segmentation, with 0.7511 Dice vs. 0.7317 Dice obtained with channels together.

4.3   Self-supervised Pretraining Vs. Fully Supervised Learning

To summarize overall performance of the method, we report results on the test set when using FSL versus initialization from SSL pretrained weights. To validate our model, we compared it with the SSL shuffle permutation pretext task (with information weighting) [13]. Model performance was compared for the labeled training dataset sizes of 100%, 45% and 25%, which respectively consist of 24, 11, and 6 volumes. There is no overlap between SSL pretraining volumes and the 45% dataset. Note that we do not conduct the experiment using pretrained weights and finetuning using the full 100% of labeled data due to the overlap in datasets providing an unfair advantage. For segmentation experiments on the neuron channel, channels were masked together, while for the vessel channel, channels were masked separately. Results are summarized for neuron and vessel channels separately in Fig. 2, and visualizations of images, ground truth (GT), and predicted segmentations for both channels can be found in Fig. 3.

We found statistically significant improvement when initializing with SSL pretrained weights versus FSL when finetuning on 25% of the labeled dataset. For both neuron and vessel channels, training with SSL weights on about half the dataset yielded better results than training with 100% of the data with the FSL model. The shuffle pretext task improved segmentation performance when finetuning using 25% of the neuron dataset, and slightly reduced performance for other experiments. Our proposed method outperformed the shuffle task in all experiments, achieving a 3.6% and 1.2% average Dice improvement when trained on 25% of labeled data on the vessel and neuron segmentation tasks respectively. Additionally, our SSL pipeline using just 25% of the labeled data outperformed the FSL model with 100% of the data on neuron segmentation.

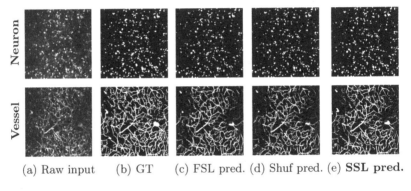

(a) Raw input   (b) GT   (c) FSL pred. (d) Shuf pred. (e) **SSL pred.**

Fig. 3. Model output visualization comparing performance of FSL, shuffle SSL task, proposed SSL method, and GT for neuron and vessel channels of a TPEM volume. All models are finetuned using 25% of the labeled dataset. All images are generated using a maximum-intensity projection along the z (depth) axis for the center 100 pixels. For columns (c) and (d), true positive predictions are in white, false positives are in red, false negatives are in blue, and true negatives are in black. (Color figure online)

5   Discussion

In this paper, we adopted and extended the data2vec target formulation to develop the first MIM-based SSL pipeline for 3D TPEM datasets. We demonstrated that this SSL pretext task provides useful features when transferred to two common downstream segmentation tasks in microscopy, and observed significant boosts in performance when comparing against typical fully-supervised models. We also introduced several intuitive masking strategies for MIM with fluorescence microscopy data by weighting masking probability using mean patch intensity and by masking individual image channels independently. This has the potential to considerably decrease labelling effort needed to develop segmentation models in microscopy, where only a subset of images in a dataset needs to be labeled to achieve similar segmentation quality.

For both neuronal and vascular data, we demonstrated that when initializing with SSL-pretrained weights, finetuning on just 45% of the labeled train set is sufficient to surpass performance when using all labels. Furthermore, for both segmentation tasks, our self-supervised pretraining pipeline made significant improvements over the fully-supervised model using only a small portion (25%) of the labeled dataset. While the improvement was greater in the neuron segmentation task than vessel segmentation, in both cases there were no significant difference in performance between SSL with 25% and FSL with 100%. We also show improved results relative to the shuffling pretext task, which intuitively provided the greatest benefit when finetuning on 25% of labeled data for a downstream task more similar to that in the original work (neuron versus axon segmentation). Similar to previous SSL studies, we found that benefits of pretraining diminish with larger quantities of available labeled TPEM data.

Intensity masking and inverse intensity masking were both shown to improve over typical random masking for TPEM data. We observed in our experiments on masking strategy and ratio that the best results on the downstream segmentation task occurred when using an inverse intensity masking strategy, which preferentially masks image *background*. Furthermore, when using inverse intensity masking, performance was more robust to the masking ratio used. This is contrary to similar studies in natural images, which have found that masking the *foreground* creates a more salient pretraining task [12], suggesting that adapting MIM from natural images to 3D microscopy requires domain-specific considerations. We hypothesize this could be jointly due to the importance of having unmasked foreground structures as context (due to task complexity), and that proper modeling of background cells and components of the neurovascular unit are key for MIM in microscopy.

6   Conclusion

In summary, we present a novel MIM-based SSL pipeline for microscopy data that can reduce the necessary labelling effort to train 3D segmentation models for TPEM, while jointly improving their analysis quality and speed. Our SSL pipeline and trained segmentation models will be made available to the research community. We expect that many of the performance improvements and insights gained in this study can be applied to related 3D microscopy modalities, enabling widespread neuroscience applications.

References

1. Albelwi, S.: Survey on self-supervised learning: auxiliary pretext tasks and contrastive learning methods in imaging. Entropy **24**(4) (2022). https://doi.org/10.3390/e24040551. https://www.mdpi.com/1099-4300/24/4/551
2. Baevski, A., Hsu, W.N., Xu, Q., Babu, A., Gu, J., Auli, M.: data2vec: a general framework for self-supervised learning in speech, vision and language (2022). https://doi.org/10.48550/arxiv.2202.03555. http://arxiv.org/abs/2202.03555

3. Bao, H., Dong, L., Piao, S., Wei, F.: Beit: bert pre-training of image transformers (2022)
4. Berg, S., et al.: ilastik: interactive machine learning for (bio)image analysis. Nat. Methods **16**(12), 1226–1232 (2019). https://doi.org/10.1038/s41592-019-0582-9
5. Cardoso, M.J., et al.: MONAI: an open-source framework for deep learning in healthcare (2022). https://doi.org/10.48550/arXiv.2211.02701
6. Caron, M., Touvron, H., Misra, I., Jégou, H., Mairal, J., Bojanowski, P., Joulin, A.: Emerging properties in self-supervised vision transformers. In: Proceedings of the International Conference on Computer Vision (ICCV) (2021)
7. Chen, T., Kornblith, S., Norouzi, M., Hinton, G.: A simple framework for contrastive learning of visual representations. arXiv preprint arXiv:2002.05709 (2020)
8. Chen, Z., Agarwal, D., Aggarwal, K., Safta, W., Balan, M., Brown, K.: Masked image modeling advances 3d medical image analysis. In: 2023 IEEE/CVF Winter Conference on Applications of Computer Vision (WACV), pp. 1969–1979. IEEE Computer Society, Los Alamitos (2023). https://doi.org/10.1109/WACV56688.2023.00201
9. Dosovitskiy, A., et al.: An image is worth 16×16 words: transformers for image recognition at scale. In: ICLR (2021)
10. Hatamizadeh, A., et al.: Unetr: transformers for 3D medical image segmentation. In: Proceedings of the IEEE/CVF Winter Conference on Applications of Computer Vision, pp. 574–584 (2022)
11. He, K., Chen, X., Xie, S., Li, Y., Dollár, P., Girshick, R.: Masked autoencoders are scalable vision learners (2021)
12. Kakogeorgiou, I., et al.: What to hide from your students: attention-guided masked image modeling. In: Avidan, S., Brostow, G., Cissé, M., Farinella, G.M., Hassner, T. (eds.) ECCV 2022. LNCS, pp. 300–318. Springer, Cham (2022). https://doi.org/10.1007/978-3-031-20056-4_18
13. Klinghoffer, T., Morales, P., Park, Y., Evans, N., Chung, K., Brattain, L.J.: Self-supervised feature extraction for 3d axon segmentation. In: 2020 IEEE/CVF Conference on Computer Vision and Pattern Recognition Workshops (CVPRW), pp. 4213–4219. IEEE Computer Society, Los Alamitos (2020). https://doi.org/10.1109/CVPRW50498.2020.00497
14. Li, Q., Shen, L.: 3d neuron reconstruction in tangled neuronal image with deep networks. IEEE Trans. Med. Imaging **39**(2), 425–435 (2020). https://doi.org/10.1109/TMI.2019.2926568
15. Li, R., Zeng, T., Peng, H., Ji, S.: Deep learning segmentation of optical microscopy images improves 3-d neuron reconstruction. IEEE Trans. Med. Imaging **36**(7), 1533–1541 (2017)
16. Taleb, A., et al.: 3d self-supervised methods for medical imaging. In: Larochelle, H., Ranzato, M., Hadsell, R., Balcan, M.F., Lin, H. (eds.) Advances in Neural Information Processing Systems, vol. 33, pp. 18158–18172. Curran Associates, Inc. (2020). https://proceedings.neurips.cc/paper/2020/file/d2dc6368837861b42020ee72b0896182-Paper.pdf
17. Tang, Y., et al.: Self-supervised pre-training of swin transformers for 3d medical image analysis. In: Proceedings of the IEEE/CVF Conference on Computer Vision and Pattern Recognition (CVPR), pp. 20730–20740 (2022)
18. Tendle, A., Hasan, M.R.: A study of the generalizability of self-supervised representations. Mach. Learn. Appl. **6**, 100124 (2021). https://doi.org/10.1016/j.mlwa.2021.100124

19. Vaswani, A., et al.: Attention is all you need. In: Guyon, I., et al. (eds.) Advances in Neural Information Processing Systems, vol. 30. Curran Associates, Inc. (2017). https://proceedings.neurips.cc/paper/2017/file/3f5ee243547dee91fbd053c1c4a845aa-Paper.pdf
20. Wang, H., et al.: Multiscale kernels for enhanced u-shaped network to improve 3d neuron tracing. In: 2019 IEEE/CVF Conference on Computer Vision and Pattern Recognition Workshops (CVPRW), pp. 1105–1113 (2019). https://doi.org/10.1109/CVPRW.2019.00144
21. Xie, Z., et al.: Simmim: a simple framework for masked image modeling (2022)
22. Zhang, C., Zhang, C., Song, J., Yi, J.S.K., Zhang, K., Kweon, I.S.: A survey on masked autoencoder for self-supervised learning in vision and beyond. arXiv preprint arXiv:2208.00173 (2022)

Automatic Quantification of COVID-19 Pulmonary Edema by Self-supervised Contrastive Learning

Zhaohui Liang⬤, Zhiyun Xue⬤, Sivaramakrishnan Rajaraman⬤, Yang Feng⬤, and Sameer Antani$^{(\boxtimes)}$ ⬤

Computational Health Research Branch, Lister Hill National Center for Biomedical Communications, National Library of Medicine, National Institutes of Health, Bethesda, MD, USA
sameer.antani@nih.gov

Abstract. We proposed a self-supervised machine learning method to automatically rate the severity of pulmonary edema in the frontal chest X-ray radiographs (CXR) which could be potentially related to COVID-19 viral pneumonia. For this we use the modified radiographic assessment of lung edema (mRALE) scoring system. The new model was first optimized with the simple Siamese network (SimSiam) architecture where a ResNet-50 pretrained by ImageNet database was used as the backbone. The encoder projected a 2048-dimension embedding as representation features to a downstream fully connected deep neural network for mRALE score prediction. A 5-fold cross-validation with 2,599 frontal CXRs was used to examine the new model's performance with comparison to a non-pretrained SimSiam encoder and a ResNet-50 trained from scratch. The mean absolute error (MAE) of the new model is 5.05 (95%CI 5.03–5.08), the mean squared error (MSE) is 66.67 (95%CI 66.29–67.06), and the Spearman's correlation coefficient (Spearman ρ) to the expert-annotated scores is 0.77 (95%CI 0.75–0.79). All the performance metrics of the new model are superior to the two comparators (P < 0.01), and the scores of MSE and Spearman ρ of the two comparators have no statistical difference (P > 0.05). The model also achieved a prediction probability concordance of 0.811 and a quadratic weighted kappa of 0.739 with the medical expert annotations in external validation. We conclude that the self-supervised contrastive learning method is an effective strategy for mRALE automated scoring. It provides a new approach to improve machine learning performance and minimize the expert knowledge involvement in quantitative medical image pattern learning.

Keywords: Self-supervised Learning · Contrastive Learning · COVID-19 · Pulmonary Edema · Deep Learning

1 Introduction

1.1 Lung Edema and COVID-19 Prognosis

Severe acute respiratory syndrome coronavirus 2 (SARS-CoV-2) caused the coronavirus disease (COVID-19) global pandemic since 2020. According to World Health Organization, the confirmed cases of COVID-19 have reached 767,518,723 and the death toll

© The Author(s), under exclusive license to Springer Nature Switzerland AG 2023
Z. Xue et al. (Eds.): MILLanD 2023, LNCS 14307, pp. 128–137, 2023.
https://doi.org/10.1007/978-3-031-44917-8_12

has accumulated to 6,947,192 [1]. As we are approaching the end of the pandemic emergency, new studies concentrate on novel methods for detection, diagnosis, evaluation, and prognosis of COVID-19 disease. For example, a cohort study in Japan found that the need of the SARS-CoV-2 patients for prolonged mechanical ventilation was quantitatively relevant to their lung ultrasound score (LUS) and radiographic assessment of the lung edema (RALE) score [2]. An international multicenter study found that the progressive increase of RALE is associated to the mortality of acute respiratory distress syndrome (ARDS) cases by COVID-19 [3]. RALE introduced by Warren MA et. al. is a quantitative tool to assess the extent and density of alveolar opacities on chest radiographs that reflect the degree of pulmonary edema [4]. As a key indicator of acute respiratory distress syndrome (ARDS), pulmonary edema is an indicator of SARS-CoV-2 severity and a predictor of prognosis [5]. A retrospective cohort study on refractory cardiogenic shock and cardiac arrest patients receiving veno-arterial extracorporeal membrane oxygenation support concluded that RALE is a discriminator for mortality and the progressive monitoring of RALE scores is a good predictor for therapeutic effects [6]. An international multicenter study in Europe observed 350 chest X-ray radiographs (CXR) from 139 COVID-19 ARDS patients in intensive care units (ICU) revealed that the progressive increase of RALE score in CXRs was associated to higher mortality and longer use time of ventilator [3]. The modified RALE scoring system (mRALE) is a non-invasive measure to evaluate the severity of pulmonary edema on CXR. It renders a total score ranging from 0 the 24 to respectively assess the extent and density of alveolar opacities of different regions of lung assessed on frontal CXRs. Thus, both RALE and mRALE are applicable to SARS-CoV-2.

1.2 Deep Learning for COVID-19 Images

Since the continuous monitoring of pulmonary edema through CXRs is an effective measure for ARDS severity and a predictor for prognosis, it can serve as an important parameter for clinical decision making, which provides a handy method for COVID-19 patient administration, particularly when CXRs were one of the most common and low-cost examinations for COVID-19 severity assessment at the peak of pandemic. Meanwhile, machine learning (ML), especially deep learning (DL) for COVID-19 images, has been widely studied since the beginning of the pandemic to enhance disease detection and management with fruitful outcomes, but it also faces multiple challenges in these critical use cases. A review on the application of DL for COVID-19 image processing found that convolutional neural networks (CNNs) have gained utmost popularity for classifying CXR images as showing COVID-19-consistent manifestations. Meanwhile, the authors pointed out the current challenges to DL for COVID-19 image analysis applications include the lack of image quality assurance, unbalance and diversity of the image datasets, and the generalization and reproducibility of the available models and algorithms, etc. [7]. A survey based on over 100 published papers on DL for COVID-19 explored the three common imaging modalities of COVID-19: CXR, computed tomography (CT) and ultrasound images. It concluded that the most effective and time-efficient method to detect COVID-19 is CXR imaging for its ease of access, low cost and low exposure to radiation compared to CT scans, and higher sensitive compared to ultrasound images. It also pointed out future research should enhance the reliability and robustness of DL applications such as using explainable AI to reduce the uncertainty and improving the accessibility of large, well-annotated image datasets [8].

One latest finding by Xie et al. is the introduction of the dense regression activation maps (dRAMs) to segment the lesion lung region from COVID-19 CT scans with the Dice coefficient of 70.2% [9]. Another is the bilateral adaptive graph-based (BA-GCN) model by Meng et al. with 2-D segmentation function for the 3-D CT scans to detect early infection of COVID-19 with significant improvement on both learning ability and generalization ability [10]. Signoroni et al. presented the BS-Net (Brixia Score Net) for weakly supervised learning to perform both classifications, scoring and segmentation simultaneously [11]. However, all the high performance of these new methods is based on the availability of large well-annotated datasets. If the models are applied to a new use case, they must be retrained with new data, or the performance will inevitably decrease. The research on adversarial network attacks supports this idea because the well-trained DL models for COVID-19 detection will become vulnerable from simple network attacks [12, 13]. This phenomenon can be explained by the randomness of pattern capturing of DL. The seemingly high performance of DL can be the random combination of basic visual patterns which cannot be interpreted by medical expertise [13, 14]. This assumption is supported by quantitative measures such as RALE or mRALE which serve a solution to these challenges in the automated quantification for COVID-19.

1.3 Deep Learning for COVID-19 Severity Quantification

The mRALE score prediction model proposed by Li et al. in 2020 is considered as a success for COVID-19 automated quantification, where a Siamese Network model was first pretrained by over 160,000 reference CXR images in the supervised mode, then it was fine-tuned by 314 frontal CXR images to predict the mRALE score for pulmonary edema severity. The model achieved high consistency with the medical expert annotation with the Spearman's correlation coefficient of 0.86 and the area under the receiver operating characteristic curve (ROC AUC) of 0.80 [15]. Another similar research by Horng et al. used semi-supervised learning to train a DenseNet architecture with a CXR dataset with 369,071 from 64,581 patients to learn the cardiopulmonary context, then the model was fine-tuned to learn the severity of chronic heart failure in four ordinal levels based on alveolar edema [16].

1.4 Study Motivation

The current success in DL mainly relies on large CXR datasets as context to guide the DL models to acquire necessary prior knowledge such as the modality significant visual patterns for the downstream tasks. Our study aims to solve the difficulty of data accessibility of DL for COVID-19 severity quantification. A new ML technology called contrastive learning is applied to learn the cardiopulmonary context patterns by comparing the similarity of identical image pairs with random augmentation. An encoder for extracting meaningful features from CXRs can be trained by this strategy for mRALE score prediction. We believe this method can reduce the data-greedy limitation of DL.

2 Material and Methods

2.1 Contrastive Learning

Contrastive learning is a machine learning approach to initialize the model training in an unsupervised learning manner to acquire meaningful representations of the training data patterns. Then the training switches to the downstream supervised learning for explicit tasks. It is considered as a transfer learning strategy to improve ML performance. The classic contrastive learning method uses both positive and negative data pairs as inputs, where the positive pairs are pulled closer in the latent space while the negative pairs are pushed apart during ML optimization. For the single input image example i, its contrastive loss is defined as:

$$L_i = -\frac{e^{s_{i,i'}}}{\sum_j e^{s_{i,j}}} = -s_{i,i'} + log\left(\sum_j e^{s_{i,j}}\right) \tag{1}$$

where $-s_{i,i'}$ is the loss term for the positive pair and $log\left(\sum_j e^{s_{i,j}}\right)$ is the loss term for the negative pair. In Eq. (1), the computation cost for the positive pair loss is obviously lower than the negative pair because the former is simply the negative cosine similarity while the latter one is the summation of all the difference of negative pairs. Note that the negative pairs loss is used to maintain the training mode, if a new method can be found to prevent mode collapse, we can remove the negative pairs loss to simplify the computation as shown by the bootstrap your own latent (BYOL) method by Tian et al., where two identical networks were paralleled to learn the image similarity in the teacher-and student mode [17]. The loss objective of BYOL is revised as:

$$L_i = -\frac{e^{s_{i,i'}}}{\sum_j e^{s_{i,j}}} = -s_{i,i'} + \beta \cdot log\left(\sum_j e^{s_{i,j}}\right) \tag{2}$$

where β is a tunable hyperparameter ranging from 0 to 1. When $\beta = 0$, the loss is only determined by the positive pair part. The BYOL method also uses the stop-gradient (stop-grad) method to prevent the teacher network from being updated by backpropagation, and a predictor is added to the student network as the learning reference for the teacher network's update using exponential moving average (EMA) weighted by β. This asymmetric architecture is effective to prevent mode collapse. The teacher network finally learns the feature similarity representations and it can act as the target encoder for any downstream tasks such as classification and regression.

The BYOL is further simplified by removing the identical paralleled architecture and replacing with a shared network for both encoder arms as the implementation of the Simple Siamese network (SimSiam) [18]. The SimSiam first used a single Siamese architecture as the backbone shared by the two sets of identical input images respectively with random augmentation. Taking the advantage that the Siamese network naturally produces "inductive biases for modeling invariance", the contrastive learning mode can be kept and progress stably. The SimSiam loss function is defined as:

$$L = \frac{1}{2}\mathcal{D}(p_1, z_2) + \frac{1}{2}\mathcal{D}(p_2, z_1) = \frac{1}{2}\mathcal{D}(p_1, stopgrad(z_2)) + \frac{1}{2}\mathcal{D}(p_2, stopgrad(z_1))$$

(3)

where z_1 and z_2 are the outputs of the projector of the p_1 and p_2 are the outputs of the predictor. Note that the stop-gradient mechanism plays a crucial role to prevent mode collapse in SimSiam optimization as mentioned in the original paper [17], where the two Siamese architecture encoders share the identical weights. The projector h and the stop-gradient mechanism form a teacher-student learning mode where the projector learns faster than the encoder to stabilize the learning mode.

In our study, we use ImageNet-pretrained ResNet-50 as the backbone of the SimSiam encoder and the projector output is a 2,048-dimensional embedding, which serves as the feature map for the downstream regression tasks. The whole architecture of the SimSiam based self-supervised model is illustrated in Fig. 1 in the next section.

2.2 Regression Based on Self-supervised Learning Features

Self-supervised learning (SSL) formulates vision patterns through the contrastive learning process. It can be used as the pattern extractor for the first part of a regressor model composed of two parts: the SimSiam network for SSL contrastive learning, and the regressor for mRALE prediction by supervised learning.

As discussed in the previous section, the SimSiam can be further divided into the encoder and the predictor, forming a structure like an autoencoder (AE). In our model, the encoder is a ResNet50 (backbone) pretrained by the ImageNet dataset. The pretrained model is easier to train to guide the filters focus on the meaningful region such as the alveoli of the lungs. It can be verified by the gradient-weighted class activation mapping (Grad-CAM). Our experiments showed that the combined strategy of transfer learning and contrastive learning can effectively keep a stable training mode compared to training from scratch. The regressor is a multi-layer perceptron (MLP) composed of two fully connected dense layers respectively with 256 neurons and followed by batch normalization. The whole architecture is illustrated in Fig. 1.

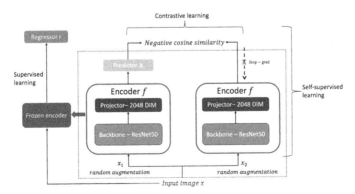

Fig. 1. Architecture of the self-supervised, contrastive learning regression model

2.3   Chest X-ray Radiograph Dataset and Experiment Setting

The CXR dataset used in our study is from the 2023 MIDRC mRALE Mastermind Challenge [19]. It contains 2,599 portable CXR images in the frontal anterior-posterior (AP) view with the mRALE scores annotated by expert radiologists and four quantitative scores representing the extent of involvement and the degree of density of each side of the lung. The images are stored in the DICOM format and accessible on the MIDRC mRALE Mastermind GitHub:

https://github.com/MIDRC/COVID19_Challenges.

The pre-processed CXR images are illustrated in Fig. 2. The images received augmentations including random flipping, color jittering, and color dropping to form two identical datasets where the index orders of each training image are the same. Note that we omitted the random cropping augmentation as recommended in the original SimSiam method because random cropping is likely to remove the alveolar opacities which are the crucial patterns for the final mRALE score.

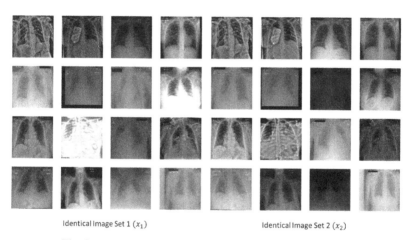

Identical Image Set 1 (x_1)   Identical Image Set 2 (x_2)

Fig. 2. Two identical image sets with random augmentations.

The retrieved images are resized to 224-by-224, 3 channels to match the input size of the pretrained ResNet-50 backbone. We split the dataset into five folds (520 images for each fold) for the cross-validation evaluation. The self-supervised contrastive learning regression model was implemented with TensorFlow version 2.12 in Python. The experiments were performed on the Amazon SageMaker Studio on a g4dn.2xlarge instance with a single Nvidia T4 tensor core GPU.

3   Results

3.1   Contrastive Learning

In the self-supervised contrastive learning phase, we used the pre-defined ResNet-50 network from the Keras API and removed the top classification layers as the backbone of the encoder. The output activation map is connected to a multi-layer perceptron

(MLP) with L2 regularization with a weight decay rate of 1×10^{-3} and layer-wise batch normalization to stabilize the contrastive learning mode. We respectively trained an encoder starting with the pretrain weights by ImageNet and another encoder starting from scratch. We first froze all the layers of the backbone and trained the encoders by stochastic gradient descent (SGD) with momentum = 0.6 and cosine decay with initial learning rate of 0.02 with 15 epochs, then we unfroze the topmost 20 layers of the backbone except for the batch normalization layers and tuned the encoders with initial learning rate of 0.002 with another 20 epochs. The training process is shown in Fig. 3.

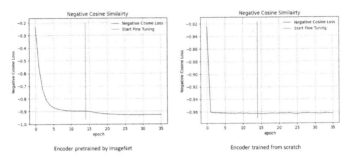

Fig. 3. Encoder optimized by self-supervised contrastive learning

Figure 3 shows that the encoder starting with the ImageNet pretrained weights (hot start) has smooth loss converge compared to the encoder trained from scratch (cold start) where the loss drop sharply to -0.96 after the second epoch and remained close to the minimum. This observation reflects the contrastive learning mode is successfully kept with the hot start while the training of the model with cold start was trapped at some local saddle points according to the original design of the SimSiam model [17].

3.2 Quantitative Prediction of mRALE

The weights of the encoders were frozen after optimized by the contrastive learning and they were connected to regressors and trained with the images and annotated scores to predict the CXR mRALE based on the lung edema patterns captured by the encoders. The regressors are MLPs with two fully connected layers with batch normalization. The regressor with encoder models were first trained for 20 epochs. Next, we unfroze the topmost 20 layers of the encoder (except from the batch normalization layers) and fine-tuned the whole regressor model with the initial learning rate of 1×10^{-5} for 15 epochs. We also trained a ResNet-50 model with the identical regressor head from scratch with 35 epochs (terminated by the early-stop mechanism at the 32nd epoch) as performance comparator to the new model. The optimization process is shown in Fig. 4.

Grad-CAM is used to indicate the regression models' focus on the images. It helps to explain the regressor behavior when combined with the performance metrics. (Fig. 5).

We performed a 5-fold cross validation to evaluate the overall performance of the three regressors with the metrics of mean squared error (MSE), mean absolute error (MAE) and the Spearman's correlation coefficient (Spearman ρ) reflecting the consistency of DL prediction to expert annotations. The mean scores with the 95% confidential

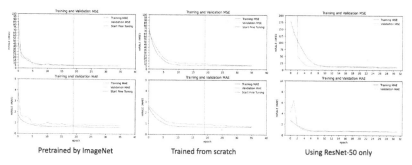

Fig. 4. Comparison of regressor training

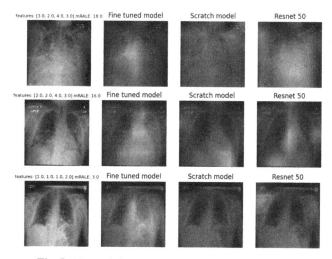

Fig. 5. Network focus regions indicated by Grad CAM

interval (95% CI) are listed in Table 1. It indicates that the proposed regressor using an encoder with pretrained weights by ImageNet and trained by self-supervised contrastive learning has the best prediction performance, but the regressor trained from cold start shows no superiority compared to directly training a ResNet-50 for the mRALE regression task. The result is also supported by the Grad CAM where the self-supervised contrastive regressor with ImageNet pretrained weights can better focus on the pulmonary regions of the CXRs (see Fig. 4). In addition, we submitted the regressor trained with the whole dataset to the MIDRC mRALE Mastermind Challenge [19] for external validation. The model achieved a prediction probability concordance of 0.811 and a quadratic weighted kappa of 0.739 with the expert annotations in the third-party test by MIDRC.

Table 1. Metrics of Model Performance

Regressor	MSE (95% CI)	MAE (95% CI)	Spearman ρ (95% CI)
Self-supervised contrastive regressor (pretrain)	5.05 (5.03–5.08)[*]	66.67 (66.29–67.06)[*]	0.77 (0.75–0.79)[*]
Self-supervised contrastive regressor (scratch)	5.71 (5.68–5.76)[*]	71.25 (70.66–71.84)[*]	0.52 (0.45–0.59)[*]
ResNet-50 regressor	5.49 (5.39–5.58)[*]	70.09 (69.00–71.18)[*▼]	0.57 (0.51–0.65)[*▼]

[*] $p < 0.01$ in t-test for mean comparison, ▼ $p < 0.05$ in t-test for mean comparison

4   Conclusion and Discussion

We propose to use the self-supervised contrastive learning strategy to train a SimSiam based encoder as feature extractor for the regression model to predict mRALE score directly from the visual pattern of frontal CXRs. The results show that the self-supervised contrastive learning strategy combined with the pretrained weights by ImageNet can achieve convincing prediction performance with a small image dataset with limit training samples.

Future work could focus on using more feature localization methods such as vision transformer (ViT) with attention to further separate the meaningful vision patterns from the background by dividing the image into small patches and using multiple segmentation models to extract the region of interest (ROI) from the medical images to filter out the noise pattern. In addition, explainable AI technology such as Grad-CAM is helpful to track and verify the DL model behaviors such that the randomness of DL can be minimized. We believe DL with self-supervised mechanism is a promising tool for automated medical image analysis and its performance can significantly improve when the knowledge acquired by AI is consistent to the long-term accumulative human expertise.

Funding. This research is supported by the Intramural Research Program of the National Library of Medicine, National Institutes of Health.

References

1. WHO, WHO Coronavirus (COVID-19) Dashboard. https://covid19.who.int/. Accessed 02 July 2023
2. Taniguchi, H., Ohya, A., Yamagata, H., Iwashita, M., Abe, T., Takeuchi, I.: Prolonged mechanical ventilation in patients with severe COVID-19 is associated with serial modified-lung ultrasound scores: a single-centre cohort study. PLoS ONE **17**(7), e0271391 (2022)
3. Valk, C.M.A., Zimatore, C., Mazzinari, G., Pierrakos, C., Sivakorn, C., Dechsanga, J., et al.: The prognostic capacity of the radiographic assessment for lung edema score in patients with COVID-19 acute respiratory distress syndrome-an international multicenter observational study. Front Med (Lausanne) **8**, 772056 (2021)

4. Warren, M.A., Zhao, Z., Koyama, T., Bastarache, J.A., Shaver, C.M., Semler, M.W., et al.: Severity scoring of lung oedema on the chest radiograph is associated with clinical outcomes in ARDS. Thorax **73**(9), 840–846 (2018)

5. Matthay, M.A., Ware, L.B., Zimmerman, G.A.: The acute respiratory distress syndrome. J. Clin. Invest. **122**(8), 2731–2740 (2012)

6. Voigt, I., Mighali, M., Manda, D., Aurich, P., Bruder, O.: Radiographic assessment of lung edema (RALE) score is associated with clinical outcomes in patients with refractory cardiogenic shock and refractory cardiac arrest after percutaneous implantation of extracorporeal life support. Intern. Emerg. Med. **17**(5), 1463–1470 (2022)

7. Aggarwal, P., Mishra, N.K., Fatimah, B., Singh, P., Gupta, A., Joshi, S.D.: COVID-19 image classification using deep learning: advances, challenges and opportunities. Comput. Biol. Med. **144**, 105350 (2022)

8. Khattab, R., Abdelmaksoud, I.R., Abdelrazek, S.: Deep convolutional neural networks for detecting COVID-19 using medical images: a survey. New Gener. Comput. **41**(2), 343–400 (2023)

9. Xie, W., Jacobs, C., Charbonnier, J.P., van Ginneken, B.: Dense regression activation maps for lesion segmentation in CT scans of COVID-19 patients. Med. Image Anal. **86**, 102771 (2023)

10. Meng, Y., Bridge, J., Addison, C., Wang, M., Merritt, C., Franks, S., et al.: Bilateral adaptive graph convolutional network on CT based Covid-19 diagnosis with uncertainty-aware consensus-assisted multiple instance learning. Med. Image Anal. **84**, 102722 (2023)

11. Signoroni, A., Savardi, M., Benini, S., Adami, N., Leonardi, R., Gibellini, P., et al.: BS-Net: learning COVID-19 pneumonia severity on a large chest X-ray dataset. Med. Image Anal. **71**, 102046 (2021)

12. Rahman, A., Hossain, M.S., Alrajeh, N.A., Alsolami, F.: Adversarial examples-security threats to COVID-19 deep learning systems in medical IoT devices. IEEE Internet Things J. **8**(12), 9603–9610 (2021)

13. Li, Y., Liu, S.: The threat of adversarial attack on a COVID-19 CT image-based deep learning system. Bioengineering (Basel) **10**(2), 194 (2023)

14. Liang, Z., Huang, J.X., Sameer, A.: Image translation by ad CycleGAN for COVID-19 X-ray images: a new approach for controllable GAN. Sensors (Basel) **22**(24), 9628 (2022)

15. Li, M.D., Arun, N.T., Gidwani, M., Chang, K., Deng, F., Little, B.P., et al.: Automated assessment and tracking of COVID-19 pulmonary disease severity on chest radiographs using convolutional siamese neural networks. Radiol. Artif. Intell. **2**(4), e200079 (2020)

16. Horng, S., Liao, R., Wang, X., Dalal, S., Golland, P., Berkowitz, S.J.: Deep learning to quantify pulmonary edema in chest radiographs. Radiol. Artif. Intell. **3**(2), e190228 (2021)

17. Tian, Y., Chen, X., Ganguli, S.: Understanding self-supervised learning dynamics without contrastive pairs. In: Proceedings of the 38th International Conference on Machine Learning, vol. 139, pp. 10268–10278. MLR Press, (2021)

18. Chen, X., He, K.: Exploring simple siamese representation learning. In: 2021 IEEE/CVF Conference on Computer Vision and Pattern Recognition (CVPR). IEEE, Nashville (2021)

19. MIDRC, MIDRC mRALE Mastermind Challenge: AI to predict COVID severity on chest radiographs. https://www.midrc.org/mrale-mastermind-2023. Accessed 02 July 2023

SDLFormer: A Sparse and Dense Locality-Enhanced Transformer for Accelerated MR Image Reconstruction

Rahul G.S.[1,2](✉), Sriprabha Ramnarayanan[1,2], Mohammad Al Fahim[1,2], Keerthi Ram[2], Preejith S.P[2], and Mohanasankar Sivaprakasam[2]

[1] Indian Institute of Technology Madras (IITM), Chennai, India
[2] Healthcare Technology Innovation Centre (HTIC), IITM, Chennai, India
{rahul.g.s,sriprabha.r}@htic.iitm.ac.in

Abstract. Transformers have emerged as viable alternatives to convolutional neural networks owing to their ability to learn non-local region relationships in the spatial domain. The self-attention mechanism of the transformer enables transformers to capture long-range dependencies in the images, which might be desirable for accelerated MRI image reconstruction as the effect of undersampling is non-local in the image domain. Despite its computational efficiency, the window-based transformers suffer from restricted receptive fields as the dependencies are limited to within the scope of the image windows. We propose a window-based transformer network that integrates dilated attention mechanism and convolution for accelerated MRI image reconstruction. The proposed network consists of dilated and dense neighborhood attention transformers to enhance the distant neighborhood pixel relationship and introduce depth-wise convolutions within the transformer module to learn low-level translation invariant features for accelerated MRI image reconstruction. The proposed model is trained in a self-supervised manner. We perform extensive experiments for multi-coil MRI acceleration for coronal PD, coronal PDFS and axial T2 contrasts with $4\times$ and $5\times$ under-sampling in self-supervised learning based on k-space splitting. We compare our method against other reconstruction architectures and the parallel domain self-supervised learning baseline. Results show that the proposed model exhibits improvement margins of (i) $\sim$1.40 dB in PSNR and $\sim$0.028 in SSIM on average over other architectures (ii) $\sim$1.44 dB in PSNR and $\sim$0.029 in SSIM over parallel domain self-supervised learning. The code is available at https://github.com/rahul-gs-16/sdlformer.git.

Keywords: MRI reconstruction · Self supervised learning · Transformers

© The Author(s), under exclusive license to Springer Nature Switzerland AG 2023
Z. Xue et al. (Eds.): MILLanD 2023, LNCS 14307, pp. 138–147, 2023.
https://doi.org/10.1007/978-3-031-44917-8_13

1   Introduction

Vision transformers have emerged as a competitive alternative to convolutional blocks in various image reconstruction tasks [9,15,20,24]. They offer a flexible mechanism to capture relationships between regions from distant neighborhoods [14], helping in relating patterns useful for image restoration. MRI acceleration can specifically benefit from this, as the imaging process involves sampling k-space trajectories, which impacts the image domain representation in a non-local manner.

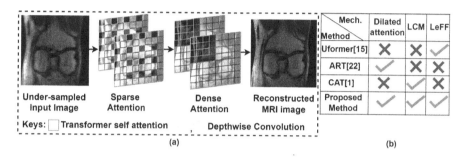

Mech. Method	Dilated attention	LCM	LeFF
Uformer[15]	✗	✗	✓
ART[22]	✓	✗	✗
CAT[1]	✗	✓	✗
Proposed Method	✓	✓	✓

Under-sampled Input Image   Sparse Attention   Dense Attention   Reconstructed MRI image

Keys: ☐ Transformer self attention   Depthwise Convolution

(a)   (b)

Fig. 1. Description of the proposed model. In the sparse attention block pixels are given in dilated manner to the input of the transformer. In dense attention block the input is given in a continuous manner. Cyan and green denote different channels. (Color figure online)

In this work, we consider the problem of MR image reconstruction using the window-based self-attention mechanism of vision transformers. Window-based transformers such as SwinMR [6] have been used for MRI reconstruction, but windowing trades-off restricted receptive field for computational complexity, which we propose to alleviate by designing a variant of the transformer module. Further, we complement the global information operations of transformers with convolutions, imparting fine-grained local feature modeling, valuable in MRI reconstruction (Fig. 1(a)).

Related Works: To increase the range over which attention is computed without increasing the computation cost, the Attention Retractable Transformer (ART) [22] uses a sparse attention block (SAB) where the input to the transformer is the windowed image regions processed in a dilated manner. On the other hand, the Cross Aggregation Transformer (CAT) [1] introduces the Locality Complementary Module (LCM) in the self-attention stage of the transformer to provide local context, but processes the input using dense neighboring windows. An alternative method of inducing locality is Locality enhanced Feed-Forward (LeFF) [15], which uses depth-wise convolutions in the transformer's feed-forward layer. While recursive dilated CNNs [13] have been applied in MRI reconstruction, an intersection of dilated or sparse self-attention mechanism with local context remains unexplored for MRI reconstruction. Figure 1b tabulates the key factors and motivations for our proposed method.

Our proposed model is a window-based self-attention transformer that incorporates sparse and dense attention blocks with convolutions. Designed to capture long-range pixel interactions and local contextual features, the proposed model is trained in a data-driven self-supervised manner [17], and demonstrated for 4× and 5× accelerations in multi-coil MRI.

We summarise our contributions as follows. **1)** We propose SDLFormer, a computationally efficient and performant transformer-based network hybridized with CNNs for accelerated multi-coil MRI reconstruction. **2)** Our proposed transformer block is designed to capture long-range dependencies via sparse attention on dilated windows in the input image domain and dense attention over neighborhood windows. The sparse and dense attention blocks are augmented with depth-wise convolutions to learn local contextual features with self-attention. **3)** We extensively evaluate the proposed network on self-supervised multi-coil MRI reconstruction using multi-coil knee datasets for three contrasts: Proton Density (PD), Proton Density with Fat Suppression (PDFS), and Axial T2. We have achieved an improvement of ∼0.6 dB in PSNR and ∼0.018 in SSIM over the best-performing model, the SwinMR transformer. We perform an ablative study to understand the contribution of each component of our proposed transformer network.

2   Method

In this section, the mathematical formulation of the MRI under-sampling process, the overall architecture pipeline, and the Locality Enhanced Transformer (LET) block are described.

Problem Formulation: Let $x \in \mathbb{C}^{N_x \times N_y}$ represent 2-D MRI image with height N_y and width N_x.

The forward model of the k-space undersampling process with N_c coils is given by,

$$y_i = M \odot \mathcal{F}(S_i \odot x); \quad i = 1, \ldots, N_c \tag{1}$$

where M is a 2-D under-sampling mask, $\odot$ represents Hadamard product, and $\mathcal{F}$ is 2-D Fourier transform respectively. S_i represents the sensitivity map that encodes the coil's spatial sensitivity and is normalized such that $\sum_{i=1}^{N} S_i^* S_i = I_n$

Our goal is to reconstruct image x from y which is formulated as an optimization problem for supervised learning given by,

$$\underset{\theta}{\operatorname{argmin}} \quad ||x - h_\theta(y)||_2^2 + \lambda ||M \odot \mathcal{F}(x) - y||_2^2 \tag{2}$$

where $x_u = \mathcal{F}^{-1}(y)$ is the undersampled image obtained by zero filling the missing k-space values, and h_θ is the image reconstruction network.

Self-supervised Learning: Following [17], we randomly partition y into two disjoint sets y_1 and y_2 as follows $y_1 = M_1 \odot y, y_2 = M_2 \odot y$, where M_1 and M_2 are the two disjoint masks used to partition the k-space y. The loss L function is defined as,

$$L(y_1, y_2) = ||M_2 \odot \mathcal{F}(h_\theta(y_1)) - y_2||_1 \qquad (3)$$

This self-supervised approach eliminates the need for fully sampled data, which requires extensive amounts of measurements for multi-coil acquisition.

Architecture Details: The overall pipeline of the proposed method is shown in Fig. 2(a). The input to the pipeline is the under-sampled k-space data which is processed using a k-space CNN. The output of k-space is converted to the image domain. Initially, two Sparse Attention Transformer modules are present, followed by two Dense Attention Transformer modules. The LET block operates as the transformer module in the sparse and dense attention blocks. The sparse attention differs from the dense attention transformer by operating in a dilated manner. K-Space CNN is a 5-layer CNN with instance normalization, ReLU activation, and a residual connection from the input to the output to enable gradient flow. The pipeline of the architecture is shown in Fig. 2(a).

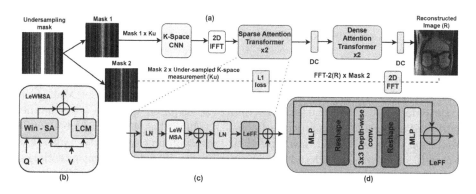

Fig. 2. Proposed Overall Pipeline. The pipeline consists of k-space CNN, Sparse attention block, dense attention block, and convolution layer in series. LeWMSA, LeFF, and LCM represent Locally enhanced Window Multi-head Self Attention, Locally enhanced Feed Forward, and Locality Complementary Module respectively. The under-sampling mask is split into two and multiplied with the k-space measurement to obtain two subsets of measured k-space. One subset is used by the model for prediction and the other subset is used as reference. L1 loss is computed between the reference k-space subset and the FFT of the image predicted by the model.

Locality Enhanced Transformer (LET): The internal architecture of the LET block is shown in Fig. 2(c). This architecture tries to address two main challenges faced by a vanilla transformer. 1) The quadratic computation cost with respect to the number of tokens. 2) The transformers show a limitation in capturing local dependencies [8,16] which are essential for image restoration.

Computational complexity is reduced using a non-overlapping Locality enhanced Window-based Multi-head Self-Attention (LeW-MSA). Here the input feature map $X \in \mathbb{R}^{(H \times W \times C)}$ is split into non-overlapping windows with window size $M \times M$ and flattened to obtain features $X_i \in \mathbb{R}^{M^2 \times C}$ from each window i. The flattened features are projected into subspace using linear projection to obtain query (Q), key (K), and Value (V). Multi-headed self-attention is applied, to the flattened features in each window using the Eq. 4a. Inspired by CAT [1], a Locality Complementary Module (LCM) is introduced in the transformer, which is a 3×3 depth-wise convolution module, used to extract local contextual features, as shown in Fig. 2(b). Following Uformer [15,19], the ability of the transformer's feed-forward layer to capture local contextual features is improved by introducing a 3×3 depth-wise convolution in the feed-forward layer, with the necessary reshaping as shown in Fig. 2(d). The architecture of the transformer block is shown in Fig. 2(c).

$$Attention(Q, K, V) = Softmax(\frac{QK^T}{\sqrt{d_r}} + B)V + LCM(V), \qquad (4a)$$

$$X' = LeWMSA(X_{in}) + X_{in}, \qquad (4b)$$

$$X_{out} = LeFF(LN(X')) + X' \qquad (4c)$$

Where X' and X_{out} are the outputs of Window-based Multi-head self-attention and $LeFF$ blocks with skip connections respectively. LN represents Layer Norm.

Dataset Details: Three protocols: coronal proton-density (PD), coronal fat-saturated PD (PDFS), and axial fat-saturated T2 from the dataset Multi-Coil Knee dataset [4], were chosen. The data was acquired through a 15-channel multi-coil setting for 20 subjects. Each 3D volume has 40 slices of 640×368 resolution complex-valued data and their corresponding sensitivity maps. The center 19 slices were considered for our experiments. The dataset was partitioned into 10 volumes containing 190 slices each for training purposes, and 10 volumes with 190 slices each for validation.

Implementation Details: The models are trained using PyTorch v1.12 on a 24 GB RTX 3090 GPU. The Adam optimizer [7] without weight decay is employed with $\beta_1 = 0.9$, $\beta_2 = 0.999$, and an initial learning rate of 1e-3, which undergo step-wise reduction using a learning rate scheduler with a step-size of 40 epochs and γ of 0.1. The training is performed for 150 epochs using the L1 loss, and the instances with the best validation loss are saved for comparison. Performance evaluation is based on Peak Signal-Noise Ratio (PSNR) and Structural Similarity Index Measure (SSIM). Since aliasing artifacts are structural, non-local processing in the image domain alone might be insufficient [10]. To address this, k-space CNN is added at the beginning of the proposed method and all the other comparison methods as suggested by [3,11,25]. For faster convergence, the weights of K-space CNN in the proposed model are initialized with the weights obtained by training KIKI-net in a self-supervised manner. The weights of the transformer are initialized with the weights obtained from the Uformer [15] model trained with natural images (SIDD dataset). The data consistency (DC) [12] in the network's output is ensured using the partition y_1. The model is also trained in parallel domain training methodology [5] and evaluated.

3   Results and Discussion

Our results are organized as follows. 1. Comparison of the proposed model with other State of the Art MRI reconstruction models. 2. Ablative study of various components in the architecture

3.1   Qualitative and Quantitative Comparison on Multi Coil Knee MRI Dataset

Table 1. Quantitative comparison of different methods on different datasets and acceleration factors. The best results for self-supervised learning [17] are highlighted in bold. The SL, PL, and SSL represent Supervised Learning, self-supervised learning in the Parallel domain training, and Self Supervised Learning with only k-space splitting respectively.

Method	Coronal PD		Coronal PDFS		Axial T2	
	4×	5×	4×	5×	4×	5×
	PSNR/SSIM	PSNR/SSIM	PSNR/SSIM	PSNR/SSIM	PSNR/SSIM	PSNR/SSIM
ZF	28.14/0.7838	25.99/0.7119	30.67/0.7848	28.84/0.7206	31.35/0.8186	30.38/0.7829
Recurrent VarNet [18]	29.49/0.8255	25.65/0.7134	30.40/0.7880	28.42/0.7237	32.44/0.8402	31.26/0.7983
VS-Net [2]	30.65/0.8431	26.71/0.7369	30.59/0.7810	28.76/0.7176	32.17/0.8269	30.82/0.7885
KIKI-net [3]	31.80/0.8617	27.42/0.7574	33.13/0.8286	30.36/0.7462	34.12/0.8564	32.65/0.8138
ISTA-Net [23]	31.94/0.8635	27.72/0.7649	32.43/0.8072	29.54/0.7320	33.73/0.8485	31.82/0.8013
ISTA-Net (PL) [5]	32.10/0.8698	27.66/0.7620	32.38/0.8067	29.56/0.7322	33.73/0.8501	31.59/0.7988
U-Net [21]	32.90/0.8884	27.90/0.7729	33.58/0.8318	30.79/0.7561	34.36/0.8596	32.67/0.8152
SwinMR [6]	33.22/0.8954	**28.43**/0.7853	33.65/0.8303	30.59/0.7508	34.38/0.8596	32.81/0.8157
Proposed (SSL)	**33.77/0.9056**	28.42/**0.8031**	**33.96/0.8359**	**30.90/0.7611**	**34.97/0.8651**	**32.97/0.8193**
Proposed (PL)	33.86/0.9065	28.71/0.8085	34.07/0.8358	30.97/0.7604	35.01/0.8656	33.08/0.8186
Proposed (SL)	36.16/0.9282	30.97/0.8495	35.09/0.8534	32.15/0.7837	36.01/0.8814	34.24/0.8393

The quantitative comparison of the proposed model with other models proposed for the Multi-Coil MRI image reconstruction is shown in Table 1. Our method outperforms other methods proposed for MRI reconstruction in PSNR and SSIM metrics on all three MRI sequences (coronal PD, coronal PDFS, and axial T2) in both 4× and 5× acceleration factors, except coronal PD with 5× acceleration in terms of PSNR. The proposed model outperforms the second-best model by 0.59 dB in PSNR and 0.0178 in SSIM, in the axial-T2 dataset for the acceleration factor of 4× and in coronal PD for the acceleration factor 5× respectively. It can be seen that in the parallel domain self-supervised training mode [5], the proposed model outperforms the ISTA-Net.

The qualitative comparison of our model with other models proposed for multi-coil MRI reconstruction for coronal PD, axial T2 dataset for acceleration factors of 4× and 5× are shown in Fig. 3(a), 3(b) respectively.

The reconstructions obtained through zero padding exhibit significant aliasing artifacts and lose important anatomical details. Although VS-Net, and Recurrent VarNet models are able to reduce the aliasing artifacts to some extent, the artifacts remain visible in the reconstructions. While the KIKI-net, U-Net, and ISTA-Net models are more effective in reducing the artifacts, they fall short in their ability to reconstruct the structures as accurately as transformer-based models. This can be attributed to their limited capability to capture long-range dependencies. Out of the transformer-based models, it can be seen that the proposed model reconstructs the image structures more accurately than the SwinMR transformer-based model. In Fig. 3(a), the SwinMR transformer-based model introduces some artifacts (region pointed to, by the blue arrow) in the

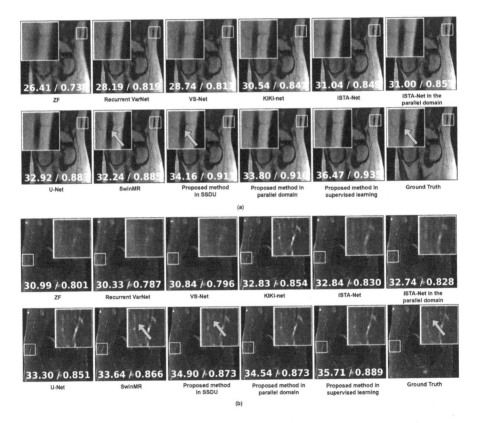

Fig. 3. (a). Coronal PD 4× acceleration. Blue arrows highlight some artifacts produced by SwinMR which is not present in the ground truth and in the result of the proposed model. (b). Coronal PDFS 4× acceleration. Blue arrows highlight the sharp reconstruction produced by the proposed method. (Color figure online)

image, which are not present in the ground truth. In Fig. 3(b), the proposed model recovers fine details better than the SwinMR model (as pointed to, by the blue arrow) when trained in self-supervised [5,17] or supervised techniques. From the results, it can be seen that increasing the receptive field by using dilated attention and complementing global information operations of transformers with fine-grained local contextual features from convolutions, positively impacts accelerated MRI image reconstruction.

3.2   Ablation Study

The impact of each block in the network is analyzed in Table 2. The results show that sparse attention blocks (SAB) significantly improve the model's performance. Dense attention block (DAB) individually performs better than SAB, but when they are combined together, they complement each other and provide the benefits of both attention methods. It can be seen that the locality-based enhancement improves the SSIM considerably, as it enables better capturing of local contextual features. This can be seen in Fig. 4.

Table 2. Comparison of different blocks in the model. The best results are highlighted in bold.

Architecture	PSNR/SSIM
CNN	31.80/0.8617
SAB	32.99/0.8863
DAB	33.10/0.8926
SAB + DAB w/o locality	33.47/0.8974
SAB + DAB	**33.77/.9056**

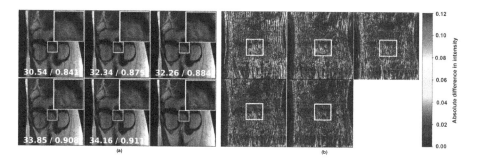

Fig. 4. (a) Qualitative comparison of different models (b). Residual map to highlight the difference. Images from left to right correspond to the output of CNN, SAB, DAB, SAB and DAB without locality, Proposed method, and ground truth respectively.

4   Conclusion

Our work increases the receptive field of the transformer without increasing the computational complexity and complements global information with local contextual features by integrating convolutions in transformers. We have trained the proposed model in a self-supervised manner to remove the necessity of fully sampled data. We have evaluated our model for the reconstruction of the multi-coil knee MRI datasets in three different acquisition protocols and show that the proposed architecture outperforms other methods. We show that the integration of local contextual features obtained from convolution, with global information obtained using dilated self-attention improves the performance of the image reconstruction.

References

1. Chen, Z., Zhang, Y., Gu, J., Kong, L., Yuan, X., et al.: Cross aggregation transformer for image restoration. Adv. Neural Inf. Process. Syst. **35**, 25478–25490 (2022)
2. Duan, J., et al.: VS-net: variable splitting network for accelerated parallel MRI reconstruction. In: Shen, D., et al. (eds.) MICCAI 2019. LNCS, vol. 11767, pp. 713–722. Springer, Cham (2019). https://doi.org/10.1007/978-3-030-32251-9_78
3. Eo, T., Jun, Y., Kim, T., Jang, J., Lee, H.J., Hwang, D.: Kiki-net: cross-domain convolutional neural networks for reconstructing undersampled magnetic resonance images. Magn. Reson. Med. **80**(5), 2188–2201 (2018)
4. Hammernik, K., et al.: Learning a variational network for reconstruction of accelerated MRI data. Magn. Reson. Med. **79**(6), 3055–3071 (2018)
5. Hu, C., Li, C., Wang, H., Liu, Q., Zheng, H., Wang, S.: Self-supervised learning for MRI reconstruction with a parallel network training framework. In: de Bruijne, M., et al. (eds.) MICCAI 2021. LNCS, vol. 12906, pp. 382–391. Springer, Cham (2021). https://doi.org/10.1007/978-3-030-87231-1_37
6. Huang, J., et al.: Swin transformer for fast MRI. Neurocomputing **493**, 281–304 (2022)
7. Kingma, D.P., Ba, J.: Adam: a method for stochastic optimization. arXiv preprint arXiv:1412.6980 (2014)
8. Li, Y., Zhang, K., Cao, J., Timofte, R., Van Gool, L.: Localvit: bringing locality to vision transformers. arXiv preprint arXiv:2104.05707 (2021)
9. Liang, J., Cao, J., Sun, G., Zhang, K., Van Gool, L., Timofte, R.: Swinir: image restoration using swin transformer. In: Proceedings of the IEEE/CVF International Conference on Computer Vision, pp. 1833–1844 (2021)
10. Ryu, K., Alkan, C., Choi, C., Jang, I., Vasanawala, S.: K-space refinement in deep learning mr reconstruction via regularizing scan specific spirit-based self consistency. In: 2021 IEEE/CVF International Conference on Computer Vision Workshops (ICCVW), pp. 3991–4000 (2021). https://doi.org/10.1109/ICCVW54120.2021.00446
11. Ryu, K., Alkan, C., Choi, C., Jang, I., Vasanawala, S.: K-space refinement in deep learning mr reconstruction via regularizing scan specific spirit-based self consistency. In: Proceedings of the IEEE/CVF International Conference on Computer Vision, pp. 4008–4017 (2021)

12. Schlemper, J., Caballero, J., Hajnal, J.V., Price, A., Rueckert, D.: A deep cascade of convolutional neural networks for MR image reconstruction. In: Niethammer, M., et al. (eds.) IPMI 2017. LNCS, vol. 10265, pp. 647–658. Springer, Cham (2017). https://doi.org/10.1007/978-3-319-59050-9_51

13. Sun, L., Fan, Z., Huang, Y., Ding, X., Paisley, J.: Compressed sensing mri using a recursive dilated network. In: Proceedings of the AAAI Conference on Artificial Intelligence, vol. 32 (2018)

14. Vaswani, A., et al.: Attention is all you need. Adv. Neural Inf. Process. Syst. **30** (2017)

15. Wang, Z., Cun, X., Bao, J., Zhou, W., Liu, J., Li, H.: Uformer: a general u-shaped transformer for image restoration. In: Proceedings of the IEEE/CVF Conference on Computer Vision and Pattern Recognition, pp. 17683–17693 (2022)

16. Wu, H., et al.: Cvt: introducing convolutions to vision transformers. In: Proceedings of the IEEE/CVF International Conference on Computer Vision, pp. 22–31 (2021)

17. Yaman, B., Hosseini, S.A.H., Moeller, S., Ellermann, J., Uğurbil, K., Akçakaya, M.: Self-supervised learning of physics-guided reconstruction neural networks without fully sampled reference data. Magn. Reson. Med. **84**(6), 3172–3191 (2020)

18. Yiasemis, G., Sonke, J.J., Sánchez, C., Teuwen, J.: Recurrent variational network: a deep learning inverse problem solver applied to the task of accelerated mri reconstruction. In: Proceedings of the IEEE/CVF Conference on Computer Vision and Pattern Recognition, pp. 732–741 (2022)

19. Yuan, K., Guo, S., Liu, Z., Zhou, A., Yu, F., Wu, W.: Incorporating convolution designs into visual transformers. In: Proceedings of the IEEE/CVF International Conference on Computer Vision, pp. 579–588 (2021)

20. Zamir, S.W., Arora, A., Khan, S., Hayat, M., Khan, F.S., Yang, M.H.: Restormer: efficient transformer for high-resolution image restoration. In: Proceedings of the IEEE/CVF Conference on Computer Vision and Pattern Recognition, pp. 5728–5739 (2022)

21. Zbontar, J., et al.: fastmri: an open dataset and benchmarks for accelerated MRI. arXiv preprint arXiv:1811.08839 (2018)

22. Zhang, J., Zhang, Y., Gu, J., Zhang, Y., Kong, L., Yuan, X.: Accurate image restoration with attention retractable transformer. arXiv preprint arXiv:2210.01427 (2022)

23. Zhang, J., Ghanem, B.: Ista-net: interpretable optimization-inspired deep network for image compressive sensing. In: Proceedings of the IEEE Conference on Computer Vision and Pattern Recognition, pp. 1828–1837 (2018)

24. Zhou, B., et al.: Dsformer: a dual-domain self-supervised transformer for accelerated multi-contrast MRI reconstruction. In: Proceedings of the IEEE/CVF Winter Conference on Applications of Computer Vision, pp. 4966–4975 (2023)

25. Zhou, B., Zhou, S.K.: Dudornet: learning a dual-domain recurrent network for fast MRI reconstruction with deep t1 prior. In: Proceedings of the IEEE/CVF Conference on Computer Vision and Pattern Recognition, pp. 4273–4282 (2020)

Robust Unsupervised Image to Template Registration Without Image Similarity Loss

Slim Hachicha, Célia Le, Valentine Wargnier-Dauchelle, and Michaël Sdika$^{(\boxtimes)}$

Univ. Lyon, INSA-Lyon, Université Claude Bernard Lyon 1, UJM-Saint Etienne, CNRS, Inserm, CREATIS UMR 5220, U1294, Lyon, France, Lyon, France
michael.sdika@creatis.insa-lyon.fr

Abstract. Although a giant step forward has been made in medical images analysis thanks to deep learning, good results still require a lot of tedious and costly annotations. For image registration, unsupervised methods usually consider the training of a network using classical registration dissimilarity metrics. In this paper, we focus on the case of affine registration and show that this approach is not robust when the transform to estimate is large. We propose an unsupervised method for the training of an affine image registration network without using dissimilarity metrics and show that we are able to robustly register images even when the field of view is significantly different in the image.

Keywords: image registration · unsupervised

1 Introduction

Image registration consists in finding a geometrical transformation to reposition an image, the moving image, in the spatial coordinate system of another image, the fixed image [5]. It has many applications such as longitudinal studies, studies on lung or cardiac motion or spatial normalization. In classical registration, an optimization problem is solved to minimize the dissimilarity between the fixed image and the moving image warped with the estimated transform [13]. The dissimilarity metric can be either geometrical or based on raw image intensities such as mutual information (MI) [9] to avoid the potentially unreliable and/or tedious geometric features extraction step. Typical problem of these optimization based methods is the lack of robustness to artifacts, to bad initialization or to the presence of abnormality as well as their long computation time.

Deep learning registration methods have also been investigated to cope with these limitations. Supervised methods [8,10,11] are indeed robust and efficient but require the ground truth transformation to be known for images in the training set. As ground truth transforms are often impossible to obtain, the training is

---

S. Hachicha and C. Le—The first two authors contributed equally to this work.

© The Author(s), under exclusive license to Springer Nature Switzerland AG 2023
Z. Xue et al. (Eds.): MILLanD 2023, LNCS 14307, pp. 148–157, 2023.
https://doi.org/10.1007/978-3-031-44917-8_14

done with either (potentially unrealistic) synthetic transforms, estimated transforms from (potentially unreliable) third party registration and sometimes using additional annotations (that can be tedious to get). In [1,7,14], the deep registration framework is unsupervised: classical registration dissimilarity losses such as MI are used to train the network. Most limits of classical registration are re-introduced. These issues are also present when the dissimilarity loss is learnt as in [2]. Most deep registration methods also use, as input tensor, the moving and fixed image concatenated in different channels. This approach is problematic as, for large displacements, first fine scale convolution layers of the network will attempt to create features from unrelated parts of the pair of images. This defect can be alleviated by using each image as an independent input of two networks as in [4]: a network estimates the position of some keypoints for each image. An affine transform is then fitted to make the positions of the keypoints match. The network is first trained using supervised training with synthetic affine transforms but then trained on real pairs of images with dissimilarity losses.

As far as we know, only in [12] is addressed the problem of unsupervised registration without image dissimilarity losses: the fixed and moving image are encoded with a separate encoder, a correlation matrix between local features is computed providing a rough displacement likelihood map for each cell and a robust fit finally outputs the estimated affine transformation matrix. Only a cycle consistency loss is used for the training. However, the computation of this correlation matrix and the subsequent fit can be computationally demanding, it cannot scale to deformable registration for example. Furthermore, as the correlation is computed with the features of the moving image before warping, these features need to be affine invariant: affine equivariant features would be more discriminative for registration.

In this paper, we propose a deep unsupervised registration method. The network only takes the moving image as input and directly outputs the affine transform to register it to a reference template. Pairwise registration can then be easily obtained by composition. For training, only unregistered images without any label are required and dissimilarity losses are not used. Our method is robust to the presence of strong artefacts or abnormalities and is robust to extreme rotations, translations, scaling or shearing. The main contributions are: 1/an unsupervised image registration method to train a network that directly outputs the affine transform of an image to an atlas 2/a two steps training procedure to enlarge the range of affine matrices that can be estimated to the most extreme cases, 3/a numerical evaluation showing the robustness of our approach even in the presence of large crops or occlusions.

2 Method

2.1 Unsupervised Registration to a Reference Template Without Dissimilarity Losses

Our goal is to train a neural network R whose input is an image I and the output is the transformation A such that $I \circ A$ is in the reference coordinate system. In other words, $I \circ R(I)$ is in the reference coordinate system. It is assumed that only a single image I_{ref} is in the reference coordinate system: $R(I_{\text{ref}}) = I_d$, all other images are neither registered nor labeled in any way. Pairwise registration is a straightforward consequence of template registration: once R is trained, the transform between a fixed image I_{fix} and a moving image I_{mov} is $R(I_{\text{mov}}) \circ [R(I_{\text{fix}})]^{-1}$.

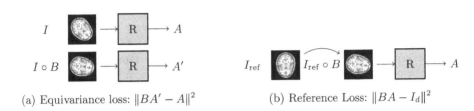

(a) Equivariance loss: $\|BA' - A\|^2$ (b) Reference Loss: $\|BA - I_d\|^2$

Fig. 1. Unsupervised registration equivariance and reference loss

Equivariance as an Unsupervised Registration Loss. As the network R registers all input images to the reference coordinate system, it should be affine equivariant. Indeed, for any input image I and transform B, the network should reposition $I \circ B$ in the reference coordinate system: $(I \circ B) \circ R(I \circ B)$ should always be registered. As $(I \circ B) \circ R(I \circ B) = I \circ (B \circ R(I \circ B)) = I \circ R(I)$, this means that for any image I and transform B, we should have:

$$B \circ R(I \circ B) = R(I). \tag{1}$$

This is a very strong structural prior of the task to solve, that is traditionally not enforced when learning registration networks. To enforce this property, for each image I of the training dataset, we draw a random affine transform B, and use the following equivariance loss (Fig. 1a):

$$L_{\text{equiv}} = \|B \circ R(I \circ B) - R(I)\|^2 \tag{2}$$

where the norm can by any matrix norm. Note that this is similar to the cycle consistency loss used in [12] for pairwise registration where their affine matrix is fitted from a correlation matrix.

The loss in Eq. 2 itself is not sufficient to train the network. First, at no point so far, the reference coordinate system was specified: at an extreme limit, equivariance could be enforced for each image independently. Second, an identically null network R will satisfy Eq. 1: some sort of regularization is required.

Regularization Loss. The regularization aims at discarding unrealistic affine transforms from the output of the neural network while retaining potentially large possible transforms. This loss L_{reg} is composed of two terms:

$$L_{\text{size}} = relu\left(\frac{1}{K} - \sigma\right) + relu(\sigma - K) \tag{3}$$

where σ are the singular values of the affine matrix predicted by the network and K is a scale hyperparameter and

$$L_{\text{anis}} = \|\log(\sigma_{\min}) - \log(\sigma_{\max})\|^2 \qquad (4)$$

where $\sigma_{\min}$ and $\sigma_{\max}$ are respectively the minimal and maximal singular value. The first term penalizes extreme size variations, the second term aims to avoid a too strong anisotropy. Translation or rotation are not penalized.

Reference Loss. We consider the unique reference image of the training dataset I_{ref}: $R(I_{\text{ref}}) = I_d$. For any affine transform B, Eq. 1 becomes $B \circ R(I_{\text{ref}} \circ B) = I_d$. Our reference loss is then (with any matrix norm) (Fig. 1b):

$$L_{\text{ref}} = \|B \circ R(I \circ B) - Id\|^2, \qquad (5)$$

where B is an affine transform randomly drawn during training.

One point is noticeable in our framework: at no point we need to compare pairs of images during the training. The reference image is fed through the network independently of all other images of the training dataset. No comparison is done between the warped image and the reference with a dissimilarity loss. No fit, that may potentially fail in some cases, need to be done between some sort of features of the moving and fixed images.

2.2 Increasing the Registration Range

Difference of field of view between the fixed and the moving images is a common registration failure reason. In order to increase the range of transformations our network is able to register, we propose a two-step training procedure. The network is first trained using our unsupervised framework on an unregistered training images that required moderate transformations to be registered. Once convergence is reached, this network is used to replace all the training images in the reference space. As all images are now registered, the network can then be trained using the loss L_{ref} with large affine parameters range on all the images of the training dataset. In the following, this training procedure will be referred as "two steps" method in opposition to the "one step" method without the supervised training with self registered images.

3 Experiments

3.1 Material and Methods

Image Data. The development of the algorithms was made using T2 brain images of the HCP database (https://www.humanconnectome.org/study/hcp-young-adult) that we split into 500 training subjects, 100 validation subjects, and 500 testing subjects. HCP images are provided registered together, we resample them to the 2 mm T1 MNI atlas that we used as the I_{ref} image. To simplify and shorten the development, the middle axial slice was extracted, resulting in a dataset of 2D 109×91 registered brain MRIs but nothing in the method limits its application to 3D images.

Evaluation Protocol. To mimic an unregistered dataset, a random affine trans-formation is applied to each image before it goes into the network. The said transformation is considered unknown during the training phase but known for the evaluation reporting. It also allows to control the transformation range for the unsupervised training phase described in Sect. 2.2. That transformation can be defined as the combination of four operations: translation, rotation, shear-ing and scaling. Several sets of hyperparameters ranges are considered in the experiments and are presented in Table 1. Note that the "easy" parameter range D_0 includes a full range of rotation.

Table 1. Affine transformation parameters range

	D_0	D_{trans}	D_{shear}	D_{scale}	D_1
Translation	± 10 pixels	± 54 pixels	± 10 pixels	± 10 pixels	± 54 pixels
Rotation	$\pm \pi$	$\pm \pi$	$\pm \pi$	$\pm \pi$	$\pm \pi$
Shearing	$\pm 10\%$	$\pm 10\%$	$\pm 50\%$	$\pm 10\%$	$\pm 50\%$
Scaling	$\pm 10\%$	$\pm 10\%$	$\pm 10\%$	$\pm 50\%$	$\pm 50\%$

During the testing phase, we apply to the registered images I_{test} a random affine transformation T' with a given parameters range of Table 1. As the ideal affine registration is the inverse of the random transform used to unregister the images, the following metrics are used for a transform T given by the network:

$$\text{Mat}_{err} = \|T \circ T' - Id\|^2 \quad \text{and} \quad \theta = \arccos \frac{tr(T \circ T')}{2}. \quad (6)$$

Robustness of the method is measured with θ_t defined as the percentage of images with a rotation error θ greater than t.

Implementation Details. The code is written in Pytorch/Monai. In our exper-iments, the network is implemented using the Monai class Regressor with six residual convolutional layers with respectively 8,16,32,64,128 and 256 channels. The convolution kernel sizes are 3×3 with the stride set to 1 for the first layer and set to 2 for the other layers. A PRELU is used after each convolutional layer. The output consists in the six coefficients of the affine transformation matrix. Note that the training is not sensitive to the hyperparameters K of L_{reg}: a value of $K = 4$ is sufficient to train the network and a scale change of 4 is already a huge global scale change between two subjects. Two matrix norms are evaluated for L_{ref}: the Froboenius norm (Frob) and the norm $\|A\| = \sum_i \|Ax_i\|$ where x_i are uniformly sampled in the image (denoted as Grid). A 3×3 grid is used here.

3.2   Results and Discussion

Ablation Study Using D_0 for the One Step Method. An ablation study was carried out to assess the importance of each loss in our one step method.

Table 2. Ablation study on the losses of our unsupervised one step method and comparison to state of the art on the D_0 parameters range.

Loss					Mat_{err}	θ_{90}	θ_{45}
L_{equiv}					1.68 ± 0.14	50.49	100.00
L_{equiv}		$+L_{size}$	$+L_{anis}$		2.18 ± 0.12	35.36	100.00
L_{equiv}		$+L_{size}$	$+L_{anis}$	$+MI$	2.56 ± 0.12	99.84	100.00
L_{equiv}	$+L_{ref}$				1.66 ± 0.13	33.39	100.00
L_{equiv}	$+L_{ref}$	$+L_{size}$			$\mathbf{0.45 \pm 0.29}$	**0.00**	**0.00**
L_{equiv}	$+L_{ref}$	$+L_{size}$	$+L_{anis}$		$\mathbf{0.45 \pm 0.27}$	**0.00**	**0.00**
L_{equiv}	$+L_{ref}$	$+L_{size}$	$+L_{anis}$	$+MI$	$\mathbf{0.39 \pm 0.26}$	**0.00**	**0.00**
				MI	3.63 ± 1.08	50.55	100.00
FSL flirt - MI					2.58 ± 1.21	49.22	98.08
supervized - L_{ref}					$\mathbf{0.32 \pm 0.22}$	**0.00**	**0.00**

Evaluation metrics for different setups are presented in Table 2 using D_0 as the affine parameters range for train and test. One can see that the combination of our three losses L_{ref}, L_{reg} and L_{equiv} is essential for our method to be robust. If one of these losses is missing, the rotation error θ_{45} will be higher than 93% and the use of MI does not help. When our three losses are used, θ_{45} drops to zero. One can also notice the very low value of Mat_{err} and that adding MI to our three losses does help here for the D_0 range of affine parameters. As a upper bound on the performance that can be achieved, a comparison was made with a model (supervized - L_{ref} trained with the L_{ref} loss used for all images (all registered) in the training dataset. Robustness error is null for this model. One can notice that Mat_{err} is the lowest for this model but our unsupervised model achieves a Mat_{err} error that is not too high compared to this upper bound model. Our results have also been compared to an unsupervised model trained only with the MI loss between the warped image and I_{ref} and to FSL - flirt [6]. As D_0 includes the full range of possible rotations, these two methods have a large rotation error. Indeed, due to the symmetry in brain images, the MI loss is not able to correctly handle large rotation. Despite this symmetry obstacle, our unsupervised method correctly register images with a full range of rotation.

Robustsness to Large Affine Parameters Ranges. To evaluate the ability of our unsupervised method to register images with large affine transforms, our model with our three losses (without MI) was trained with several affine parameter ranges for L_{ref} and L_{equiv}. Results are presented in Table 3. As already noticed, despite D_0 includes the full range of possible rotations, our method is able to correctly find the correct transform with no rotation error and a low Mat_{err}. Our method is also robust to large shear although Mat_{err} is higher in this case. One can also note that our method is more robust to an increase in range for the L_{ref} loss than for the L_{equiv} loss. This last point could be expected as L_{ref}

Table 3. Influence of the affine parameter range of the B matrix on our method

Range		Mat_{err}	θ_{90}	θ_{45}
L_{ref}	L_{equiv}			
D_0	D_0	0.41 ± 0.27	0.00	0.00
D_{shear}	D_{shear}	1.29 ± 0.68	0.00	0.00
D_{trans}	D_{trans}	2.96 ± 1.70	49.51	84.70
D_{scale}	D_{scale}	3.27 ± 0.58	83.39	83.39
D_1	D_0	20.33 ± 17.11	7.89	44.08
D_0	D_1	11.71 ± 6.06	46.71	86.68
D_1	D_1	12.08 ± 5.70	41.78	81.10

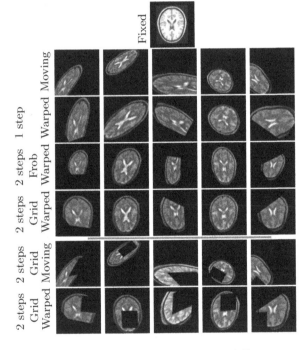

Fig. 2. Large affine transform registration: comparison with D_1 parameter range of our unsupervised one step method and our two steps method with differents losses in the second step. Results with/without occlusions.

is a supervised loss (but with only a single image). As a conclusion, although it is remarkable that a regular training of the network with L_{equiv}, L_{ref} and L_{reg} enables to obtain a robust template registration for large shear and rotation, it is not sufficient for general large affine transform and the training procedure of Sect. 2.2 should be used.

Table 4. Large affine transform registration: comparison with D_1 parameter range of our unsupervised one step method and our two steps method with differents losses in the second step, with and without occlusions.

Method	Mat_{err}	θ_{90}	θ_{45}
One step	12.08 ± 5.70	41.78	81.10
Two steps - MI	10.28 ± 5.59	38.98	56.09
Two steps - Frob	$\mathbf{1.88 \pm 0.90}$	0.49	8.55
Two steps - Grid	3.69 ± 3.54	**0.00**	**1.32**
Two step - Frob - w. occ	4.55 ± 4.68	3.78	18.91
Two step - Grid - w. occ	$\mathbf{3.79 \pm 3.67}$	**0.00**	**1.64**

Large Transform Registration with the Two Steps Training. In Table 4, a comparison of our one step and our two steps method is presented. The D_0 parameter range was used for the first step, D_1 was used for the second step and the evaluation. For the second step, the L_{ref} loss was implemented using either the Frob. or the Grid norm. A two steps method with MI in the second step was also evaluated. Large occlusions were also added during train and test to test the robustness to abnormalities.

One can see that both "one step" and "two steps with MI" are unable to correctly register the images for the D_1 range of affine parameters. In contrast, the robustness error drops considerably for our two steps approaches with both Frob. or Grid matrix norm. Note that although Mat_{err} is lower for Frob, both θ_{45} and θ_{90} are lower with Grid. Superiority of Grid for the training is confirmed by visual inspection: one can clearly see in Fig. 2, that "two steps - Grid" is the only method that correctly realign the images in the reference coordinate system despite the large initial misalignment, even for the extreme case where a large part of the image is cropped. Note that the superiority of Grid over Frob was also reported in [3] for homography estimation. Finally, one can see using both the quantitative metrics and the visual inspection, that the two steps procedure with the Grid norm is able to correctly register images when both large abnormalities are present on the image and the affine transform is very large.

4 Conclusion

In this paper, we proposed an unsupervised image registration method to train a network that directly outputs the affine transform of an image to an atlas. Our method does not rely on dissimilarity metrics but on three losses that enforce prior on the registration tasks: equivariance, invertibility of the output and the positioning of a unique given template. This simple method is able to robustly register when full range of rotation and large shear are present. For large translation, large scale change, a two steps training procedure is used to enlarge the range of affine matrixes that can be estimated to the most extreme cases.

Numerical evaluation shows the robustness of our approach even in the presence of large crops or occlusions. In a future work, we plan to extend our approach to the deformable registration case.

Acknowledgments. This work was supported by the LABEX PRIMES (ANR-11-LABX-0063) of Université de Lyon, by the "Projet Emergence" CNRS-INS2I APID-IFF, by the INSA BQR SALVE and by the France Life Imaging network (ANR-11-INBS-0006). Experiments were carried out using HPC resources from GENCI-IDRIS (AD011012544/AD011012589).

References

1. Balakrishnan, G., Zhao, A., Sabuncu, M.R., Guttag, J., Dalca, A.V.: Voxelmorph: a learning framework for deformable medical image registration. IEEE Trans. Med. Imaging **38**(8), 1788–1800 (2019)

2. Czolbe, S., Pegios, P., Krause, O., Feragen, A.: Semantic similarity metrics for image registration. Med. Image Anal. **87**, 102830 (2023). https://doi.org/10.1016/j.media.2023.102830

3. DeTone, D., Malisiewicz, T., Rabinovich, A.: Deep image homography estimation. In: RSS Workshop: Are the Sceptics Right? Limits and Potentials of Deep Learning in Robotics (2016)

4. Evan, M.Y., Wang, A.Q., Dalca, A.V., Sabuncu, M.R.: Keymorph: robust multi-modal affine registration via unsupervised keypoint detection. In: Medical Imaging with Deep Learning (2022)

5. Hill, D., Batchelor, P., Holden, M., Hawkes, D.: Medical image registration. Phys. Med. Biol. **46**, R1–45 (2001). https://doi.org/10.1088/0031-9155/46/3/201

6. Jenkinson, M., Bannister, P., Brady, M., Smith, S.: Improved optimization for the robust and accurate linear registration and motion correction of brain images. Neuroimage **17**(2), 825–841 (2002)

7. Li, H., Fan, Y.: Non-rigid image registration using self-supervised fully convolutional networks without training data. In: 2018 IEEE 15th International Symposium on Biomedical Imaging (ISBI 2018), pp. 1075–1078. IEEE (2018)

8. Liao, R., et al.: An artificial agent for robust image registration. Proceedings of the AAAI Conference on Artificial Intelligence, vol. 31, no. 1 (2017). https://doi.org/10.1609/aaai.v31i1.11230

9. Mattes, D., Haynor, D.R., Vesselle, H., Lewellyn, T.K., Eubank, W.: Nonrigid multimodality image registration. In: Medical Imaging 2001: Image Processing, vol. 4322, pp. 1609–1620. Spie (2001)

10. Miao, S., Wang, Z.J., Liao, R.: Real-time 2d/3d registration via cnn regression (2016)

11. Rohé, M.-M., Datar, M., Heimann, T., Sermesant, M., Pennec, X.: SVF-net: learning deformable image registration using shape matching. In: Descoteaux, M., Maier-Hein, L., Franz, A., Jannin, P., Collins, D.L., Duchesne, S. (eds.) MICCAI 2017. LNCS, vol. 10433, pp. 266–274. Springer, Cham (2017). https://doi.org/10.1007/978-3-319-66182-7_31

12. Siebert, H., Hansen, L., Heinrich, M.P.: Learning a metric for multimodal medical image registration without supervision based on cycle constraints. Sensors **22**(3), 1107 (2022)

13. Sotiras, A., Davatzikos, C., Paragios, N.: Deformable medical image registration: a survey. IEEE Trans. Med. Imaging **32**(7), 1153–1190 (2013). https://doi.org/10. 1109/TMI.2013.2265603
14. de Vos, B.D., Berendsen, F.F., Viergever, M.A., Sokooti, H., Staring, M., Išgum, I.: A deep learning framework for unsupervised affine and deformable image registration. Med. Image Anal. **52**, 128–143 (2019)

A Dual-Branch Network with Mixed and Self-Supervision for Medical Image Segmentation: An Application to Segment Edematous Adipose Tissue

Jianfei Liu$^{(\boxtimes)}$, Omid Shafaat, and Ronald M. Summers

Imaging Biomarkers and Computer-Aided Diagnosis Laboratory, Radiology and Imaging Sciences, Clinical Center, National Institutes of Health, Bethesda, MD, USA
`jianfei.liu@nih.gov`

Abstract. In clinical applications, one often encounters reduced segmentation accuracy when processing out-of-distribution (OOD) patient data. Segmentation models could be leveraged by utilizing either transfer learning or semi-supervised learning on a limited number of strong labels from manual annotation. However, over-fitting could potentially arise due to the small data size. This work develops a dual-branch network to improve segmentation on OOD data by also applying a large number of weak labels from inaccurate results generated by existing segmentation models. The dual-branch network consists of a shared encoder and two decoders to process strong and weak labels, respectively. Mixed supervision from both labels not only transfers the guidance from the strong decoder to the weak one, but also stabilizes the strong decoder. Additionally, weak labels are iteratively replaced with the segmentation masks from the strong decoder by self-supervision. We illustrate the proposed method on the adipose tissue segmentation of 40 patients with edema. Image data from edematous patients are OOD for existing segmentation methods, which often induces under-segmentation. Overall, the dual-branch segmentation network yielded higher accuracy than two baseline methods; the intersection over union (IoU) improved from 60.1% to 71.2% ($p < 0.05$). These findings demonstrate the potential of the dual-branch segmentation network with mixed- and self-supervision to process the OOD data in clinical applications.

Keywords: Self-supervision · Mixed supervision · Dual-branch · Residual U-Net · Edema

1 Introduction

Deep learning has proven successful for medical image segmentation [3], especially for supervised segmentation in which anatomical structures are fully labeled. The recent development of nnU-Net [4] provides a systematic approach for supervised medical image segmentation. It can accurately segment over

© The Author(s), under exclusive license to Springer Nature Switzerland AG 2023
Z. Xue et al. (Eds.): MILLanD 2023, LNCS 14307, pp. 158–167, 2023.
https://doi.org/10.1007/978-3-031-44917-8_15

100 anatomical structures on CT images [13]. However, in clinical applications, existing segmentation methods often fail on out-of-distribution (OOD) diseased data. One important clinical application is the segmentation of adipose tissue in patients with edema (Fig. 1) [2]. Edema is swelling characterized by fluid retention within subcutaneous tissue. Adipose tissue can be accurately segmented on patients without edema by the residual U-Net [8] (Fig. 1). However, if edema is present, the subcutaneous fat tends to be under-segmented.

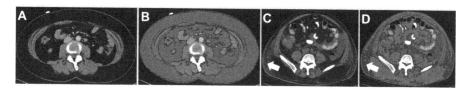

Fig. 1. Comparison of adipose tissue segmentation on patients with and without edema. (A) Adipose tissue manifests as homogenous regions in patients without edema. (B) These homogeneous regions can be easily segmented. (C) In contrast, edema presents as substantial heterogeneity (arrow) that is out-of-distribution (OOD) leading to (D) under-segmentation.

Transfer learning is often used to expand model generality on OOD data. The application to image segmentation is to fine-tune decoder weights on a small number of strong labels from manual annotation [5]. It assumes that feature maps from the frozen encoder are general enough to represent OOD data, which could potentially arise over-fitting issue. Semi-supervised learning [1] is another approach to handle a few strong labels, such as the dual-network structures through cross-teaching [11], mean-teacher [15], and multi-task training [12]. The segmentation accuracy could be further improved if weak labels, such as scribble, are added [7,10]. It is also called mixed supervision because both supervised and weakly-supervised labels are used. Dual-branch network is often used for mixed supervision with a shared encoder and two decoders to process strong and weak labels, respectively [9]. It is so effective that even training only with weak labels for both decoders can still generate reasonable segmentation results [10]. The segmentation accuracy could be further improved by using strong labels and enforcing consistent segmentation masks between strong and weak decoders [7].

However, all these methods [7,9,10,14] still need manual annotations to create weak labels, such as scribbles. Instead, weak labels in this work were automatically created from existing segmentation methods (Fig. 1D) [6]. It combines thresholding and level set segmentation methods to create weak labels. During training, they were iteratively updated with the segmentation masks from the strong decoder in a self-supervision way. Last but not least, the encoder and decoders of the dual-branch network are backboned with the residual U-Net [17]. A combinatorial loss of cross entropy and Dice coefficient functions is utilized to leverage the segmentation accuracy. All these improvement helps to accurately segment adipose tissue on the OOD patient data with edema, where weak labels are created from existing segmentation models that fail to process them.

2   Methodology

Figure 2 shows the overview of the dual-branch network. It has a shared encoder backboned with the residual U-Net, and two duplicated decoders to process strong labels $D_s = (\mathbf{X}_i^s, \mathbf{Y}_i^s)_N$ and weak labels $D_w = (\mathbf{X}_i^w, \mathbf{Y}_i^w)_M$, respectively. $\mathbf{X}_i^s \in \mathbb{R}^\Omega$ is the i-th image and $\mathbf{Y}_i^s \in \{0, 1\}^\Omega$ is its manually labeled mask. $\mathbf{Y}_i^w$ is the segmentation mask of $\mathbf{X}_i^w$, which is automatically generated by an adipose tissue segmentation method [8] (Fig. 1D). Here, $M \gg N$.

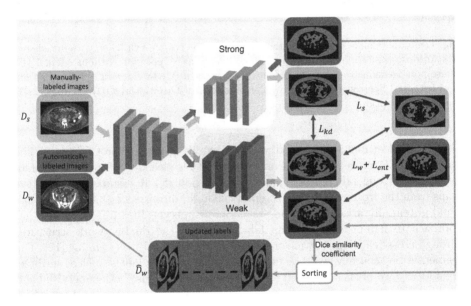

Fig. 2. Overview of dual-branch network to segment edematous adipose tissue on CT images. It has a shared encoder from a residual U-Net to extract feature maps, and two duplicated strong and weak decoders to process strong and weak labels, D_s and D_w. Two pipelines to process D_s and D_w are highlighted in green and red, respectively. The dual-branch network is optimized by a combinatory loss of data terms L_s and L_w, a cross training term L_{kd}, and a Shannon-entropy term L_{ent}. Self-supervision (cyan path) iteratively improves D_w with the segmentation masks from the strong decoder. The process starts with calculating Dice similarity coefficient (DSC) between the masks from strong and weak decoders. The masks from the strong encoder are then sorted according to DSC. Finally, the ones with high DSC values are selected to form the updated $\hat{D}_w$. (Color figure online)

The dual-branch segmentation network has three data processing pipelines. The pipeline to process strong labels is highlighted in green, and the one for weak labels is in red. The pipeline of self-supervision in cyan iteratively updates weak labels D_w with more accurate labels $\hat{D}_w$ from the strong decoder. We elaborate these pipelines in below.

2.1   Mixed Supervision for Dual-Branch Network Training

The purpose of this step is to train the dual-branch segmentation network in the green and red pipelines. D_s and D_w are processed separately for edematous adipose tissue segmentation in these two pipelines.

The first term L_{sup} in the loss function is to utilize the input data labels to train the dual-branch network. L_{sup} contains two components, including L_s to train both strong and weak decoders by $D_s = (\mathbf{X}_i^s, \mathbf{Y}_i^s)_N$ and L_w to only train the weak decoder by $D_w = (\mathbf{X}_i^w, \mathbf{Y}_i^w)_M$. Let $\mathbf{Z}_i^{s,s} \in [0,1]^\omega$ and $\mathbf{Z}_i^{w,s} \in [0,1]^\omega$ be the segmentation masks of an image $\mathbf{X}_i^s \in D_s$ from strong and weak decoders, respectively. $\mathbf{Z}_i^{s,w} \in [0,1]^\omega$ and $\mathbf{Z}_i^{w,w} \in [0,1]^\omega$ are the masks of the image $\mathbf{X}_i^w \in D_w$. Both L_s and L_w are defined as the combination of binary cross entropy and Dice coefficient loss.

$$L_{sup} = L_s + L_w = \sum_{i=1}^{N} (F(\mathbf{Y}_i^s, \mathbf{Z}_i^{s,s}) + F(\mathbf{Y}_i^s, \mathbf{Z}_i^{w,s})) + \sum_{j=1}^{M} F\left(\mathbf{Y}_j^w, \mathbf{Z}_j^{w,w}\right) \quad (1)$$

where

$$F(\mathbf{Y}_i, \mathbf{Z}_i) = -\frac{1}{2}\left(\mathbf{Y}_i \log \mathbf{Z}_i - (1 - \mathbf{Y}_i)1 - \log(\mathbf{Z}_i)\right) - \frac{2\mathbf{Y}_i \mathbf{Z}_i}{\mathbf{Y}_i^2 + \mathbf{Z}_i^2} \quad (2)$$

The second term L_{kd} is to is to ensure the segmentation masks of the same image generated by the strong and weak decoders to be consistent for both D_s and D_w. In other words, $Z_i^{s,s}$ and $Z_i^{w,s}$ should be similar, so are $Z_i^{s,w}$ and $Z_i^{w,w}$. The Kullback-Leibler divergence is used to compare two segmentation masks.

$$K(\mathbf{Z}_i^s, \mathbf{Z}_i^w) = \mathbf{Z}_i^{sT} \log \frac{\mathbf{Z}_i^s}{\mathbf{Z}_i^w} \quad (3)$$

Here, T denotes the transpose operator and

$$L_{kd} = \sum_{i=1}^{N} K(\mathbf{Z}_i^{s,s}, \mathbf{Z}_i^{w,s}) + \sum_{j=1}^{M} K(\mathbf{Z}_j^{s,w}, \mathbf{Z}_j^{w,w}) \quad (4)$$

The last term L_{ent} is to encourages high confidence of the segmentation masks from the weak decoder. The weak decoder is primarily trained by weak labels. It causes inaccurate segmentation masks potentially with low probability values. The Shannon-entropy minimization is used to leverage the probability values of the segmentation mask from the weak decoder.

$$L_{ent} = -\sum_{i=1}^{N} \mathbf{Z}_i^{s,wT} \log \mathbf{Z}_i^{s,w} - \sum_{j=1}^{M} \mathbf{Z}_j^{w,wT} \log \mathbf{Z}_j^{w,w} \quad (5)$$

Combining Eqs. 1, 4, and 5 leads to the final loss function.

$$L = L_{sup} + \lambda_1 L_{kd} + \lambda_2 L_{ent} \tag{6}$$

Here, $\lambda_1 = 0.001$ and $\lambda_2 = 1$ are two constant weights to balance different loss terms. Minimizing Eq. 6 can conduct mixed supervision of strong and weak labels to train green and red pipelines in Fig. 2.

2.2 Self-Supervision for Updating Weak Labels

Weak labels D_w were initially created on the OOD patient data with edema (Fig. 1D) by a segmentation model that are trained on the patients without edema. The weak decoder trained by inaccurate D_w is prone to causing segmentation errors. In contrast, the strong decoder is trained on D_s from manual annotation and it is high likely to generate accurate adipose tissue segmentation. It motivates to iteratively update D_w with the segmentation masks from the strong decoder. The updating pipeline is highlighted in cyan in Fig. 2.

We select the segmentation mask $\mathbf{Z}_i^{s,w}$ to replace the existing weak label $\mathbf{Y}_j^w$ if $\mathbf{Z}_i^{w,w}$ is consistent with $\mathbf{Z}_i^{s,w}$. It means that $\mathbf{Z}_i^{s,w}$ is stable to both decoders, which is more likely because $\mathbf{Z}_i^{s,w}$ is close to the actual segmentation masks. Based on this assumption, we first calculate the Dice similarity coefficient (DSC) values of $\mathbf{Z}_i^{s,w}$ and $\mathbf{Z}_i^{w,w}$, and DSC values are then sorted. $\mathbf{Z}_i^{s,w}$ with high DSC value is kept formulating new weak labels $\hat{D}_w$ according to a truncation ratio. In this work, D_w is empirically updated every 3 epochs considering 10 epochs total are used to train the dual-branch network. In Fig. 3, the missing adipose tissue regions (yellow arrows) due to edema are gradually recovered by using the segmentation masks from the strong decoder at different epochs. Iterative self-supervision not only improves the segmentation accuracy, but also reduces the training time as some inaccurate weak labels are eliminated.

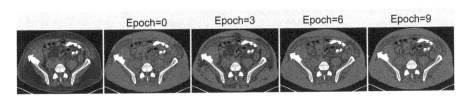

Fig. 3. Self-supervision process of enhancing adipose tissue regions (yellow arrows) from the strong decoder at different training epochs. The original weak label is illustrated at epoch = 0. (Color figure online)

Once the dual-branch segmentation network is trained, the segmentation mask $\mathbf{Z}^s$ from the strong decoder is used for inference on the testing images.

2.3   Dataset and Validation Methods

A total of 150 contrast-enhanced CT scans were collected from 150 unique patients with edema. The image spacing and slice thickness ranges from 0.66 mm to 0.98 mm, and 0.5 mm to 1 mm, respectively. The number of slices spans from 273 to 903. Among them, 50 CT scans were randomly selected, and 5–10 slices were also randomly picked to manually annotate in each scan. The process of manual annotation involves thresholding the CT slice and cleaning non-edematous regions by ITK-SNAP [16]. Annotated CT slices from 10 annotated CT scans were used to create strong labels D_s. The remaining 40 annotated scans were used to validate the segmentation accuracy. Adipose tissue from 100 unannotated CT scans were automatically extracted by an existing segmentation model. They were used to create weak labels D_w with 61,011 CT slices. We used three segmentation metrics to evaluate accuracy: intersection over union (IoU), Dice similarity coefficient (DSC), absolute volume difference (AVD).

Three types of experiments were designed to determine the setup of D_s and D_w as well as to evaluate the segmentation accuracy of the dual-branch network. Firstly, we created three types of D_s with 65 slices from 5 CT scans, 95 slices from 8 CT scans, and 116 slices from 10 CT scans. The comparison of segmentation accuracy helped to select the number of strong labels in D_s. Secondly, we tested three truncation ratios of self-supervised learning to reduce the number of images in D_w by 20%, 50%, and 80%. The larger the value, the smaller number of weak labels were kept in each iterative update. Lastly, we compared the proposed dual-branch network with mixed and self-supervision (DBMS) against two baseline approaches, transfer learning (TF) [5] and conventional dual-branch method (DB) [7]. TF was trained on the same strong labels D_s that was also used by DBMS. DB was also trained on the same D_s and D_w.

3   Experimental Results

3.1   Training Dataset Determination

Table 1 shows that the strong labels increase segmentation accuracy. D_s with 116 images achieved the best segmentation accuracy. IoU, DSC, and AVD of D_s with 116 images were all not statistically significantly better than D_s with 65 and 95 images ($p > 0.05$). However, IoU already achieved 68.7% with only 5 CT volumes, and the addition of five more volumes only improved it to 71.2%. Such marginal accuracy increase has the cost of more manual annotations. This result suggests that ten labeled CT volumes are a good starting point.

Regarding the number of weak labels in D_w, it was surprising that IoU dropped to 57.6% after 80% of D_w were removed although these labels have segmentation errors. It increased to 69.5% after 50% were removed and continually climbed to 71.2% after 20% in Table 2. IoU, DSC, and AVD for the truncation ratio of 20% were all statistically significantly better than for the ratio of 80% ($p < 0.05$). However, only IoU for the ratio of 20% is better than for the ratio of 50% ($p = 0.04$). Still, it was only a marginal improvement (2%)

Table 1. Edematous adipose tissue segmentation accuracy versus number of strong labels in D_s.

# labeled images	IoU (%)	DSC (%)	AVD (%)
65	68.7 ± 14.7	80.5 ± 11.2	**18.0 ± 21.5**
95	70.4 ± 17.4	81.1 ± 15.0	26.7 ± 41.3
116	**71.2 ± 16.1**	**81.9 ± 13.4**	19.4 ± 23.4

Data are (mean ± SD). Bold font indicates best result.

of IoU after less than 50% of weak labels were removed. Therefore, D_s is empirically set with 116 CT images from 10 CT volumes, and the truncation ratio of D_w is 20%.

Table 2. Edematous adipose tissue segmentation accuracy versus truncation ratios for D_w.

Truncation ratio	IoU (%)	DSC (%)	AVD (%)
20%	**71.2 ± 16.1**	**81.9 ± 13.4**	**19.4 ± 23.4**
50%	69.5 ± 18.8	80.3 ± 16.5	26.1 ± 43.0
80%	57.6 ± 15.9	71.7 ± 13.9	26.1 ± 20.3

Data are (mean ± SD). Bold font indicates best result.

3.2   Segmentation Accuracy Evaluation

Table 3 compared the segmentation accuracy between two baseline approaches, TF [5] and DB [7], with the proposed DBMS method. DBMS outperformed both baseline approaches ($p < 0.01$).

Table 3. Edematous adipose tissue segmentation accuracy for proposed and two baseline approaches.

Methods	IoU (%)	DSC (%)	AVD (%)
TF	67.2 ± 17.2	78.9 ± 15.5	32.7 ± 55.9
DB	60.1 ± 15.4	73.9 ± 13.5	23.2 ± 19.6
DBMS	**71.2 ± 16.1**	**81.9 ± 13.4**	**19.4 ± 23.4**

Data are (mean ± SD). Bold font indicates best result.

Figure 4 illustrated the segmentation results from TF, DB, and DBMS on three patients. TF and DB still left parts of edematous adipose tissue regions with holes while they were successfully segmented by DBMS (Fig. 4C1–4E1).

TF missed part of subcutaneous adipose tissue region while DB missed visceral adipose tissue region in the abdomen of the second patient (Fig. 4C2–4E2). The same errors also occurred in the pelvis of the third patient. In contrast, DBMS successfully segmented adipose tissue region in all three cases.

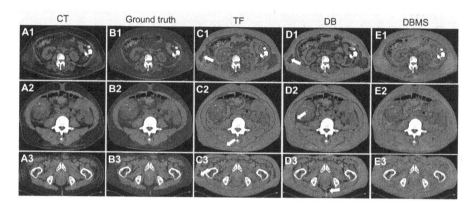

Fig. 4. Comparison of edematous adipose tissue segmentation results using transfer learning (TF), dual-branch network (DB), and the proposed dual-branch with mixed and self-supervision (DBMS). Each row corresponds to a different patient. Both TF and DB methods failed to cover edema regions in the first patient; the regions were successfully segmented by DBMS. TF missed some edema regions, while DB under-segmented visceral tissue in both second and third rows. DBMS achieved the highest segmentation accuracy in comparison with TF and DB.

4 Conclusion and Future Work

This paper introduces a dual-branch network with mixed and self-supervision for the segmentation of OOD data. The method starts by using a segmenter trained on patients without edema. The weak labels produced by this segmenter are combined with a limited number of strong labels from manual annotation. The weak labels are then iteratively self-improved. The combination of mixed and self-supervision outperformed both transfer learning and the original dual-branch method. The proposed method is a general framework for the segmentation of OOD data. Future work includes a comparison with existing supervised adipose tissue segmentation methods [8,13] to show its efficacy on OOD data. We expect that it can be readily applied to other complex medical image segmentation problems that are poorly addressed by existing approaches.

Acknowledgments. This research was supported by the Intramural Research Program of the National Institutes of Health Clinical Center.

References

1. Cheplygina, V., de Bruijne, M., Pluim, J.P.: Not-so-supervised: a survey of semi-supervised, multi-instance, and transfer learning in medical image analysis. Med. Image Anal. **54**, 280–296 (2019)
2. Having, K., Bullock, S.: Fetal anasarca. J. Diagn. Med. Sonography **27**(1), 19–25 (2011)
3. Hesamian, M.H., Jia, W., He, X., Kennedy, P.: Deep learning techniques for medical image segmentation: achievements and challenges. J. Dig. Imaging **32**, 582–596 (2019)
4. Isensee, F., Jaeger, P.F., Kohl, S.A.A., Petersen, J., Maier-Hein, K.H.: nnu-net: a self-configuring method for deep learning-based biomedical image segmentation. Nat. Methods **18**, 203–211 (2020)
5. Karimi, D., Warfield, S.K., Gholipour, A.: Transfer learning in medical image segmentation: new insights from analysis of the dynamics of model parameters and learned representations. Artif. Intell. Med. **116**, 102078 (2021)
6. Lee, S.J., Liu, J., Yao, J., Kanarek, A., Summers, R.M., Pickhardt, P.J.: Fully automated segmentation and quantification of visceral and subcutaneous fat at abdominal ct: application to a longitudinal adult screening cohort. Br. J. Radiol. **91**(1089), 20170968 (2018)
7. Liu, B., Desrosiers, C., Ayed, I.B., Dolz, J.: Segmentation with mixed supervision: confidence maximization helps knowledge distillation. Med. Image Anal. **83**, 102670 (2023)
8. Liu, J., Shafaat, O., Summers, R.M.: Development of multiscale 3d residual u-net to segment edematous adipose tissue by leveraging annotations from non-edematous adipose tissue. In: The 18th International Symposium on Medical Information Processing and Analysis (2022)
9. Luo, W., Yang, M.: Semi-supervised semantic segmentation via strong-weak dual-branch network. In: Vedaldi, A., Bischof, H., Brox, T., Frahm, J.-M. (eds.) ECCV 2020. LNCS, vol. 12350, pp. 784–800. Springer, Cham (2020). https://doi.org/10.1007/978-3-030-58558-7_46
10. Luo, X., Hu, M., Liao, W., Zhai, S., Song, T., Wang, G., Zhang, S.: Scribblesupervised medical image segmentation via dual-branch network and dynamically mixed pseudo labels supervision. In: International Conference on Medical Image Computing and Computer-Assisted Intervention, vol. 13431, pp. 528–538 (2022). https://doi.org/10.1007/978-3-031-16431-6_50
11. Luo, X., Hu, M., Song, T., Wang, G., Zhang, S.: Semi-supervised medical image segmentation via cross teaching between cnn and transformer. In: International Conference on Medical Imaging with Deep Learning (2022)
12. Wang, D., et al.: A novel dual-network architecture for mixed-supervised medical image segmentation. Computer. Med. Imaging Graph. **89**, 101841 (2021)
13. Wasserthal, J., Meyer, M., Breit, H.C., Cyriac, J., Yang, S., Segeroth, M.: Totalsegmentator: robust segmentation of 104 anatomical structures in ct images (2022). https://doi.org/10.48550/ARXIV.2208.05868. https://arxiv.org/abs/2208.05868
14. Wu, Y., Xu, M., Ge, Z., Cai, J., Zhang, L.: Semi-supervised left atrium segmentation with mutual consistency training. In: de Bruijne, M., et al. (eds.) MICCAI 2021. LNCS, vol. 12902, pp. 297–306. Springer, Cham (2021). https://doi.org/10.1007/978-3-030-87196-3_28
15. Xiang, J., Qiu, P., Yang, Y.: Fussnet: fusing two sources of uncertainty for semi-supervised medical image segmentation. In: International Conference on Medical

Image Computing and Computer-Assisted Intervention, vol. 13438, pp. 481–491 (2022). https://doi.org/10.1007/978-3-031-16452-1_46

16. Yushkevich, P.A., et al.: User-guided 3D active contour segmentation of anatomical structures: significantly improved efficiency and reliability. Neuroimage **31**(3), 1116–1128 (2006)

17. Zhang, Z., Liu, Q., Wang, Y.: Road extraction by deep residual u-net. IEEE Geosci. Remote Sens. Lett. **15**(5), 749–753 (2018)

Weakly-Supervised, Semi-supervised, and Multitask Learning

Combining Weakly Supervised Segmentation with Multitask Learning for Improved 3D MRI Brain Tumour Classification

Sajith Rajapaksa[1], Khashayar Namdar[1,2], and Farzad Khalvati[1,2,3,4,5,6](✉)

[1] Neurosciences and Mental Health Research Program, The Hospital for Sick Children, Toronto, Canada
[2] Institute of Medical Science, University of Toronto, Toronto, Canada
farzad.khalvati@utoronto.ca
[3] Department of Medical Imaging, University of Toronto, Toronto, Canada
[4] Department of Computer Science, University of Toronto, Toronto, Canada
[5] Department of Mechanical and Industrial Engineering, University of Toronto, Toronto, Canada
[6] Vector Institute, Toronto, Canada

Abstract. Segmentation plays a crucial role in computer-aided medical image diagnosis, as it enables the models to focus on the region of interest (ROI) and improve classification performance. However, medical image datasets often lack segmentation masks due to cost. In this work, we have introduced a novel end-to-end pipeline that enhances classification by incorporating ROIs generated by a weakly supervised method as an auxiliary task in a deep multitask learning framework. We have demonstrated that our approach outperforms conventional methods that only rely on classification. By using weakly supervised segmentation, we are able to leverage pixel-wise information, which ultimately leads to improved classification performance.

Keywords: Weakly Supervised Learning · Multitask Learning · Tumour Classification · Brain Cancer

1 Introduction

To provide rapid and accurate patient care, computer-assisted diagnostic systems (CAD) are crucial in the radiology decision-making process. Deep learning techniques have demonstrated significant improvements in CADs. However, training these systems requires large and finely annotated datasets, including segmentation of regions of interest (ROIs) such as the tumour. Unfortunately,

Supplementary Information The online version contains supplementary material available at https://doi.org/10.1007/978-3-031-44917-8_16.

© The Author(s), under exclusive license to Springer Nature Switzerland AG 2023
Z. Xue et al. (Eds.): MILLanD 2023, LNCS 14307, pp. 171–180, 2023.
https://doi.org/10.1007/978-3-031-44917-8_16

acquiring such annotated datasets can be challenging due to manual annotation costs, inter- and intra-reader variability, and privacy regulations, which hinder the fast development of deep learning-based approaches in medical imaging [15]. These have resulted in an excellent opportunity to explore methods beyond fully supervised techniques. This study addresses two questions: A) Can 3D ROIs be extracted from a classifier that has only been trained using global labels, such as tumour type? B) Can the extracted ROIs enhance the classifier's performance on the same classification task?

To address the first question, we investigate weakly supervised semantic segmentation (WSSS). Through learning binary classification, the convolutional neural network (CNN) can also learn to focus on the ROI [9]. By perturbing regions in the input image and comparing the effect on the performance of the classification model with the non-perturbed classification, we can understand the model's reliance on a particular region, which may represent the ROI, such as tumour [12]. An iterative approach was recently proposed to obtain segmentation masks by perturbing segmented superpixels in the image [11]. The authors also showed that an optimal perturbation extracts the most helpful local information from the pre-trained classification model for a given image, which is referred to as the optimal local perturbation in this paper. However, since the proposed work is based on an iterative localized perturbation approach, it demands substantial computational resources. This work significantly improves the pipeline by replacing the iterative superpixel-based perturbation with an optimal global perturbation mask generation. This results in an iteration-less approach that generates a map indicating which regions are more relevant to the classification task (i.e., Relevance Maps). We apply the proposed method to brain tumour segmentation in 3D MRI and show that our method outperforms optimal local perturbations [11], local interpretable model-agnostic explanations (LIME) [12], and GradCAM [14].

As for the second question, this work proposes combining the optimal global perturbation WSSS method with deep multitask learning (dMTL). WSSS allows the use of globally annotated data, leveraging semantic segmentation to provide pixel-level annotations. By combining WSSS with multitask learning, the model can be jointly trained on both classification and segmentation tasks, leading to improved overall performance by leveraging the strengths of each task. This approach enables the classification model to benefit from the additional information provided by the segmentation task, helping to outperform traditional classification methods that rely on a single task.

In this work, we focus on classifying brain tumour types. Radiology-based methods aim to reduce the number of biopsies needed to plan treatment. As discussed earlier, deep learning-based CAD systems can provide more clinical insights. In that regard, we make two main contributions. First, we propose a novel end-to-end pipeline that utilizes global labels to generate weakly supervised ROIs and enhance the classification of brain tumour types. This is achieved by combining ROI candidates as auxiliary tasks within a multitask classification architecture. This approach helps improve the model's accuracy. Second, we introduce a novel objective function incorporating pre-trained binary classification to produce optimal perturbation masks containing important localized regions. This method generates masks that are optimal to highlight the most relevant features in the input data, which then are used to generate segmentation of ROI, with no need for manual ROI masks for training.

2   Methods

Dataset: The Multimodal Brain Tumour Segmentation Challenge 2020 dataset was used as our primary dataset [2–4,8]. 3D volumes of T1-weighted (T1w), T1-weighted with contrast enhancement (T1wCE), T2-weighted (T2w) and fluid-attenuated inversion recovery (FLAIR) sequences were available for each patient, along with tumour segmentation and type. The dataset included 369 3D scans, with 263 High-grade Glioma (HGG) and 106 Low-grade Glioma (LGG) classes, which included 133 in training, 19 in validation, 38 in test, maintaining a 60% HGG and 40% LGG tumour ratio. Each sequence was independently normalized using min-max normalization and then center-cropped to 128 × 128 × 128 volumes.

2.1   Overview

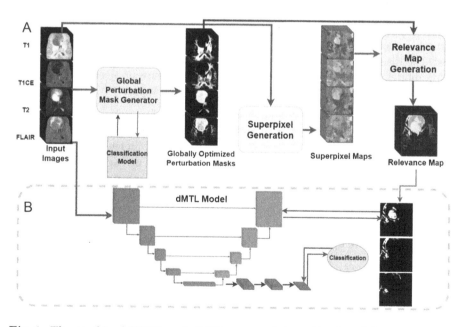

Fig. 1. The combined WSSS and dMTL approach is outlined as follows. Section A describes the WSSS pipeline, which extracts ranked ROI from MRI sequences. Section B then utilizes the generated ranked ROI as training data.

As shown in Fig. 1, this paper presents a two-part approach that combines dMTL and WSSS to improve the performance of brain tumour classification models. The first part involves candidate region generation, which utilizes relevance maps to generate ranked ROIs for input to a classification model [10]. This process generates ROIs without requiring manual ROI masks for training that can be used as input in the next phase. In the second part, we focus on the multitask classification model, training it with the generated ranked ROIs as auxiliary tasks. This approach enables us to leverage the benefits of both multitask learning and WSSS.

2.2 Candidate Region Generation

The candidate ROI generation algorithm includes two parts, as shown in Fig. 1A. The first is to generate whole image perturbation. We utilize a classification model only trained using tumour labels on the BraTS2020 dataset to generate a perturbation mask that is the most effective in changing the class probability. The second part is the Relevance Map generation. In this step, we create superpixel maps using the input images and assign the value of the perturbation mask to generate the ranked regions. This allows for using the top-ranking regions as the segmentation mask.

Whole Image Perturbation Generation. In this step, our objective is to generate a perturbation mask that will have the greatest effect on classification probability but will have the least change to the original input image. To accomplish this, we utilize a GAN-like approach [5] to train our generative model. First, the discriminator is replaced with a pre-trained 3D tumour-type classification model. The generator is then trained with our novel objective function to produce the optimal perturbation mask for the given input.

Objective Function. We introduce a novel objective function, modified perturbation loss, which maximizes the difference between the classification probability (generated by the pre-trained model) of the perturbed image and the original image, combined with L1 loss and Indecisive penalty. For each batch, the loss is calculated by applying (multiplying) the generated perturbations mask onto the original MRI and generating a classification using the pre-trained model. Then we calculate the difference between the predictions of perturbed and non-perturbed images to determine the effectiveness of that generated perturbation. In the following, we explain each component of the loss function in detail.

Perturbation Loss. $\frac{1}{n}\sum_{i=1}^{n} log(\frac{1}{|y_p - y_{np}|})$ Where p means perturbed, and np is non-perturbed, n is the number of samples, and y is the highest probability of the given class derived from the pre-trained classifier. The goal of the perturbation loss penalty is to encourage the generator model to confuse the pre-trained classification model. Therefore, we calculate the difference between the predicted classification for the perturbed and non-perturbed image as the score. Then we take the log of the inverse of that score as we look to minimize the loss score.

L1 Loss. $\frac{1}{n}\sum_{i=1}^{n}|MRI_p - MRI_{np}|$ Where MRI_p is the perturbation-applied MRI volume and MRI_{np} is the original MRI volume. During the initial experimentation, we observed that perturbation loss alone was not able to generate localized perturbation regions. To ensure we generated images that are more than random noise, we incorporated the L1 loss. L1 loss or Least Absolute Deviation loss minimizes the sum error of the two given images. This forces the model to learn to generate a perturbation map with the least amount of change to the original image, thus learning more localized regions. In the context of an adversely generative model, this acts as the minimizing element.

Indecisive Penalty. $\frac{1}{n}\sum_{i=1}^{n}(-\alpha(y_p - \beta)^2 + \delta)$ Where α, β and δ are hyperparameters for the parabolic function based on experiments and y_p is the probability of a given class using generated perturbed input. After the initial experimentation, we observed the model training would plateau once it learned to predict at the center point (pretrained classification predicting 0.5). To penalize this behaviour, we introduced indecisive loss, which is a parabolic function with the highest penalty at the center point, which encourages the model to move towards 0 or 1.

Final Loss Function

$$\frac{1}{n}(\sum_{i=1}^{n}log(\frac{1}{|y_p - y_{np}|}) + \sum_{i=1}^{n}-\alpha(y_p - \beta)^2 + \delta + \sum_{i=1}^{n}|MRI_p - MRI_{np}|) \qquad (1)$$

The final loss function is the sum of the indecisive penalty, L1 loss, and perturbation loss.

Generator. We selected a modified U-Net [13] architecture as our generator model. The model was modified to have a lower-dimensional bottleneck to reduce the likelihood of forming an identity function. The model was then trained with the input of $128 \times 128 \times 128 \times 4$ MRI volumes to output a mask with the same shape. Using the previously discussed loss function, the model was trained with a learning rate of 0.1 and Adam optimizer [7] for 200 epochs.

Classifier. We selected a 3D ResNet [6] model as our classification architecture. The model was trained with a learning rate of 0.01 and the Adam optimizer for 100 epochs using binary cross-entropy as the loss function on HGG vs LGG classification. The trained model at epoch 81 was selected for evaluation as it achieved the highest validation area under the ROC curve (AUC) of 0.86. The model achieved an AUC of 0.83 on the test set.

Relevance Map Generation. First, we generated the optimal perturbation mask for a given MRI scan, as described above. Next, we used the SLIC algorithm [1] to produce a superpixel map for each MRI sequence. For every superpixel, we computed the sum of voxel values within the region of the previously generated perturbation mask. Subsequently, we combined all the MRI sequences by adding the volumes together to form a single 3D volume. Then after normalization, we used binning to generate ranked regions from the combined superpixel maps. This enables us to identify the top-ranking regions as the candidate ROI, which are most relevant to a given classification.

2.3   Multitask Learning Architecture

We propose a multitask learning architecture with a U-Net and a classifier combined, shown in Fig. 1B. The inputs to our model are multimodal 3D volumes of brain MRI sequences (T1, T1CE, T2, and FLAIR). This allows our model to make use of the complementary information provided by each modality to improve performance. At the end of the encoder, our architecture is split into two sections: one for classification (3 fully connected layers) and one for segmentation (standard U-net decoder). The classification section uses convolutional layers to extract features from the input data, while the segmentation section uses upsampling to generate pixel-level annotations. As the segmentation output, we allow the model to output N separate masks, where N is determined by the number of ranked ROIs used to train the model. For example, if we include three ranked ROIs, our model will output three separate masks. The model is trained using a multitask learning objective as described below, which allows the U-Net and the classifier to share knowledge and learn common features from the data. This allows our model to make use of the additional information provided by the segmentation task to improve the performance on the classification task.

Multitask Learning Objective. Our objective function or the multitask learning architecture is a combination of binary cross-entropy loss and dice loss, defined in Eq. 2. This allows us to improve both the segmentation and the classification at the same time. The final loss is calculated by taking the average loss of all segmentation tasks and summing it with the classification loss.

$$(w) * -(y \log(p) + (1-y) \log(1-p)) + (1-w) * \frac{1}{n} (\sum_{i=1}^{n} \frac{2|X \cap Y|}{|X| + |Y|}) \qquad (2)$$

where log is the natural log, y is the ground truth binary label for the classification task (0 or 1), and p is the predicted probability by the classifier of the given class. $|X|$ represents the predicted set of pixels as the segmentation mask, and $|Y|$ is the ground truth segmentation, which is the 3D relevance map in our WSSS-based method. As the segmentation output, we allow the model to output N separate masks. Where N is determined by the number of ranked ROIs used to train the model and w represents the weight given to the main task (between 0 and 1). We have selected classification as the main task, and therefore we have set the weight w to 0.8, giving the classification task loss more weight.

3   Experiments and Results

3.1   WSSS Method Evaluation

We perform the following evaluations to evaluate the effectiveness of the proposed WSSS method.

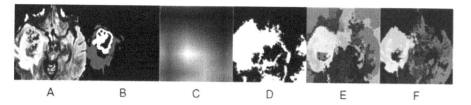

Fig. 2. Visual comparison of globally perturbed Relevance Maps (F) to the original image (A), expert annotation (B), GradCAM (C) [14], LIME (D) [12], and locally perturbed Relevance Maps (E) [11].

Table 1. Average DSC score comparison between methods using best superpixel groupings.

	LIME [12]	Grad-CAM [14]	Relevance Maps (Blank) [10]	Relevance Maps (OLP [10])	OGP (Ours)
Average DSC score	0.06	0.11	0.40	0.45	**0.72**

Table 2. Average DSC on ranked superpixels generated on optimal global and optimal local perturbations.

Rank	OLP [10]	OGP
1	0.31	**0.39**
2	0.18	0.24
3	0.10	0.21

Table 3. Average DSC evaluation on cumulative top ranking superpixels.

Rank	OLP [10]	OGP
1	0.31	0.39
1+2	**0.34**	0.40
1+...+3	0.32	0.45
1+...+4	0.29	0.49
1+...+5	0.25	**0.50**

1. We evaluated the relevance maps produced by generating segmentations with the best superpixel groupings. The highest achievable Dice similarity coefficient (DSC) was found by iterating through the superpixels from highest ranked to lowest to find the best grouping for a given image when compared against the expert annotation. We compared optimal local perturbations (OLP) [10], LIME [12], and Grad-CAM [14] with the proposed optimal global perturbation (OGP). Using 100 superpixels generated on the T2w sequence, the OLP method achieved a DSC score of 0.45. The proposed OGP method achieved a higher DSC score of **0.72** using all sequences, as shown in Table 1. LIME and Grad-CAM methods achieved significantly lower DSC scores of 0.06 and 0.11, respectively, using the best thresholding for each image. Figure 2 shows the visual comparison of proposed globally perturbed Relevance Maps (OGP) to expert annotation, GradCAM and LIME methods, and locally perturbed Relevance Maps (OLP) [11].

2. We calculated the average Dice similarity coefficient (DSC) for each ranked superpixel, where rank one means the superpixel with the highest value that had the most effect on the tumour classification. The selection of ranked superpixels does not require any human input. Table 2 shows the average DSC scores for the ranked superpixels. Using 100 superpixels generated on the T2w sequence, the OLP superpixels achieved an average DSC score of 0.31. The highest-ranking OGP superpixel achieved a higher average DCS score of 0.39.

3. We assessed whether combining lower-ranked superpixels with top-ranked ones improved segmentation. The results in Table 3 show that the proposed OGP method achieved an average DSC score of 0.50 by combining the first five superpixels, outperforming the OLP method that reduced the average DSC to 0.25. The proposed OGP method is better at selecting secondary superpixels containing tumour regions.

3.2   dMTL Method Evaluation

An ablation study was performed to assess the effectiveness of the dMTL + WSSS model. The average AUC was calculated using a randomly selected dataset sampling consisting of 190 3D scans (training: 133, validation: 19, test: 38), maintaining a 60% HGG and 40% LGG tumour ratio to balance the training classes. All models were trained for 50 epochs using SGD optimizer ($lr = 0.01$, momentum $= 0.9$). First, we trained a tumour classification network without an auxiliary task, and then trained models with different auxiliary tasks, namely expert segmentation, rank 1 ROI generated by our proposed WSSS, and multiple rank ROIs generated by the WSSS. As shown in Table 4, the classification-only model performed poorly with an AUC of 0.70. However, combining classification with expert segmentation as an auxiliary task improved the results to 0.92 AUC. Using only the rank 1 generated ROI (through WSSS) as an auxiliary task achieved 0.85 AUC, and combining the top 3 ranks further improved performance to 0.87 AUC. These results demonstrate the effectiveness of our proposed approach for improving medical imaging classification with no need for manual ROI segmentation for training. We also observed that auxiliary tasks improved learning over the validation set, and using only rank 1 ROI had noisier learning compared to expert annotation or combining the top 3 ROIs.

Table 4. Multitask learning experiment results.

Task	AUC
Classification Only	0.70
Classification + Expert Segmentation	0.92
Classification + Rank 1 ROI Segmentation	0.85
Classification + Rank 1 + Rank 2 + Rank 3 ROI Segmentation	0.87

4   Conclusions

In this work, we presented a novel end-to-end pipeline that improves classification by utilizing ranked ROI segmentation generated by WSSS as an auxiliary task in multitask learning. By combining the strengths of WSSS and classification techniques, our approach outperforms traditional classification methods that rely only on a single task. The proposed approach allows our model to capture the nuances of the data better and improves overall classification performance while generating ROIs without requiring manual ROI segmentation for training. However, one limitation of the proposed method is the performance of the WSSS method relies on the selection of the initial classification task, as it requires some success in initial classification performance, which may only be suitable for some classification problems. This can be mitigated by selecting an easier initial classification task, such as a tumour or no tumour. Our pipeline represents a promising new approach to classification that has the potential to significantly advance the field by allowing to leverage large datasets that do not have fine-grain annotations. We aim to expand the evaluation for future work by including additional datasets and more recent WSSS methods for comparison with the state-of-the-art. Furthermore, an in-depth exploration of the produced segmentation's ability to capture clinically meaningful information will be conducted.

Acknowledgement. This research has been supported by Huawei Technologies Canada Co., Ltd.

References

1. Achanta, R., Shaji, A., Smith, K., Lucchi, A., Fua, P., Süsstrunk, S.: Slic superpixels. Technical report (2010)
2. Bakas, S., et al.: Segmentation labels and radiomic features for the pre-operative scans of the TCGA-LGG collection. Cancer Imaging Arch. **286** (2017)
3. Bakas, S., et al.: Advancing the cancer genome atlas glioma MRI collections with expert segmentation labels and radiomic features. Sci. Data **4**(1), 1–13 (2017)
4. Bakas, S., et al.: Identifying the best machine learning algorithms for brain tumor segmentation, progression assessment, and overall survival prediction in the brats challenge. arXiv preprint arXiv:1811.02629 (2018)
5. Goodfellow, I.J., et al.: Generative adversarial networks. arXiv preprint arXiv:1406.2661 (2014)
6. He, K., Zhang, X., Ren, S., Sun, J.: Deep residual learning for image recognition. Corr abs/1512.03385 (2015)
7. Kingma, D.P., Ba, J.: Adam: a method for stochastic optimization. arXiv preprint arXiv:1412.6980 (2014)
8. Menze, B.H., et al.: The multimodal brain tumor image segmentation benchmark (BRATS). IEEE Trans. Med. Imaging **34**(10), 1993–2024 (2014)
9. Niu, Z., Zhong, G., Yu, H.: A review on the attention mechanism of deep learning. Neurocomputing **452**, 48–62 (2021)
10. Rajapaksa, S., Khalvati, F.: Localized perturbations for weakly-supervised segmentation of glioma brain tumours. arXiv preprint arXiv:2111.14953 (2021)

11. Rajapaksa, S., Khalvati, F.: Relevance maps: a weakly-supervised segmentation method for 3D brain tumour in MRIs. Front. Radiol. **2**, 1061402 (2022)
12. Ribeiro, M.T., Singh, S., Guestrin, C.: "Why should i trust you?" explaining the predictions of any classifier. In: Proceedings of the 22nd ACM SIGKDD International Conference on Knowledge Discovery and Data Mining, pp. 1135–1144 (2016)
13. Ronneberger, O., Fischer, P., Brox, T.: U-Net: convolutional networks for biomedical image segmentation. In: Navab, N., Hornegger, J., Wells, W.M., Frangi, A.F. (eds.) MICCAI 2015. LNCS, vol. 9351, pp. 234–241. Springer, Cham (2015). https://doi.org/10.1007/978-3-319-24574-4_28
14. Selvaraju, R., Cogswell, M., Das, A., Vedantam, R., Parikh, D., Batra, D.: Grad-cam: visual explanations from deep networks via gradient-based localization. arxiv Preprint posted online 7 (2016)
15. Willemink, M.J., et al.: Preparing medical imaging data for machine learning. Radiology **295**(1), 4–15 (2020)

Exigent Examiner and Mean Teacher: An Advanced 3D CNN-Based Semi-Supervised Brain Tumor Segmentation Framework

Ziyang Wang$^{(\boxtimes)}$ and Irina Voiculescu

Department of Computer Science, University of Oxford, Oxford, UK
{ziyang.wang,irina}@cs.ox.ac.uk

Abstract. With the rise of deep learning applications to medical imaging, there has been a growing appetite for large and well-annotated datasets, yet annotation is time-consuming and hard to come by. In this work, we train a 3D semantic segmentation model in an advanced semi-supervised learning fashion. The proposed SSL framework consists of three models: a *Student* model that learns from annotated data and a large amount of raw data, a *Teacher* model with the same architecture as the student, updated by self-ensembling and which supervises the student through pseudo-labels, and an *Examiner* model that assesses the quality of the student's inferences. All three models are built with 3D convolutional operations. The overall framework mimics a collaboration between a consistency training Student ↔ Teacher module and an adversarial training Examiner ↔ Student module. The proposed method is validated with various evaluation metrics on a public benchmarking 3D MRI brain tumor segmentation dataset. The experimental results of the proposed method outperform pre-existing semi-supervised methods. The source code, baseline methods, and dataset are available at https://github.com/ziyangwang007/CV-SSL-MIS.

Keywords: Semi-Supervised Learning · Image Semantic Segmentation · Mean Teacher · Adversarial Training · Brain Tumour Segmentation

1 Introduction

When applying deep-learning-based techniques to medical image segmentation, there has been a growing need for large and well-annotated datasets which, in turn, has come with a high cost in time and labor [1,13,17,26,30]. Semi-Supervised Learning (SSL) allows a model to be trained with a small amount of labeled data and a large amount of unlabeled data, has been widely explored in medical image analysis [9,18,22,29,33].

© The Author(s), under exclusive license to Springer Nature Switzerland AG 2023
Z. Xue et al. (Eds.): MILLanD 2023, LNCS 14307, pp. 181–190, 2023.
https://doi.org/10.1007/978-3-031-44917-8_17

Consistency training is the most popular study in semantic segmentation with SSL. The consistency regularization is under the assumption when the perturbation is applied to the unlabeled data, the predictions should not change significantly, i.e. training a model with a consistent output. The perturbation is explored normally with feature perturbation [2,16,18,22], and network perturbation [11,27]. A series of feature perturbations come with data augmentation such as CutMix [9] is developed to sufficiently varied perturbation, MixMatch [6] introduces low-entropy labels for data-augmented unlabeled examples and then mixes labeled and unlabeled data via MixUp [23], and FixMatch [12] utilises pseudo labels on weak augmentation to supervise the labeling on strong augmentation. On the other side, network perturbation studies normally come up with various network architectures such as dual-students [11] introducing stabilization constraint to an additional student for Student-Teacher style SSL [22], TriNet [7] explores three different decoders with a shared encoder and diversing data for classification, and triple-view learning [27] further explores multi-view learning for image semantic segmentation.

A self-ensembling SSL method named Mean Teacher [22], which is an extension of temporal ensembling [18], has been widely adopted in semi-supervised learning (SSL) for medical image segmentation [5,19,25,28]. This method typically consists of a student model and a teacher model, with the same architecture. The student model learns from annotated data with feature perturbation, and the teacher model is updated by the average model weight from the student model. The teacher model is usually more robust than the student model and can supervise the student with pseudo-labels under a consistency-aware concern.

Alongside consistency training, another common SSL technique is adversarial training [10,15,21]. It normally involves developing an additional discriminator model to extract statistical features which aim to distinguish the quality of inferences of the model. Its standalone performance is still not serviceable in the clinical domain, especially not when only a limited amount of labeled data is available [8,14].

In response to the above concerns, we explore a training scheme which involves consistency-training-based SSL with further adversarial training; this extends the Student-Teacher style prototype with an Examiner paradigm, creating an Examiner↔Student↔Teacher SSL framework. To the best of our knowledge, this is the first work in medical image segmentation which explores consistency training and adversarial training simultaneously with 3D convolutional operations. The contribution can be considered threefold: (i) The proposed framework consists of three models i.e. Examiner, Student, and Teacher, which are all based on 3D convolutions that can make the most of a training set which includes some annotated images as well as some unannotated raw data; (ii) Adversarial training and consistency regularization are proposed via Examiner ↔ Student, and Teacher ↔ Student respectively during the training process. (iii) Our framework has been validated on the public benchmark MRI brain tumor segmentation dataset [13] using comprehensive evaluation metrics. The results show that it outperforms seven other semi-supervised methods under the same hyper-parameter setting, segmentation backbone, and feature information distribution.

2   Approach

In this paper, $\mathbf{L}$, $\mathbf{U}$ and $\mathbf{T}$ denote a labeled training set, an unlabeled training set, and a test set. A batch of labeled training set is denoted as $(\boldsymbol{X}_l, \boldsymbol{Y}_{gt}) \in \mathbf{L}$, a batch of testing set as $(\boldsymbol{X}_t, \boldsymbol{Y}_{gt}) \in \mathbf{T}$, and unlabeled training as $(\boldsymbol{X}_u) \in \mathbf{U}$, where $\boldsymbol{X}_l, \boldsymbol{X}_t, \boldsymbol{X}_u \in \mathbb{R}^{h \times w}$, and $\boldsymbol{Y}_{gt} \in [0,1]^{h \times w}$ represent 2D grey-scale images, and their corresponding ground-truth annotations, respectively. A prediction $\boldsymbol{Y}_p \in [0,1]^{h \times w}$ is generated by a segmentation model $f(\theta) : \boldsymbol{X} \mapsto \boldsymbol{Y}_p$ using the parameters θ of the model f. This $\boldsymbol{Y}_p$ can also be considered as a batch of unlabeled data with pseudo labels $(\boldsymbol{X}_u) \in \mathbf{U}$, and the set of pairs $(\boldsymbol{X}_u, \boldsymbol{Y}_p)$ can be used to retrain a model f. The Examiner, Student and Teacher are denoted by $f_E(\theta_e), f_S(\theta_s), f_T(\overline{\theta})$ respectively, where θ represents the parameters of each model, and $\overline{\theta}$ represents the average model weights constructed by the Teacher. The training of the Examiner $\leftrightarrow$ Student $\leftrightarrow$ Teacher composite minimizes the supervision loss $Loss_{sup}$ and the semi-supervision loss $Loss_{semi}$ of the Student and Examiner, respectively. $Loss_{sup}$ and $Loss_{semi}$ differ from each other through the use of genuine ground truth $\boldsymbol{Y}_{gt}$ or generated pseudo labels $\boldsymbol{Y}_p$. Our proposed SSL framework is briefly illustrated in Fig. 1, and the individual models $f_E(\theta_e)$, $f_S(\theta_s)$, and $f_T(\overline{\theta})$ are detailed in the following sections.

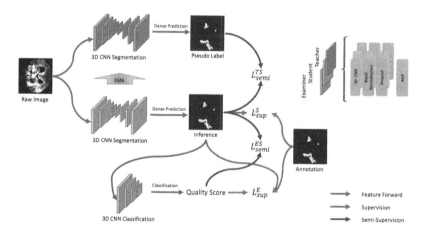

Fig. 1. The Examiner$\leftrightarrow$Student$\leftrightarrow$Teacher Framework for Brain Tumor Segmentation.

2.1   Student Model

In order to exploit the 3D nature of the MRI scans, a 3DUNet [4] is used as the Student model $f_S(\theta)$. Each network block of this UNet is based on 3D convolutional operations, Batch Normalization and DropOut shown in Fig. 1. Like in [22], $f_S(\theta)$ learns directly from data with annotations $(\boldsymbol{X}_l, \boldsymbol{Y}_{gt})$, and supervised by the Teacher via pseudo labels $(\boldsymbol{X}_u, \boldsymbol{Y}_p)$. The crucial difference is that,

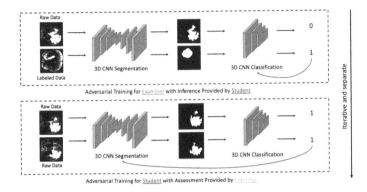

Fig. 2. The Illustration of Adversarial Training Between Examiner and Student.

at the same time, $f_S(\theta)$ is also validated against the Examiner via adversarial training. The inference of student model $f_S(\theta)$ is given in Eq. 1, where Gaussian noise is applied to all input data (both labeled and unlabeled) $\mathbf{X} = \mathbf{X}_l \cup \mathbf{X}_u$ during training.

$$\mathbf{Y}_p = f_s(\mathbf{X} + Noise; \theta_s) \tag{1}$$

2.2   Teacher Model

The architecture of the Teacher $f_T(\overline{\theta})$ is similar to $f_S(\theta)$, except the Teacher does not learn from data directly. It is updated from the exponential moving average (EMA) of $f_S(\theta)$ (illustrated in Eq. 2), and it is more likely than the Student to predict the correct inference. Under the consistency-aware concern of inference from the same input data [22], the Teacher's predictions are considered as the pseudo labels to supervise the Student.

$$\overline{\theta} = \alpha\theta_{t-1} + (1 - \alpha)\theta_t \tag{2}$$

where $\overline{\theta}$ is updated based on the Student parameter θ_t from the previous training step t; weight factor $\alpha = 1 - \frac{1}{t+1}$. The pseudo labels are generated by the Teacher without noise as:

$$\mathbf{Y}_p = f_T(X_u; \overline{\theta}). \tag{3}$$

Thus the unlabeled training set X_u can be utilized to train the Student with $(\mathbf{X}_u, \mathbf{Y}_p)$.

2.3   Examiner Model

In order to capitalize on adversarial learning [33], a 3D-CNN-based discriminator is put in place to assess the quality of the Student's inference. This matches the metaphor for an Examiner which checks the quality of the learning. The Examiner consists of four 3D CNN layers, a down-sampling operation, and multi-linear layers shown in Fig. 1. Its architecture is following the classical VGGNet [20].

The Examiner and Student are trained against each other repeatedly for the duration of the training (seen in Fig. 2). The Examiner classifies the quality of its input as indicated as Eq. 4.

$$Y_e = f_E(Y_p; \theta_e) \tag{4}$$

where a segmentation mask predicted by Student Y_p originating from the ground-truth label Y_{gt} is marked as a 1:*pass*, whereas a Student inference from pseudo label is marked as a 0:*fail* $Y_e \in [pass, fail]$. As the adversarial training progresses, the student provides increasingly higher-quality inferences, the examiner provides an increasingly strict assessment.

2.4   Objective

The training objective of the proposed SSL approach is to minimize the sum of the supervision loss $\mathcal{L}_{sup}$ and the semi-supervision loss $\mathcal{L}_{semi}$ of two models $f_E(\theta), f_S(\theta)$ as shown in Eq. 5:

$$\mathcal{L} = \underbrace{\mathcal{L}_{sup}^S + \mathcal{L}_{sup}^E}_{sup} + \lambda \underbrace{(\mathcal{L}_{semi}^{TS} + \mathcal{L}_{semi}^{ES})}_{semi} \tag{5}$$

where the losses are split as $\mathcal{L}_{sup}$ or $\mathcal{L}_{semi}$ depending on whether the feeding data is from a labeled training set or not, and the loss is controlled by a ramp-up weight factor λ [28]. S, E, TS, ES indicate the loss of the Student model, Examiner model, Student model with the help of the Teacher, and the Student model with the assessment of the Examiner, respectively. The overall segmentation loss is based on the Dice Coefficient, denoted Dice(.), and on Cross-Entropy CE(.). Loss $\mathcal{L}_{sup}^S$ is used to train the Student with labeled data $(X_l, Y_{gt}) \in \mathbf{L}$, as per Eq. 6:

$$\mathcal{L}_{sup}^S = CE(Y_{gt}, f_S(X_l; \theta)) + Dice(Y_{gt}, f_S(X_l; \theta)) \tag{6}$$

Loss $\mathcal{L}_{sup}^E$ is used to train the Examiner with inferences from either the labeled or the unlabeled training set, illustrated in Eq. 7. The score $f_E(\theta) \in \{0, 1\}$, where 1 and 0 stand for *pass*, and *fail*.

$$\mathcal{L}_{sup}^E = CE(f_E(f_S(X_l; \theta_S); \theta_E), 1) \\ + CE(f_E(f_S(X_u; \theta_S); \theta_E), 0) \tag{7}$$

Loss $\mathcal{L}_{semi}^{TS}$ is used to train the Student under the Teacher's supervision. A hybrid loss is utilized as shown in Eq. 8.

$$\mathcal{L}_{semi}^{TS} = CE(f_S(X_u; \theta), f_T(X_U; \theta)) \\ + Dice(f_S(X_u; \theta), f_T(X_U; \theta)) \tag{8}$$

Loss $\mathcal{L}_{semi}^{ES}$ is used to train the Student under the 'exigent' assessment of Examiner via adversarial learning. The training objective of $\mathcal{L}_{semi}^{ES}$ for $f_S(\theta)$ is for *all* the inferences to be *passed* by the Examiner. This makes the Examiner 'exigent' in that it repeats the examination process until all, or at least as many

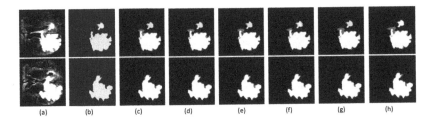

Fig. 3. Two sample images, corresponding annotations, and related inferences against annotations. (a) Raw image, (b) annotations, (c) ADVENT, (d) ICT, (e) UAMT, (f) CPS, (g) TVL, (h) ours. (Color figure online)

students as possible, have received a *pass*. In our experience, this can require as many as $O(10^4)$ iterations.

$$\mathcal{L}_{\text{semi}}^{ES} = -\text{CE}(f_E(f_s(\boldsymbol{X}_u; \theta_S); \theta_E), 0) \tag{9}$$

Table 1. The Direct Comparison Between Each SSL Method on Brain Tumor MRI Testing Set When 10% of Training Set is Annotated.

Model	Dice↑	Acc↑	Pre↑	Sen↑	Spe↑	HD↓	ASD↓	SBD↑
ADVENT [24]	0.8458	0.9901	0.8935	0.8029	0.9967	12.8024	2.4089	0.5395
ICT [23]	0.8422	0.9900	0.8997	0.7917	0.9969	18.3787	2.5350	0.5399
UAMT [32]	0.8578	0.9908	0.8973	0.8217	0.9967	11.7392	2.4667	0.5547
CPS [3]	0.8580	0.9907	0.8882	**0.8298**	0.9963	12.9194	**2.0330**	0.5598
TVL [27]	0.8508	0.9903	0.8824	0.8214	0.9962	18.5677	2.2680	0.5955
Ours	**0.8605**	**0.9911**	**0.9135**	0.8134	**0.9973**	**8.7455**	2.1574	**0.6013**

3 Experiments

Implementation Details. The Examiner↔Student↔Teacher SSL method has been validated on the MRI Brain Tumor Segmentation (BraTS) from MICCAI Challenge 2019 [13]. It contains routine clinically-acquired 3T multimodal MRI scans, with accompanying ground-truth masks annotated by neuro-radiologists. We select flair images for whole tumor segmentation, with 80% selected for training (10% of which are labeled and the rest assumed unlabeled), and the remainder 20% for testing. The experiments are conducted with Pytorch on an Nvidia GeForce RTX 3090 GPU, and Intel(R) Intel Core i9-10900K. The 3D CNN segmentation is based on a modified 3DUNet [4,17]. Runtimes average around 11.5 seconds per iteration. The dataset is processed for 3D semantic segmentation, with all images resized to 96 × 96 × 96. All baseline methods and our proposed method are trained with the same hyperparameter settings including training for 30,000 iterations then being tested with the model which had performed best on the validation set, batch size of 2, the optimizer for the

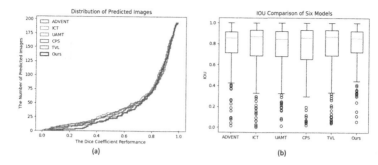

Fig. 4. The Dice and IoU Distribution of Each Inference by Six SSL Methods with Line and Box Chart.

Student is SGD, and the learning rate is initially set to 0.01 with 0.9 momentum and 0.0001 weight decay; the optimizer for the Examiner is Adam, and the learning rate is 0.0001. The Student with the best performance on validation set is for final testing.

Table 2. The Direct Comparison Between Each SSL Method on Brain Tumor MRI Testing Set Under Different Data Situations.

Labeled	10%			30%			50%		
Model	Dice↑	HD↓	ASD↓	Dice↑	HD↓	ASD↓	Dice↑	HD↓	ASD↓
ADVENT [24]	0.8458	12.8024	2.4089	0.8772	7.8178	2.1462	0.8769	8.1860	1.9881
ICT [23]	0.8422	18.3787	2.5350	0.8750	8.7348	1.9811	0.8741	7.3740	1.8393
UAMT [32]	0.8578	11.7392	2.4667	0.8793	7.6906	1.9216	0.8885	10.4160	1.7932
CPS [3]	0.8580	12.9194	**2.0330**	0.8770	7.2425	**1.7739**	0.8842	8.3445	1.8786
TVL [27]	0.8508	18.5677	2.2680	0.8798	11.1982	2.0076	0.8864	7.1704	1.8076
Ours	**0.8605**	**8.7455**	2.1574	**0.8830**	7.0310	1.8910	**0.8920**	6.9425	**1.7628**

Compare with Baseline Methods. Our proposed method is compared with other SSL including Deep Adversarial Network (DAN) [33], Adversarial Entropy Minimization for Domain Adaptation (ADVENT) [24], Interpolation Consistency Training (ICT) [23], Mean Teachers (MT) [22], Uncertainty-Aware Mean Teachers (UAMT) [32], Cross Pseudo Supervision (CPS) [3], and Triple-View Learning (TVL) [27]. All the baseline SSL methods are with the *same* segmentation backbone i.e. 3DUNet for a fair comparison [4]. The comparisons are conducted with a variety of evaluation metrics including Dice Coefficient (Dice), Accuracy (Acc), Precision (Pre), Sensitivity (Sen), Specificity (Spe), Hausdorff Distance (HD) 95% with millimeter, and Average Surface Distance (ASD). We further report the extent to which the boundaries of the segmentations match the annotations [31], using the Symmetric Boundary Dice (SBD). ↑ and ↓ denote the performance number (by similarity metrics or difference metrics) as the higher the better, or the lower the better, respectively. **Results** The qualitative results are

Table 3. The Ablation Study with Two Separate Semi-Supervision Schemes and Fully Supervised Learning on Brain Tumor MRI Testing Set.

Supervision			Performance						
St	Te	Ex	Dice↑	Acc↑	Pre↑	Sen↑	Spe↑	HD↓	ASD↓
✓	(10% Full)		0.8405	0.9898	0.8889	0.7970	0.9965	12.2822	2.2771
✓	✓		0.8546	0.9906	0.8995	0.8139	0.9968	12.4331	**2.1487**
✓		✓	0.8555	0.9906	0.8917	**0.8222**	0.9965	12.3674	2.5333
✓	✓	✓	**0.8605**	**0.9911**	**0.9135**	0.8134	**0.9973**	**8.7455**	<u>2.1574</u>
100% Full			0.9073	0.9931	0.9130	0.9018	0.9968	7.4953	1.9241

sketched in Fig. 3 illustrating two randomly selected raw images, annotations, and inference against the published annotations accordingly. , Red, and Black show true positive (TP), false positive (FP), false negative (FN) and true negative (TN) pixels against published annotations. Some of the quantitative results are detailed in Table 1 with various metrics. The best performance are highlighted with **Bold**, and the second best of ours are <u>Underlined</u>. *It is worth noting that high Precision and low Sensitivity are not necessarily a good combination, nor are low Sensitivity and high Specificity.* Increasing Sensitivity (by 1.6% in Table 1) is desirable here as more of the tumour gets detected. Most of the results of our proposed methods are with **Bold** seen in Table 1. Except for reporting the average evaluation performance, each predicted image is also evaluated with Dice Coefficient seen in Fig. 4(a) and (b). The (a) line chart illustrates the number of the predicted images on Y-Axis depending on the Dice threshold on X-Axis. The more curved the line, the more likely to predict segmentation with high Dice. The line of the best method (Ours) is highlighted with a **Thick** line. The (b) box plot directly illustrates the IoU distribution of predicted images of six different SSL methods. The qualitative and quantitative results demonstrate the competitive performance of the proposed method against other SSL methods. The quantitative results shown in Table 1 are under the assumption that 10% of the training set is annotated. We further explored different data situations when 30% and 50% of the training set are with annotations shown in Table 2. **Ablation Study** To analyze the individual effects of each proposed contribution, as well as their combined effects, we conducted extensive ablation experiments, which are detailed in Table 3. ✓ with Teacher or Examiner indicates the only consistency training or adversarial training SSL scheme, which are both able to help the Student model learn from unannotated data. Further experiments of fully supervised learning of the student model with 10% annotated data and 100% annotated data are validated as the lower-bound and upper-bound performance, respectively. In the lower-bound experiment, only the Student model is with a single ✓, which has no feature learning for raw data but with only 10% provided annotated data. In the upper-bound experiment, all three models are deployed with 100% of annotated data provided. Table 3 presents the promising improvement for Student with the help of Teacher and Examiner model.

4   Conclusion

Leveraging the power of adversarial training in the form of an Examiner model in conjunction with the Mean Teacher consistency regularization paradigm makes for a powerful combination which offers an improvement to semi-supervised learning for medical image segmentation. This has been validated on the widely used BraTS database but is easy to generalise to any semantic segmentation and, indeed, to other classes of downstream tasks.

References

1. Bernard, O., et al.: Deep learning techniques for automatic MRI cardiac multi-structures segmentation and diagnosis: is the problem solved? IEEE TMI **37**(11), 2514–2525 (2018)
2. Chen, L.-C., et al.: Naive-student: leveraging semi-supervised learning in video sequences for urban scene segmentation. In: Vedaldi, A., Bischof, H., Brox, T., Frahm, J.-M. (eds.) ECCV 2020. LNCS, vol. 12354, pp. 695–714. Springer, Cham (2020). https://doi.org/10.1007/978-3-030-58545-7_40
3. Chen, X., et al.: Semi-supervised semantic segmentation with cross pseudo supervision. In: CVPR (2021)
4. Çiçek, Ö., Abdulkadir, A., Lienkamp, S.S., Brox, T., Ronneberger, O.: 3D U-Net: learning dense volumetric segmentation from sparse annotation. In: Ourselin, S., Joskowicz, L., Sabuncu, M.R., Unal, G., Wells, W. (eds.) MICCAI 2016. LNCS, vol. 9901, pp. 424–432. Springer, Cham (2016). https://doi.org/10.1007/978-3-319-46723-8_49
5. Cui, W., et al.: Semi-supervised brain lesion segmentation with an adapted mean teacher model. In: IPMI (2019)
6. David, B., et al.: Mixmatch: a holistic approach to semi-supervised learning. In: NeurIPS (2019)
7. Dong-DongChen, et al.: Tri-net for semi-supervised deep learning. In: IJCAI (2018)
8. Fang, K., Li, W.-J.: DMNet: difference minimization network for semi-supervised segmentation in medical images. In: Martel, A.L., et al. (eds.) MICCAI 2020. LNCS, vol. 12261, pp. 532–541. Springer, Cham (2020). https://doi.org/10.1007/978-3-030-59710-8_52
9. French, G., et al.: Semi-supervised semantic segmentation needs strong, varied perturbations. In: BMVC (2019)
10. Hung, W.C., et al.: Adversarial learning for semi-supervised semantic segmentation. In: BMVC (2018)
11. Ke, Z., et al.: Dual student: breaking the limits of the teacher in semi-supervised learning. In: CVPR (2019)
12. Kihyuk, S., et al.: Fixmatch: simplifying semi-supervised learning with consistency and confidence. In: NeurIPS (2020)
13. Menze, B.H., et al.: The multimodal brain tumor image segmentation benchmark (BraTS). IEEE TMI **34**(10), 1993–2024 (2014)
14. Mittal, S., Tatarchenko, M., Brox, T.: Semi-supervised semantic segmentation with high-and low-level consistency. IEEE TPAMI **43**(4), 1369–1379 (2019)
15. Nasim, S., et al.: Semi supervised semantic segmentation using generative adversarial network. In: ICCV (2017)

16. Ouali, Y., et al.: Semi-supervised semantic segmentation with cross-consistency training. In: CVPR (2020)
17. Ronneberger, O., Fischer, P., Brox, T.: U-Net: convolutional networks for biomedical image segmentation. In: Navab, N., Hornegger, J., Wells, W.M., Frangi, A.F. (eds.) MICCAI 2015. LNCS, vol. 9351, pp. 234–241. Springer, Cham (2015). https://doi.org/10.1007/978-3-319-24574-4_28
18. Samuli, L., Aila, T.: Temporal ensembling for semi-supervised learning. In: ICLR (2016)
19. Shanis, Z., Gerber, S., Gao, M., Enquobahrie, A.: Intramodality domain adaptation using self ensembling and adversarial training. In: Wang, Q., et al. (eds.) DART/MIL3ID-2019. LNCS, vol. 11795, pp. 28–36. Springer, Cham (2019). https://doi.org/10.1007/978-3-030-33391-1_4
20. Simonyan, K., Zisserman, A.: Very deep convolutional networks for large-scale image recognition. In: ICLR (2015)
21. Takeru, M., et al.: Virtual adversarial training: a regularization method for supervised and semi-supervised learning. IEEE TPAMI $41(8)$, 1979–1993 (2018)
22. Tarvainen, A., et al.: Mean teachers are better role models: weight-averaged consistency targets improve semi-supervised deep learning results. In: NeurIPS (2017)
23. Verma, V., et al.: Interpolation consistency training for semi-supervised learning. In: IJCAI (2019)
24. Vu, T.H., et al.: ADVENT: adversarial entropy minimization for domain adaptation in semantic segmentation. In: CVPR (2019)
25. Wang, K., et al.: Semi-supervised medical image segmentation via a tripled-uncertainty guided mean teacher model with contrastive learning. MedIA (2022)
26. Wang, Z., et al.: RAR-U-net: a residual encoder to attention decoder by residual connections framework for spine segmentation under noisy labels. In: ICIP. IEEE (2021)
27. Wang, Z., et al.: Triple-view feature learning for medical image segmentation. In: MICCAI-W (2022)
28. Wang, Z., et al.: Uncertainty-aware transformer for MRI cardiac segmentation via mean teachers. In: MIUA (2022)
29. Wang, Z., Dong, N., Voiculescu, I.: Computationally-efficient vision transformer for medical image semantic segmentation via dual pseudo-label supervision. In: ICIP. IEEE (2022)
30. Wang, Z., Voiculescu, I.: Dealing with unreliable annotations: a noise-robust network for semantic segmentation through a transformer-improved encoder and convolution decoder. Appl. Sci. $13(13)$, 7966 (2023)
31. Yeghiazaryan, V., et al.: Family of boundary overlap metrics for the evaluation of medical image segmentation. SPIE JMI $5(1)$, 015006–015006 (2018)
32. Yu, L., Wang, S., Li, X., Fu, C.-W., Heng, P.-A.: Uncertainty-aware self-ensembling model for semi-supervised 3D left atrium segmentation. In: Shen, D., et al. (eds.) MICCAI 2019. LNCS, vol. 11765, pp. 605–613. Springer, Cham (2019). https://doi.org/10.1007/978-3-030-32245-8_67
33. Zhang, Y., Yang, L., Chen, J., Fredericksen, M., Hughes, D.P., Chen, D.Z.: Deep adversarial networks for biomedical image segmentation utilizing unannotated images. In: Descoteaux, M., Maier-Hein, L., Franz, A., Jannin, P., Collins, D.L., Duchesne, S. (eds.) MICCAI 2017. LNCS, vol. 10435, pp. 408–416. Springer, Cham (2017). https://doi.org/10.1007/978-3-319-66179-7_47

Extremely Weakly-Supervised Blood Vessel Segmentation with Physiologically Based Synthesis and Domain Adaptation

Peidi Xu[1(✉)], Blaire Lee[2], Olga Sosnovtseva[2], Charlotte Mehlin Sørensen[2], Kenny Erleben[1], and Sune Darkner[1]

[1] Department of Computer Science, University of Copenhagen, Copenhagen, Denmark
peidi@di.ku.dk

[2] Department of Biomedical Sciences, University of Copenhagen, Copenhagen, Denmark

Abstract. Accurate analysis and modeling of renal functions require a precise segmentation of the renal blood vessels. Micro-CT scans provide image data at higher resolutions, making deeper vessels near the renal cortex visible. Although deep-learning-based methods have shown state-of-the-art performance in automatic blood vessel segmentations, they require a large amount of labeled training data. However, voxelwise labeling in micro-CT scans is extremely time-consuming, given the huge volume sizes. To mitigate the problem, we simulate synthetic renal vascular trees physiologically while generating corresponding scans of the simulated trees by training a generative model on unlabeled scans. This enables the generative model to learn the mapping implicitly without the need for explicit functions to emulate the image acquisition process. We further propose an additional segmentation branch over the generative model trained on the generated scans. We demonstrate that the model can directly segment blood vessels on real scans and validate our method on both 3D micro-CT scans of rat kidneys and a proof-of-concept experiment on 2D retinal images. Code and 3D results are available at (https://github.com/diku-dk/RenalVesselSeg).

Keywords: Blood vessel · Renal vasculature · Semantic segmentation · Physiological simulation · Generative model · Domain adaptation

1 Introduction

The vasculature in each organ has a characteristic structure tailored to fulfill the particular requirements of the organ. The renal vasculature serves as a resource distribution network and plays a significant part in the kidney's physiology and pathophysiology. Not only does it distribute blood to individual nephrons and

Supplementary Information The online version contains supplementary material available at https://doi.org/10.1007/978-3-031-44917-8_18.

© The Author(s), under exclusive license to Springer Nature Switzerland AG 2023
Z. Xue et al. (Eds.): MILLanD 2023, LNCS 14307, pp. 191–201, 2023.
https://doi.org/10.1007/978-3-031-44917-8_18

regulates the filtration of blood in the kidney, but it also allows neighboring nephrons to interact through electrical signals transmitted along the vessels as a communication network [16]. Automatic segmentation of renal blood vessels from medical scans is usually the essential first step for developing realistic computer simulations of renal functions.

General Deep-Learning Based Segmentation of Blood Vessels: Deep learning models have been widely used for automatic blood vessel segmentations and have shown state-of-the-art performances applied on lungs, liver, and eyes [5,11,12,27]. However, only a few efforts were made for renal blood segmentation. Recently, He et al. proposed Dense biased networks [9] to segment renal arteries from abdominal CT angiography (CTA) images by fusing multi-receptive fields and multi-resolution features for the adaptation of scale changes. However, the limited resolution of CTA images only allows the models to reach interlobar arteries and enables the estimation of blood-feeding regions, which is useful for laparoscopic partial nephrectomy but not for analyzing realistic renal functions. Therefore, there is a need for imaging with higher resolution, e.g., micro-computed tomography (micro-CT) scans.

Micro-Computed Tomography and Related Deep-Learning Works: Micro-CT shares the same imaging principle as conventional clinical CT, but with a much smaller field of view, such that microscale images of high spatial resolution can be obtained [20]. Micro-CT scans are commonly used to study various microstructures, including blood vessels [1]. Few existing research on the auto-segmentation of micro-CT scans focuses on segmenting internal organs of the heart, spinal cord, right and left lung [15], and blood vessels on colorectal tissue [19] using either nn-UNet [10] or variant 3DUNet [4,21]. There is, however, no prior work in segmenting vasculatures in organs like kidneys from micro-CT scans. Crucially, most of the above deep learning methods require a large number of label maps to train the segmentation network. Manual labeling of micro-CT scans is extremely time-consuming given the huge volume size. Therefore, in our case, we do not have any clean label maps to train a segmentation model.

Synthetic Training Data for Blood Vessel Segmentation: Transfer learning from artificially generated data is one possible technique to train deep learning models in a data scarcity setting. The process involves pre-training models on synthetic data, which are then fine-tuned on a small set of labeled real data. In medical image segmentation, this strategy has been widely applied to tumor segmentations [13]. Since blood vessels do follow certain physiological and anatomical properties, e.g., Murray's law [18], this approach has also been applied to train segmentation models for mouse brain vasculature with physiologically synthesized vessels [25]. However, these works only pre-train the models on synthetic data and still require real labeled data for fine-tuning. Recently, Menten et al. [17] synthesize retinal vasculature and then emulate the corresponding optical coherence tomography angiography (OCTA) images. They show that a UNet trained on these emulated image-label pairs can directly segment real OCTA images. However, the way they generate scans from synthesized labels is completely explicit, which includes a series of physics-based image transformation functions that emulate the image acquisition process (e.g., OCTA). These functions clearly require expert knowledge and do not translate to micro-CT settings.

Generative Models for Domain Adaptation: In practice, a relatively large number of unlabeled scans are usually available. Thus, a more general way to generate scans without emulating image acquisition explicitly is to utilize these unlabeled scans via a generative model, i.e., domain adaptation. Medical image segmentation with domain adaptation is an active research area, and a popular method is Generative Adversarial Networks (GANs). In particular, CycleGAN [29] has been used to perform domain adaptation for medical image segmentation such as liver and tumor segmentation in CT images, where the goal is to train a segmentation model on one domain and then apply it to another domain with missing or scarce annotated data [2,8]. Recently, Chen et al. [3] segment cerebral vessels in 2D Laser speckle contrast imaging (LSCI) images using public fundus images with segmentation labels as the source domain and a CycleGAN for domain adaptation. The ability of CycleGAN to perform translation without paired training data makes it a powerful tool for domain adaptation.

Our Contribution: We propose a framework with two main components: 1) a physiology-based simulation that synthesizes renal vascular trees and 2) a generative model with an additional segmentation branch that adapts the synthesized vascular trees to real scans while performing segmentation simultaneously. For 1), we extend the work [26] from physiologically synthesizing renal arterial tree to venous tree. Since a small prebuilt tree needs to be manually provided in the initialization step of the process, we call our method *extremely weakly-supervised.* For 2), we aim to "emulate" corresponding scans using CycleGANs. Specifically, we follow the idea in [3] to train a vessel segmentation network over the output from CycleGAN while extending to 3D on kidney micro-CT images. Notably, although 3D CycleGAN has been adopted for segmenting brain tissues and heart chambers [2,8,28], no similar work exists on subtle structures like blood vessels in 3D. Moreover, these works still require scans or segmentations from other sources, modalities, or time points as the source domain. Instead, our source domain is purely physiologically synthesized vascular trees. We show that our combined model can directly segment blood vessels in real scans from the target domain and demonstrate the validity of our approach to segmenting vasculatures both on 3D micro-CT scans of rat kidneys and 2D retinal images.

2   Method

2.1   Physiologically-Based Simulation of Renal Blood Vessels

Constraint Constructive Optimization (CCO) [22] and its variant Global Constructive Optimization (GCO) [7] are widely used fractal-based methods that simulate the growth of vascular trees. These methods turn tree growth into an optimization problem based on the biological, physiological, and hemodynamic factors involved in the process. Here, the vascular tree is modeled by a directed acyclic graph $\mathcal{G} \equiv (\mathcal{V}, \mathcal{E})$ where $\mathcal{V}$ is a set of nodes in the two endpoints of each vessel centerline with its coordinates in Euclidean space as node features, and $\mathcal{E}$ is a set of directed edges representing each vessel segment as a cylindrical tube with its radius as edge features. Boundary conditions such as terminal radius and flow distributions are imposed to represent physiologic conditions. The algorithms then find a vascular tree that minimizes the system's overall cost function while fulfilling several constraints.

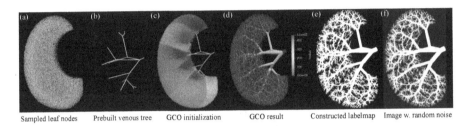

| Sampled leaf nodes | Prebuilt venous tree | GCO initialization | GCO result | Constructed labelmap | Image w. random noise |

Fig. 1. Physiologically based vessel synthesizing pipeline. Details are given in [26]. The last two subfigures are shown with maximum intensity projection (MIP).

Here we follow [26], which adopts GCO as the backbone model for generating the renal vascular trees with optimal branching structures by performing multi-scale optimizations through iterating several operations such as splitting and relaxation [7]. However, instead of the arterial tree presented in [26], we only focus on the venous tree because it constitutes most of the vessel foreground. In summary, veins follow a similar pattern to arteries but are thicker, which is accomplished by sampling more terminal nodes with large radii (Fig. 1a). Detailed modifications over boundary conditions from arterial to venous trees are given in supplementary material, including tuning the weighting factors of the loss defined in [26]. Together with inherent randomnesses in the GCO process itself, the generated tree (Fig. 1d) will look different each run. This enables a variety of synthesized vascular trees to train the later deep-learning model.

Note that though a prebuilt tree $\mathcal{G}_0 \equiv (\mathcal{V}_0, \mathcal{E}_0)$ is required to guide the GCO process as noted in [26], $\mathcal{G}_0$ involves less than 20 nodes, as shown in Fig. 1b, which can be manually selected. This node selection process should take much less time than a voxel-wise manual annotation of the whole blood vessels. Therefore, we call our pipeline *extremely weakly-supervised* with a partially annotated tree structure but without any real segmentation label maps.

2.2 CycSeg: CycleGAN with Additional Segmentation Branch

To create a synthetic image dataset, the reconstructed vascular tree structures $\mathcal{G} \equiv (\mathcal{V}, \mathcal{E})$ (Fig. 1d) are then remapped to 3D binary label maps (Fig. 1e) by voxelization, the detail of which is given in [26]. We then generate the corresponding gray-scale synthetic images (Fig. 1f) by simply assigning vessel foreground and background with random integers in $[128, 255]$ and $[0, 127]$ respectively. Of course, a segmentation model trained on these image-label pairs (Fig. 1f & e) will not work on real scans because of this oversimplified scan construction.

In order to adapt corresponding scans that emulate the micro-CT acquisition process out of the label maps from the previous step, unlabeled real micro-CT scans are utilized to train a generative model. Our backbone model is CycleGAN [29], which we extend to 3D while integrating an additional segmentation branch with segmenter S using a standard 3D UNet [4], as shown in Fig. 2(Left). We refer to our model as CycSeg later. The only modification we make in 3D is that 32 filters are used in the first layer instead of 64 to ease the computational load. Please refer to the supplementary material for detailed model architectures.

We strictly follow the original design [29] while extending to 3D for the loss functions definition and training procedure. Briefly, the two-way GAN loss $\mathcal{L}_{GAN}(G_{A \to B}, D_B)$ and $\mathcal{L}_{GAN}(G_{B \to A}, D_A)$ is to encourage the generator network to produce samples that are indistinguishable from real samples. Besides, cycle-consistency loss $\mathcal{L}_{cyc}(G_{A \to B}, G_{B \to A})$ is to assure the property $a \sim p_{data}(a) : G_{B \to A}(G_{A \to B}(a)) = a$ and $b \sim p_{data}(b) : G_{A \to B}(G_{B \to A}(b)) = b$. In our case, $p_{data}(a)$ and $p_{data}(b)$ denotes the real micro-CT scans distribution and the synthetic scans distribution from the physiologically generated trees, respectively. A final identity loss $\mathcal{L}_{id}(G_{A \to B}, G_{B \to A})$ is to stabilize the two generators. Please refer to [29] for the exact definition and computation of the above losses.

As shown in Fig. 2, instead of being trained on the synthesized scans (real B) directly, the segmenter (S) is trained on the adapted output (fake A) from the generator $G_{B \to A}$. Because the generator $G_{B \to A}$ learns to adapt realistic noise to the synthesized scans from unlabeled real scans (real A in Fig. 2), the segmenter (S) trained on the output from $G_{B \to A}$ will be able to segment unseen real scans. This introduces the segmentation loss $\mathcal{L}_{seg}(S, G_{B \to A})$. Thus, the final loss $\mathcal{L}_{tot}$ is defined as

$$
\begin{aligned}
\mathcal{L}_{tot} &= \mathcal{L}(G_{A \to B}, G_{B \to A}, D_A, D_B, S) \\
&= \mathcal{L}_{GAN}(G_{A \to B}, D_B) + \mathcal{L}_{GAN}(G_{B \to A}, D_A) \\
&+ \lambda_1 \mathcal{L}_{cyc}(G_{A \to B}, G_{B \to A}) + \lambda_2 \mathcal{L}_{id}(G_{A \to B}, G_{B \to A}) + \lambda_3 \mathcal{L}_{seg}(S, G_{B \to A})
\end{aligned}
\tag{1}
$$

Here $\mathcal{L}_{seg}(S, G_{B \to A})$ is an unweighted combination of a dice loss and standard cross-entropy loss. Specifically, the segmenter S takes the output from the generator $G_{B \to A}$ as input. Thus, given the physiologically generated label map g and its corresponding synthetic gray-scale image $x \sim p_{data}(b)$, the segmenter outputs $p = S(G_{B \to A}(x))$, and $\mathcal{L}_{seg}(S, G_{B \to A})$ is defined as

$$
\mathcal{L}_{seg}(S, G_{B \to A}) = \frac{1}{N}\left(-\sum_i^N g_i \log p_i + 1 - \frac{2\sum_i^N p_i g_i}{\sum_i^N p_i + \sum_i^N g_i}\right)
\tag{2}
$$

where N is the total number of voxels in each sampled 3D patch.

We follow [29] by setting the weights $\lambda_1 = 10$ and $\lambda_2 = 5$ while setting $\lambda_3 = 3$ experimentally. Note that although $G_{B \to A}$ is one of the input models to compute $\mathcal{L}_{\text{seg}}(S, G_{B\to A})$, all the CycleGAN components including $G_{B\to A}$ are frozen when training the segmenter S by blocking backpropagation. Moreover, since the generator, discriminator, and segmenter are trained alternately, λ_3 does not strongly impact the training and only affects early stopping.

During inference, all CycleGAN components are discarded, while real scans (domain A) are directly passed to segmenter S to output segmentation maps.

3   Experiments and Results

Dataset: The kidney cast was prepared as described in [1] in agreement with approved protocols (approval granted from the Danish Animal Experiments Inspectorate under the Ministry of Environment and Food, Denmark). The rat kidneys were *ex vivo* scanned in a ZEISS XRadia 410 Versa μCT scanner with an isotropic voxel size of 22.6 μm [1], with a fixed dimension of $1000 \times 1024 \times 1014$. To ease the computational load, scans are auto-cropped to $(692 \pm 33) \times (542 \pm 28) \times (917 \pm 28)$ by intersected bounding cubes from Otsu's thresholding in each dimension [26]. Here, we use 7 unlabeled scans (domain A) for training and 4 labeled scans for testing. The synthesized dataset (domain B) has 15 image-label pairs by tuning parameters used in GCO and running multiple times as discussed in Sect. 2.1.

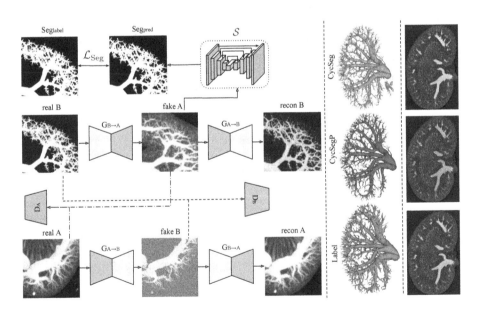

Fig. 2. Left: An illustration of CycleGAN with an additional segmentation branch working on adapted (fake) domain A images by $G_{B\to A}$. All 3D patches are shown with MIP. Computations for $\mathcal{L}_{\text{GAN}}$, $\mathcal{L}_{\text{id}}$, $\mathcal{L}_{\text{cyc}}$ are not shown for simplicity. Middle: An example result in 3D. Right: A sample slice overlaid with segmentation.

Pre-processing: Each generated patch is only preprocessed by simple min-max normalization $X_{\text{scale}} = (x_i - x_{\text{min}})/(x_{max} - x_{min})$.

Experimental Setup and Training Process: The network is implemented in PyTorch and trained on NVIDIA A100 with a batch size of 1 and patch size of 208 for 200 epochs. All three components are optimized using the Adam optimizer with the same learning rate of 2×10^{-4} and reduced by 1% for every epoch. We apply early stopping if $\mathcal{L}_{\text{tot}}$ (cf. Eq. (1)) of ten consecutive epochs does not decrease. Training takes approximately three days to reach convergence, while segmentation during inference takes only around two minutes per scan.

3.1   Results

As shown in Fig. 2, the CycleGAN successfully adapts realistic noise during micro-CT acquisition to the synthesized images (from real B to fake A), while a UNet trained over the adapted image with the corresponding synthesized label maps can segment real micro-CT scans. Although the ex-vivo scan separates the organ of interest from other parts, the segmentation of venous trees is still challenging due to various noises during the micro-CT acquisition and efficacy of the contrast media. Despite of few false positives, the 3D results in Fig. 2 show a smooth and clear venous tree structure, which indicates that the segmenter is trained to recognize veins from noises in real scans by the adapted images from $G_{B \to A}$. Since the result should anatomically be a connected tree, we also apply a simple connected component post-processing to the model's output (CycSegP), which removes the floating points and produces visually better results.

Table 1. Segmentation result on private renal and public retina dataset (in %).

Training data		Model	Acc	DICE	clDICE
Renal	Synthetic label + Raw scan	CycSeg	99.1 ± 0.1	74.3 ± 1.7	64.7 ± 5.0
		CycSegP	99.1 ± 0.1	74.9 ± 1.9	71.3 ± 4.4
Retinal	CHASE label + DRIVE image	Cyc Seg	96.1 ± 0.1	74.8 ± 0.4	76.3 ± 0.1
	DRIVE label + DRIVE image	UNet2D	96.5 ± 0.1	79.6 ± 0.5	78.9 ± 0.8

Table 1 shows the quantitative evaluation of the segmentation performance on the test set of four labeled scans, including accuracy, DICE score, and the topology-aware centerline DICE (clDICE) [23]. Although the test data size is too small to do a train-test split for training fully-supervised segmentation models, we believe that the visual inspection in Fig. 2 and relatively high quantitative results in Table 1 over 3D vessel segmentation task demonstrate the potential of our method in segmenting and building 3D renal models from micro-CT scans.

As a further qualitative evaluation, Fig. 3 shows one test sample with ground truth and our segmentation result (CycSeg) with MIP. These small vessels near the renal cortex are not labeled by human experts since manually reaching such details is too challenging and can take months to label a single scan. On the contrary, the small vessels are successfully recovered in our results since the model is trained on physiologically generated vascular trees that can reach as deep as possible. This is a major rationale behind creating a synthetic renal vascular dataset. Therefore, our results have potentially significantly better performance than those reported in Table 1 because these small vessels are currently regarded as false positives. Similar behavior has also been noticed in [17].

3.2   Proof-of-Concept on Retinal Blood Vessel Segmentation

We acknowledge that the quantitative analysis above may not be thorough with four test data. Thus, we conduct a proof-of-concept on a 2D retinal blood vessel segmentation task. We follow the previous experimental setups but with a patch size of 256 and batch size of 32 due to the ease of computational load in 2D.

Dataset and Domain Construction: We adopt the DRIVE dataset [24] as the target domain, which includes 40 digital fundus images captured by a Canon CR5 3CCD camera with a resolution of 584×565 pixels. However, the 3D vascular structure will not be physiologically correct when projecting to 2D images, and some works argue against compliance with Murray's law in retinal blood vessels [14]. Thus, we do not physiologically synthesize retinal blood vessels but only focus on the validity of the segmentation power with domain adaptation. Thus, we directly adopt label maps from another dataset (CHASE [6]) as the source domain. Specifically, we use 20 from 40 images of the DRIVE dataset without label maps to form the target domain (real A), together with 28 label maps from the CHASE dataset to form the source domain (real B) in analog to Fig. 2. These unpaired data are used to train the CycSeg jointly. Note that DRIVE label maps and CHASE images are discarded. The remaining 20 labeled images from DRIVE are used for testing.

Fig. 3. An example test sample shown with MIP. Small vessels near the cortex are not labeled but correctly detected by CycSeg.

An illustration of retinal domain adaptation and visual results in analog to Fig. 2 is in the supplementary material. As an ablation study, we adopt the same train-test split to directly train a fully-supervised UNet [21] using real image-label pairs from the DRIVE training set. From Table 1, the fully-supervised UNet still outperforms domain adaptation, but the difference is acceptable, as our goal is not to outperform the state-of-the-art but to propose a pipeline that can do segmentation without any labeled images from the target domain.

4   Conclusion

We have presented a pipeline that segments blood vessels from real scans without any manually segmented training data. The pipeline first synthesizes label maps of renal vasculatures using a physiologically based model and then generates corresponding scans implicitly via a 3D CycleGAN from unlabeled scans. Simultaneously, an additional segmentation branch on top of CycleGAN enables the segmentation of blood vessels on real scans. This removes any need for expert knowledge of scanning settings compared to [17]. We believe our pipeline can crucially reduce annotations needed to segment blood vessels and easily adapt to other organs or modalities.

Since segmentation is the final objective, the intermediate image adaptation task is only visually inspected. Future work could include numerical tests like image structure clustering and Amazon Mechanical Turk perceptual studies [29]. A modification over [26] is necessary to model the pair-wise coupling of veins and arteries and to train an Artery/Vein multi-class segmentation model in the future, which is far beyond the scope of this work. Nonetheless, more clean ground truth labels should enable a more thorough validation and benchmark test with standard segmentation models.

References

1. Andersen, S.B., et al.: Evaluation of 2D super-resolution ultrasound imaging of the rat renal vasculature using ex vivo micro-computed tomography. Sci. Rep. **11**(1), 1–13 (2021)
2. Bui, T.D., Wang, L., Lin, W., Li, G., Shen, D.: 6-month infant brain MRI segmentation guided by 24-month data using cycle-consistent adversarial networks. In: 2020 IEEE 17th International Symposium on Biomedical Imaging (ISBI), pp. 359–362. IEEE (2020)
3. Chen, H., et al.: Real-time cerebral vessel segmentation in laser speckle contrast image based on unsupervised domain adaptation. Front. Neurosci. 1523 (2021)
4. Çiçek, Ö., Abdulkadir, A., Lienkamp, S.S., Brox, T., Ronneberger, O.: 3D U-Net: learning dense volumetric segmentation from sparse annotation. In: Ourselin, S., Joskowicz, L., Sabuncu, M.R., Unal, G., Wells, W. (eds.) MICCAI 2016. LNCS, vol. 9901, pp. 424–432. Springer, Cham (2016). https://doi.org/10.1007/978-3-319-46723-8_49
5. Cui, H., Liu, X., Huang, N.: Pulmonary vessel segmentation based on orthogonal fused U-Net++ of chest CT images. In: Shen, D., et al. (eds.) MICCAI 2019. LNCS, vol. 11769, pp. 293–300. Springer, Cham (2019). https://doi.org/10.1007/978-3-030-32226-7_33
6. Fraz, M.M., et al.: An ensemble classification-based approach applied to retinal blood vessel segmentation. IEEE Trans. Biomed. Eng. **59**(9), 2538–2548 (2012)
7. Georg, M., Preusser, T., Hahn, H.K.: Global constructive optimization of vascular systems (2010). https://openscholarship.wustl.edu/cse_research/36
8. Gilbert, A., Marciniak, M., Rodero, C., Lamata, P., Samset, E., Mcleod, K.: Generating synthetic labeled data from existing anatomical models: an example with echocardiography segmentation. IEEE Trans. Med. Imaging **40**(10), 2783–2794 (2021)

9. He, Y., et al.: Dense biased networks with deep priori anatomy and hard region adaptation: semi-supervised learning for fine renal artery segmentation. Med. Image Anal. **63**, 101722 (2020)

10. Isensee, F., Jaeger, P.F., Kohl, S.A., Petersen, J., Maier-Hein, K.H.: nnU-Net: a self-configuring method for deep learning-based biomedical image segmentation. Nat. Methods **18**(2), 203–211 (2021)

11. Jia, D., Zhuang, X.: Learning-based algorithms for vessel tracking: a review. Comput. Med. Imaging Graph. **89**, 101840 (2021)

12. Keshwani, D., Kitamura, Y., Ihara, S., Iizuka, S., Simo-Serra, E.: TopNet: topology preserving metric learning for vessel tree reconstruction and labelling. In: Martel, A.L., et al. (eds.) MICCAI 2020. LNCS, vol. 12266, pp. 14–23. Springer, Cham (2020). https://doi.org/10.1007/978-3-030-59725-2_2

13. Lindner, L., Narnhofer, D., Weber, M., Gsaxner, C., Kolodziej, M., Egger, J.: Using synthetic training data for deep learning-based GBM segmentation. In: 2019 41st Annual International Conference of the IEEE Engineering in Medicine and Biology Society (EMBC), pp. 6724–6729. IEEE (2019)

14. Luo, T., Gast, T.J., Vermeer, T.J., Burns, S.A.: Retinal vascular branching in healthy and diabetic subjects. Investig. Ophthalmol. Vis. Sci. **58**(5), 2685–2694 (2017)

15. Malimban, J., et al.: Deep learning-based segmentation of the thorax in mouse micro-CT scans. Sci. Rep. **12**(1), 1822 (2022)

16. Marsh, D.J., Postnov, D.D., Sosnovtseva, O.V., Holstein-Rathlou, N.H.: The nephron-arterial network and its interactions. Am. J. Physiol.-Renal Physiol. **316**(5), F769–F784 (2019)

17. Menten, M.J., Paetzold, J.C., Dima, A., Menze, B.H., Knier, B., Rueckert, D.: Physiology-based simulation of the retinal vasculature enables annotation-free segmentation of oct angiographs. In: Wang, L., Dou, Q., Fletcher, P.T., Speidel, S., Li, S. (eds.) MICCAI 2022. LNCS, vol. 13438, pp. 330–340. Springer, Cham (2022). https://doi.org/10.1007/978-3-031-16452-1_32

18. Murray, C.D.: The physiological principle of minimum work: I. the vascular system and the cost of blood volume. Proc. Natl. Acad. Sci. **12**(3), 207–214 (1926)

19. Ohnishi, T., et al.: Three-dimensional vessel segmentation in whole-tissue and whole-block imaging using a deep neural network: proof-of-concept study. Am. J. Pathol. **191**(3), 463–474 (2021)

20. Ritman, E.L.: Current status of developments and applications of micro-CT. Annu. Rev. Biomed. Eng. **13**, 531–552 (2011)

21. Ronneberger, O., Fischer, P., Brox, T.: U-Net: convolutional networks for biomedical image segmentation. In: Navab, N., Hornegger, J., Wells, W.M., Frangi, A.F. (eds.) MICCAI 2015. LNCS, vol. 9351, pp. 234–241. Springer, Cham (2015). https://doi.org/10.1007/978-3-319-24574-4_28

22. Schreiner, W., Karch, R., Neumann, F., Neumann, M.: Constrained constructive optimization of arterial tree models. Scaling Biol. **145**, 65 (2000)

23. Shit, S., et al.: clDice-a novel topology-preserving loss function for tubular structure segmentation. In: Proceedings of the IEEE/CVF Conference on Computer Vision and Pattern Recognition, pp. 16560–16569 (2021)

24. Staal, J., Abràmoff, M.D., Niemeijer, M., Viergever, M.A., Van Ginneken, B.: Ridge-based vessel segmentation in color images of the retina. IEEE Trans. Med. Imaging **23**(4), 501–509 (2004)

25. Todorov, M.I., et al.: Machine learning analysis of whole mouse brain vasculature. Nat. Methods **17**(4), 442–449 (2020)

26. Xu, P., et al.: A hybrid approach to full-scale reconstruction of renal arterial network. Sci. Rep. **13**(1), 7569 (2023)
27. Zhang, J., Zhang, Y., Xu, X.: Pyramid u-net for retinal vessel segmentation. In: ICASSP 2021-2021 IEEE International Conference on Acoustics, Speech and Signal Processing (ICASSP), pp. 1125–1129. IEEE (2021)
28. Zhang, Z., Yang, L., Zheng, Y.: Translating and segmenting multimodal medical volumes with cycle-and shape-consistency generative adversarial network. In: Proceedings of the IEEE Conference on Computer Vision and Pattern Recognition, pp. 9242–9251 (2018)
29. Zhu, J.Y., Park, T., Isola, P., Efros, A.A.: Unpaired image-to-image translation using cycle-consistent adversarial networks. In: Proceedings of the IEEE International Conference on Computer Vision, pp. 2223–2232 (2017)

Multi-task Learning for Few-Shot Differential Diagnosis of Breast Cancer Histopathology Images

Krishna Thoriya[1(✉)], Preeti Mutreja[2], Sumit Kalra[3,4], and Angshuman Paul[3]

[1] Department of Electrical Engineering, Indian Institute of Technology Jodhpur,
Jodhpur, India
krishna.4@iitj.ac.in
[2] Novealthy Innovations Pvt. Ltd., Jodhpur, India
[3] Department of Computer Science Engineering, Indian Institute of Technology
Jodhpur, Jodhpur, India
[4] Interdisciplinary Research Platform - Smart Healthcare, Indian Institute of
Technology Jodhpur, Jodhpur, India

Abstract. Deep learning models may be useful for the differential diagnosis of breast cancer histopathology images. However, most modern deep learning methods are data-hungry. But, large annotated dataset of breast cancer histopathology images are elusive. As a result, the application of such deep learning methods for the differential diagnosis of breast cancer is limited. To deal with this problem, we propose a few-shot learning approach for the differential diagnosis of the histopathology images of breast tissue. Our model is trained through two stages. We initially train our model for a binary classification task of identifying benign and malignant tissues. Subsequently, we propose a multi-task learning strategy for the few-shot differential diagnosis of breast tissues. Experiments on publicly available breast cancer histopathology image datasets show the efficacy of the proposed method.

Keywords: Few-shot learning · Multi-task learning · Histopathology images

1 Introduction

An early diagnosis is often a key factor in the successful treatment of breast cancer. Deep learning-based models have made incredible strides in the diagnosis of breast cancer histopathology images. However, most modern deep learning methods are data-hungry. Annotating histopathology images is time-consuming and requires a domain expert. Therefore, large-scale datasets of breast cancer histopathology images are elusive. Most research works on breast cancer histopathology images focus on the classification of benign and malignant breast cancer tissues. However, a more precise diagnosis requires a fine-grained classification of histopathology images. Fine-grained classification of breast cancer histopathology images with limited annotation is even more challenging.

© The Author(s), under exclusive license to Springer Nature Switzerland AG 2023
Z. Xue et al. (Eds.): MILLanD 2023, LNCS 14307, pp. 202–210, 2023.
https://doi.org/10.1007/978-3-031-44917-8_19

In this work, we propose a technique for few-shot fine-grained classification of breast cancer histopathology images utilizing multi-task learning. To that end, we first train a CNN architecture on a histopathology image dataset (subsequently referred to as the source dataset) of breast tissues with annotations for benign and malignant tissues. This dataset contains a large number of annotated images. Subsequently, we perform a few-shot training of our model with another dataset (subsequently referred to as the target dataset) using a small number of histopathology images of breast tissues with fine-grained labels for benign and malignant classes. Our model is designed in such a way that during the few-shot training, our model can simultaneously learn two tasks, namely binary classification (benign vs malignant) and fine-grained classification. Thus, we design a multi-task learning setup by transferring knowledge of binary (benign vs malignant) classification from the source dataset and utilizing multi-task learning for fine-grained classification from the target dataset. Our approach is aimed to overcome the problem of a large breast cancer histopathology dataset with a fine-grained annotation. The fine-grained classification of histopathology images may be helpful in the differential diagnosis of breast cancer histopathology images.

In this work, our major contributions are as follows.

- We propose a few-shot learning technique for the fine-grained classification of breast cancer histopathology images.
- Our model utilizes transfer learning from the source dataset for binary classification to learn fine-grained classification in a target dataset.
- We design a multi-task learning strategy to facilitate the few-shot fine-grained classification.

The rest of the paper is organized as follows. In Sect. 2, we discuss the proposed method followed by the details of the experiments and results in Sect. 3. Finally, we conclude the paper in Sect. 4.

2   Methods

We propose a model for few-shot fine-grained classification of breast histopathology images. Our model is first trained on a source dataset (of breast histopathology images) containing a large number of images with binary annotations (benign and malignant) (stage 1 of training). After that, we retrain our model on a target dataset (of breast histopathology images) by utilizing only a few images of with fine-grained annotations, namely, Adenosis, Fibroadenoma, Phyllodes Tumor, Tubular Adenoma, Ductal Carcinoma, Lobular Carcinoma, Mucinous Carcinoma, and Papillary Carcinoma for differential diagnosis (stage 2 of training). The first four labels represent fine-grained classes of benign tumors and the rest represent fine-grained classes of malignant tumors.

During stage 2, our model is trained in a multi-task learning setting where it learns a binary classification (benign vs malignant) and a fine-grained classification of the aforementioned eight classes. During stage 2, the model also exploits the learning of stage 1 for benign vs malignant classification to facilitate the fine-grained classification. In stage 2 of the proposed method, we use only 10 images from each fine-grained class from the BreakHis dataset to train our model. That is why our method is a few-shot learning method. Next, we discuss the stages of the training. A block diagram of stage 2 of the proposed method is presented in Fig. 1.

2.1   Stage 1: Training for Binary Classification

We use ResNet [6] for designing our method. The choice of ResNet is motivated by its ability to perform better feature propagation. We take ResNet-50 model pretrained on ImageNet [4]. We train this ResNet model with our source dataset for benign vs malignant classification. In this stage, we use the ResNet model with one output layer that produces one of the two possible class labels (benign or malignant) as output. For binary classification, we use binary cross-entropy loss as our loss function. Therefore, to train the models for binary classification, we minimize binary cross-entropy loss.

2.2   Stage 2: Training Few-Shot Multi-task Learning

In stage 2 of training, we take the model trained on stage 1 and further train it with fine-grained labels from the target dataset. We design a multi-task learning strategy with two output heads of our model. The first output head produces benign or malignant as output label. The second output head produces one of the fine-grained labels as output label. To that end, we add one more classification head to our model of stage 1 (see Fig. 1). With this architecture we exploit the learning of stage 1 to aid the fine-grained classification with a few training images per fine-grained class. Thus, we utilize a transfer learning from the source dataset of stage 1 to facilitate few-shot fine-grained classification of the images of the target dataset.

Since we plan to use multi-task learning in stage 2, we design a loss function that combines losses computed from both the output heads of our model. We compute binary cross-entropy loss (L_1) from the outputs of the binary classification head (i.e., for task 1) and categorical cross-entropy loss [15] (L_2) from the outputs of the fine-grained classification head (i.e., for task 2). Subsequently, the total loss is

$$L = L_1 + \beta L_2, \tag{1}$$

where β is a hyperparameter representing the relative weight assigned to the loss components. We minimize the total loss L to train our model. We choose the value of β based on the validation performance of the model. Table 1 indicates data distribution of the target dataset used in stage 2. We use data augmentation to increase the size of the training set.

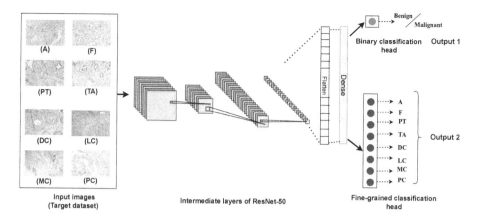

Fig. 1. A block diagram of stage 2 of the proposed method. Images representing different classes (Adenosis(A), Fibroadenoma (F), Phyllodes Tumor (PT) and Tubular Adenoma (TA), Ductal Carcinoma (DC), Lobular Carcinoma (LC), Mucinous Carcinoma (MC), and Papillary Carcinoma (PC)) from the target dataset are shown as input.

2.3   Experimental Settings

In stage 1, we split the source dataset in 60:10:30 ratio for training, validation, and testing, respectively. After that, we use a few data augmentation techniques [12] to enlarge the training dataset size. The augmentation techniques that are used are zooming, height shifting, width shifting, rotation, vertical flip, salt pepper, gaussian noise, shearing and elastic deformation. After applying data augmentation techniques, we get a total of 2400 images containing 1200 images from each of the benign and malignant classes. We use SGD [11] optimizer with learning rate of 0.001 to train our model through 70 epochs and a batch size of 4. In the last layer, we initialize 'He Normal' [5] weights. 30% of the images from the source dataset has been used for testing and 10% of the total images has been used for validation.

In stage 2, our model is trained with 10 images for every fine-grained class. In the target dataset, we choose 10 images randomly for training from each class ensuring that these images are from different patients. In stage 2, we use 5 different types of augmentation techniques, namely rotation, zooming, width shift (shifting image horizontally), height shift (shifting image vertically), and shearing. Adam [8] optimizer with a learning rate of 0.00001 is used. After every four epochs, the learning rate decays by a factor of 0.7. Loss weights in binary and fine-grained classification heads are set to 0.1 and 0.9 respectively. The value of β is chosen accordingly. The weight initialization parameter is set to 'He normal' for the last two layers of the classification heads in both tasks. The number of neurons in the dense layers is set to 4096. The classification layers of the heads for binary classification and fine-grained classification use the Sigmoid activation function and the LeakyReLu function, respectively.

Table 1. Distribution of images in the target (BreakHis [13]) dataset for binary classification (Benign(B) or Malignant (M)) and for fine-grained classification. For fine-grained classification, eight types of tumors, namely, Adenosis(A), Fibroadenoma (F), Phyllodes Tumor (PT) and Tubular Adenoma (TA), Ductal Carcinoma (DC), Lobular Carcinoma (LC), Mucinous Carcinoma (MC), and Papillary Carcinoma (PC) are considered.

Data type		Classification Type										Total number of instances
		Binary		Fine-grained								
		B	M	A	F	PT	TA	DC	LC	MC	PC	
Train	Original	40	40	10	10	10	10	10	10	10	10	80
	Augmented	200	200	50	50	50	50	50	50	50	50	400
	Total	240	240	60	60	60	60	60	60	60	60	480
Validation		20	20	5	5	5	5	5	5	5	5	40
Test		562	1314	98	238	94	132	857	140	188	129	1876

Test instance				
Ground-truth label	Adenosis	Fibroadenoma	Phyllodes Tumor	Tubular Adenoma
Predicted label	**Adenosis**	**Fibroadenoma**	**Phyllodes Tumor**	**Tubular Adenoma**
Test instance				
Ground-truth label	Ductal Carcinoma	Mucinous Carcinoma	Lobular Carcinoma	Papillary Carcinoma
Predicted label	**Ductal Carcinoma**	**Papillary Carcinoma**	**Lobular Carcinoma**	**Fibroadenoma**

Fig. 2. Sample images from the BreakHis dataset with their ground-truth labels and the predicted labels by the proposed method.

3   Experimental Results and Comparison

3.1   Datasets

The Source Dataset (ICIAR 2018): We use ICIAR 2018 grand challenge on BreAst Cancer Histology (BACH) [2] image dataset (referred to as ICIAR) as our source dataset for binary classification. We use histopathology images categorized into 4 classes, namely, Normal, Benign, In Situ carcinoma, and Invasive carcinoma. The dataset contains a total of 400 microscopic images. Each class consists of 100 microscopic images and their corresponding ground truth labels. Benign and Normal tumors are considered in the benign class while In situ carcinoma and Invasive carcinoma fall under malignant class. In stage 1, the model is trained to perform benign vs malignant classification.

The Target Dataset (BreakHis): For stage 2 of the proposed method, we use images from the Breast Cancer Histopathology Database (BreakHis) [13]. This dataset consists of histopathology images of different types of benign and malignant breast tumors. Adenosis (A), Fibroadenoma (F), Phyllodes Tumor (PT), and Tubular Adenoma (TA) are the types of benign tumors considered in this dataset. On the other hand, this dataset contains histopathology images of several types of malignant tumors, namely, Ductal Carcinoma (DC), Lobular Carcinoma (LC), Mucinous Carcinoma (MC), and Papillary Carcinoma (PC). The dataset has a total of 9109 microscopic slides. We use the data corresponding to 40× magnification for our experiment. Since our model executes two tasks on this dataset at stage 2, we consider the tumors for benign vs malignant and also for fine-grained classification into one of the eight aforementioned classes. Thus the BreakHis dataset is used at stage 2 for multi-task few-shot learning with few images for each of the fine-grained classes.

3.2 Comparative Performances

We evaluate the performance of our method using F1 score and area Under the ROC curve (AUC) [1]. On the BreakHis dataset, we compute the AUC score for fine-grained classification in two ways. First, the AUC score for each class is calculated against the remaining classes (one-vs-rest or OvR). The average AUC score is then computed for all possible pairwise combinations of classes (one-vs-one or OvO). We calculate macro average of AUC score by calculating AUC scores for each label and finding their unweighted mean. This does not take label imbalance into account. So, we also calculate the weighted mean value of AUC scores.

After training the model as described in stage 1, our model achieved 84.17% test accuracy on the ICIAR dataset for binary classification. Using this model

Table 2. Performances of different methods for fine-grained classification in the BreakHis dataset in terms of 'Macro' and 'Weighted' average of AUC scores using One-vs-one (OvO) and One-vs-rest (OvR) strategies.

Methods	AUC score			
	One Vs One		One Vs Rest	
	Macro	Weighted	Macro	Weighted
IRV2	0.70	0.70	0.70	0.69
RN50	0.47	0.48	0.47	0.48
BCDN-C	0.50	0.50	0.50	0.50
BCDN-A	0.59	0.60	0.58	0.61
DN	0.53	0.53	0.52	0.56
ENB3	0.50	0.50	0.50	0.50
Proposed	**0.71**	**0.70**	**0.71**	**0.68**

with its saved weights, we evaluated the model on the test images from BreakHis dataset for the two tasks of stage 2. Figure 2 shows sample images from each of the eight fine-grained classes from the BreakHis dataset with their ground truth labels and the predicted labels by our model.

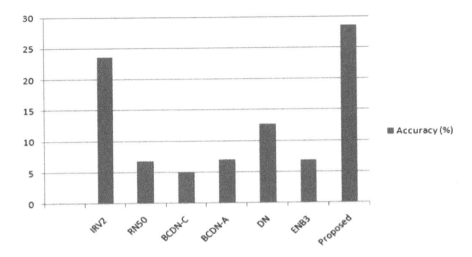

Fig. 3. Average classification accuracies of different methods for fine-grained classification in the BreakHis dataset.

We compare our method with several state-of-the-art approaches. These are Inception-ResNet-V2 (**IRV2**) [14], ResNet-50 (**RN50**) [10], DenseNet **DN** [9], EfficientNet-B3 (**ENB3**) [3], and BCDNet (**BCDN**) [7]. In one BCDN, features from VGG-16 and ResNet-50 backbones are concatenated which is denoted by **BCDN-C**. In another architecture, the features before the classification layer are added, abbreviated by **BCDN-A**. As a part of the comparison, we choose the existing classification models. We then fine-tune those models for our multi-class classification. The comparisons of these methods for fine-grained classification in BreakHis dataset in terms of the AUC scores are reported in Table 2. The average classification accuracies of different methods for the fine-grained classification in the BreakHis dataset are presented in Fig. 3. Notice that our method outperforms most of the competing methods in terms of the AUC scores and average classification accuracy.

Next, we compare the performance of different methods in terms of their performance for each of the individual fine-grained classes. Table 3 presents a comparison of the F1 scores achieved by the proposed method and the competing methods for each of the fine-grained classes in the BreakHis dataset. Thus, we observe the superiority of the proposed method in terms of different performance metrics for the fine-grained classification in the BreakHis dataset.

Table 3. F1 scores for different methods for fine-grained classification in the BreakHis dataset.

Methods	F1 Score							
	Benign				Malignant			
	A	F	PT	TA	DC	LC	MC	PC
IRV2	0.20	0.29	0.18	0.23	0.25	0.25	0.21	0.14
RN50	0.08	0.10	0.08	0.05	0.02	0.08	0.09	0.04
BCDN-C	0.0	0.0	0.10	0.0	0.0	0.0	0.0	0.0
BCDN-A	0.0	0.0	0.0	0.13	0.0	0.0	0.0	0.0
DN	0.0	0.22	0.0	0.0	0.0	0.0	0.0	0.0
ENB3	0.0	0.0	0.0	0.0	0.0	0.0	0.0	0.13
Proposed	**0.14**	**0.29**	**0.23**	**0.25**	**0.15**	**0.21**	**0.12**	**0.15**

4   Conclusions

We propose a method for few-shot differential diagnosis of breast cancer histopathology images. Our method is trained in two stages. In the first stage, our model learns benign vs malignant classification in a source dataset. Subsequently, in stage 2, we implement a multi-task learning setup where a target dataset is used for training the model a binary (benign vs malignant) and a fine-grained classification simultaneously. Our method outperforms several state-of-the-art approaches on a publicly available dataset with fine-grained labels. Our method has the potential to significantly reduce the task of annotation and help in the future development of a clinically applicable system for the differential diagnosis of breast cancer histopathology images. In the future, we will try to utilize auxiliary information about different fine-grained classes to facilitate the few-shot diagnosis. We will also look into designing generalizable few-shot learning models for the diagnosis of histopathology images.

References

1. Bradley, A.P.: The use of the area under the roc curve in the evaluation of machine learning algorithms. Pattern Recognit. **30**(7), 1145–1159 (1997). https://doi.org/10.1016/S0031-3203(96)00142-2
2. Aresta, G., et al.: Bach: grand challenge on breast cancer histology images. Med. Image Anal. **56**, 122–139 (2019). https://doi.org/10.1016/j.media.2019.05.010
3. Chandrasekar, M., Ganesh, M., Saleena, B., Balasubramanian, P.: Breast cancer histopathological image classification using efficientnet architecture. In: 2020 IEEE International Conference on Technology, Engineering, Management for Societal impact using Marketing, Entrepreneurship and Talent (TEMSMET), pp. 1–5 (2020). https://doi.org/10.1109/TEMSMET51618.2020.9557441
4. Deng, J., Dong, W., Socher, R., Li, L.J., Li, K., Fei-Fei, L.: Imagenet: a large-scale hierarchical image database. In: 2009 IEEE Conference on Computer Vision and

Pattern Recognition, pp. 248–255 (2009). https://doi.org/10.1109/CVPR.2009. 5206848

5. He, K., Zhang, X., Ren, S., Sun, J.: Delving deep into rectifiers: surpassing human-level performance on imagenet classification. In: 2015 IEEE International Conference on Computer Vision (ICCV), pp. 1026–1034 (2015)

6. He, K., Zhang, X., Ren, S., Sun, J.: Deep residual learning for image recognition. In: Proceedings of the IEEE Conference on Computer Vision and Pattern Recognition, pp. 770–778 (2016)

7. He, Q., Cheng, G., Ju, H.: BCDnet: parallel heterogeneous eight-class classification model of breast pathology. PLoS ONE **16**, e0253764 (2021)

8. Kingma, D., Ba, J.: Adam: a method for stochastic optimization. In: International Conference on Learning Representations (2014)

9. Nawaz, M.A., Sewissy, A.A., Soliman, T.H.A.: Multi-class breast cancer classification using deep learning convolutional neural network. Int. J. Adv. Comput. Sci. Appl. **9**, 316–332 (2018)

10. Nishant Behar, M.S.: Resnet50-based effective model for breast cancer classification using histopathology images. Comput. Model. Eng. Sci. **130**(2), 823–839 (2022)

11. Ruder, S.: An overview of gradient descent optimization algorithms. arXiv abs/1609.04747 (2016)

12. Shorten, C., Khoshgoftaar, T.M.: A survey on image data augmentation for deep learning. J. Big Data **6**, 1–48 (2019)

13. Spanhol, F.A., Oliveira, L.S., Petitjean, C., Heutte, L.: A dataset for breast cancer histopathological image classification. IEEE Trans. Biomed. Eng. **63**(7), 1455–1462 (2015)

14. Xie, J., Liu, R., Luttrell, J., Zhang, C.: Deep learning based analysis of histopathological images of breast cancer. Front. Genet. **10**, 80 (2019). https://doi.org/10.3389/fgene.2019.00080

15. Zhang, Z., Sabuncu, M.: Generalized cross entropy loss for training deep neural networks with noisy labels (2018)

Active Learning

Test-Time Augmentation-Based Active Learning and Self-training for Label-Efficient Segmentation

Bella Specktor-Fadida[1]([✉]), Anna Levchakov[2], Dana Schonberger[2,3], Liat Ben-Sira[4,5], Dafna Ben Bashat[2,5,6], and Leo Joskowicz[1,7]

[1] School of Computer Science and Engineering, The Hebrew University of Jerusalem, Jerusalem, Israel
bella.specktor@mail.huji.ac.il
[2] Sagol Brain Institute, Tel Aviv Sourasky Medical Center, Tel Aviv-Yafo, Israel
[3] Department of Biomedical Engineering, Tel Aviv University, Tel Aviv, Israel
[4] Division of Pediatric Radiology, Tel Aviv Sourasky Medical Center, Tel Aviv, Israel
[5] Faculty of Medicine, Tel Aviv University, Tel Aviv, Israel
[6] Sagol School of Neuroscience, Tel Aviv University, Tel Aviv, Israel
[7] Edmond and Lily Safra Center for Brain Sciences, The Hebrew University of Jerusalem, Jerusalem, Israel

Abstract. Deep learning techniques depend on large datasets whose annotation is time-consuming. To reduce annotation burden, the self-training (ST) and active-learning (AL) methods have been developed as well as methods that combine them in an iterative fashion. However, it remains unclear when each method is the most useful, and when it is advantageous to combine them. In this paper, we propose a new method that combines ST with AL using Test-Time Augmentations (TTA). First, TTA is performed on an initial teacher network. Then, cases for annotation are selected based on the lowest estimated Dice score. Cases with high estimated scores are used as soft pseudo-labels for ST. The selected annotated cases are trained with existing annotated cases and ST cases with border slices annotations. We demonstrate the method on MRI fetal body and placenta segmentation tasks with different data variability characteristics. Our results indicate that ST is highly effective for both tasks, boosting performance for in-distribution (ID) and out-of-distribution (OOD) data. However, while self-training improved the performance of single-sequence fetal body segmentation when combined with AL, it slightly deteriorated performance of multi-sequence placenta segmentation on ID data. AL was helpful for the high variability placenta data, but did not improve upon random selection for the single-sequence body data. For fetal body segmentation sequence transfer, combining AL with ST following ST iteration yielded a Dice of 0.961 with only 6 original scans and 2 new sequence scans. Results using only 15 high-variability placenta cases were similar to those using 50 cases. Code is available at: https://github.com/Bella31/TTA-quality-estimation-ST-AL.

Supplementary Information The online version contains supplementary material available at https://doi.org/10.1007/978-3-031-44917-8_21.

© The Author(s), under exclusive license to Springer Nature Switzerland AG 2023
Z. Xue et al. (Eds.): MILLanD 2023, LNCS 14307, pp. 213–223, 2023.
https://doi.org/10.1007/978-3-031-44917-8_21

Keywords: Self-training · Active learning · Test-time augmentation · Fetal MRI

1   Introduction

Segmentation of anatomical structures in CT and MRI scans is a key task in many clinical applications. However, manual annotation requires expertise, is tedious, time-consuming, and is subject to annotator variability. State-of-the-art automatic volumetric segmentation methods are based on deep neural networks. While effective, these methods require a large, high-quality dataset of expert-validated annotations, which is difficult to obtain. A variety of methods have been proposed to address annotation scarcity in semantic segmentation [18].

Self-training (ST), also called pseudo-labeling, is a method for iterative semi-supervised learning (SSL). In ST, a model improves the quality of the pseudo-annotations by learning from its own predictions [4]. It is performed by alternatively training two or more networks with an uncertainty-aware scheme [4,15,18]. Nie et al. [13] describe an adversarial framework with a generator segmentation network and a discriminator confidence network. Xia et al. [20] propose a method for generating pseudo-labels based on co-training multiple networks. Consistency regularization (CR) [3,14], another popular SSL method, relies on various perturbation techniques to generate disagreement on the same inputs, so that models can be trained by enforcing prediction consistency on unlabeled data without knowing the labeled information.

Active learning (AL) aims to identify the best samples for annotation during training. The most common criterion for sample selection is based on prediction uncertainty estimation, following the premise that more information can be learned by the model using uncertain samples [2]. AL often uses ensembled uncertainty measurements that require training multiple models or Monte-Carlo dropout [9,22]. Ensemble-based methods measure the agreement between different models, with higher model disagreement potentially implying more uncertainty and less informativeness. Jungo et al. [9] indicated the need for subject-level uncertainty for quality estimation.

Segmentation quality estimation is used in ST to discard low-quality pseudo-labels and in AL to select low-quality samples for manual annotation. Wang et al. [19] show that aleatory uncertainty scoring with Test-Time Augmentations (TTA) provides a better uncertainty estimation than test-time dropout-based model uncertainty. They show that TTA helps to eliminate overconfident incorrect predictions. Specktor et al. [16] discard low-quality pseudo-labels for ST with TTA-based Dice estimation. Others use TTA-based error estimation for AL with the Volume Overlap Distance and the Jensen-Shannon divergence [5,7].

Frameworks that combine SSL and AL have been recently proposed for both natural and medical images [6–8,10,12,23]. Zhang et al. [23] propose a closed loop pseudo-labeling and informative active annotation framework. Nath et al. [12] describe a two-stage learning framework for each active iteration where the unlabeled data is used in the second stage for semi-supervised fine-tuning. Gaillochet et al. [7] applies cross-augmentation consistency during training and inference at each iteration to both improve model learning in a semi-supervised fashion and identify the most relevant unlabeled samples to annotate next. However, these methods do not take into account the data properties at each iteration. A key question remains whether it is always best to combine SSL and AL, and when it is better to use each separately.

Recently, an offline self-training scheme with one or two teacher-student iterations has been reported to yield superior segmentation results [21,25]. It consists of teacher training on annotated data followed by pseudo-labels generation on unlabeled data and student training that jointly learns from the manual and the high-quality generated pseudo-labels.

In this paper we present a new human-in-the-loop method based on TTA for a combined training of actively selected and offline-calculated self-trained examples. It performs simultaneous computation of pseudo-labels for self-training and segmentation quality estimation for an active selection of samples and filtering of unreliable pseudo-labels. The method also uses border slices annotations to improve the pseudo-labels and the quality estimation accuracy.

2   Method

The method consists of: 1) training a teacher network on a small number of examples; 2) training a student model using a fully-automatic ST module (optional); 3) training a second student model with a combined AL and ST module using the base network from step 1 or 2. The combined AL and ST iteration is performed either directly after the initial model training or after ST iteration.

2.1   ST Module

The fully automatic ST iteration is optionally performed before the combined AL and ST module iteration. It uses soft teacher predictions instead of hard teacher predictions, as these were found to perform better [1,24]. See the Supplementary Material (Sect. 1, Table A1). The pseudo-labels are either network predictions without post-processing (soft network predictions) or TTA predictions medians for each voxel, depending on the benefit of using TTA for a given segmentation task. Unreliable training examples are filtered out with quality estimation ranking using a threshold. The threshold is selected so that the number of pseudo-labels will be at least the same as the number of labeled examples.

The student self-training network is trained with the original data of the initial network and with the new self-training examples using an optimization scheme with learning rate restarts [11].

TTA-Based Quality Estimation: The quality estimation is obtained by computing the mean Dice score between the median prediction and each of the augmentation results [16]. For TTA we use flipping, rotation, transpose and contrast augmentations. A median prediction is first assigned for each voxel, and then the estimated Dice score is obtained by computing the median Dice score between the median and each one of the augmentation results.

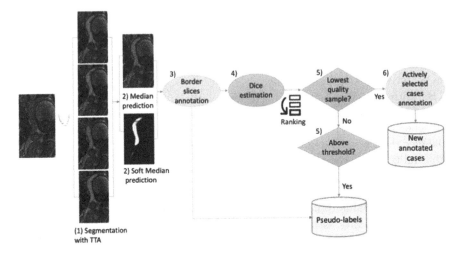

Fig. 1. Flow diagram of the combined active learning and self-training method illustrated on the placenta (dark green). The human annotation steps are marked in yellow; light green steps are automatic. (Color figure online)

2.2   Combined AL and ST Module

The combined AL and ST module consists of five steps: 1) TTA inference is performed with a base network; 2) border slices of the region of Interest (ROI) are annotated for the TTA inference data; 3) cases are selected for annotation and unreliable pseudo-labels are filtered using TTA-based quality estimation on the slices of the structure of interest; 4) manual correction of the selected cases is performed for annotation; and 5) training is performed with the newly selected annotated cases, existing annotated cases, and additional ST cases.

The new network uses the original data in combination with new actively selected cases and pseudo-labels. Let D be the set of all cases. The training set $D_{train} \subset D$ is $D_{train} = D_{base} \cup D_{AL} \cup D_{ST}$, where D_{base} is the set of training examples of the initial network, D_{AL} is the set of actively selected examples, and D_{ST} is the set of selected pseudo-labeled examples. Training is performed by fine-tuning the base network with learning rate restarts optimization [11].

Figure 1 illustrates the process of generating the new training datasets D_{AL} and D_{ST}. The process includes: 1) segmentation inference with TTA using the base network; 2) calculation of the median of TTA results for each voxel (soft median prediction) and thresholding with t = 0.5 to produce the final median prediction mask (median prediction); 3) manual annotation of border slices; 4) TTA Dice estimation and ranking of new unlabeled cases by estimated Dice metric; 5) selection of cases with the lowest estimated Dice for annotation, and from the rest of the cases selection of pseudo labels above an estimated Dice threshold; 6) manual annotation of the actively selected cases.

Both the AL and ST cases use the quality estimation method described in [10], similar to the quality estimation in the fully automatic self-training module.

The cases with the lowest estimated Dice score are selected for annotation and cases with estimated quality above a threshold are used as pseudo-labels. See the Supplementary Material for illustrations (Sect. 2, Fig. A1-A2).

2.3   Border Slices Annotation

For this human-in-the-loop method, various types of manual annotations are performed on the unlabeled cases. To decrease errors in the background slices outside of the structure of interest, the uppermost and lowermost slices of the ROI that includes the structure of interest are manually selected by the annotator [17]. This is an easy task that, and unlike segmentation annotations, can be quickly performed for a large number of cases. These annotations are used to correct the self-training result outside of the structure of interest and to estimate more accurately the Dice score in the selected region.

3   Experimental Results

To evaluate our method, we retrospectively collected fetal MRI scans and conducted three studies. The fetal MRI body scans were acquired with the FIESTA and the TRUFI sequences as part of routine fetal assessment of fetuses with gestational ages (GA) of 28–39 weeks from the Tel-Aviv Sourasky Medical Center, Israel. They included the segmentation of the fetal body or the fetal placenta.

Datasets and Annotations: The FIESTA sequence fetal body dataset consists of 104 cases acquired on a GE MR450 1.5T scanner with a resolution range of $1.48 - 1.87 \times 1.48 - 1.87 \times 2 - 5.0$ mm^3. The TRUFI sequence fetal body dataset consists of 101 cases acquired on Siemens Skyra 3T, Prisma 3T, and Aera 1.5T scanners, with a resolution range of $0.6 - 1.34 \times 0.6 - 1.34 \times 2 - 4.8$ mm^3.

The placenta in-distribution (ID) dataset includes 88 cases, 50 TRUFI and 38 FIESTA. The TRUFI scans were acquired on Siemens Prisma and Vida scanners with a resolution of $0.781 \times 0.781 \times 2$ mm^3. The FIESTA sequence scans were acquired on a GE MR450 1.5T scanner with a resolution range of $1.48 - 1.87 \times 1.48 - 1.87 \times 2 - 5.0$ mm^3. For placenta segmentation, an additional Out-Of-Distribution (OOD) dataset with 24 TRUFI scans and restricted field of view not including the entire placenta was used. The OOD cases were acquired with Siemens Prisma and Vida scanners with a resolution of $0.586 \times 0.586 \times 4$ mm^3.

Both the annotations and the corrections were performed by a clinical trainee. All segmentations were validated by an expert fetal radiologist with >20 years of experience in fetal imaging.

Studies: We conducted three studies, two with fetal body segmentation data and one with placenta data. To address the high variability in segmentation quality of the low-data regime, we performed all the experiments with four different randomizations and averaged between them. In all experiments, we used 16 TTA variations. We evaluated the experiments with the Dice score, 2D average symmetric surface distance (ASSD), and Hausdorff robust (95 percentile)

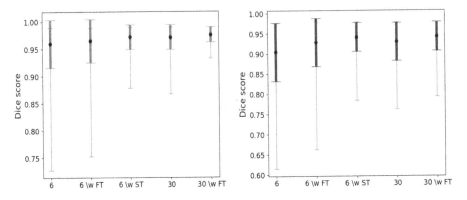

Fig. 2. Experimental results for the self training method on FIESTA ID and TRUFI OOD data averaged across four runs. Dots represent the mean Dice scores; grey bars show the minimum and the maximum; standard deviation: ID data (blue bar), OOD data (green bar). FT: Fine-tuning, ST: Self-training. Comparison between (x-axis): 1) 6 training examples (baseline); 2) 6 training examples with FT; 3) 6 training examples with ST 4) 30 training examples; 5) 30 training examples with FT (Color figure online)

metrics. A network architecture similar to Dudovitch et al. [5] was utilized with the Keras and Tensorflow frameworks.

Study 1: We evaluate the performance of the ST method alone on the fetal body segmentation ID and OOD data. Baseline networks with 6 training examples were first trained with cases randomly selected from the 30 FIESTA scans dataset. The ST was applied to the remaining 24 cases. Performance of the automatic ST method was tested on 68 ID FIESTA scans and 58 OOD TRUFI scans. Since sometimes longer training may result in improved performance [17], the performance of the ST method was also compared to that of fine-tuned networks without ST using learning rate restarts optimization scheme.

For ID data, using self-training (ST) improved the Dice score from 0.964 to 0.971, the ASSD from 1.88 mm to 1.52 mm and the Hausdorff distance from 6.15 mm to 4.8 mm. For the OOD data, the difference in performance was higher, with the self-training method improving the Dice score from 0.920 to 0.941, the ASSD from 4.7 mm to 3.67 mm, and the Hausdorff distance from 21.01 mm to 15.76 mm. Figure 2 shows the results with the Dice score. The self-training also improved the standard deviation from 0.04 to 0.023 and from 0.06 to 0.036 for ID and OOD data respectively, and achieved the same performance of a network trained on manually segmented 30 cases for both ID and OOD data.

Study 2: We evaluate the performance of the combined AL and ST method for FIESTA to TRUFI sequence transfer for fetal body segmentation. We subsequently performed sequence transfer for the TRUFI sequence using the ST network from the previous experiment as the initial network. To evaluate the differences in performance between the four runs, this time we calculated the average, STD, minimum, and maximum for the average performance of each one

Table 1. Fetal body segmentation results comparison with the Dice, Hausdorff 95 percentile and 2D ASSD metrics between: 1) 6 FIESTA cases and additional 3 randomly selected TRUFI scans; 2) 6 FIESTA cases and 3 additional actively selected TRUFI scans; 3) 6 FIESTA cases and 3 additional actively selected TRUFI scans in combination with ST; 4) 6 FIESTA cases and 2 additional actively selected TRUFI scans in combination with ST and with additional annotations of border slices. 5) a network trained without the automatic ST step using 6 FIESTA cases and 3 additional TRUFI actively selected scans with ST and border slices annotations, and; 6) a baseline of 30 fully annotated TRUFI scans. For (1–5), average ± STD and min-max range are listed for the four runs.

	Dice	Hausdorff	ASSD
1. 6 FIESTA + 3 TRUFI Random	0.957 ± 0.005	8.36 ± 0.35	2.51 ± 0.28
	$0.950 - 0.963$	$7.76 - 8.67$	$2.29 - 2.97$
2. 6 FIESTA + 3 TRUFI AL	0.957 ± 0.003	8.85 ± 0.74	2.53 ± 0.14
	$0.953 - 0.961$	$7.6 - 9.58$	$2.34 - 2.74$
3. 6 FIESTA + 3 TRUFI AL ST	0.959 ± 0.002	7.84 ± 1.16	2.45 ± 0.15
	$0.956 - 0.962$	$6.29 - 9.54$	$2.23 - 2.65$
4. 6 FIESTA + 2 TRUFI AL ST \ w borders	$\mathbf{0.961 \pm 0.001}$	$\mathbf{6.40 \pm 0.41}$	$\mathbf{2.20 \pm 0.14}$
	$\mathbf{0.960} - 0.963$	$5.73 - \mathbf{6.78}$	$2.00 - \mathbf{2.38}$
5. 6 FIESTA + 3 TRUFI AL ST \ w borders \ wo ST iteration	0.959 ± 0.003	8.09 ± 1.14	2.37 ± 0.25
	$0.955 - 0.963$	$6.23 - 9.08$	$1.95 - 2.59$
6. 30 Baseline scans	0.964	6.99	2.14

of the runs. We added either: 1) 3 additional randomly selected TRUFI scans; 2) 3 additional AL TRUFI scans; 3) 3 additional AL TRUFI scans in combination with ST, or; 4) 2 additional AL TRUFI scans in combination with ST and with border slices annotations. We also obtained results for: 5) a network trained without the automatic ST step using 3 additional TRUFI AL scans and with ST that includes border slices annotations, and; 6) a baseline of 30 fully annotated TRUFI scans.

Table 1 lists the results. The best results were achieved using only two additional labeled TRUFI scans with border slices annotations, yielding a mean Dice score of 0.961, close to that of the 30 fully annotated TRUFI scans baseline of 0.964. There was almost no difference between active versus random scan selection. Using the combined AL and ST method without the automatic ST step yielded very good results, although slightly worse than those of a network trained following the ST step, despite an additional annotated TRUFI scan. The worse network performance without the automatic ST iteration yielded an average Dice score of 0.955 vs. 0.960 using the ST iteration.

Study 3: This study evaluates ST method and the combined AL and ST method on the high-variability data of placenta segmentation with both FIESTA and TRUFI sequences. Four initial networks were trained with 10 randomly selected training examples out of the 50 FIESTA and TRUFI scans, with the rest 40 cases used for ST and AL. The combined FIESTA and TRUFI data was split into 50/4/34 train/validation/test cases. An additional 24 scans were used for OOD data validation. Again, we evaluated the average, STD, minimum, and maximum for the average performances of the four runs. We compared between

Table 2. Placenta segmentation results for ID and OOD data using the Dice, Hausdorff percentile 95, and 2D ASSD metrics.

		ID Data			OOD Data		
		Dice	Hausdorff	ASSD	Dice	Hausdorff	ASSD
1. 10 Baseline	Mean	0.806	20.98	7.64	0.641	35.53	17.65
	STD	0.003	1.13	0.26	0.021	8.12	1.62
	Min	0.803	19.08	7.34	0.628	25.53	15.12
	Max	0.811	22.00	8.03	0.678	46.46	19.48
2. 10 ST	Mean	0.819	19.75	7.11	0.703	29.23	18.86
	STD	0.010	2.24	0.35	0.028	7.08	1.93
	Min	0.806	16.95	6.65	0.656	23.22	16.49
	Max	0.833	23.21	7.47	0.727	40.74	21.56
3. 10+5 Random	Mean	0.821	19.30	7.02	0.688	29.29	13.68
	STD	0.008	1.25	0.33	0.039	6.64	0.90
	Min	0.809	17.81	6.68	0.620	23.81	12.50
	Max	0.832	21.06	7.46	0.717	40.35	14.91
4. 10+5 AL	Mean	**0.827**	**17.34**	**6.59**	**0.710**	**25.49**	12.88
	STD	0.006	1.10	0.46	0.030	**1.76**	1.35
	Min	0.819	16.52	5.96	0.661	23.59	11.52
	Max	0.835	19.21	7.11	0.743	27.98	15.12
5. 10+5 AL + ST	Mean	0.822	19.69	6.90	**0.711**	26.50	**12.59**
	STD r	0.006	1.25	0.12	**0.014**	3.35	**0.92**
	Min	0.813	18.33	6.76	**0.691**	21.82	11.48
	Max	0.829	21.68	7.09	0.728	31.29	13.82
6. 50 Baseline	Mean	0.825	18.34	7.16	0.710	24.32	13.81

six scenarios: 1) a baseline network trained on 10 scans; 2) a network trained on 10 initial scans and additional ST scans; 3) a network trained on 10 initial scans and additional 5 randomly selected scans; 4) a network trained with 10 initial scans and additional 5 AL scans; 5) a network trained with 10 initial scans, 5 AL scans, and additional ST scans; 6) a network trained on 50 scans.

Table 2 lists the results. Using ST alone improved segmentation results from a mean Dice score of 0.806 to 0.819 for ID data and from 0.641 to 0.703 for OOD data. Using actively selected scans performed better than random selection, with a much smaller STD, reaching the performance of a network trained on 50 annotated scans. For ID data, the mean and minimum average Dice scores with actively selected scans were 0.827 and 0.819, respectively, and a mean and minimum average Dice scores of random selection were 0.821 and 0.809, respectively. For OOD data, the mean and minimum average Dice scores of actively selected scans were 0.710 and 0.661, compared to a mean of 0.688 and a minimum of 0.620 using random selection.

Combining ST with AL did not improve the results, except for the OOD data Dice score STD, which was the lowest of all setups, and a minimum Dice score of 0.691, which was the highest. It slightly hurt performance on ID data, indicating that ST might induce excessive noise in the pseudo-labels. Adding automatic ST iteration may improve the pseudo-labels quality, but the effect may be negligible as the results are already on-par with a network trained on 50 cases.

4 Conclusion

We presented a novel TTA-based framework for combined training with AL and ST in one iteration. The ST uses soft labels acquired from TTA results and border slices annotations when appropriate. Our experimental results show the effectiveness of the ST method alone for both low and high variability data regimes of fetal body and placenta segmentation, respectively. The combined iteration of AL and ST was effective when applied to the low data variability of the fetal body segmentation, especially with border slices annotations which have a low annotation cost, yielding a Dice score of 0.961 for sequence transfer using 6 examples from the original sequence and only 2 examples from the new sequence, close to that of 30 annotated cases from the new sequence. In this scenario of low variability data, AL did not improve upon random selection. However, AL was effective for the high data variability setup, but adding ST to AL resulted in slight performance decline for ID data, indicating that ST might induce excessive noise in the pseudo-labels. In this case, AL may be better without ST. This suggests that for methods that combine AL with ST or CR SSL, a supervised network iteration with AL cases can be beneficial before the semi-supervised fine-tuning. Future work can explore this for different data variability settings.

References

1. Arazo, E., Ortego, D., Albert, P., O'Connor, N., McGuinness, K.: Pseudo-labeling and confirmation bias in deep semi-supervised learning. In: Proceedings of International Joint Conference on Neural Networks (IJCNN), pp. 1–8 (2020)
2. Budd, S., Robinson, E., Kainz, B.: A survey on active learning and human-in-the-loop deep learning for medical image analysis. Med. Image Anal. **71**, 102062 (2021)
3. Chen, X., Yuan, Y., Zeng, G. & Wang, J. Semi-supervised semantic segmentation with cross pseudo supervision. In: Proceedings of IEEE/CVF Conference On Computer Vision and Pattern Recognition, pp. 2613–2622 (2021)
4. Cheplygina, V., Bruijne, M., Pluim, J.: Not-so-supervised: a survey of semi-supervised, multi-instance, and transfer learning in medical image analysis. Med. Image Anal. **54**, 280–296 (2019)
5. Dudovitch, G., Link-Sourani, D., Ben Sira, L., Miller, E., Ben Bashat, D., Joskowicz, L.: Deep learning automatic fetal structures segmentation in MRI scans with few annotated datasets. Medical Image Computing And Computer Assisted

Intervention-MICCAI 2020: 23rd International Conference, Lima, Peru, October 4–8, 2020, Proceedings, Part VI 23, pp. 365–374 (2020)

6. Fathi, A., Balcan, M., Ren, X., Rehg, J.: Combining self training and active learning for video segmentation. Technical report, Georgia Institute of Technology (2011)

7. Gaillochet, M., Desrosiers, C., Lombaert, H.: TAAL: test-time augmentation for active learning in medical image segmentation. Data Augmentation, Labelling, And Imperfections: Second MICCAI Workshop, DALI 2022, Held In Conjunction With MICCAI 2022, Singapore, September 22, 2022, Proceedings. pp. 43–53 (2022)

8. Guan, L., Yuan, X.: Iterative Loop Learning Combining Self-Training and Active Learning for Domain Adaptive Semantic Segmentation. ArXiv Preprint ArXiv:2301.13361 (2023)

9. Jungo, A., Reyes, M.: Assessing reliability and challenges of uncertainty estimations for medical image segmentation. In: Medical Image Computing And Computer Assisted Intervention-MICCAI 2019: 22nd International Conference, Shenzhen, China, October 13–17, 2019, Proceedings, Part II 22, pp. 48–56 (2019)

10. Lai, Z., Wang, C., Oliveira, L., Dugger, B., Cheung, S., Chuah, C.: Joint semi-supervised and active learning for segmentation of gigapixel pathology images with cost-effective labeling. In: Proceedings IEEE/CVF International Conference On Computer Vision, pp. 591–600 (2021)

11. Loshchilov, I., Hutter, F.: Sgdr: stochastic gradient descent with warm restarts. ArXiv Preprint ArXiv:1608.03983 (2016)

12. Nath, V., Yang, D., Roth, H., Xu, D.: Warm start active learning with proxy labels and selection via semi-supervised fine-tuning. In: Medical Image Computing And Computer Assisted Intervention-MICCAI 2022: 25th International Conference, Singapore, September 18–22, 2022, Proceedings, Part VIII, pp. 297–308 (2022)

13. Nie, D., Gao, Y., Wang, L., Shen, D.: ASDNet: attention based semi-supervised deep networks for medical image segmentation. In: Frangi, A.F., Schnabel, J.A., Davatzikos, C., Alberola-López, C., Fichtinger, G. (eds.) MICCAI 2018. LNCS, vol. 11073, pp. 370–378. Springer, Cham (2018). https://doi.org/10.1007/978-3-030-00937-3_43

14. Ouali, Y., Hudelot, C., Tami, M.: Semi-supervised semantic segmentation with cross-consistency training. In: Proceedings Of The IEEE/CVF Conference On Computer Vision and Pattern Recognition, pp. 12674–12684 (2020)

15. Shen, W., et al.: A survey on label-efficient deep image segmentation: bridging the gap between weak supervision and dense prediction. IEEE Trans. Pattern Anal. Mach. Intell. (2023)

16. Specktor-Fadida, B., et al.: A bootstrap self-training method for sequence transfer: state-of-the-art placenta segmentation in fetal MRI. Uncertainty For Safe Utilization Of Machine Learning In Medical Imaging, And Perinatal Imaging, Placental And Preterm Image Analysis: 3rd International Workshop, UNSURE 2021, And 6th International Workshop, PIPPI 2021, Held In Conjunction With MICCAI 2021, Strasbourg, France, October 1, 2021, Proceedings 3. pp. 189–199 (2021)

17. Specktor-Fadida, B., Link-Sourani, D., Ben-Sira, L., Miller, E., Ben-Bashat, D., Joskowicz, L.: Partial annotations for the segmentation of large structures with low annotation cost. Medical Image Learning With Limited And Noisy Data: First International Workshop, MILLanD 2022, Held In Conjunction With MICCAI 2022, Singapore, September 22, 2022, Proceedings. pp. 13–22 (2022)

18. Tajbakhsh, N., Jeyaseelan, L., Li, Q., Chiang, J., Wu, Z., Ding, X.: Embracing imperfect datasets: a review of deep learning solutions for medical image segmentation. Med. Image Anal. 63, 101693 (2020)

19. Wang, G., Li, W., Aertsen, M., Deprest, J., Ourselin, S., Vercauteren, T.: Aleatoric uncertainty estimation with test-time augmentation for medical image segmentation with convolutional neural networks. Neurocomputing **338**, 34–45 (2019)
20. Xia, Y., Yang, D., Yu, Z., Liu, F., Cai, J., Yu, L., Zhu, Z., Xu, D., Yuille, A., Roth, H.: Uncertainty-aware multi-view co-training for semi-supervised medical image segmentation and domain adaptation. Med. Image Anal. **65**, 101766 (2020)
21. Yang, L., Zhuo, W., Qi, L., Shi, Y., Gao, Y.: St++: make self-training work better for semi-supervised semantic segmentation. Proceedings of the IEEE/CVF Conference On Computer Vision And Pattern Recognition, pp. 4268–4277 (2022)
22. Yang, L., Zhang, Y., Chen, J., Zhang, S., Chen, D.: Suggestive annotation: a deep active learning framework for biomedical image segmentation. Medical Image Computing And Computer Assisted Intervention- MICCAI 2017: 20th International Conference, Quebec City, QC, Canada, September 11–13, 2017, Proceedings, Part III 20, pp. 399–407 (2017)
23. Zhang, W., Zhu, L., Hallinan, J., Zhang, S., Makmur, A., Cai, Q., Ooi, B.: Boostmis: Boosting medical image semi-supervised learning with adaptive pseudo labeling and informative active annotation. Proceegings of IEEE/CVF Conference On Computer Vision and Pattern Recognition, pp. 20666–20676 (2022)
24. Zhu, Y., et al.: Improving semantic segmentation via efficient self-training. IEEE Trans. Pattern Anal. Mach. Intell. (2021)
25. Zoph, B., Ghiasi, G., Lin, T., Cui, Y., Liu, H., Cubuk, E., Le, Q.: Rethinking pre-training and self-training. Adv. Neural. Inf. Process. Syst. **33**, 3833–3845 (2020)

Active Transfer Learning for 3D Hippocampus Segmentation

Ji Wu, Zhongfeng Kang, Sebastian Nørgaard Llambias,
Mostafa Mehdipour Ghazi, and Mads Nielsen[✉]

Pioneer Centre for AI, Department of Computer Science, University of Copenhagen,
Copenhagen, Denmark
`madsn@di.ku.dk`

Abstract. Insufficient data is always a big challenge for medical imaging that is limited by the expensive labeling cost, time-consuming and intensive labor. Active learning aims to reduce the annotation effort by training a model on actively selected samples, most of them adopt uncertainty measures as instance selection criteria. However, uncertainty strategies underperform in most active learning studies. In addition, inaccurate selections worse than random sampling in initial stage referred to as "cold start" problem is also a huge challenge for active learning. Domain adaptation aims at alleviating the cold start problem and also reducing the annotation effort by adapting the model from a pre-trained model trained on another domain. Our work focuses on whether active learning can benefit from domain adaptation and the performance of uncertainty strategy compared to random selection. We studied 3D hippocampus images segmentation based on 3D UX-Net and four MRI datasets *Hammers, HarP, LPBA40,* and *OASIS*. Our experiments reveal that active learning with domain adaptation is more efficient and robust than without domain adaptation at a low labeling budget. The performance gap between them diminishes as we approach to that half of the dataset is labeled. In addition, entropy sampling also converges faster than random sampling, with slightly better performance.

Keywords: Active learning · medical image segmentation · domain adaptation · entropy sampling

1 Introduction

Hippocampus [20] is a small, medial, subcortical brain structure, as a part of limbic system, playing a crucial role in consolidation of information from short-term to long-term memory, and in spatial memory that enables navigation. Neurodegeneration [9] indicates that the shape and volume of hippocampus will be affected longitudinally by different pathologies associated to Alzheimer's disease. Therefore, hippocampal segmentation from 3D MRI is of great importance for many researches of neuropsychiatric disorders, e.g., Epilepsy [3] and trauma [27].

Supplementary Information The online version contains supplementary material available at https://doi.org/10.1007/978-3-031-44917-8_22.

© The Author(s), under exclusive license to Springer Nature Switzerland AG 2023
Z. Xue et al. (Eds.): MILLanD 2023, LNCS 14307, pp. 224–234, 2023.
https://doi.org/10.1007/978-3-031-44917-8_22

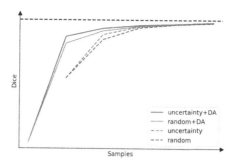

Fig. 1. An illustration of the objective of this study for an improvement of the segmentation performance of domain adaptation and uncertainty sampling for active learning. It is hypothesized that knowledge transferred from source domains and uncertainty sampling can help enhance the performance.

Deep learning methods, e.g., FCN [32], Unet [29], and DeepLab [5], nowadays has made great achievements for image segmentation on the labeled datasets. Nevertheless, most of these deep learning based segmentation tasks are pixel-level, particularly for the medical industry [12,13,26], as the urgent demand for high accuracy and precision in delineating regions of interest, anomalies, and structures within medical images further underscores the necessity of pixel-level annotation. However, this pixel-level demand rather than patches or regions-level gives a notable challenge-considerable expense associated with annotating images at pixel level. The process of manually assigning labels to each pixel often requires expert input and extensive time commitments. This remains a resistance that labeled data is far from enough that is limited by the expensive labeling cost, time-consuming and intensive labor compared to massive unlabeled data [4,7]. Therefore, it is eager to explore the potential methods that reduce the amount of annotated data required to train the optimal model on limited budget.

Active learning (AL) [22,35,36] is used extensively to reduce the annotation effort on actively selected informative or representative samples. By training a model, it selects a new set of samples that are considered most useful and effective for concrete machine learning tasks to be annotated at the end of each circle via the acquisition function until the annotation budget is spent out. This method is widely used for image tasks [1,19]. Uncertainty sampling [28] has been proposed to seek for most uncertain samples, which encourages to choose a biased distribution to sample more frequently from those regions of the input space that have a larger impact on the parameter being estimated. However, uncertainty sampling perform poorly in most active learning studies [1,14,30] and hardly outperforms random sampling.

Besides, due to that active learning is a gradual process starting with zero labeled samples, without any labeled data at the beginning, the model can not make accurate predictions, therefore, can not select informative samples for labeling. These inaccurate predictions and selections worse than random selection in initial stage referred to as the "cold start" problem [6] is also a huge challenge for

Table 1. Test segmentation Dice scores (DSCs). the results from 3D UX-Net are bolded. Note that model names denote "source data (model-pipeline)", where *HHL* refers to the datasets *Hammers, HarP*, and *LPBA40*. B and X indicate the baseline (nnU-Net) and 3D UX-Net pipelines.

Model	Dataset				
	Hammers	HarP	LPBA40	OASIS	Avg
HHL (B)	0.86 ± 0.02	0.85 ± 0.20	0.86 ± 0.01	0.77 ± 0.04	0.84 ± 0.07
HHL (X)	**0.89 ± 0.01**	**0.92 ± 0.01**	**0.87 ± 0.03**	**0.84 ± 0.06**	**0.88 ± 0.03**
HarP (B)	0.72 ± 0.03	0.89 ± 0.08	0.57 ± 0.09	0.74 ± 0.20	0.73 ± 0.10
HarP (X)	**0.79 ± 0.05**	**0.92 ± 0.02**	**0.62 ± 0.05**	**0.83 ± 0.02**	**0.79 ± 0.04**
OASIS (B)	0.70 ± 0.05	<u>0.37 ± 0.32</u>	<u>0.27 ± 0.25</u>	0.83 ± 0.19	0.54 ± 0.20
OASIS (X)	**0.77 ± 0.03**	**0.82** ± <u>0.07</u>	**0.70** ± <u>0.10</u>	**0.89 ± 0.02**	**0.80 ± 0.06**

active learning. To alleviate this problem, we propose to utilize domain adaptation (DA) skills [11] that can adapt the model on the target domain by the model pre-trained on the source domain, where the target domain is different from but related to the source domain. Energy-based Active Domain Adaptation (EADA) [36] also gives the potential for active learning under domain adaptation. This inspires that the knowledge from the source hippocampus dataset may help reduce the annotation effort by being used as an initial point for active learning on the target hippocampus dataset.

In this paper, we explore the impact of domain adaptation, along with the performances between entropy sampling and random sampling on hippocampus datasets in active learning. The core of the study is 3D hippocampus segmentation, and we use four datasets incurring severe domain shifts. We expect to have an ideal result similarly to Fig. 1, which is presumed that domain adaptation and uncertainty sampling can reduce annotation effort.

The rest of this paper is organized as follows. Section 2 introduces all methodologies. Sections 3 and 4 present the experimental setup and the experimental results, respectively. Finally, Sect. 5 discusses some findings we observed in our work and Sect. 6 concludes this paper.

2   Methods

2.1   3D UX-Net

Model selection [33] is a critical component of active learning and has a significant impact on the effectiveness and efficiency of active learning process. The goal of active learning is to minimize the number of labeled samples required to achieve a certain level of performance. An accurate and great model can select informative samples with high uncertainty and avoid selecting redundant or uninformative samples, such to reduce labeling effort required and save time and resources.

3D UX-Net [16], which is a recently proposed 3D medical image segmentation model published at ICLR 2023, is an extension of UX-Net [25] that adapts the

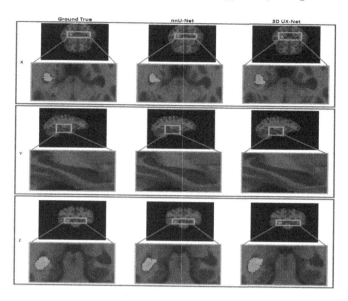

Fig. 2. Qualitative representations of 3D hippocampus across *OASIS* dataset. 3D UX-Net shows the better segmentation quality compared to nnU-Net.

capability of hierarchical transformers and preserves the advantages of using ConvNet modules such as inductive biases. It consistently achieves improvement in both scenarios across all ConvNets and transformers SOTA with fewer model parameters on the three challenging public datasets, FeTA 2021 [26], FLARE 2021 [18] and AMOS 2022 [13].

nnU-Net [12] is a widely used 3D fully convolutional neural network (CNN) that has also achieved excellent results on various MIS challenges in 2020 including highly specialized solutions on 23 public datasets used in international biomedical segmentation competitions. Table 1 shows the result of comparison between 3D UX-Net and nnU-Net on MIS, 3D UX-Net exhibits superior performance on all datasets. Particularly for the performance of the *OASIS* [21] model on datasets *HarP* [2] and *LPBA40* [31] (marked with underline), 3D UX-Net achieves significant improvement and robustness with DSCs of 0.82 ± 0.07 and 0.70 ± 0.10 respectively, compared to only 0.37 ± 0.32 and 0.27 ± 0.25 for nnU-Net. Apart from quantitative representations, Fig. 2 further provides an additional vision of demonstrating the quality improvement in segmentation with 3D UX-Net. The morphology of hippocampus are well segmented compared to nnU-Net.

Algorithm 1: The framework of pool-based active learning algorithm

---

Input: $\mathcal{L} \subset \mathcal{D} = \{< x, y >\}$: Labelled set,
$U = \mathcal{D} \backslash \mathcal{L} = \{< x, ? >\}$: Unlabelled set,
θ: Segmentation model,
ϕ: Active Learning query function
while $|U| > 0 \wedge no\ stopping\ criterion$ **do**
    $\theta = train(\mathcal{L})$;
    for $all < x, ? > \in U$ **do**
        | Compute Active Learning metric $\phi(x)$ under θ
    end
    Choose x^* with highest magnitude of $\phi(x^*)$
    Annotate y^*
    update labelled set $\mathcal{L} \leftarrow \mathcal{L} \cup \{< x^*, y^* >\}$
    update unlabelled set $U \leftarrow U \backslash \{< x^*, y^* >\}$
end

2.2 Active Learning

We use the standard framework of pool-based active learning [34] as Algorithm 1 shown.

It computes metrics $\phi(x)$ based on the training model θ and chooses the samples x^* with high magnitude of $\phi(x^*)$ from unlabeled pool for each iteration until stopping criterion.

2.3 Importance Sampling

Importance sampling [23] is a significant technique for reducing the variance in statistical analysis. The basic idea is to select more frequent samples from those regions of input space that have a larger impact on the parameter being estimated. In order to achieve this, a biased distribution is chosen that encourages the important regions of the input variables.

However, the importance in latent space is a very abstract concept, especially in deep learning tasks, complicated network frameworks, and high dimension makes the latent space basically unexplorable. Instead, **uncertainty sampling** is proposed in active learning, which aims to select data samples that are characterized by high uncertainty. The underlying principle is based on the assumption that the most informative and important samples for model improvement are those for which the model is least confident in its predictions.

Entropy Sampling is one of the methods for uncertainty sampling. In information theory, entropy is defined as expected value of the information contained in a data source. For a sample X with n possible outcomes and probabilities $p_1, p_2, ..., p_n$, where each outcome and probability is for each pixel, we have entropy $H(x)$,

$$H(x) = H(p_1, p_2, ..., p_n) = -\sum_{i=1}^{n} p_i \log_2 p_i \tag{1}$$

Table 2. Overview of the datasets used in this study.

Dataset	Train	Test	Age	Strength	Manufacturer
Hammers	20	10	20–54	1.5T	GE
HarP	100	35	55–90	1.5T & 3T	GE, Siemens, Philips
LPBA40	30	10	19–40	1.5T	GE
OASIS	15	20	18–90	1.5T	Siemens

We use entropy sampling to select the most uncertain samples with highest entropy such to match important regions of the unlabeled pool that have a larger impact on the segmentation of model.

2.4 Domain Adaptation

Active learning potentially enhances annotation efficiency by iteratively selecting the most important data to be annotated. However, a striking contradiction to this promise is that it fails to select at the first few choices due to no labeled data in pool, even worse than random selection, which may also have an impact on the final performance. We identify this as cold start problem in active learning.

To alleviate this problem, we utilized domain adaptation [11], which is a technique used to adapt a machine learning model trained on one domain, named as source domain, to another related but different domain, named as target domain. The basic idea behind it is to train a model on a source domain with labeled data, and then use the knowledge learned from the source domain to adapt the model to a target domain with unlabeled data.

We take full advantage of the 4 datasets of hippocampus that we have, and train the models using 100% samples of them. Those 4 100% models are used as the pre-trained models to transfer knowledge from a labeled source domain to an unlabeled target domain gradually by the active learning process. By adapting the models to the target domain, it is possible to make more accurate predictions with fewer labeled instances, and thus overcome the cold start problem.

3 Experimental Setup

3.1 Data

In order to assess the effectiveness of the active learning method on 3D images, we utilized 240 T1-weighted MRI scans from the *Hammers* [10], *HarP* [2], *LPBA40* [31] and *OASIS* [15] as datasets. The heterogeneous datasets are independently collected, annotated, and label-corrected for this study. Table 2 provides details of the datasets on acquisition methods, labeling techniques, and demographics, serving to avoid overfitting specific domains. All datasets include only normal subjects, with the exception of *HarP*, which included scans from patients with mild cognitive impairment and Alzheimer's disease.

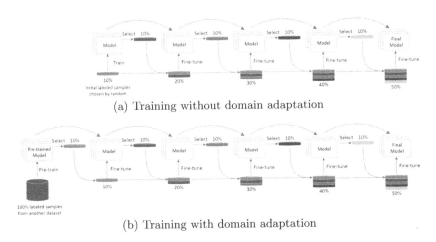

(a) Training without domain adaptation

(b) Training with domain adaptation

Fig. 3. Overview of two AL experiments. (a) is the first experiment, (b) is the second. they are conducted with both entropy sampling and random sampling.

3.2 Experimental Setup

Overall, our study comprises two comparison experiments (see Fig. 3). The first experiment involves training a model using 10% of the initial labeled data and budget sizes. The second experiment involves training a model adapted from three other pre-trained models that were trained based on 100% of the labeled data of their pool. In both experiments, random sampling is set as the baseline method and is compared with entropy sampling. Prior to initiating the active learning cycles, the pre-trained models are trained on each of the datasets used in this study. Furthermore, the budget size per cycle is set equal to the initial labeled data size for the first experiment.

Implementation Details. Our method is implemented in PyTorch [24]. For the pre-trained models, The Dice [8] loss is used as the cost function for training, and the AdamW [17] optimizer was employed with the learning rate of 0.0001. We train models for 8000 epochs with batch-size of 2 as in [16]. The models are used in the pool-based active learning framework, where 5 cycles were performed, and 10% of the unlabeled pool was selected in each cycle, ultimately selecting 50% of the pool by the end of the process. The same approach was used for training the models from scratch, with the exception that a random 10% of initial labeled data was provided. Each experiment was repeated 10 times to ensure robustness and minimize the effects of random fluctuations.

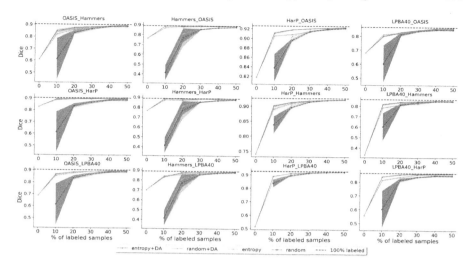

Fig. 4. AL performance on *Hammers*, *HarP*, *LPBA40*, *OASIS*. Performance comparison between domain adaptation to AL method (solid lines) and AL method (dashed lines). The initial and per cycle budget are equal in all the curves.

4   Results

To evaluate domain adaptation on active learning method, we consider several pre-trained models varied by datasets. In this section we inspect the contribution of domain adaptation pre-training in active learning.

Figure 4 shows active learning results on *Hammers*, *HarP*, *LPBA40*, and *OASIS* for each column. The evaluated methods are divided into two groups: methods with domain adaptation represented by solid lines, methods using models trained from scratch represented by dashed lines. Initial and per cycle budgets are 10% labeled data. Black dashed line is the dice for training directly on 100% labeled datasets. As can be seen, domain adaptation significantly improves both entropy sampling and random sampling on all datasets. Methods using models trained from scratch have huge fluctuations, particularly before 30% labeled samples, instead, domain adaptation greatly improves the robustness. Both types of methods achieve almost the full performance training on 100% labeled datasets and close the gap as we approach to that half of the dataset is labeled.

From the active learning perspective, the entropy sampling transitioned to higher performance compared to random sampling both with and without domain adaptation for most of cases from 10% budget. However, for a small number of cases, limited by the data, entropy will also select samples that are not the best in the domain. AL on *Hammers* adapted on *LPBA40* pre-trained model and AL on *LPBA40* adapted on *OASIS* pre-trained model, this transition happens after labeling 20% of data.

5   Discussion

The experiments above shows that although in most of cases, entropy sampling method outperforms random sampling. However, we still noticed that for a small number of cases, limited by the data, entropy will also select not important samples in the domain, worse than random sampling. And due to the constraints of our 3D hippocampus datasets, we only explore 10% initial labeled data and budget sizes per cycle rather than smaller scales. There are possibly more interesting results if using smaller scales per cycle, such as 1% or 2%. Besides, we conduct these experiments with famous and widely used entropy sampling. Then how about using other methods in uncertainty strategy, or other strategies, such as diversity-based, consistency-based, or hybrid, etc.

6   Conclusion

In this paper, we analyzed entropy sampling and random sampling in active learning respectively, and investigate how active learning benefits from domain adaptation. Our experiments indicate that active learning with domain adaptation is more efficient and robust than without domain adaptation at a low labeling budget. The performance gap between them diminishes as we approach to that half of the dataset is labeled. Besides, entropy sampling also converges faster than random sampling, with slightly better performance.

Acknowledgements. This project has received funding from Pioneer Centre for AI, Danish National Research Foundation, grant number P1.

References

1. Bengar, J.Z., van de Weijer, J., Twardowski, B., Raducanu, B.: Reducing label effort: self-supervised meets active learning (2021)
2. Boccardi, M., et al.: Training labels for hippocampal segmentation based on the EADC-ADNI harmonized hippocampal protocol. Alzheimer's Dementia **11**(2), 175–183 (2015). https://doi.org/10.1016/j.jalz.2014.12.002
3. Carmo, D., Silva, B., Yasuda, C., Rittner, L., Lotufo, R.: Hippocampus segmentation on epilepsy and Alzheimer's disease studies with multiple convolutional neural networks. Heliyon **7**(2), e06226 (2021). https://doi.org/10.1016/j.heliyon.2021.e06226
4. Casanova, A., Pinheiro, P.O., Rostamzadeh, N., Pal, C.J.: Reinforced active learning for image segmentation (2020)
5. Chen, L.C., Papandreou, G., Kokkinos, I., Murphy, K., Yuille, A.L.: DeepLab: semantic image segmentation with deep convolutional nets, atrous convolution, and fully connected CRFs. IEEE Trans. Pattern Anal. Mach. Intell. **40**(4), 834–848 (2018). https://doi.org/10.1109/TPAMI.2017.2699184
6. Chen, L., et al.: Making your first choice: to address cold start problem in medical active learning. In: Medical Imaging with Deep Learning (2023). https://openreview.net/forum?id=5iSBMWm3ln

7. Chen, L., Fu, Y., You, S., Liu, H.: Hybrid supervised instance segmentation by learning label noise suppression. Neurocomputing **496**, 131–146 (2022). https://doi.org/10.1016/j.neucom.2022.05.026

8. Dice, L.R.: Measures of the amount of ecologic association between species. Ecology **26**(3), 297–302 (1945). https://www.jstor.org/stable/1932409

9. Dubois, B., Hampel, H., Feldman, H.H., Carrillo, M.C., Cummings, J., Jack, C.R., Jr.: Preclinical Alzheimer's disease: definition, natural history, and diagnostic criteria. Alzheimers Dement. **12**(3), 292–323 (2016)

10. Faillenot, I., Heckemann, R.A., Frot, M., Hammers, A.: Macroanatomy and 3D probabilistic atlas of the human insula. Neuroimage **150**, 88–98 (2017). https://doi.org/10.1016/j.neuroimage.2017.01.073

11. Farahani, A., Voghoei, S., Rasheed, K., Arabnia, H.R.: A brief review of domain adaptation (2020)

12. Isensee, F., Jaeger, P.F., Kohl, S.A.A., Petersen, J., Maier-Hein, K.H.: nnU-Net: a self-configuring method for deep learning-based biomedical image segmentation. Nat. Methods **18**(2), 203–211 (2021)

13. Ji, Y., et al.: AMOS: a large-scale abdominal multi-organ benchmark for versatile medical image segmentation. arXiv preprint arXiv:2206.08023 (2022)

14. Konyushkova, K., Sznitman, R., Fua, P.: Learning active learning from data (2017)

15. Landman, B.A., Warfield, S.K.: MICCAI 2012: grand challenge and workshop on multi-atlas labeling. In: International Conference on MICCAI (2012)

16. Lee, H.H., Bao, S., Huo, Y., Landman, B.A.: 3D UX-Net: a large kernel volumetric convnet modernizing hierarchical transformer for medical image segmentation (2022). https://doi.org/10.48550/ARXIV.2209.15076

17. Loshchilov, I., Hutter, F.: Decoupled weight decay regularization (2019)

18. Ma, J., et al.: Fast and low-GPU-memory abdomen CT organ segmentation: the flare challenge. Med. Image Anal. **82**, 102616 (2022)

19. Makili, L.E., Sánchez, J.A.V., Dormido-Canto, S.: Active learning using conformal predictors: application to image classification. Fusion Sci. Technol. **62**(2), 347–355 (2012). https://doi.org/10.13182/FST12-A14626

20. Martin, J., Radzyner, H., Leonard, M.: Neuroanatomy: Text and Atlas. Ovid ebook collection, McGraw-Hill Companies, Incorporated (2003). https://books.google.dk/books?id=OUC4igr3O4sC

21. Mehdipour Ghazi, M., Nielsen, M.: FAST-AID brain: fast and accurate segmentation tool using artificial intelligence developed for brain. arXiv preprint (2022). https://doi.org/10.48550/ARXIV.2208.14360

22. Nath, V., Yang, D., Landman, B.A., Xu, D., Roth, H.R.: Diminishing uncertainty within the training pool: active learning for medical image segmentation. IEEE Trans. Med. Imaging **40**(10), 2534–2547 (2021). https://doi.org/10.1109/tmi.2020.3048055

23. Owen, A.B.: Monte Carlo theory, methods and examples (2013)

24. Paszke, A., Gross, S., Massa, F., Bai, J., Chintala, S.: PyTorch: an imperative style, high-performance deep learning library. In: Advances in Neural Information Processing Systems, vol. 32, pp. 8024–8035. Curran Associates, Inc. (2019). https://papers.neurips.cc/paper/9015-pytorch-an-imperative-style-high-performance-deep-learning-library.pdf

25. Patel, K., Kovalyov, A., Panahi, I.: UX-Net: filter-and-process-based improved u-net for real-time time-domain audio separation (2022). https://doi.org/10.48550/ARXIV.2210.15822

26. Payette, K., de Dumast, P., Kebiri, H., Ezhov, I., Bach Cuadra, M., Jakab, A.: An automatic multi-tissue human fetal brain segmentation benchmark using the fetal tissue annotation dataset. Sci. Data **8**(1), 167 (2021). https://doi.org/10.1038/s41597-021-00946-3

27. Postel, C., et al.: Variations in response to trauma and hippocampal subfield changes. Neurobiol. Stress **15**, 100346 (2021). https://doi.org/10.1016/j.ynstr.2021.100346

28. Raj, A., Bach, F.: Convergence of uncertainty sampling for active learning (2021). https://doi.org/10.48550/ARXIV.2110.15784

29. Ronneberger, O., Fischer, P., Brox, T.: U-Net: convolutional networks for biomedical image segmentation (2015). https://doi.org/10.48550/ARXIV.1505.04597

30. Scheffer, T., Decomain, C., Wrobel, S.: Active hidden Markov models for information extraction. In: Hoffmann, F., Hand, D.J., Adams, N., Fisher, D., Guimaraes, G. (eds.) IDA 2001. LNCS, vol. 2189, pp. 309–318. Springer, Heidelberg (2001). https://doi.org/10.1007/3-540-44816-0_31

31. Shattuck, D., et al.: Construction of a 3D probabilistic atlas of human cortical structures. NeuroImage **39**, 1064–1080 (2008). https://doi.org/10.1016/j.neuroimage.2007.09.031

32. Shelhamer, E., Long, J., Darrell, T.: Fully convolutional networks for semantic segmentation (2016). https://doi.org/10.48550/ARXIV.1605.06211

33. Sugiyama, M., Kawanabe, M.: Active learning with model selection, pp. 215–224 (2012)

34. Wu, D.: Pool-based sequential active learning for regression (2018)

35. Wu, T.H., et al.: D2ADA: dynamic density-aware active domain adaptation for semantic segmentation (2022)

36. Xie, B., Yuan, L., Li, S., Liu, C.H., Cheng, X., Wang, G.: Active learning for domain adaptation: an energy-based approach. In: Proceedings of the AAAI Conference on Artificial Intelligence, vol. 36, no. 8 (2022)

Transfer Learning

Using Training Samples as Transitive Information Bridges in Predicted 4D MRI

Gino Gulamhussene[1]($\boxtimes$) (iD), Oleksii Bashkanov[1], Jazan Omari[2], Maciej Pech[2] (iD), Christian Hansen[1] (iD), and Marko Rak[1]

[1] Faculty of Computer Science, Otto-von-Guericke University, Universitätsplatz 2, 39106 Magdeburg, Germany
gino.gulamhussene@ovgu.de

[2] Department of Radiology and Nuclear Medicine, University Hospital Magdeburg, Leipziger Straße 44, 39120 Magdeburg, Germany

Abstract. The lack of real-time techniques for monitoring respiratory motion impairs the development of guidance systems for image-guided interventions. Recent works show that U-Net based real-time 4D MRI prediction methods are promising, but prone to bad image quality when small training data sets and inputs with multiple MR contrast are used. To overcome this problem, we propose a more efficient use of the spare training data and re-utilize 2D training samples as a secondary input for construction of transitive information bridges between the navigator slice primary input and the data slice prediction. We thus remove the need for a separate 3D breath-hold MRI with different MR contrast as the secondary input. Results show that our novel construction leads to improved prediction quality with very sparse training data, with a significant decrease in root mean squared error (RMSE) from 0.3 to 0.27 (p< $2.2e^{-16}$, d=0.19). Additionally, removing 3D imaging reduces prior acquisition time from 3 to 2 min.

Keywords: 4D MRI · free breathing · time-resolved · Deep Learning

1 Introduction

Spatially limited capturing of organ motion, i.e., just one slice instead of the whole organ volume, and consequently, insufficient organ motion compensation are a problem during image-guided interventions. Especially when computer assistance systems are utilized, like navigation systems, that process interventional images, insufficient motion compensation may lead to inaccuracies in instrument navigation to the target and thus impair treatment results. In MRI-guided procedures, real-time 4D MRI (3D + t), i.e., real-time imaging of a large volume is not feasible yet. It requires either large amounts of reference data or reconstruction times are long. On the other hand very short acquisition times lead to very small training data sets and a reduction in prediction quality. Thus, 4D MRI is not yet intervention-ready.

© The Author(s), under exclusive license to Springer Nature Switzerland AG 2023
Z. Xue et al. (Eds.): MILLanD 2023, LNCS 14307, pp. 237–245, 2023.
https://doi.org/10.1007/978-3-031-44917-8_23

Table 1. Related work: P/R (Pro-/Retrospective), TR (time-resolved), Phases (breathing phases), vps (volumes/s), Recon. (reconstruction time), Acq (prior acquisition time).

	P/R	Matrix size	Resolution in mm³	TR	Phases		vps		Recon. in s/vol	Acq in min	RMSE median (95%)
					P	R	P	R			
[1]	R	256 × 166	1.5 × 1.5 × 5	no	–	4	–	–	–	–	–
[8]	R	250 × 176x32	1.5 × 1.5 × 5	no	–	4	–	–	–	3	–
[13]	R	175 × 190 × 9	2 × 2x5	no	–	10	–	–	–	13	–
[10]	R	256 × 224x20	1.28 × 1.28 × 5	no	–	8	–	–	–	1.2	–
[7]	R	416 × 250x125	**1.2 × 1.2 × 1.6**	no	–	8	–	–	75	5	–
[9]	R	138 × 208x30	2 × 2x5	no	–	10	–	–	30	5	–
[14]	R	–	1.67 × 1.67 × 5	no	–	10	–	–	–	–	–
[11]	R	192 × 192 × 25	1.8 × 1.8 × 4	yes	–	36	–	5	73	60	–
[12]	R	224 × 224 × 53	1.3 × 1.3 × 5	yes	–	36	–	4.4	–	10	–
[15]	R	128 × 128 × 56	2.7 × 2.7 × 4	yes	–	9.78	–	1.63	20	**0.33**	–
[3]	R	140 × 176 × 47	1.82 × 1.82 × 4	yes	–	36	–	6	27	60	–
[4]	**P/R**	128 × 128 × 209	1.8 × 1.8 × 1.8	yes	10.5	36	1.75	6	0.57	24	0.29 (0.45)
[6]	**P/R**	128 × 128 × 209	1.8 × 1.8 × 1.8	yes	10.5	36	1.75	6	0.57	3	0.31 (0.47)
our	**P/R**	128 × 128 × 50	1.8 × 1.8 × 4	yes	10.5	36	1.75	6	0.57	2	**0.27 (0.48)**

4D MRI methods can be classified as either respiratory phase-resolved (PR) or time-resolved (TR) (see Table 1). The former usually reconstruct up to ten phases of one breathing cycle with typically short acquisition times around 5 min but do not account for irregular breathing. [1,7–10,13,14] The other class uses clinical 2D MRI sequences alternating between so called navigator- and data slices for time-resolved 4D imaging, based on von Siebenthal [11]. Data slices are sorted into 3D MRIs based on navigator similarity. The drawbacks are: long acquisition and reconstruction times (up to 60 min and 73 s). Several works partially address these shortcomings [3,12,15].

To overcome the lack of real-time capabilities in previous methods, we proposed an end-to-end trainable deep learning framework [4]. It achieves sub-second 3D reconstruction times by learning the relationship between navigator and data slices. Because acquiring sufficient training data (24 min) is challenging in real-life clinical scenarios, we showed that transfer learning can reduce the prior acquisition time to 3 min with a slight compromise in prediction quality [6]. In this work, we propose a more efficient utilization of sparse training data to reduce prior acquisition time and restore compromised 4D MRI prediction quality by reusing training samples as transitive information bridges.

2   Materials and Methods

2.1   MRI Data

The liver MRI data of 20 healthy subjects were acquired on a MAGNETOM Skyra MRI scanner (Siemens Medical Solutions, Erlangen, Germany), following the protocol and sequence parameters outlined in the study by Gulamhussene et

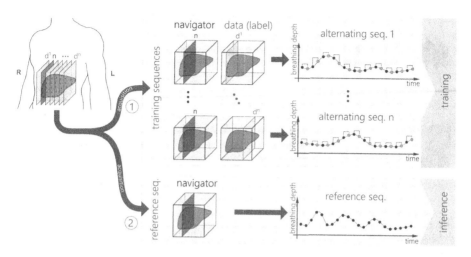

Fig. 1. The data set contains two types of data for each subject. 1) around 50 training sequences and 2) two reference sequences. While the first are an alternating sequence of navigator and data slices, the second contains only navigators. (based on Fig. 1 in [6])

al. [3]. In their work, they translated the Philips based MRI acquisition proposed by von Siebenthal et al. [11] to the equivalent acquisition on a Siemens machine. The data, study information, and MR protocols are publicly available [2,5]. In this work the training sequences and the references sequences from the data set are used (see gray boxes in Fig. 1). For each subject the data set contains around 50 training sequences and two reference sequences.

Training sequences consist of 2D images acquired under free-breathing conditions. It contains to different types of images. First navigator slices (short navigators) and second, data slices. The two types of images are acquired alternatingly in the sequence. The navigator has a fixed slice position in the right liver lobe and serves as an image based respiratory surrogate during training. The data slice position is also fixed within one training sequence but is changed for each training sequence. The first sequence has the data slice position p_1, the second one has $p_1 + 4\,\text{mm}$, the Nth sequence at $p_1 + N \times 4\,\text{mm}$. Together, all training sequences sample the liver equidistantly in 4 mm steps. Each sequences contains 175 image pairs. The number of slice positions depends on the liver size, ranging from 38 to 57. Acquisition time for each slice was 166 ms.

Reference sequences acquire 513 navigators under free-breathing, capturing the progression of the breathing states, including variations such as shallow/deep or thoracic/abdominal breathing, encompassing around 20 breathing cycles. They serve as surrogate during inference. The navigator position of the reference sequence and all training sequences is the same.

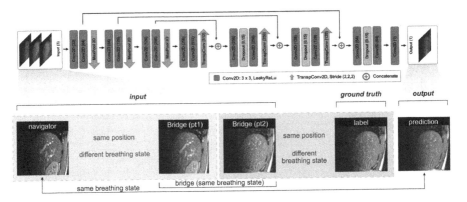

Fig. 2. Network architecture and transitive information bridging using reserved samples from the training data, i.e., the bridge split. The three input channels of the UNet get 1) a navigator from the training sample, 2) a navigator from the bridge sample, 3) the label from the bridge sample.

2.2 Deep Learning Framework

We propose an update to our deep learning-based 4D MRI framework [4]. Figure 2 shows the updated form. In the previous formulation, we proposed to use the training sequences together with slices of a 3D breath-hold volume, which are available in the data set as well but have a different MR contrast than the MR slices, to predict a 4D MRI. The network was fed by three input channels getting 1) a navigator slice, 2) a slice of the 3D volume at navigator position, and 3) a slice of the 3D volume at label position, which is the position we seek to predict. The slices of the 3D volume in channel two and three thereby serve as a transitive information bridge. We call this volume bridging (VB). Let B be the breathing state, which is visible in the navigator in channel one. Let ΔB be the difference in breathing states between the images in channel one and two. The network can learn the effect of ΔB, and, since the inputs in channels two and three share the same breathing state, the network can learn to apply the inverse effect to the third channel, thus predicting the breathing state B for that slice position. The data slices from the navigator-data pairs serve as labels. Using batching, a 3D volume can be predicted in a single forward pass by letting each batch entry indicate another slice position by adjusting the third channel. However, this learning task not only involved learning ΔB but also learning the apparent difference in MR contrast between the breath-hold volume and the label.

2.3 Improved Formulation

In this work, we propose to reuse the training samples from the training sequences as bridges instead of requiring a separate breath-hold volume with a different MR contrast and call this sample bridging (SB). The relation of the inputs and output regarding the slice position and breathing state are depicted in Fig. 2. For the new method the samples are split into four instead of three splits, namely: training, validation, test, and bridge split. In a forward pass of the new method, input channel one is still fed by the navigator of the training sample, however, the second and third channel are fed by a navigator and data slice of a bridge sample from the bridge pool from the same training sequence as the current training sample. There are notable differences between VB and SB. First, in SB, channels two and three have a time offset of 166 ms due to the acquisition time. We hypothesize that the effect is negligible or compensated by the network. Second, in VB, the bridges not only have a different MR contrast but also lack image detail compared to the label. In SB, all inputs and outputs share the same MR contrast and level of image detail. We hypothesize that this simplifies the learning task. Third, SB avoids the need for a 3D volume, which reduces the beforehand acquisition time significantly by 1 min. Within the framework, for comparability, we use the same network architecture and training setup as described in our earlier work, please see [6] for details. We differentiate two SB flavors: 1) fixed sample bridging (FSB) where each slice position has its own and fixed navigator-data pair as a bridge, and 2) random sample bridging (RSB) where the bridges for each slice position are randomly chosen for each forward pass during training. For FSB, the bridge split is small and contains only one bridge sample for each slice position. For RSB, the size of the bridge split is a hyper parameter. It contains two or more bridge samples per slice position. All source code is publicly available: https://github.com/gulamhus/SampleBridges-MILLanD2023

2.4 Experiments

Data is split into source domain **S** (16 subjects) and target domain **T** (4 subjects). The experiment design requires a second split per training sequence into: training (50%), validation (2%), and test (48%) sets. The framework was evaluated on two aspects: the use of source and target domain data, and the type of bridging. Configurations are denoted as XX+YYY, where XX+ indicates the used data and can be empty, DL+ (direct learning), or TL+. They mean: only source data, only target data or both were used, respectively. The bridge type is denotes as YYY and can be VB, RSB, FSB, or FRSB. The latter means, RSB was used in the base model and FSB was used during fine-tuning. That results in three configuration groups for evaluation: (VB, RSB, FSB), (DL+VB, DL+RSB, DL+FSB), and (TL+VB, TL+RSB, TL+FSB).

Table 2 summarises the research questions. Out-of-domain performance refers to testing a model trained in **S** on **T** without fine-tuning. T-tests and Cohen's d were performed.

Exp 1.1 (addressing RQ 1.1, 1.2 and 4): Utilizing VB, RSB, and FSB respectively, three sets of 7 models each were trained with data of every subject in **S**. Each of the 7 models per set were trained at decreasing levels of training data amounts (decreasing from 24 min to 0.25 min). The out-of-domain performance of the models was evaluated for each subject in **T**.

Table 2. Research questions (RQ)

RQ 1.1:	Do FSB and RSB improve out-of-domain performance over VB?
RQ 1.2:	If so, does this effect depend on training data size?
RQ 2.1:	Does TL+FSB and TL+RSB improve performance over TL+VB models?
RQ 2.2:	If so, does the effect depend on the base model's training data size?
RQ 2.3:	And does it depend on data availability in **T** for fine-tuning?
RQ 3.1:	Does FSB and RSB improve models directly learned in **T**?
RQ 3.2:	If so, is the effect dependent on data availability in **T**?
RQ 4 :	If FSB and RSB have an effect, do the effects differ?

Exp 1.2 (RQ 2.1, 2.2 and 4): All pre-trained models of Exp 1.1 were fine-tuned for each subject in **T** separately, using 2 min of training data. This resulted in three sets (TL+VB, TL+RSB, TL+FSB) in which the same bridge types are used as in the base models. A fourth set (TL+RFSB) was fine-tuned using RSB in the base model and FSB during fine-tuning. All models were evaluated on the test data from the same target subject used for fine-tuning.

Exp 2.1 (RQ 3.1, 3.2 and 4): Three sets (DL+VB, DL+RSB, DL+FSB) of models were trained directly and separately on every subject in **T**. In this context only, DL denotes direct learning in the target domain, in reference to the term TL. Each set contains 7 models per target subject, trained at decreasing training data amount (decreasing from 47 min to 1 min). The performance of the models was evaluated on the test data of the subject used for training.

Exp 2.2 (RQ 2.3): Those pre-trained models from Exp 1.1, that were trained with 2 min of training data, were fine-tuned on each subject in **T** separately at the same training data amount levels defined in Exp 2.1, resulting in four sets (TL+VB, TL+RSB, TL+FSB and TL+RFSB), each containing 6 models per target subject. The performance of the models was evaluated on the test data of the subject used for fine-tuning.

3   Results

The results are depicted in Fig. 3 and Table 3. For better readability, the TL+FSB set was omitted from Fig. 3, showing no significant difference to TL+RSB.

Exp 1.1 and 1.2, SB increases out-of-domain performance compared to VB [RQ 1.1 Yes], regardless of source domain data size, reducing meadian RMSE significantly ($p< 2.2e^{-16}$, d=-1.22) from 0.50 to 0.31 (at the 2 min data availability level). Improvements are comparable to TL ($p< 2.2e^{-16}$, d=-1.67). The effect size depends on data availability but becomes nearly constant for training data sizes of 5 min and larger [RQ 1.2 Yes]. Without TL, we find that RSB performs slightly better than FSB ($p=2.069e^{-7}$, d=-0.025) [RQ 4 Yes]. Both TL+FSB and TL+RSB reduce meadian RMSE compared to TL+VB from 0.3 to 0.28

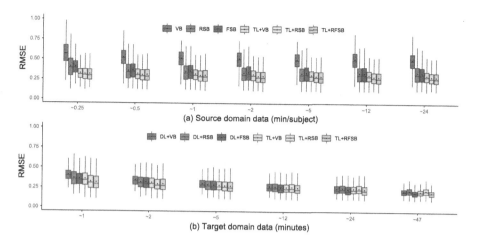

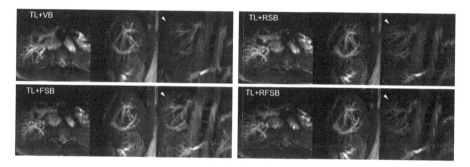

Fig. 3. Box plots of (a) **Exp 1.1** and **1.2** and (b) **Exp 2.1** and **2.2**

Fig. 4. Visual comparison of TL+VB (previously best) and all TL+SB flavors. The white arrows indicate places, where the change in image detail is well recognizable.

(p< $2.2e^{-16}$, d=-0.14 and d=-0.19) [RQ 2.1 Yes]. However, in this experiment, TL+FSB and TL+RSB show no significant difference (p=0.4846, d=0.04).

Exp 2.1 and 2.2, both DL+FSB and DL+RSB improve meadian RMSE over DL+VB from 0.4 to 0.34 and 0.35 respectively (p< $2.2e^{-16}$, d=-0.21 and d=-0.13) [RQ 3.1 Yes]. Target domain data availability has a major influence on found effects [RQ 3.2 Yes]. The effect size of DL+RSB inverts for training data sizes of 12 min and beyond. The effects of TL+FSB and TL+RSB are dependent on target domain data availability during fine tuning [RQ 2.3 Yes]. Similar to DL+RSB, the effect of TL+RSB inverts for larger training sizes. TL+RFSB yields the best over all performance. In a qualitative comparison of TL+VB, TL+FSB, TL+RSB, and TL+RFSB (see Fig. 4) we gain detail (arrows) over TL+VB for all alternatives using the same amount of training data.

Table 3. Median RMSE (95th RMSE percentile). [a] from [4], [b] from [6]

Error by source domain data availability (in min)							
	0.25	0.5	1	2	5	12	24
VB[a]	0.57 (0.83)	0.51 (0.78)	0.5 (0.77)	0.5 (0.77)	0.49 (0.76)	0.5 (0.76)	0.49 (0.75)
RSB	0.39 (0.68)	0.34 (0.58)	0.33 (0.55)	0.31 (0.55)	0.31 (0.55)	0.31 (0.57)	0.32 (0.58)
FSB	0.39 (0.61)	0.35 (0.59)	0.33 (0.57)	0.32 (0.55)	0.31 (0.55)	0.31 (0.55)	0.31 (0.55)
TL+VB[b]	0.31 (0.48)	0.3 (0.49)	0.3 (0.48)	0.3 (0.48)	0.29 (0.47)	0.29 (0.46)	0.29 (0.46)
TL+RSB	0.3 (0.48)	0.29 (0.47)	**0.28 (0.47)**	0.28 (0.46)	**0.27 (0.46)**	0.27 (0.45)	**0.27 (0.45)**
TL+FSB	**0.29 (0.5)**	**0.28 (0.5)**	0.28 (0.49)	0.28 (0.49)	0.27 (0.48)	0.27 (0.48)	0.27 (0.47)
TL+RFSB	0.29 (0.51)	**0.28 (0.5)**	0.28 (0.49)	**0.27 (0.48)**	0.27 (0.47)	**0.26 (0.45)**	**0.27 (0.45)**
Error by target domain data availability (in min)							
	1	2	5	12	24	47	
DL+VB[a]	0.4 (0.58)	0.33 (0.49)	0.29 (0.45)	0.25 (0.41)	0.22 (0.38)	0.2 (0.29)	
DL+RSB	0.35 (0.57)	0.3 (0.49)	0.27 (0.44)	0.25 (0.4)	0.23 (0.37)	0.21 (0.31)	
DL+FSB	0.34 (0.55)	0.3 (0.51)	0.26 (0.45)	0.23 (0.42)	0.21 (0.39)	0.19 (0.28)	
TL+VB[b]	0.34 (0.55)	0.3 (0.47)	0.26 (0.43)	0.23 (0.4)	0.22 (0.38)	0.2 (0.28)	
TL+RSB	0.3 (0.52)	0.28 (0.46)	0.26 (0.43)	0.24 (0.4)	0.23 (0.37)	0.21 (0.32)	
TL+FSB	0.3 (0.52)	0.28 (0.48)	0.25 (0.46)	0.23 (0.42)	0.21 (0.39)	**0.19 (0.27)**	
TL+RFSB	**0.29 (0.51)**	**0.27 (0.48)**	**0.25 (0.45)**	**0.23 (0.41)**	**0.21 (0.38)**	**0.19 (0.27)**	

4   Discussion and Conclusion

While both RSB and FSB significantly improve model performance in all experiments, TL+RSB is unsuitable for larger training data sizes. TL+RFSB with 2 min per subject in both source domain and target domain provides the best balance of efficiency and performance. If fine-tuning is not possible, FSB still greatly improves prediction performance, almost as much as TL alone. While the resolution is dependent on the thickness of the training slices, this is easy to handle by distributing the same number of slice to more positions, e.g., acquiring 2 samples every 1 mm instead of 8 samples every 4 mm. This increases resolution while keeping the acquisition time. The current work has limitations that should be addressed in future work. A clinical validation involving medical experts and real interventional scenarios has to be performed yet and will offer stronger evidence of the method's effectiveness. Also evaluating performance using additional metrics and conducting the evaluation with cross-validation techniques will improve the accuracy of results. For example investigating whether the network fills in erroneous details in the prediction. **Conclusion:** Our approach re-utilizes training samples as transitive information bridges, improving prediction quality and eliminating the need for a prior 3D scan, thereby reducing acquisition time.

Acknowledgements. The authors acknowledge the financial support from the Federal Ministry for Economics and Energy of Germany (project number 16KN093921). This work was carried out as part of the STIMULATE research campus.

References

1. Cai, J., Chang, Z., Wang, Z., Paul Segars, W., Yin, F.F.: Four-dimensional magnetic resonance imaging (4D-MRI) using image-based respiratory surrogate: a feasibility study. Med. Phys. **38**(12), 6384–6394 (2011)
2. Gulamhussene, G., Joeres, F., Rak, M., Lübeck, C., Pech, M., Hansen, C.: 2D MRI liver slices with navigator frames. a test data set for image based 4D MRI reconstruction (2019). https://doi.org/10.24352/UB.OVGU-2019-093
3. Gulamhussene, G., Joeres, F., Rak, M., Pech, M., Hansen, C.: 4D MRI: robust sorting of free breathing MRI slices for use in interventional settings. PLoS ONE **15**(6), e0235175 (2020)
4. Gulamhussene, G., et al.: Predicting 4D liver MRI for MR-guided interventions. Comput. Med. Imaging Graph., 102122 (2022). https://doi.org/10.1016/j.compmedimag.2022.102122, https://www.sciencedirect.com/science/article/pii/S0895611122000921
5. Gulamhussene, G., et al.: 2D MRI liver slices with navigator frames. a test data set for image based 4D MRI reconstruction. Part II (2021). https://doi.org/10.24352/UB.OVGU-2021-071
6. Gulamhussene, G., et al.: Transfer-learning is a key ingredient to fast deep learning-based 4D liver MRI reconstruction (2022)
7. Han, F., Zhou, Z., Cao, M., Yang, Y., Sheng, K., Hu, P.: Respiratory motion-resolved, self-gated 4D-MRI using rotating cartesian k-space (ROCK). Med. Phys. **44**(4), 1359–1368 (2017)
8. Hu, Y., Caruthers, S.D., Low, D.A., Parikh, P.J., Mutic, S.: Respiratory amplitude guided 4-dimensional magnetic resonance imaging. Int. J. Radiat. Oncol.* Biol.* Phys. **86**(1), 198–204 (2013)
9. van de Lindt, T., et al.: A self-sorting coronal 4D-MRI method for daily image guidance of liver lesions on an MR-LINAC. Int. J. Radiat. Oncol.* Biol.* Phys. **102**(4), 875–884 (2018)
10. Paganelli, C., Summers, P., Bellomi, M., Baroni, G., Riboldi, M.: Liver 4DMRI: a retrospective image-based sorting method. Med. Phys. **42**(8), 4814–4821 (2015)
11. von Siebenthal, M., Szekely, G., Gamper, U., Boesiger, P., Lomax, A., Cattin, P.: 4D MR imaging of respiratory organ motion and its variability. Phys. Med. Biol. **52**(6), 1547 (2007)
12. Tanner, C., Samei, G., Székely, G.: Improved reconstruction of 4D-MR images by motion predictions. In: Golland, P., Hata, N., Barillot, C., Hornegger, J., Howe, R. (eds.) Medical Image Computing and Computer-Assisted Intervention – MICCAI 2014: 17th International Conference, Boston, MA, USA, September 14-18, 2014, Proceedings, Part I, pp. 146–153. Springer International Publishing, Cham (2014). https://doi.org/10.1007/978-3-319-10404-1_19
13. Tryggestad, E., et al.: Respiration-based sorting of dynamic MRI to derive representative 4D-MRI for radiotherapy planning. Med. Phys. **40**(5), 051909 (2013)
14. Yang, Z., Ren, L., Yin, F.F., Liang, X., Cai, J.: Motion robust 4D-MRI sorting based on anatomic feature matching: a digital phantom simulation study. Radiat. Med. Prot. **1**(1), 41–47 (2020)
15. Yuan, J., Wong, O.L., Zhou, Y., Chueng, K.Y., Yu, S.K.: A fast volumetric 4D-MRI with sub-second frame rate for abdominal motion monitoring and characterization in MRI-guided radiotherapy. Quant. Imaging Med. Surg. **9**(7), 1303 (2019)

To Pretrain or Not to Pretrain? A Case Study of Domain-Specific Pretraining for Semantic Segmentation in Histopathology

Tushar Kataria[1,2]([✉]), Beatrice Knudsen[3], and Shireen Elhabian[1,2]([✉])

[1] Kahlert School of Computing, University of Utah, Salt Lake City, USA
[2] Scientific Computing and Imaging Institute, University of Utah,
Salt Lake City, USA
{tushar.kataria,shireen}@sci.utah.edu
[3] Department of Pathology, University of Utah, Salt Lake City, USA
beatrice.knudsen@path.utah.edu

Abstract. Annotating medical imaging datasets is costly, so fine-tuning (or transfer learning) is the most effective method for digital pathology vision applications such as disease classification and semantic segmentation. However, due to texture bias in models trained on real-world images, transfer learning for histopathology applications might result in underperforming models, which necessitates the need for using unlabeled histopathology data and self-supervised methods to discover domain-specific characteristics. Here, we tested the premise that histopathology-specific pretrained models provide better initializations for pathology vision tasks, i.e., gland and cell segmentation. In this study, we compare the performance of gland and cell segmentation tasks with histopathology domain-specific and non-domain-specific (real-world images) pretrained weights. Moreover, we investigate the dataset size at which domain-specific pretraining produces significant gains in performance. In addition, we investigated whether domain-specific initialization improves the effectiveness of out-of-distribution testing on distinct datasets but the same task. The results indicate that performance gain using domain-specific pretrained weights depends on both the task and the size of the training dataset. In instances with limited dataset sizes, a significant improvement in gland segmentation performance was also observed, whereas models trained on cell segmentation datasets exhibit no improvement. Github Code Repository.

Keywords: Domain Specific pretraining · Gland and Cell Segmentation · Transfer Learning

Supplementary Information The online version contains supplementary material available at https://doi.org/10.1007/978-3-031-44917-8_24.

© The Author(s), under exclusive license to Springer Nature Switzerland AG 2023
Z. Xue et al. (Eds.): MILLanD 2023, LNCS 14307, pp. 246–256, 2023.
https://doi.org/10.1007/978-3-031-44917-8_24

1 Introduction

Deep learning models typically require a substantial amount of data to effectively learn generalized latent space representations [4]. However, acquiring large medical image datasets is more challenging compared to real-world image datasets for three primary reasons. Firstly, the annotation process for medical images involves domain-specific knowledge from pathologists and radiologists to manually outline anatomical structures. This is challenging given the global scarcity of pathology and radiology experts [12,19,23]; Secondly, the image annotation interfaces are inefficient in generating labor-intensive workflows. Thirdly, inter-observer disagreement among medical professionals necessitates the involvement of multiple experts to repeat each annotation task [5,7,21]. Lastly, in addition to the annotation challenges there are biases in medical data. Biases in histopathology images arise from variations in tissue quality, staining protocols leading to difference in color and texture [11], scanning protocols and slide scanners [11,14,17].

These biases are often site-specific and can cause major distribution shifts between different data sets, which in turn reduces the generalization of deep learning models [11,17].

Other forms of distribution shifts for histopathology in cancer cohorts include discrepancies between cancer and normal tissue histology, the proportion of histologic cancer subtypes, grades and stages, and variations in clinical, demographic, and race-related variables [15,25]. These variables generate data imbalances that can degrade the performance of deep learning models during testing.

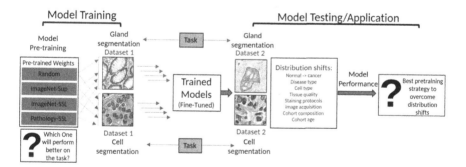

Fig. 1. Do different weight initialization matter? The study is designed from the perspective of an AI user who can choose between multiple pretrained models (domain or non-domain, supervised or self-supervised) options for a given task. The best pretrained model is the one that has the highest accuracy on the task and is least affected by distribution shifts. This study provides a framework to choose amongst pretrained models and select the most advantageous for the task.

In medical image vision tasks, fine-tuning pretrained models (also known as transfer learning) has become a common approach [6,18]. These tasks are important for automated diagnosis, cancer grading and predictions of patients outcomes across all cancer types.

Using supervised or self-supervised methods, deep learning models exhibit strong capabilities to learn effective latent representations [3]. However, they may suffer from domain-specific texture bias [10], which can impede their performance [22]. Previous research indicates that if sufficient data is available for training, a model trained de-novo (i.e., from scratch) may outperform a fine-tuned model [18,22]. This suggests a potential benefit of domain-specific pretraining [13,29] over transfer learning from ImageNet [9].

Because large, annotated data sets are difficult to obtain for pretraining on histopathology images, self-supervised (SSL) and annotation free methods provide an alternative strategy for pretraining models to learn valid representation in the latent space [1,2,28]. Models can then be further fine-tuned with a few annotations to produce acceptable results on test datasets. However, no studies systematically evaluated the impact of domain-specific pretaining for histopathology models that are tasked to learn cell and gland segmentation. The closest matching work to this study is an investigation of pretraining on classification and instance segmentation tasks [13].

As gland and cell segmentation differ from instance segmentation and classification, the effect of pretraining on the analysis of out-of-distribution (OOD) datasets also remains unknown. The contributions of this paper are as follows:-

– Comparison of de-novo trained models with pretrained models on the ImageNet dataset using class supervision [9] and self-supervision [28] for semantic segmentation tasks in histopathology.
– Finetuning pretrained domain-specific (histopathology) models [13] for gland and cell segmentation. These comparisons will indicate whether domain-specific pretraining aids cell and gland segmentation.
– Determining the effect of compute resources and data quantity on model performance improvements.
– Investigating whether domain-specific training leads to a better generalization of models to data distribution shifts.

2   Different Pretrained Weights Used

To investigate whether domain-specific pretraining leads to generalization in gland and cell segmentation tasks, the study aims to address the following research questions:

– *Is domain pretraining, which involves initializing the weights trained with domain-specific images(histopathology), more effective for transfer learning compared to pretrained weights from ImageNet data?*
– *Do self-supervised outperform supervised weight initializations?*
– *Does domain-specific pretraining enhance the quality of features and improve the model's performance on datasets with distribution shifts?*

All initializations are compared against random initialization (i.e., training from scratch), which serves as the baseline to identify initializations (mentioned below) that outperform random. The flow diagram of the study is shown in Fig. 1.

Models are trained with 3 different types of initializations: (1) **pretrained weights using class supervision on ImageNet data**: default weights are provided in Pytorch for *ImageNetV1* and *ImageNetV2*. The top-1 accuracies in the initialization amount to 76.13 and 80.85, respectively. These weights are obtained by training a ResNet50 [9] model with class supervision. For two other initialization, weights are obtained using a self-supervised technique called Barlow Twins [28]. (2) **Pretrained weights with ImageNet data using SSL (SSLImage)**: Self-supervised weights were obtained after training on data from ImageNet without using labels. (3) **Histopathology Domain-Specific pretraining using SSL (SSLPathology)**: This model is released as part of the study in [13] for domain-specific pretraining on histopathology data. The model was pretrained using more than three million histopathology image patches sampled from various cancers at different magnifications. More details about the pretraining method and the dataset can be found in [13].

2.1 Dataset Details

We have experimented with gland and cell segmentation tasks on these five histopathology datasets:

Gland Segmentation Datasets: Colon cancer datasets, GlaS and CRAG [8, 26], possess ground truth gland segmentation annotations for normal and colon cancer glands. The GlaS dataset has 88 training & 80 testing images of size less 700×600 pixels, whereas the CRAG dataset has 160 training & 40 testing images of size 1512×1512 pixels.

Cell Segmentation Datasets: Three cell segmentation datasets are used for experimentation KUMAR [16], CPM17 [27] and TNBC [20] possess ground truth annotations of nuclear outlines (Table 1).

Table 1. Cell Segmentation Dataset Details. Sample examples of the dataset are shown in supplementary Fig. 9.

Datasets	Train Imgs	Test Imgs	Img Size	No. of Annotated Nuclei
KUMAR [16]	16	14	1000×1000	21623
CPM17 [27]	31	31	500×500	7570
TNBC [20]	34	16	512×512	4022

2.2 Implementation Details

A U-Net [24] model is used with *Resnet50* [9] backbone for semantic segmentation application(gland & cell both). The decoder is always the same for all models. Details of implementation can be found in the associated github[1]. Models are

---

[1] GitHub Repository.

trained using PyTorch and a data split of 80-20 for training and validation. The best model possessing a minimum loss on validation data is further evaluated on the test dataset. Testing data is only used for inference.

During training the patch size is 256×256, sampled randomly in the whole image. At inference, predictions are averaged over a window size of 128 pixels. The learning rate is fixed to 0.0001 and the number of epochs for all experiments is set to 4000 for gland segmentation and 2000 for cell segmentation. The models are trained five times and average metrics are reported, this ensures that variations due to stochasticity caused by the dataset loader are factored out. Data augmentation includes horizontal and vertical flips, random rotation, and translation. All models are trained on NVIDIA V100 GPUs.

Evaluation Metrics: Dice and Jaccard scores (also known as the intersection over union) serve as metrics for segmentation tasks [24, 26].

3   Results

Gland Segmentation Results: The line plots (standard deviation marked as shading) of performance measures for different initialization are shown in Fig. 2-A and 6-A. We trained models with different backbone initializations on an increasing amount of data. The following observations emerged from these experiments:- (a) Increasing the quantity of data improves performance for all initializations and decreases variation. (b) For different training dataset sizes, models with pretrained weight initializations outperform those with random initializations, but the performance gap between models trained with random initialization and pretrained weights decreases as the quantity of data increases. (c) For small datasets, finetuning domain-specific pretrained weights has a significant performance advantage over other initializations. However, as dataset size increases, the effect diminishes[2].

Variations in performance due to different amounts of training epochs for all datasets are shown in Fig. 2-B and 6-B. For very small datasets(10% and 30% graph), finetuning domain-specific pretrained weights outperforms all other initializations at all epochs. However, for larger datasets(100% data), ImageNet supervised weights also outperform at lower epochs. This show that domain-specific pretraining is not dependent on computational power but rather on dataset diversity. If a dataset is not diverse or small in size, then domain-specific pretrained weights are beneficial, but other initialization can be better for higher diversity and epochs. Qualitative results are shown in supplementary Fig. 8, domain-specific fine-tuned models have more accurate gland outlines and fewer false positive pixels than other models.

Cell Segmentation Results: The performance of various initializations is depicted in Fig. 3. Even though some of the observations are similar to those of previous experiments, novel observations emerge from cell segmentation results:-

---

[2] All images are best viewed on a digital device following magnification.

(a) Model performances with KUMAR [16] data are an exception where random initialization is outperforming or competitive with other initializations. (b) Domain-specific pretraining is performing similar to or worse than ImageNet initialization for most cases. Altogether our results demonstrate that fine-tuning domain-specific pretrained weights does not improve the performance of the U-Net/ResNet model for cell segmentation tasks. Qualitative results are shown in supplementary Fig. 9.

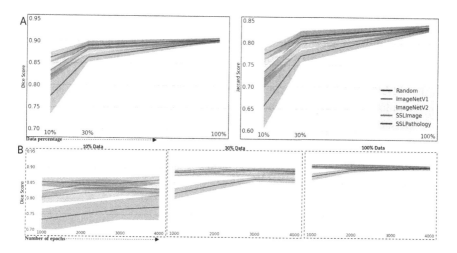

Fig. 2. Gland Segmentation Results for Different Initializations on GlaS[26]. (**A**) Dice and Jaccard Score for different percentage of training data used. Solid line shows the mean performance metrics, where as color shading shows the variance. We can clearly observe that increasing data increases model performance, but with more data domain specific pretraining doesn't have a significant effect on performance. (**B**) Average dice score variations with different amounts of training time, i.e., number of epochs. We clearly see a difference in performance for different initialization for low dataset size and lesser epochs. Results on CRAG dataset are shown in Supplementary Fig. 6.

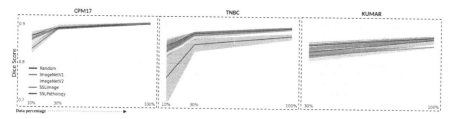

Fig. 3. Cell Segmentation Results. Different initialization has similar patterns, i.e., with increasing data variation in performance decreases and mean performance increases. But for cell segmentation domain specific pretraining doesn't seem to be better than image-net pretrained weights for different data sizes.

UMAP Results: We sampled 300 random patches from the test sets of GlaS and CRAG to generate projections for encoders and decoders shown in Fig. 4. Feature values were extracted from the first encoder layer in U-Net, the deepest encoder layer, and the last decoder layer.

In the network's first layer, the projections of features from various initializations form clouds that overlap. We interpret this observation to conclude that the initial layers of deep neural networks capture low-level statistics and that all initializations capture comparable attributes. As encoding depth increases, the representations become more distinct and the overlap decreases, indicating that networks pretrained in different ways may be learning different representations of the same data. This is counterintuitive, as we would expect that each of the pretrained models generates similar high-level representations when performing identical tasks and using the same dataset. However, the distribution of features in the UMAP projection of latent layer representations appears to have topological similarity across initializations which indicates that features for different initialization may be related via a rigid transformation in latent space. A similar conclusion is valid for the decoder UMAP. Together, these results suggest that distinct initializations, despite being clustered at different locations in the UMAP, might learn similar relational feature characteristics between samples in the dataset.

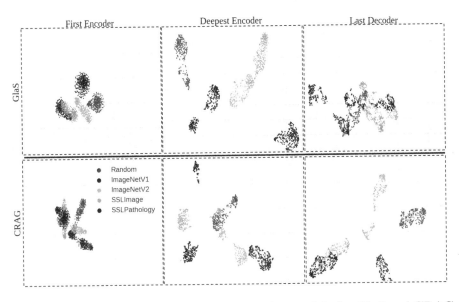

Fig. 4. UMAP for different Gland Segmentation models for GlaS and CRAG datasets. We generate UMAP with nearest neighbor=25, distance=0.1, and metric=cosine. Comparing the latent representation of the initial encoder to that of the deepest encoder, there is substantially less overlap between initializations, but the distribution of points is topologically similar.

3.1 Out of Distribution Testing Results

For OOD testing, we use the fine-tuned segmentation models (source dataset, Dataset 1) with different initialization for out-of-distribution testing on other datasets (target dataset, Dataset 2) without fine-tuning on the second dataset. This analysis reveals the distribution bias various initializations learned during the training (fine-tuning) process.

Gland Segmentation Results. The results for OOD testing for the gland segmentation task are shown in Fig. 5. At a low amount of data, the domain-specific, finetuned models perform best and using random initializations results in the greatest relative performance drop compared to all other initializations.

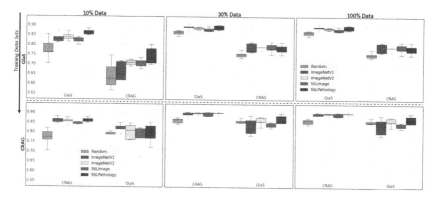

Fig. 5. Average dice score for OOD testing. Y-axis shows the dataset used for training of the model. X-axis is the performance on the corresponding test sets without any fine-tuning. A model trained on CRAG datasets transfers effectively to GlaS, but not vice versa. Domain-specific pretrained models are generally better at out-of-domain performance.

Cell Segmentation Results: The results of OOD testing for different datasets are shown in supplementary Fig. 7 and lead to the following observations: (a) pretrained models are better than models with random initialization at the same task on unseen datasets from KUMAR [16] and CPM17 [27]). In contrast, models with random initialization and trained on TNBC [20] outperform or perform the same as the pretrained initialized model. (b) A drop in performance exists on TNBC data for models trained on KUMAR [16] and CPM17 [27] but not for models trained on TNBC [20] or KUMAR [16] and applied to CPM17. (c) Domain-specific pretrained models when tested on OODdata demonstrate a lesser drop in performance compared to other pretraining approaches.

4 Conclusion and Future Work

In this study, we demonstrate that a using domain-specific pretrained backbone can be beneficial for gland segmentation when data are limited or of low diversity data for the task at hand. However, the performance gap for fine-tuned domain-specific pretrained weights compared to random initialization decreased as the amount of training data increased. The results of cell segmentation indicate that domain-specific pretrained weights may not be advantageous for all types of tasks. The results of UMAP projections indicate that the initial layers of domain-specific and non-domain-specific models learn similar features, but that the deeper encoders are distinct. Although the topology of latent feature representations is similar for the different initialization, models may be learning similar high-level characteristics within the latent feature spaces. Lastly, during out-of-distribution testing, models initialized with domain-specific pretrained weights suffered the same performance degradation as other initializations. Therefore, domain-specific pretrained weight initialization may not be effective at learning site-independent features. Our final conclusion from this study is that fine-tuning domain-specific pretrained weights may be beneficial for specific tasks and datasets, but benefits are not universal. Domain-specific pretrained weights suffer from the same issues as weights on image-net. Lastly, we would like to make the reader aware that this study did not cover medical vision tasks such as multi-class semantic segmentation and cell detection. We also did not utilize models pretrained using vision-language models. Both these comparisons are left for future work.

Acknowledgments. We thank the Department of Pathology and the Kahlert School of Computing at the University of Utah for their support of this project.

References

1. Caron, M., Misra, I., Mairal, J., Goyal, P., Bojanowski, P., Joulin, A.: Unsupervised learning of visual features by contrasting cluster assignments. Adv. Neural Inf. Proc. Syst. **33**, 9912–9924 (2020)
2. Chen, T., Kornblith, S., Norouzi, M., Hinton, G.: A simple framework for contrastive learning of visual representations. In: International Conference on Machine Learning, pp. 1597–1607. PMLR (2020)
3. Chen, T., Kornblith, S., Swersky, K., Norouzi, M., Hinton, G.E.: Big self-supervised models are strong semi-supervised learners. Adv. Neural Inf. Proc. Syst. **33**, 22243–22255 (2020)
4. Deng, J., Dong, W., Socher, R., Li, L.J., Li, K., Fei-Fei, L.: ImageNet: a large-scale hierarchical image database. In: 2009 IEEE Conference on Computer Vision and Pattern Recognition, pp. 248–255. IEEE (2009)
5. Eaden, J., Abrams, K., McKay, H., Denley, H., Mayberry, J.: Inter-observer variation between general and specialist gastrointestinal pathologists when grading dysplasia in ulcerative colitis. J. Pathol.: J. Pathol. Soc. G. B. Irel. **194**(2), 152–157 (2001)
6. Erhan, D., Courville, A., Bengio, Y., Vincent, P.: Why does unsupervised pretraining help deep learning? In: Proceedings of the Thirteenth International Conference on Artificial Intelligence and Statistics, pp. 201–208. JMLR Workshop and Conference Proceedings (2010)

7. Farmer, M., Petras, R.E., Hunt, L.E., Janosky, J.E., Galandiuk, S.: The importance of diagnostic accuracy in colonic inflammatory bowel disease. Am. J. Gastroenterol. **95**(11), 3184–3188 (2000)
8. Graham, S., et al.: MILD-Net: minimal information loss dilated network for gland instance segmentation in colon histology images. Med. Image Anal. **52**, 199–211 (2019)
9. He, K., Zhang, X., Ren, S., Sun, J.: Deep residual learning for image recognition. In: Proceedings of the IEEE Conference on Computer Vision and Pattern Recognition, pp. 770–778 (2016)
10. Hermann, K., Chen, T., Kornblith, S.: The origins and prevalence of texture bias in convolutional neural networks. Adv. Neural Inf. Proc. Syst. **33**, 19000–19015 (2020)
11. Howard, F.M., et al.: The impact of site-specific digital histology signatures on deep learning model accuracy and bias. Nat. Commun. **12**(1), 4423 (2021)
12. Jajosky, R.P., Jajosky, A.N., Kleven, D.T., Singh, G.: Fewer seniors from united states allopathic medical schools are filling pathology residency positions in the main residency match, 2008–2017. Hum. Pathol. **73**, 26–32 (2018)
13. Kang, M., Song, H., Park, S., Yoo, D., Pereira, S.: Benchmarking self-supervised learning on diverse pathology datasets. In: Proceedings of the IEEE/CVF Conference on Computer Vision and Pattern Recognition, pp. 3344–3354 (2023)
14. Kataria, T., Knudsen, B., Elhabian, S.: Unsupervised domain adaptation for semantic segmentation via feature-space density matching. arXiv preprint arXiv:2305.05789 (2023)
15. Kataria, T., et al.: Automating ground truth annotations for gland segmentation through immunohistochemistry (2023)
16. Kumar, N., Verma, R., Sharma, S., Bhargava, S., Vahadane, A., Sethi, A.: A dataset and a technique for generalized nuclear segmentation for computational pathology. IEEE Trans. Med. Imaging **36**(7), 1550–1560 (2017)
17. Liu, Q., Dou, Q., Yu, L., Heng, P.A.: Ms-Net: multi-site network for improving prostate segmentation with heterogeneous MRI data. IEEE Trans. Med. Imaging **39**(9), 2713–2724 (2020)
18. Mensink, T., Uijlings, J., Kuznetsova, A., Gygli, M., Ferrari, V.: Factors of influence for transfer learning across diverse appearance domains and task types. IEEE Trans. Pattern Anal. Mach. Intell. **44**(12), 9298–9314 (2021)
19. Metter, D.M., Colgan, T.J., Leung, S.T., Timmons, C.F., Park, J.Y.: Trends in the us and canadian pathologist workforces from 2007 to 2017. JAMA Netw. Open **2**(5), e194337–e194337 (2019)
20. Naylor, P., Laé, M., Reyal, F., Walter, T.: Segmentation of nuclei in histopathology images by deep regression of the distance map. IEEE Trans. Med. Imaging **38**(2), 448–459 (2018)
21. Nir, G., et al.: Automatic grading of prostate cancer in digitized histopathology images: learning from multiple experts. Med. Image Anal. **50**, 167–180 (2018)
22. Raghu, M., Zhang, C., Kleinberg, J., Bengio, S.: Transfusion: understanding transfer learning for medical imaging. In: Advances in Neural Information Processing Systems 32 (2019)
23. Robboy, S.J., et al.: Reevaluation of the us pathologist workforce size. JAMA Netw. Open **3**(7), e2010648–e2010648 (2020)

24. Ronneberger, O., Fischer, P., Brox, T.: U-Net: convolutional networks for biomedical image segmentation. In: Navab, N., Hornegger, J., Wells, W.M., Frangi, A.F. (eds.) Medical Image Computing and Computer-Assisted Intervention – MICCAI 2015: 18th International Conference, Munich, Germany, October 5-9, 2015, Proceedings, Part III, pp. 234–241. Springer International Publishing, Cham (2015). https://doi.org/10.1007/978-3-319-24574-4_28

25. Shi, L., et al.: EBHI-Seg: a novel enteroscope biopsy histopathological hematoxylin and eosin image dataset for image segmentation tasks. Front. Med. **10** (2023). https://doi.org/10.3389/fmed.2023.1114673

26. Sirinukunwattana, K., et al.: Gland segmentation in colon histology images: the GlaS challenge contest. Med. Image Anal. **35**, 489–502 (2017). https://doi.org/10.1016/j.media.2016.08.008

27. Vu, Q.D., et al.: Methods for segmentation and classification of digital microscopy tissue images. Front. Bioeng. Biotechnol., 53 (2019)

28. Zbontar, J., Jing, L., Misra, I., LeCun, Y., Deny, S.: Barlow Twins: self-supervised learning via redundancy reduction. In: International Conference on Machine Learning, pp. 12310–12320. PMLR (2021)

29. Zhang, S., et al.: Large-scale domain-specific pretraining for biomedical vision-language processing. arXiv preprint arXiv:2303.00915 (2023)

Large-Scale Pretraining on Pathological Images for Fine-Tuning of Small Pathological Benchmarks

Masakata Kawai[1]([envelope]) [ORCID], Noriaki Ota[2], and Shinsuke Yamaoka[2]

[1] Department of Pathology, University of Yamanashi, Yamanashi, Japan
mkawai@yamanashi.as.jp
[2] Systems Research and Development Center, Technology Bureau, NS Solutions Corp, Tokyo, Japan
{ota.noriaki.4qp,yamaoka.shinsuke.5ke}@jp.nssol.nipponsteel.com

Abstract. Pretraining a deep learning model on large image datasets is a standard step before fine-tuning the model on small targeted datasets. The large dataset is usually general images (e.g. imagenet2012) while the small dataset can be specialized datasets that have different distributions from the large dataset. However, this "large-to-small" strategy is not well-validated when the large dataset is specialized and has a similar distribution to small datasets. We newly compiled three hematoxylin and eosin-stained image datasets, one large (PTCGA200) and two magnification-adjusted small datasets (PCam200 and segPANDA200). Major deep learning models were trained with supervised and self-supervised learning methods and fine-tuned on the small datasets for tumor classification and tissue segmentation benchmarks. ResNet50 pretrained with MoCov2, Sim-CLR, and BYOL on PTCGA200 was better than imagenet2012 pretraining when fine-tuned on PTCGA200 (accuracy of 83.94%, 86.41%, 84.91%, and 82.72%, respectively). ResNet50 pretrained on PTCGA200 with MoCov2 exceeded the COCOtrain2017-pretrained baseline and was the best in ResNet50 for the tissue segmentation benchmark (mIoU of 63.53% and 63.22%). We found supervised re-training imagenet-pretrained models (ResNet50, BiT-M-R50x1, and ViT-S/16) on PTCGA200 often improved downstream benchmarks.

Keywords: Large-scale training · Pathological benchmark · Self-supervised learning · Vision transformer

1 Introduction

Large-scale pretraining benefits large neural nets for fine-tuning downstream tasks. One success story is imagenet (including imagenet2012 and imagenet-21k, or in21k) [12] for supervised and self-supervised learning of deep neural models in computer vision

---

Codes: https://github.com/enigmanx20/PatchTCGA
Datasets: http://bit.ly/3KCzkCA

Supplementary Information The online version contains supplementary material available at https://doi.org/10.1007/978-3-031-44917-8_25.

© The Author(s), under exclusive license to Springer Nature Switzerland AG 2023
Z. Xue et al. (Eds.): MILLanD 2023, LNCS 14307, pp. 257–267, 2023.
https://doi.org/10.1007/978-3-031-44917-8_25

[1, 7, 17, 20, 25, 33]. Pretraining on large datasets before fine-tuning on small datasets, we call this "large-to-small" strategy, is a common strategy in deep learning [13, 15, 23, 32]. However, the effect of pretraining on large specialized pathological image datasets with different distributions from general images is not well systematically compared due to the lack of magnification-adjusted large and small datasets. Here, we conducted a large-scale pretraining of deep learning models on pathological hematoxylin and eosin (H&E) stained images. After pretraining, the models were fine-tuned on small magnification-adjusted pathological datasets, benchmarking the downstream classification and semantic segmentation performances (Fig. 1).

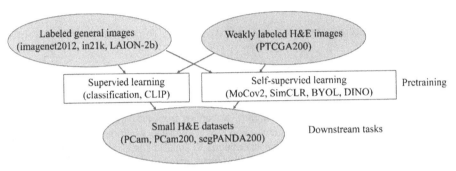

Fig. 1. Upstream large-scale supervised and self-supervised pretraining on general image datasets and an H&E image dataset (PTCGA200). The model performance of classification and tissue segmentation was measured on the downstream small H&E image datasets.

Our findings and contributions are as follows:

- We compiled three public magnification-adjusted pathological H&E image datasets, one large (PTCGA200) and two small datasets (PCam200 and segPANDA200), organized for deep learning pretraining and benchmarking. We conducted systematic benchmarking using six major models and four self-supervised learning methods.
- Self-supervised learning frameworks benefit from PTCGA200 pretraining and often exceed imagenet2012 supervised and self-supervised pretraining, but don't outperform in21k supervised pretraining.
- Supervised re-training for organ classification on PTCGA200 of imagenet2012/in21k-pretrained models often boosts the downstream task performances.

2   Related works

Several studies [1, 25, 32] showed large models pretrained on large image datasets are better in the downstream performance than small models and small datasets pairs. However, specialized image domains including H&E images in digital pathology are distinct from general images. Particularly, contrastive self-supervised learning [2, 5, 7–9, 17, 20] leveraging content-preserving augmentations needs care for these image domain differences. The success of transfer learning from general images to H&E images [10, 24], although it is a common approach, is not obvious [27]. As such, we were motivated to fill the gap of the "large-to-small strategy" in digital pathology, a large H&E dataset to small H&E datasets. We compiled a large patch-based H&E image dataset ourselves as there are no public large H&E datasets comparable with imagenet2012. Instead, several studies [6, 21, 30] used a large repository of whole slide H&E images (WSIs) from the Cancer Genome Atlas (TCGA) project. However, WSIs are gigapixel images including many uninformative white backgrounds. A patch-based dataset is handy, compact, and memory efficient in the deep learning pipeline and improves reproducibility. For the above reasons, we newly introduced a large patch-based dataset cropped from TCGA WSIs named Patch TCGA in 200μm (PTCGA200) that is comparable with imagenet2012. Model performance is often measured by downstream task performance using learning visual task adaptation benchmark (VTAB) [41], a suit of 19 distinct small datasets to benchmark transfer learning capability [1, 25, 32]. VTAB includes a pathological dataset, Patch Camelyon (denotes PCam) [14, 38], as one of the specialized datasets. However, the 96px images at 0.24 microns per pixel (MPP) in PCam are small for the recent computational environment and hard to adjust to the magnification of PTCGA200. To benchmark classification and segmentation performances, two small magnification-adjusted patch-based datasets (PCam200 and segPANDA200) were newly introduced. Contrary to studies [2, 6] that employ self-supervised learning on over a million patches using ad hoc datasets for training and validation, our public datasets enhance reproducibility and facilitate comparisons against various benchmarks.

3 Methods

We benchmarked supervised and self-supervised pretraining on a large pathological image dataset and validated the fine-tuning performance on downstream pathological tasks. We randomly cropped 500 patches in the 200μm scale per slide from the tissue region of around 10220 diagnostic slides from TCGA and resized them into 512×512px using bicubic interpolation. Training, validation, and test sets were split so that patches from the same slide be in the same set (slide-level split). The RGB means and standard deviations of the whole PTCGA200 are (0.7184, 0.5076, 0.6476) and (0.0380, 0.0527, 0.0352), respectively. Patch Camelyon in 200μm (PCam200) was made in the same manner from Camelyon2016 challenge dataset [14]. Segmentation PANDA in 200μm (SegPANDA200) was made in the same manner but the patch size was 1024px at the same MPP from the prostate cancer grade assessment (PANDA) challenge dataset [3] from Radboud. Training, validation, and test sets were split so that the proportion of International Society of Urological Pathology (ISUP) grade is balanced in each set. The supervised pretraining task on PTCGA200 is a 20-class organ classification, while the downstream tasks are binary tumor or normal classification (PCam200 and PCam), and 6-class semantic segmentation of prostate biopsy (segPANDA200). They are in the same H&E image domain but, by definition, are distinct and almost independent tasks of each other. The datasets used in this study are tabulated in Table 1.

Almost the same image augmentation suit was used in training throughout the study. The experiments were conducted almost only once except for a minor hyperparameter search on validation sets (up to 5 trials). The experiments were conducted with multiple NVIDIA V100 GPUs except for ViT-S/16 supervised scratch training with two A6000 NVIDIA GPUs. PyTorch and torchvision versions were 1.7.1 and 0.8.2, respectively.

Table 1. Properties of the datasets used in this study. MPP: microns per pixel

Dataset	Classes	Training	Validation	Test	Image size	MPP
imagenet2012	1000	1281167	50000	100000	Variable	–
in21k	21841	Total 14197122			Variable	–
LAION-2b	–	Total 2b			Variable	–
PTCGA200	20	4945500	107500	57000	512	0.39
PCam200	2	28539	10490	17674	512	0.39
PCam	2	262144	32768	32768	96	0.97
segPANDA200	6	70878	15042	15040	1024	0.39

Fine-Tuning Details. We replaced the classification head with a D × N fully connected layer in PTCGA200, PCam200, and PCam, where D is the dimension of the encoder output and N is the number of classes. We reset the running means and variances in the batch normalization layers before fine-tuning. We adopted the same hyperparameters in each task, prioritizing model varieties over better performance by hyperparameter search. The optimizer was SGD with momentum = 0.9 and Nesterov = False without weight decay. The batch size was 512. The learning rate was 0.05 and decayed according to the cosine annealing schedule. The images were normalized using the same means and standard deviations as pretraining. The RGB means and standard deviations of (0.5, 0.5, 0.5) and (0.5, 0.5, 0.5) respectively were used when fine-tuning from randomly initialized weights. Some models were fine-tuned on larger input images (384px) than pretraining as recommended in [1, 25]. The positional embedding of ViT was resized to the targeted size by bicubic interpolation. Linear classification protocols [19, 40] are often used to evaluate the backbone model. Nevertheless, we fine-tuned the whole model to simulate real applications requiring better overall performance.

4 Experiments

4.1 PTCGA200 Scratch Pretraining

We trained ResNet18/50 [18], InceptionV3 [35], EfficientNet-b3 [36], ViT-S/16 [1], and ViT-B/32 [1] as the deep learning models for scratch pretraining. We excluded VGG-16 [34] although they are popular in digital pathology applications. They lack batch normalization layers [22] and have nearly five times the number of parameters as compared to ResNet50 (130M versus 22M, respectively), so the direct comparison seemed inappropriate. We included vision transformers (ViTs) [1] as recent studies report their utility in digital pathology [6, 11, 26]. All the models were trained on PTCGA200 for the 20-class classification task minimizing cross-entropy loss. The weights were randomly initialized. The images were normalized using PTCGA200 means and standard deviations. The optimizer was AdamW [29] with beta1 = 0.9 and beta2 = 0.999. The batch size was 4k. The learning rates were increased in the warmup epochs [16] and decayed with the cosine annealing schedule in the remaining epochs. The base learning rate was increased during warmup epochs until the peak learning rate was equal to the base learning rate multiplied by (batch size)/256. We report top-1 accuracies in % in Table 2.

Table 2. Top-1 accuracies (in %) supervised scratch training on PTCGA200

Model	Test accuracy	Best validation accuracy	Epochs	Image size	Weight decay	Base LR	Warmup epochs
ResNet18	84.01	83.94	60	224	5e-5	0.001	10
ResNet50	85.30	85.32	60	224	5e-5	5e-4	10
InceptionV3	85.98	85.66	60	299	5e-5	1e-4	10
EfficientNet-b3	**88.35**	88.11	60	300	5e-5	1e-4	10
ViT-S/16	84.44	86.63	80	224	0.03	1e-4	15
ViT-B/32	84.10	84.83	100	224	0.03	1e-4	20

All the models obtained over 84.01% accuracy. EfficientNet-b3 obtained the best accuracy of 88.35%, which was the best among all the models including the following fine-tuning part.

Self-supervised Scratch Pretraining. We included self-supervised learning as it recently attracts attention [2, 6, 11, 37] in digital pathology where detailed patch-level labels are hard to obtain. We chose MoCov2 [20], SimCLR [7], BYOL [17], and DINO [5] as the self-supervised methods. They seek invariant representation across two differently augmented views encoded by a pair of slightly different encoders [4]. The backbone models were Res-Net50 in SimCLR, MoCov2, and BYOL, and ViT-S/16 in DINO. We trained Mo-Cov2, SimCLR, BYOL, and DINO on PTCGA200 training set from scratch for 40 epochs. We modified SimCLRv1 [7] to have 3-layer MLP and made the first layer of the MLP the encoder output as proposed in SimCLRv2 [8]. We implemented BYOL in PyTorch following the original implementation in JAX. We froze patch embedding of ViT in DINO as in [9]. The images were normalized using PTCGA200 means and standard deviations. The hyperparameters were set default in the original repositories.

4.2 PTCGA200 Fine-Tuning of Pretrained Models

We fine-tuned imagenet2012-, in21k-, and LAION-2b-pretrained models downloaded from PyTorch Hub, PyTorch Image Models [39], or official repositories (re-training) as well as PTCGA200-pretrained models on PTCGA200 for 30k iterations. Pretrained ViT-B/32 using Contrastive Language-Image Pretraining (CLIP) [32] on LAION-2b was included. Supervised re-training was inspired by self-supervised re-training in REMEDIS [2]. We included Big Transfer (BiT) [25] models pretrained on in21k (BiT-M in the original paper) as the state-of-the-art models for transfer learning. BiT-R50x1 has a ResNetv2 [19] architecture characterized by group normalization [40] and weight standardization [31] instead of batch normalization. We report top-1 accuracies in % in Tables 3 and 4.

Table 3. PTCGA200 top-1 accuracies (in %) fine-tuned from supervised pretraining on general images

Model	Test accuracy	Image size	Pretraining dataset
ResNet18	79.27/81.79	224/384	imagenet2012
ResNet50	81.46/82.72	224/384	imagenet2012
InceptionV3	83.05	384	imagenet2012
EfficientNet-b3	83.39	384	imagenet2012
ViT-S/16	85.13/**87.21**	224/384	in21k
ViT-B/32	82.36/85.87	224/384	in21k
ViT-B/32-CLIP	66.06/75.13	224/384	LAION-2b
BiT-R50x1	85.64	384	in21k → imagenet2012

Table 4. PTCGA200 top-1 accuracies (in %) fine-tuned from self-supervised pretraining

Model	Test accuracy	Image size	Pretraining dataset
ResNet50-McCov2	81.06/83.09	224/384	imagenet2012
ResNet50-McCov2	82.83/83.94	224/384	PTCGA200
ResNet50-SimCLR	86.31/**86.41**	224/384	PTCGA200
ResNet50-BYOL	83.73/84.91	224/384	PTCGA200
ViT-S/16-DINO	69.09/72.97	224/384	imagenet2012
ViT-S/16-DINO	83.60/85.05	224/384	PTCGA200

ViT-S/16 pretrained on in21k obtained the best performance of 87.21% accuracy in fine-tuned models. PTCGA200-pretrained ResNet50 with SimCLR fine-tuned on 384px images was the best in ResNet50 including scratch training. Fine-tuned ViT-S/16, ViT-B/32, and BiT-R50x1 on 384px images as well as ResNet50 pretrained on PTCGA200 with SimCLR exceeded the ResNet50 scratch training baseline of 85.30%. Fine-tuning on 384px images improved the performance invariably. PTCGA200-pretrained self-supervised models (MoCov2 and DINO) exceeded the corresponding imagenet2012-pretrained models.

4.3 PCam200 Fine-Tuning

We fined-tuned models used in PTCGA200 on PCam200 for 1k iterations. We report accuracies in % in Tables 5 and 6. PCam fine-tuning results are found in the Supplemental Material.

Table 5. PCam200 accuracies (in %) fine-tuned from supervised pretraining on PTCGA200 and general images. Pretraining dataset None indicates random initialization of weights. The right side of the arrow indicates the re-training dataset

Model	Test accuracy	Image size	Pretraining dataset
ResNet18	92.72/82.14	384	imagenet2012/PTCGA200
ResNet50	79.10	224	None
ResNet50	91.97/92.56	224/384	imagenet2012
ResNet50	91.89/92.48	224/384	PTCGA200
ResNet50	**93.24**	384	imagenet2012 → PTCGA200
InceptionV3	92.57/91.80	384	imagenet2012/PTCGA200
EfficientNet-b3	90.51/89.69	384	imagenet2012/PTCGA200
ViT-S/16	92.91/88.80	384	in21k/PTCGA200
ViT-S/16	93.22	384	in21k → PTCGA200
ViT-B/32	91.65/89.62	384	in21k/PTCGA200
ViT-B/32-CLIP	76.75	384	LAION-2b
BiT-R50x1	93.24/**93.67**	384	in21k → imagenet2012/in21k
BiT-R50x1	93.49	384	in21k → imagenet2012 → PTCGA200

Table 6. PCam200 accuracies (in %) fine-tuned from self-supervised pretraining on PTCGA200 and general images

Model	Test accuracy	Image size	Pretraining dataset
ResNet50-MoCov2	91.70/91.94	384	imagenet2012/PTCGA200
ResNet50-SimCLR	92.07	384	PTCGA200
ResNet50-BYOL	**92.15**	384	PTCGA200
ViT-S/16-DINO	76.16/91.79	384	imagenet2012/PTCGA200

BiT-R50x1 pretrained on in21k obtained the best accuracy of 93.67%. Re-training of imaget2012/in21k-pretrained models on PTCGA200 improved the accuracies by 0.68% (ResNet50) and 0.25% (BiT-R50x1). Re-training on PTCGA200 from imagenet2012-pretraining was the best in ResNet50 with an accuracy of 93.24%. Imagenet2012/in21k-pretrained models exceeded PTCGA200-pretrained supervised models, but competing in ResNet50 (92.56% and 92.48%), InceptionV3 (92.57% and 91.80%) and EfficientNet-b3 (90.51% and 89.69%). Fine-tuning on 384px images improved the performance. PTCGA200-pretrained self-supervised models (MoCov2 and DINO) exceeded the corresponding imagenet2012-pretrained models (91.94% and 91.70%, and 91.79% and 76.16%, respectively).

4.4 SegPANDA200 Fine-Tuning

We fined-tuned models used in PTCGA200 fine-tuning as well as COCOtrain2017-pretrained models on segPANDA200 for 1k iterations. In segPANDA200 a fully convolutional network (FCN) [28] head was attached to the feature maps or the ViT maps defined as the following. ViT is a convolution-free network and has no feature maps, so we retiled the output sequence excluding **CLS** token as the original patch positions. This is the reverse operation of flattening before patch embedding. We call this feature map like intermediate output the ViT map. We used the last layer (12th layer of ViT-S and ViT-B) output and zero-initialized the positional embedding. We examined which layer output to use and the effect of zero-initializing positional encoding (not shown) and found the last layer output is good when the positional embedding is zero-initialized. We report mIoU (mean intersection over union) in % in Tables 7 and 8.

Table 7. SegPANDA200 mIoU (in %) fine-tuned from supervised pretraining on PTCGA200 and general images. Pretraining dataset None indicates random initialization of weights. The right side of the arrow indicates the re-training dataset. Feature/ViT map size is intermediated output size in pixels on the validation/test 1024px image before FCN or DeepLabv3 heads

Model	Test mIoU	Pretraining dataset	Feature/ViT map size
ResNet18	57.76/48.71	imagenet2012/PTCGA200	32
ResNet50	43.27	None	32
ResNet50	58.76/49.79	imagenet2012/PTCGA200	32
ResNet50	59.93	imagenet2012 → PTCGA200	32
InceptionV3	58.70/50.12	imagenet2012/PTCGA200	30
EfficientNet-b3	61.31/51.42	imagenet2012/PTCGA200	32
ViT-S/16	61.57/57.70	in21k/PTCGA200	64
ViT-S/16	61.23	in21k → PTCGA200	64
ViT-B/32	59.21/58.04	in21k/PTCGA200	32
ViT-B/32-CLIP	40.08	LAION-2b	32
BiT-R50x1	67.16/67.07	in21k → imagenet2012/in21k	32
BiT-R50x1	**67.60**	in21k → imagenet2012 → PTCGA200	32
ResNet50	63.22	COCOtrain2017 (PASCAL VOC)	32
ResNet50-DeepLabv3	**69.61**	COCOtrain2017 (PASCAL VOC)	32

In21k-pretrained BiT-R50x1 re-trained on PTCGA200 obtained the best mIoU of 67.60%. Re-training of imaget2012 pretrained models on PTCGA200 improved the mIoUs by 1.17% (ResNet50) and 0.44% (BiT-R50x1). But it degraded the mIoU by 0.34% in ViT-S/16. PTCGA200-pretrained self-supervised ResNet50 with MoCov2

Table 8. SegPANDA200 mIoU (in %) fine-tuned from self-supervised pretraining on PTCGA200 and general images. Feature/ViT map size is intermediated output size in pixels on the validation/test 1024px image before FCN heads

Model	Test mIoU	Pretraining dataset	Feature/ViT map size
ResNet50-MoCov2	62.76/**63.53**	imagenet2012/PTCGA200	32
ResNet50-SimCLR	53.50	PTCGA200	32
ResNet50-BYOL	56.01	PTCGA200	32
ViT-S/16-DINO	36.21/59.26	imagenet2012/PTCGA200	64

obtained the best mIoU of 63.53% in ResNet50 and exceeded the imagenet2012-pretrained mIoU of 58.76% and COCOtrain2017-pretrained mIoU of 63.22%.

5   Conclusion

We explored the "large-to-small" strategy in pathological images through systematic benchmarking with various models and learning techniques. Large-scale training on PTCGA200 benefits not only self-supervised models trained from scratch but also imagenet2012/in21k-pretrained models by re-training. Magnification-adjusted datasets (PCam200 and segPANDA) strengthened benchmark reliability for classification and segmentation.

Acknowledgment. The results shown here are in part based upon data generated by the TCGA Research Network: https://www.cancer.gov/tcga. We follow the original licenses to share the compiled datasets. We share PTCGA200 by acknowledging NIH Genomic Data Sharing (GDS) Policy. We share PCam200 dataset under CC0 license. We share segPANDA200 dataset under CC BY-SA-NC 4.0 license. This paper is based on results obtained from a project, JPNP20006, commissioned by the New Energy and Industrial Technology Development Organization (NEDO).

References

1. Dosovitskiy, A. et al.: An image is worth 16 × 16 words: transformers for image recognition at scale. Presented at the (2021)
2. Azizi, S. et al.: Robust and efficient medical imaging with self-supervision (2022). https://doi.org/10.48550/arxiv.2205.09723
3. Bulten, W., et al.: Artificial intelligence for diagnosis and Gleason grading of prostate cancer: the PANDA challenge. Nat. Med. **28**(1), 154–163 (2022). https://doi.org/10.1038/s41591-021-01620-2
4. Cao, Y.-H., Wu, J.: Rethinking self-supervised learning: small is beautiful (2021). arXiv: 2103.13559 [cs]
5. Caron, M., et al.: Emerging properties in self-supervised vision transformers. Presented at the (2021)

6. Chen, R.J., et al.: Scaling vision transformers to gigapixel images via hierarchical self-supervised learning. Presented at the (2022). https://doi.org/10.1109/CVPR52688.2022.01567

7. Chen, T., et al.: A simple framework for contrastive learning of visual representations (2020)

8. Chen, T., et al.: Big self-supervised models are strong semi-supervised learners (2020)

9. Chen, X., et al.: An empirical study of training self-supervised vision transformers. CoRR. abs/2104.02057 (2021)

10. Coudray, N., et al.: Classification and mutation prediction from non–small cell lung cancer histopathology images using deep learning. Nat. Med. **24**(10), 1559–1567 (2018). https://doi.org/10.1038/s41591-018-0177-5

11. Deininger, L., et al.: A comparative study between vision transformers and CNNs in digital pathology

12. Deng, J., et al.: ImageNet: a large-scale hierarchical image database. In: IEEE, pp. 248–255 (2009)

13. Devlin, J., et al.: BERT: pre-training of deep bidirectional transformers for language understanding. Presented at the June (2019). https://doi.org/10.18653/v1/N19-1423

14. Ehteshami Bejnordi, B., et al.: Diagnostic assessment of deep learning algorithms for detection of lymph node metastases in women with breast cancer. JAMA **318**(22), 2199 (2017). https://doi.org/10.1001/jama.2017.14585

15. Esteva, A., et al.: Dermatologist-level classification of skin cancer with deep neural networks. Nature **542**(7639), 115–118 (2017). https://doi.org/10.1038/nature21056

16. Goyal, P., et al.: Accurate, Large Minibatch SGD: Training ImageNet in 1 Hour (2018). arXiv:1706.02677 [cs]

17. Grill, J.-B., et al.: Bootstrap your own latent - a new approach to self-supervised learning. Presented at the (2020)

18. He, K., et al.: Deep residual learning for image recognition. Presented at the (2016). https://doi.org/10.1109/CVPR.2016.90

19. He, K., et al.: Identity mappings in deep residual networks. arXiv:1603.05027 [cs]. (2016)

20. He, K., et al.: Momentum contrast for unsupervised visual representation learning. Presented at the (2020). https://doi.org/10.1109/CVPR42600.2020.00975

21. Howard, F.M., et al.: The impact of site-specific digital histology signatures on deep learning model accuracy and bias. Nat. Commun. **12**(1), 4423 (2021). https://doi.org/10.1038/s41467-021-24698-1

22. Ioffe, S., Szegedy, C.: Batch normalization: accelerating deep network training by reducing internal covariate shift (2015). https://arxiv.org/abs/1502.03167

23. Alayrac, J.B., et al.: Flamingo: a visual language model for few-shot learning. Presented at the (2022)

24. Kather, J.N., et al.: Deep learning can predict microsatellite instability directly from histology in gastrointestinal cancer. Nat. Med. **25**(7), 1054–1056 (2019). https://doi.org/10.1038/s41591-019-0462-y

25. Kolesnikov, A., et al.: Big transfer (BiT): general visual representation learning (2020). arxiv:1912.11370 [cs]

26. Li, Z., et al.: Vision transformer-based weakly supervised histopathological image analysis of primary brain tumors. iScience **26**, 1, 105872 (2023). https://doi.org/10.1016/j.isci.2022.105872

27. Liu, Y., et al.: Detecting cancer metastases on gigapixel pathology images. https://arxiv.org/abs/1703.02442

28. Long, J., et al.: Fully convolutional networks for semantic segmentation. https://arxiv.org/abs/1411.4038

29. Loshchilov, I., Hutter, F.: Decoupled weight decay regularization (2017). arxiv.org.

30. Lu, M.Y., et al.: AI-based pathology predicts origins for cancers of unknown primary. Nature **594**, 106–110 (2021). https://doi.org/10.1038/s41586-021-03512-4
31. Qiao, S., et al.: Micro-batch training with batch-channel normalization and weight standardization (2020). arXiv:1903.10520 [cs]
32. Radford, A., et al.: Learning transferable visual models from natural language supervision. Presented at the (2021)
33. Russakovsky, O., et al.: ImageNet large scale visual recognition challenge. Int. J. Comput. Vis. (IJCV). **115**, 211–252 (2015). https://doi.org/10.1007/s11263-015-0816-y
34. Simonyan, K., Zisserman, A.: Very deep convolutional networks for large-scale image recognition. In: 3rd International Conference on Learning Representations (ICLR 2015), pp. 1–14 Computational and Biological Learning Society (2015)
35. Szegedy, C., et al.: Rethinking the inception architecture for computer vision. Presented at the (2016). https://doi.org/10.1109/CVPR.2016.308
36. Tan, M., Le, Q.: EfficientNet: rethinking model scaling for convolutional neural networks. Presented at the (2019)
37. Uegami, W., et al.: MIXTURE of human expertise and deep learning—developing an explainable model for predicting pathological diagnosis and survival in patients with interstitial lung disease. Mod. Pathol. **35**(8), 1083–1091 (2022). https://doi.org/10.1038/s41379-022-01025-7
38. Veeling, B.S., et al.: Rotation equivariant CNNs for digital pathology (2018). arxiv.org.
39. Wightman, R.: PyTorch image models. GitHub repository (2019). https://doi.org/10.5281/zenodo.4414861
40. Wu, Y., He, K.: Group Normalization. https://openaccess.thecvf.com/content_ECCV_2018/html/Yuxin_Wu_Group_Normalization_ECCV_2018_paper.html
41. Zhai, X., et al.: A large-scale study of representation learning with the visual task adaptation benchmark (2019)

Author Index

© The Editor(s) (if applicable) and The Author(s), under exclusive license
to Springer Nature Switzerland AG 2023
Z. Xue et al. (Eds.): MILLanD 2023, LNCS 14307, pp. 269–270, 2023.
https://doi.org/10.1007/978-3-031-44917-8

Printed in the United States
by Baker & Taylor Publisher Services